W9-BHT-405

CANADA'S GDP BY EXPENDITURES, 2010
SOURCE: STATISTICS CANADA, CANSIM TABLE 380-0017.

		($ BILLIONS)
Consumption		
Consumer expenditure on goods and services		940.6
Investment		
Business investment in plant and equipment	178.5	
Residential construction	112.7	
Addition to inventories	2.3	
Total investment		293.5
Government		
Government expenditure on goods and services		420.9
Exports and Imports		
Exports of goods and services	478.1	
Imports of goods and services	508.7	
Balance		−30.6
Gross Domestic Product		**1624.6**

CANADA'S GDP BY INCOMES, 2010
SOURCE: STATISTICS CANADA, CANSIM TABLE 380-0016.

	($ BILLIONS)
Wages, salaries, and supplementary labour income	849.6
Corporation profits before taxes	180.7
Government enterprise profits	15.6
Interest and miscellaneous investment income	70.0
Accrued net income of farm operators from farm production	1.4
Net income of non-farm unincorporated business including rent	103.6
Inventory valuation adjustment	1.9
Indirect taxes less subsidies on products	172.6
Capital consumption allowances	229.3
Gross Domestic Product	**1624.6**

PEARSON

ALWAYS LEARNING

Brian Lyons

Canadian Macroeconomics
Problems & Policies
Tenth Edition

Cover Art: Courtesy of PhotoDisc/Getty Images, brandX pictures.

Copyright © 2012 by Pearson Learning Solutions
All rights reserved.

This copyright covers material written expressly for this volume by the editor/s as well as the compilation itself. It does not cover the individual selections herein that first appeared elsewhere. Permission to reprint these has been obtained by Pearson Learning Solutions for this edition only. Further reproduction by any means, electronic or mechanical, including photocopying and recording, or by any information storage or retrieval system, must be arranged with the individual copyright holders noted.

Previously published as:

Canadian Macroeconomics: Problems and Policies, Eighth Edition
by Brian Lyons
Copyright © 2007, 2004, 2001, 1998, 1995, 1991, 1987, 1983 by Pearson Education Canada
Published by Prentice Hall
Toronto, Ontario

Statistics Canada information is used with the permission of Statistics Canada. Users are forbidden to copy this material and/or redisseminate the data, in an original or modified form, for commercial purposes, without the expressed permission of Statistics Canada. Information on the availability of the wide range of data from Statistics Canada can be obtained from Statistics Canada's Regional Offices, its World Wide Web site at http://www.statcan.gc.ca, and its toll-free access number 1-800-263-1136.

All trademarks, service marks, registered trademarks, and registered service marks are the property of their respective owners and are used herein for identification purposes only.

Pearson Learning Solutions, 501 Boylston Street, Suite 900, Boston, MA 02116
A Pearson Education Company
www.pearsoned.com

Printed in the United States of America

6 7 8 9 10 V3NL 16 15 14 13

000200010271269324

SD/FC

ISBN 10: 1-256-43244-X
ISBN 13: 978-1-256-43244-9

For Barb, Amber, Colin, Parker, Reid, Marnie, Brent, Dylan, Liam, Ryan, Brady, and Jack

Brief Contents

Contents

1   What Is Economics?   1

5   Money and the Economic System   101

6   Booms, Recessions, and Inflation ... 124

9   International Trade ... 209

10   The Canadian Dollar in Foreign Exchange Markets ... 234

11   The Global Economy ... 261

12   Canada in the Global Economy ... 291

13　Into the Future ... 315

"IN THE NEWS" BOXES

"YOU DECIDE" BOXES

Preface

Introduction

Canadian Macroeconomics: Problems and Policies, Tenth Edition, is an introductory text that addresses itself to the economic opportunities and challenges facing Canada today and the policy choices for governments in dealing with these issues. It is not oriented toward rigorous, abstract, or elegant economic theory, nor to a mathematical approach to economics—most students of introductory economics neither want nor need these. Rather, its approach tends to be practical and real world–based, using economic theory not for its own sake so much as to develop an understanding of the issues being discussed.

The text is ideally suited for a student's first course in macroeconomics and is used in this role at the secondary school, community college, and university levels.

New to This Edition

The challenge for this tenth edition is that at the time of writing (fall 2011), the economic situation was very uncertain. The recovery following the economy's sharp downturn in 2008–09 had started out at a quite promising pace in 2009; however, by 2011 it was losing momentum in both the United States and Canada. The outlook was clouded by the prospect of significant cuts to U.S. government spending in 2012 and beyond, and a growing number of observers were speaking in terms of about a 50 percent risk of a "double-dip" recession in the USA. In this edition, we deal with this situation in three ways.

First, we have added several new "In the News" and "You Decide" boxes that will try to capture basic issues that are likely to persist (or at least remain important as background items to the current situation) for the life of the edition. These include boxes on the recession, the monetary policy response (plus a section of text on the fiscal policy response), how the recession affected the exchange rate of the Canadian dollar, and the role of the interrelationship between the Chinese and American economies that underlay the recession.

Second, we have added various *Critical Thinking* questions and *Use the Web* exercises that not only focus on recent and current economic events, but also provide the URLs for students to update themselves on these developments.

And third, we will post on the Canadian Microeconomics and Macroeconomics website (http://www.pearsoncustom.com/can/micro_macro_econ) regular updates on economic developments as they occur.

In addition to these major updates, we have undertaken a number of updates and improvements for this edition. These include clarification of the marginal tax rate, improved explanation of the 2008–09 recession, much improved and more current coverage of the leading indicator, and improved and updated coverage of "full employment". Parts of Chapter 9 have been extensively rewritten to reflect recent developments, including Canada's trade with China and the role of exports in the 2008-09 recession. Chapter 11 has also been extensively rewritten to update the inter-relationship between the Chinese and American economies leading up to the financial crisis and recession of 2008–09, and Chapters 12 and 13 have been updated to reflect the changes in the global economic situation since the ninth edition in early 2009, which now seems like a very long time ago.

In this tenth edition, we continue to try to make the text more interactive with the student. The main aspect of this effort is the **Integrated Study Guide** following the end-of-chapter questions in each chapter. The Integrated Study Guide consists of three types of questions:

(a) **Review Questions** These are based closely on the material in the chapter, and are mostly short answer in nature. The answers are provided at the end of the book, which makes these questions into a "self-check" on the content of the chapter. Answers to all of these questions are provided in Appendix B.

(b) **Critical Thinking Questions** (CTQs) These are more complex, and lend themselves more to discussion and debate. Some are based on real world situations; others are based on "what if" scenarios. Answers to asterisked CTQs are provided in Appendix B; the remaining answers are available in the Instructor's Manual that accompanies *Canadian Macroeconomics*.

(c) **Use the Web** These require the same thinking skills as the CTQs, but are based on real world information that students can dig out themselves from the internet.

Also, the text retains the familiar "In the News" and "You Decide" boxes, many of which are new for the tenth edition. The questions that accompany these boxes also require critical thinking skills.

Features

According to both students and teachers, a major feature of *Canadian Macroeconomics* is its readability, which helps considerably in the learning and teaching of a subject that has an undeserved reputation of being formidable. Other aspects of the text include

- **Organization** The material is organized in a manner that students find logical and easy to follow.
- **Structure** The number of chapters fits well into most schools' programs, and if time is short, Chapter 13 can be omitted.
- **Interactivity** The boxes described above, together with the discussion questions at the end of each chapter and in the Study Guide, provide extensive opportunities for students to interact with the material, both in groups and on their own.
- **Pedagogical Tools** Learning Objectives, "You Decide" and "In the News" boxes, and end-of-chapter questions all help students focus on and apply the important points in each chapter.
- **Current Economic Developments** By posting these on the portal website and updating them regularly, students can be apprised of changes in the economic situation.

Organization

For the main body of the book, the structural changes of the previous edition have stood up well, and the updates for this tenth edition have created a more focused and cleanly flowing presentation of macroeconomics. Following the introductory material in the first two chapters, the supply side of the economy is presented, followed by the demand side, providing a structured overview of the economy on a macroeconomic scale at an early point in the text. Money and banking are then covered, expanding on the coverage of the demand side and providing a link to the major topic of economic instability in Chapter 6. In the next chapter, the monetary and fiscal policies used to stabilize the economy are covered, followed by a chapter on the realities that limit what can be achieved by these policies in the Canadian context.

Chapter 9 introduces international trade, emphasizing the importance of trade in the Canadian economy and the basic principles concerning trade and trade restrictions. Chapter 10 deals with exchange rates and government exchange rate policy, and the relationship of these to trade performance. In Chapter 11 the globalization of the world economy is addressed, using the two main themes of international agreements concerning the topics of Chapters 9 and 10: trade (the GATT/WTO) and exchange rates (the IMF). In addition, Chapter 11 reviews recent major developments in the world economy, stressing the emergence of China as a major player. Chapter 12 focuses on Canada's involvement in the globalized world economy, examining Canadian trade policy, the North American Free Trade Agreement (NAFTA) and its effects on Canada, Canada's international competitiveness, and the importance of fluctuations in Canada's exchange rate.

Chapter 13 summarizes Canada's economic position and prospective government policy directions for the future with respect to trade, productivity, and monetary and fiscal policy. Chapter 13 concludes with a brief review of some of the longer-term economic challenges facing Canada, including the exchange rate, the retirement of the baby boomers, and productivity growth, as well as the challenge of the recession of 2008–09 and its possible aftermath, which will be updated on the Canadian Microeconomics and Macroeconomics website.

Supplements

The following supplements have been carefully prepared to aid instructors and students in using this edition:

Resources for Instructors

Instructor's Resource CD-ROM: This invaluable resource includes the following instructor supplements:

- An **Instructor's Solutions Manual** provides teaching tips, the answers to all end-of-chapter questions, and answers to Critical Thinking Questions.
- **Pearson TestGen** is a testing software that enables instructors to view and edit the existing questions, add questions, generate tests, and distribute tests in a variety of formats. Powerful search and sort functions make it easy to locate questions and arrange them in any order desired. TestGen also enables instructors to administer tests on a local area network, have the tests graded electronically, and have the results prepared in electronic or printed reports. TestGen is compatible

with Windows and Macintosh operating systems, and can be downloaded from the TestGen website located at **www.pearsoned.com/testgen**. Contact your local sales representative for details and access.

- **PowerPoint Slides:** A collection of transparencies, culled from the textbook or specifically designed to complement chapter content, is also available electronically in PowerPoint software on the Instructor's Resource CD-ROM.
- **Image Library:** A collection of transparency masters is available for all the figures, tables, and graphs in the text.

These instructor supplements are offered on CD-ROM.

Resources for Students

In addition to the Interactive Study Guide at the end of each chapter in *Canadian Macroeconomics*, the following online study material is also provided:

Companion Website (www.pearsoncustom.com/can/micro_macro.econ): The CW includes a chapter outline, self-assessment quizzes, and links to other relevant and engaging websites for each part of the text.

Acknowledgments

Anyone undertaking a project of this magnitude and duration feels indebtedness to many people. In particular, I would like to express my gratitude to Bill Trimble, who said I should do it, Len Rosen, who refused to let me say I wouldn't, and all those teachers and students who used the first seven editions and offered helpful comments and suggestions.

I would also like to thank the people whose reviews of all eight editions of the manuscript were so helpful: for the first edition, Ray Canon, Gord Cleveland, Ward Levine, Jim Thompson, and Ian Wilson; for the second, Alan Idiens and Chuck Casson; for the third, Linda Nitsou, Bo Renneckendorf, Gord Enemark, L.W. Van Niekerk, Stephen Wise, and Ann Dunkley; for the fourth, Carol Ann Waite, Izhar Mirza, John Parry, and Byron Eastman; for the fifth, Valerie Beckingham, Michael Loconte, Pauline A. Lutes, Peter J. MacDonald, Karen Murkar, John Parry, Don Pepper, Judith Skuce, Don Wheeler, and Peter Young; for the sixth edition, Peter Peters of University College of the Cariboo, Karen Murkar of DeVry Institute of Technology, Ian Wilson of St. Lawrence College, Don Wheeler of College of the North Atlantic, Jean Cormier of New Brunswick Community College (Moncton), Martin Moy and Bill Gallivan of University College of Cape Breton, Terri Anderson of Mohawk College, and Jane Taylor of Nova Scotia Community College; for the seventh edition, Worku Aberra of Dawson College, Frances Ford of New Brunswick Community College (Moncton), Carl Graham of Assiniboine Community College, Donald Howick of St. Clair College, Alan Idiens of College of New Caledonia, Peter J. MacDonald of Cambrian College, Raimo Marttala of Malaspina College, Martin Moy of University College of Cape Breton, A. Gyasi Nimarko of Vanier College, John Pirrie of St. Lawrence College, and Charles Walton of Nova Scotia Community College. For the eighth edition: Aurelia Best of Centennial College, Bob Holland and Elizabeth Evans of Nova Scotia Community College, Alan Idiens, George Kennedy, and Ekaterina Gregory of College of New Caledonia, Shirley Pasieka of SAIT, Lance Shandler of Kwantlen University College, and Andrew Wong of the University of Alberta. Many thanks to the reviewers of this, the ninth edition: George Kennedy, Alan Idiens, Ekaterina Gregory, Ron Gallagher, Carol Derken, and Bruno Fullone.

Finally, I want to express my appreciation to my immediate family—Barb, Marnie, and Amber—who have provided support and understanding over unduly long periods of time.

I have no doubt that there are many improvements that can be made to this book, and welcome suggestions from teachers and students. Please write to me at Sheridan College, 7899 McLaughlin Road, Brampton, Ontario L6Y 5H9, or email me at **brian.lyons@sheridanc.on.ca**.

Brian Lyons
November 2011

A Great Way to Learn and Instruct Online

The Pearson Education Canada Companion Website is easy to navigate and is organized to correspond to the chapters in this textbook. Whether you are a student in the classroom or a distance learner you will discover helpful resources for in-depth study and research that empower you in your quest for greater knowledge and maximize your potential for success in the course.

Companion
Website

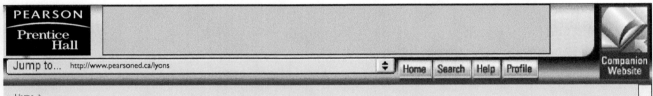

[http://www.pearsoncustom.com/can/micro_macro_econ]

PEARSON
Prentice
Hall

Companion
Website

Jump to...   http://www.pearsoned.ca/lyons   ⬍   Home | Search | Help | Profile

Home >

Companion Website

Canadian Macroeconomics: Problems and Policies, Ninth Edition, and *Canadian Microeconomics: Problems and Policies*, Ninth Edition, by Brian Lyons

Student Resources
The modules in this section provide students with tools for learning course material. These modules include:
- Chapter Objectives
- Destinations
- Quizzes
- Net Search
- Glossary

In the quiz modules students can send answers to the grader and receive instant feedback on their progress through the Results Reporter. Coaching comments and references to the textbook may be available to ensure that students take advantage of all available resources to enhance their learning experience.

Instructor Resources
Links will direct instructors to a secure, password-protected site that provides access to a variety of teaching aids, including PowerPoint Presentations, downloadable Instructor's Manual, and TestGen test bank. To get a password, simply contact your Pearson Education Canada Representative or call Faculty Sales and Services at 1-800-850-5813.

What Is Economics?

After studying this chapter, you should be able to

1. Explain why scarcity is regarded as the basic *economic problem*.

2. Explain the meaning and the significance of the terms *opportunity cost, productivity, efficiency,* and *effectiveness*.

3. Explain the three basic questions of economics.

4. Explain how a market system economy provides answers to each of the three basic questions of economics.

5. Explain how profits and the profit motive contribute to the effective and efficient use of economic resources.

6. Explain how competition contributes to the effective and efficient use of economic resources.

7. State three types of problems that tend to occur in market system economies.

8. Explain why Canada's economic system is described as a *mixed free-enterprise* system, and describe three major types of roles played by government in the Canadian economy.

Living in a world of 24-hour news channels and the internet, it is easy to feel overwhelmed by the constant stream of events being reported to us. Many of these events are of an economic nature, and they are often reported only briefly and with minimal explanations of the *reasons why* they have happened. This often leaves people feeling that economic changes just happen to them, and that they are at the mercy of forces beyond their understanding.

This need not be the case. Economic events don't just happen; they happen because something has *caused* them to happen. And a basic understanding of economics will let you understand not only *what* is happening, but also *why* it's happening. Doing this does not require mastering difficult economic theories—much of this book involves organizing things that you already know into a "tool kit," or a framework that can help you to understand the cause–effect connections underlying economic events. And this tool kit will help you not only to understand why things have happened, but also (with a little bit of luck) maybe even to foresee what is likely to happen in the future.

Let's start by getting a clear idea of what economics is all about.

What is economics? To the householder, economics is the difficult task of balancing the family budget, so that there is not too much month left over at the end of the money. To the business leader, economics is the problem of producing a product at a low enough cost that it can be marketed profitably in competition with the products of other producers. To a government leader, economics means difficult policy choices between goals that too often are in conflict, making it impossible to please everyone and difficult to ensure re-election. To the general public, economics is usually associated with incomprehensible and often contradictory pronouncements of people called *economists*, who many people suspect were created in order to make weather forecasters look good.

Each viewpoint, representing a particular group (householders, business leaders, and government leaders), is only one aspect of the real meaning of economics. To the economist, however, the topic involves the broader question of how well a society's economic system satisfies the economic needs and wants of its people.

Economics, then, is about many matters both small and large. On a small scale, *microeconomics* (after the Greek word *micro*, meaning "small") focuses on various *parts* of the economy, such as consumers, business, labour, and government. These topics and other issues are covered in my companion text, *Canadian Microeconomics: Problems and Policies*.

On a wider scale, *macroeconomics* (after the Greek word *macro*, meaning "big") deals with broader matters pertaining to the performance of the economy *as a whole*, such as recessions, unemployment, government finances and debt, inflation, interest rates, and international trade and finance. This book deals with matters such as these.

The Varied Nature of Economics

Some aspects of economic issues raise *philosophical questions*; for instance, should the government provide employment insurance benefits to people who earn considerable income through seasonal work? Other aspects of economics, however, involve more *technical economic analysis*. For example, if the Bank of Canada reduces interest rates, by how much could we expect unemployment to decrease? In other situations, economics becomes involved with *value judgments*. For example, suppose an economic analysis estimates that if the government restricts imports of eggs in order to protect jobs on Canadian farms, higher egg prices in Canada will cost consumers roughly $120 000 for every job saved through this policy. Is this a worthwhile price to pay for the jobs that are saved? This question involves a value judgment, in the sense that even people who agree about the economic analysis of the issue may disagree on what policy the government should follow. One person may be more concerned about the effect of job losses, while another may place greater emphasis on the higher prices that Canadian consumers will have to pay for eggs.

The Limitations of Economic Analysis

Because it deals with the behaviour of people (consumers, workers, business people, government policy-makers), economics is not a precise science like mathematics. And with respect to important economic policy issues, economic analysis does not provide clear and simple *answers*, such as, "reduce interest rates by 0.5 of a percentage point." However, economic analysis can greatly *clarify the choices* to be made by estimating what would happen if interest rates were (or were not) reduced. So, while economic analysis does not provide us with *decisions*, it does provide us with a much better *basis for making* decisions.

Can Economists Agree on Anything?

"Ask five economists what should be done about a problem and you'll get six different recommendations" is a jibe frequently directed at economists. Given the disagreements among economists (and others loosely described as such) on important matters, it is easy to get the impression that the field of economics involves more unsubstantiated opinion than systematic analysis.

In fact, however, economics is in considerably better condition than the naysayers think. First, to add controversy to news coverage, the media often try to create controversy by seeking out dissenting opinions on economic issues, giving even illogical opinions an undeserved appearance of legitimacy. Second, many public pronouncements on economic matters are made not by economists, but rather by politicians whose goal is not to discuss economic issues rationally, but rather to score (or obscure) points politically. Most disagreements among economists arise not from *economic analysis* of issues but rather from differences concerning *policy recommendations* (value judgments) that arise from that analysis. In fact, there are many generally accepted facts, concepts, and theories that constitute a sort of "mainstream" of economic thought that is less publicized but much more important than disagreements between individual economists. This book attempts to build around this mainstream of thought, while considering the major alternatives to it where these are important.

Isn't This All Terribly Difficult?

Not really. Probably the most insightful observation ever made about economics as a field of study is that it is a *complex* subject but not a *difficult* one. Unlike nuclear physics or differential calculus, there is little in economics that many people find conceptually difficult. Rather, economics deals with people and their behaviour and decisions as consumers, workers, business people, and government policy-makers. Much of this behaviour is already known to the student of introductory economics; what needs to be done is to organize these fragments of knowledge into a framework for analyzing and understanding economic events. This book attempts to do this in a way that does not require abstract theories and complex mathematics, and focuses instead on developing an understanding of real and relevant Canadian macroeconomic issues in a readable and, hopefully, enjoyable way. Before examining these issues, however, we will consider the basic problems of economics and the nature of Canada's economic system.

The Economic Problem: Too Many Wants, Not Enough Resources

The fundamental problem of economics—so basic that it is known as *the economic problem*—is the simple fact that we cannot have everything that we would like. And because of this reality, we are forced to make some difficult decisions.

All too often, however, this and other key economic realities become lost in the confusing complexity of our modern economy. A modern economy can seem very bewildering, because it consists of numerous factors, such as consumers, small businesses, big businesses, ebusinesses, labour unions, and governments. In addition, there are external factors such as exports, imports, trade policy, and the international value of the Canadian dollar. And a modern economy generates seemingly countless statistics concerning output, employment, unemployment, the money supply, interest rates, prices, government tax revenues and spending, consumer spending and saving, banks, profits, stock markets, and so on. Furthermore, each of these factors is related to the others in ways that are often subtle and complex. Such complexities often make understanding an issue difficult because they obscure the basic economic principles of the issue.

In order to better understand an economic situation, it is helpful to eliminate the many complexities associated with a modern economy, so that we can focus on the basic economic principles involved. As a way to eliminate complexity, suppose that a group of people is stranded on a deserted island. With none of the complexities of a modern economy to distract it, this group must come to grips with the most basic economic problem: the people in the group have *economic needs and wants*, but there are only certain *economic resources* available to them. The group needs and wants things such as food, shelter, clothing, security, and so on. To produce these things, the group has three basic types of **economic resources**, or **inputs**—the skills of the people in the group, the equipment they have, and the natural resources of the island.

The Skills of the People (Labour)

The largest and most important single economic resource available to any society is the skills of its people, which economists refer to as **labour**. Labour includes all types of skills: manual labour, skilled work, management, and professional services. In our island mini-society, people will have various useful skills, such as hunting, fishing, farming, building, planning, and managing.

Capital Equipment

Another vitally important economic resource is society's stock of **capital equipment** (also simply called **capital**), by which we mean its tools, equipment, machinery, factories, computers, and so on. Capital equipment is crucially important because it increases **productivity**, or output per worker per hour. And when each worker produces more, the society can enjoy more economic prosperity, or a higher **standard of living**—more goods and services per person. Figure 1-1 illustrates the importance of capital equipment.

---

economic resources
Labour, capital equipment, and natural resources that are used to produce goods and services.

inputs
The same as economic resources.

labour
The largest single productive input available to any economy, labour includes all of the productive talents of the people of a society, mental as well as physical.

capital equipment
The tools, equipment, machinery, and factories used to increase production per worker, and thus improve living standards.

productivity
Output per worker per hour; one measure of efficiency.

standard of living
A measure of the economic prosperity of the people of a society, usually expressed in terms of the volume of goods and services consumed per person per year.

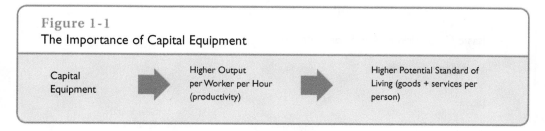

Figure 1-1
The Importance of Capital Equipment

Capital Equipment → Higher Output per Worker per Hour (productivity) → Higher Potential Standard of Living (goods + services per person)

"If you were asked to choose just one test of an economy's performance, one of the strongest candidates would be growth in productivity. In the long run, increases in productivity—that is, in output per worker—are the only way for a country to raise its living standards."
— THE ECONOMIST

While a modern industrial economy possesses a vast array of factories, machinery, equipment, and computers, our island mini-society will have only a few basic tools, such as spears, fishnets, and plows. As a result, productivity will be low, and the people of the mini-society will have relatively few goods to enjoy. So in order to increase their productivity and standard of living, they might, for example, build more capital equipment.

Natural Resources (Land)

The third economic resource available to a society is natural resources, which economists refer to as **land**. In our island mini-society, these natural resources would likely be few and simple—waterways, fish, land, trees, plants, and so on. In a modern economy, natural resources are often much more complex. For example, using energy resources such as oil, natural gas, and atomic energy involves sophisticated technology.

People tend to think of natural resources as finite (and depleting). But some natural resources, such as forests and fish, can be renewable if managed effectively, and technology is capable of creating entirely new resources, such as natural gas and nuclear power. For example, until the development of nuclear reactors, uranium could not reasonably be considered an economic resource. In a similar way, improvements in technology made the Athabasca Tar Sands of northern Alberta into a major energy resource. So, while some natural resources are becoming depleted, new resources can be developed through technology.

land
Short form for all the natural resources available to a society's economy as economic inputs.

The Task of an Economic System

The task of the economic system of any society is to organize and use these economic resources, or productive inputs, to produce goods and services (**output**) of the types and quantities that will best satisfy the needs and wants of the people of the society. This process is shown in Figure 1-2.

In our island mini-society, the process shown in Figure 1-2 would be quite simple: people with various skills would use simple tools such as spears, nets, and plows to produce products to satisfy basic needs such as food, shelter, and security. In a modern economy, this process is much more sophisticated, involving a wide range of skills and "high-tech" equipment and resources to produce a tremendous volume and variety of both goods and services. However, the basic task is the same in both economies: to use our economic resources to our best advantage.

output
The goods and services produced by a society using its productive inputs.

The Basic Economic Problem of Scarcity

Using our economic resources to our best advantage is particularly important because we do not have enough economic resources to produce everything that we would like

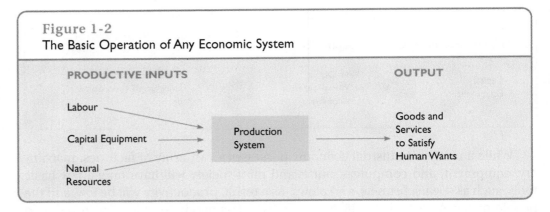

Figure 1-2
The Basic Operation of Any Economic System

scarcity

The problem that, while economic inputs (and thus potential output) are limited in availability, people's wants and needs are apparently unlimited.

to have. This is the basic economic problem of **scarcity**: the economic resources (inputs) on the left side of Figure 1-2 are in limited supply, while the amounts of goods and services wanted by people on the right side of Figure 1-2 seem to be unlimited. Since we cannot have everything that we want, we are forced to *make choices*, some of which might be difficult.

The island mini-economy illustrates this reality particularly clearly, because the choices are so limited. Suppose there are ten people available for work, and the group decides to use five of them for getting food, three for getting fuel, and two for taking care of security by maintaining fences and standing watch against certain threatening creatures that roam the island. If the group finds that they don't have enough food, they can increase food production by 20 percent by adding another person to the food team. However, this addition would require removing that person from one of the subgroups who are either getting fuel or providing security. While the group would be better fed, it would have either less comfort or less security. So having more of any one of these items means having less of another, forcing the group to make difficult choices.

YOU DECIDE

Opportunity Cost

opportunity cost

The concept that the real economic cost of producing something is the forgone opportunity to produce something else that could have been produced with the same inputs.

Economists use the term **opportunity cost** to describe the choices that scarcity forces upon us. That is, opportunity cost refers to what you *could have had* if you had used your resources for something else. ∎

QUESTIONS

1. Suppose that in the island mini-economy you had four people working: two people catching a total of six fish per day and two others picking a total of 8 kg of fruit per day. If you decided that you wanted to have three more fish each day, what would be a reasonable estimate of the opportunity cost of that decision?

2. As a consumer in a modern economy, your economic resources consist of the money available to you. Suppose that you had only $150 and your mother was expecting a Mother's Day gift (tickets to yet another Rolling Stones concert) that cost $150; however, your car had just broken down, and it would cost $150 to repair it.

   (a) What would be the opportunity cost of buying your mother the gift?

   (b) What would be the opportunity cost of getting your car fixed?

These are the same issues that Canadian households face in managing their budgets. Since your income can't buy everything that you would like, you have to make choices about what you will have and what you will forgo. Taking that dream vacation would be wonderful, but it will mean that you cannot buy the car that you really want. See the accompanying "You Decide" box for a look at the concept of opportunity cost in making choices.

And an entire nation, through its government, must come to grips with the same problems. The public wants the best health-care and education systems as well as other government services, but governments lack the tax revenues to provide the ideal levels of all services. Since using more tax resources for one service would leave less for other services, we must accept less than ideal levels of all services.

So the basic economic problem of scarcity is a universal one, affecting all societies. In the following sections, let's consider some of the implications of the problem of scarcity.

Effectiveness and Efficiency

Because we cannot have everything that we would like, it is very important that we use our scarce economic resources wisely, by producing as much as we can of things that are needed and wanted. This brings us to the concepts of *effectiveness* and *efficiency*, which are the two most basic measures of the performance of any economic operation, from an individual business to a nation's entire economy.

Effectiveness refers to producing goods and services that are *needed and wanted*. If an economic system achieves these goals, it is said to be effective. **Efficiency** refers to using the economic resources available to you to produce a *high volume of output* at a *low production cost per unit*. One common measure of efficiency is productivity, or output per worker per hour. Societies with efficient economies that produce a high volume of goods and services per worker tend to have a high standard of living, or consumption per person.

To recap, it is important that an economy be *both* effective *and* efficient. The more effectively and efficiently a society uses its economic resources, the more successful it will be in making available to its people larger volumes of goods and services that are needed and wanted—and at lower prices. As a result, its people will enjoy a higher standard of living.

effectiveness
A measure of how well an economy performs in terms of producing goods and services that meet the needs and wants of people.

efficiency
A measure of how well an economy performs in terms of producing high volumes of goods and services at a low cost per item.

The Three Basic Questions of Economics

As we have seen, the task of any economic system is to use its scarce economic resources efficiently and effectively in order to best satisfy the needs and wants of its people. Since economic resources are scarce and we cannot have everything that we want, we are forced to make certain very basic choices:
- What goods and services will we produce?
- How should we produce these goods and services?
- How will we divide up our output of goods and services among ourselves? That is, who will get how much?

These are the three most basic economic questions that every society must face, regardless of its stage of development or the nature of its economic system.

What to Produce?

Because economic resources (or productive inputs) are scarce, no society can have all the goods and services it would like to have. Instead, it must *make choices*, or set priorities. For example, the people in our island mini-society would have to decide whether to produce fish, vegetables, shelter, fuel, security, or more equipment to make their work more efficient.

What makes such choices difficult is that they involve deciding not only what *will* be produced, but also what *will not* be produced. If the group decides to use six people to farm vegetables, those six people will not be available to gather fuel or build shelter. So, a decision to produce *more* of one thing necessarily means accepting *less* of other things. This type of decision forces us to set priorities, or decide what is most important to us. Obviously, making such decisions relates to the goal of *effectiveness*, as discussed in the previous section, because the priorities we set will reflect our needs and wants, or how much we value each product.

Consumer Goods or Capital Goods?

One of the most basic what-to-produce decisions that must be made is whether *consumer goods* or *capital goods* will be produced. Consumer goods (such as food and fuel) can be enjoyed *in the present*, but are used up quickly and do not contribute to longer-term economic prosperity. Capital goods (such as tools and equipment), on the other hand, cannot be consumed and enjoyed *today*, but they will increase our productive efficiency *in the future*. In this way, capital goods will contribute to our future production and prosperity, by increasing our productivity for the many years that they will last. Figure 1-3 illustrates this choice.

These decisions will have a crucial influence on the prosperity of a society both in the present and in the future. If our island mini-society emphasizes the production of consumer goods, its people will enjoy a higher standard of living in the present. However, if the inhabitants emphasize consumer-goods production to the point of neglecting capital-goods production, they will enjoy less prosperity in the future. On the other hand, if the people are willing to make do with fewer consumer goods in the present in order to build more capital goods, they can look forward to higher levels of economic prosperity in the future. In the second half of the twentieth century, Japan and Germany stressed the production of capital goods to achieve economic growth; more recently, this has been a high priority for China.

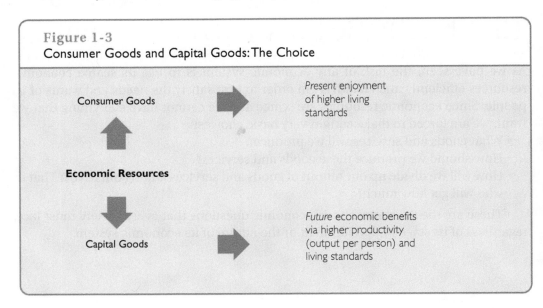

Figure 1-3
Consumer Goods and Capital Goods: The Choice

Consumer Goods → *Present* enjoyment of higher living standards

Economic Resources

Capital Goods → *Future* economic benefits via higher productivity (output per person) and living standards

How to Produce It?

Once we have decided *what* we want to produce, we must decide *how* each product or service is to be produced. This is a question of production methods: How should we combine our scarce inputs of labour, capital equipment, and natural resources for use in production?

As a simple example, suppose our island mini-society has decided to produce (cultivate) vegetables. The next question is, How should the group do this? Should people cultivate by hand? Or use simple tools such as hoes? Or use more sophisticated equipment such as plows? Before the vegetables that the group wants can be produced, the group will have to decide how to produce them.

Generally speaking, our goal will be to develop production methods that result in *higher efficiency* in order to increase our economic prosperity. However, the decision becomes more complicated if we need to use economic resources to build capital equipment in order to increase output per worker. If the amount of capital equipment we can build is limited, would it be better, for example, to build a plow for cultivating vegetables or a net for fishing? This decision would be easier to make if we could find a way to measure the *costs* of using the plow and the net (in terms of the hours, materials, and equipment needed to build each of them) against the *benefits* of each (in terms of the increased output each would bring).

Obviously, in deciding the answer to this question, we are pursuing the goal of *efficiency*, as discussed earlier. By being efficient, we avoid wasting our scarce economic resources, and so increase our economic prosperity.

Most running shoes are manufactured in Asia by large companies using low-wage labour, but New Balance also has plants in the United States, using higher-paid workers with computerized equipment.

Who Gets How Much? (Dividing the Economic Pie)

The last of our three basic questions is, How we will divide up our output of goods and services among our people? Who will receive what share of what we have produced?

Should everyone receive an equal share? Or should some people receive more than others? If some are to receive a larger share, why should they get more, and how much more should they get?

We have seen that a society will prosper economically if the work of its people is *effective* and *efficient*. An unequal distribution of income can promote better economic performance by rewarding people who work effectively and efficiently with a larger share of the "economic pie." If everyone knew that they were going to receive the same share as everyone else, why should anyone make an extra effort or contribution?

In addition to effectiveness and efficiency, however, there is the goal of *fairness*. How wide a gap between the rich and the poor are we prepared to accept? What if some people cannot produce enough to live decently without help from the others? Should the most productive people give up some of what they have produced (earned) in order to help the less productive ones? And if our answer to this question is yes, how much should the better-off people give up in order to help the less fortunate (or less capable)?

This question of how to divide up the economic pie is certainly the most controversial of the three basic economic questions. In a modern economy such as Canada's, a person's share of the economic pie depends on his or her *income*. If an accountant's income (after taxes) is twice as large as a labourer's, the accountant's share of the economic pie will be twice that of the labourer.

But by what standards should we *decide* who gets higher incomes and a larger share of the pie? Should hockey players receive a larger share than doctors? Should lawyers have a larger share than social workers? Should firefighters get a larger share than that of daycare workers? Somehow, every society has to work out the question of how to divide up the economic pie.

Answering the Three Questions

In this section, we have considered the three basic questions of economics that every society must answer—what to produce, how to produce it, and how to divide it up. Different societies answer these questions in very different ways. In the next section, we will consider how Canada's economic system deals with these most basic questions.

Canada's Economic System

We have seen that the basic economic problem of scarcity forces upon every society the need to address three questions: what to produce (and not produce), how to produce it, and how to divide it up among the people of the society. To deal with these questions, a society has to organize its economic resources (labour, capital equipment, and natural resources) in order to use them both effectively (produce things that are needed and wanted) and efficiently (produce them in high volume and at low cost and price), thereby generating economic prosperity for its people.

Effective and efficient organization of resources is no small task. The Canadian economy—the ninth largest in the world—includes over 33 million consumers with their own wants and needs, over two million business enterprises producing millions of different goods and services, and a labour force of 18 million people with a wide variety of skills. How, then, does the Canadian economy organize all these economic resources to produce over $1.6 trillion ($1 600 000 000 000) of goods and services annually, and in the process manage to provide its people with one of the highest standards of living in the world?

The Market System

market system
An economic system in which economic decisions are made in a decentralized manner mainly by consumers and privately owned producers.

Most of Canada's economic system is organized according to a *market system*. In the **market system** (also known as the *free enterprise system*), privately owned businesses (*free enterprises*) produce goods and services for profit in response to the demand of buyers. Nearly 80 percent of the total output of the Canadian economy is produced by such businesses, which are collectively known as the *private sector*. In the private sector, the key economic decisions are made by consumers and businesses.

In addition to its private sector, the Canadian economy has a substantial *government sector*, in which the key decisions are made by governments. The government sector accounts for roughly 22 percent of the output of the economy, consisting mostly of public services such as health care, education, and public security. In addition, governments play a number of other important roles in the economy, which we will examine later.

First let's examine what a market is and how it operates, and how a market system functions.

What Is a Market?

Simply stated, a *market* is where buyers and sellers come together to exchange goods and services for money, or to buy and sell things. Figure 1-4 illustrates this concept more formally, using the market for candles as an example. The figure shows that the market for candles consists of

(a) a number of sellers offering to sell candles, in competition with each other (economists call this side the *supply side* of the market), and

(b) many buyers offering to buy candles, in competition with each other (economists call this side the *demand side* of the market).

The interaction between buyers and sellers in the marketplace determines the *price* of candles ($5.00 each) and the *sales* of candles (100 000 per day). If the willingness of buyers to buy candles or the willingness of sellers to sell them were to change, the price and sales of candles would also change.

How Do Markets Work?

Markets respond to changes in buyers' demand. For instance, if the demand for candles increased (because there were more buyers, or buyers had more money, or candles became more popular than before), the increased demand would cause the *price* of candles to increase, say, from $5 to $7. This higher price, together with higher sales, would make it more profitable to produce candles. Because of this potential for higher profit, more candles would be produced and offered for sale, perhaps 110 000 per day instead of 100 000.

In the same way, if the demand for candles were to fall, then the price would fall, making candle production less profitable. With lower prices and lower sales, producers would produce fewer candles, in response to the lower demand of consumers.

The "classic" form of market is a farmers' market or a flea market, where many producers and consumers come directly together to buy and sell various products. However, markets take many other forms. To most people, the most familiar form of market is at the retail level, where consumers buy goods and services from retailers. In addition, there are wholesale markets and commodity markets, where the buyers are businesses that bid for the products in an auction environment; labour markets, where people's time and skills are purchased, and the price paid is a wage rate or salary; capital markets (or markets for loans), where the use of someone else's money is purchased, and the price paid is the interest rate; and stock markets, where the shares of corporations are bought and sold.

Some markets (such as the market for babysitters) are extremely local in nature, while others (such as the market for wheat or oil) are worldwide in scope. In some markets, buyers and sellers interact face to face; in other markets they never see each other. Regardless of its particular form, however, any market consists of a supply side and a demand side, as pictured in Figure 1-4.

Some markets are conducted over the internet. For examples, visit **www.trader.ca** and **www.expedia.ca**.

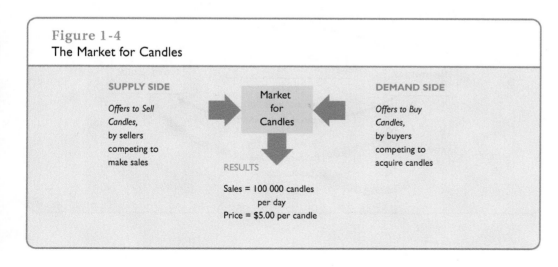

Figure 1-4
The Market for Candles

SUPPLY SIDE		DEMAND SIDE
Offers to Sell Candles, by sellers competing to make sales	Market for Candles → RESULTS ↓ Sales = 100 000 candles per day Price = $5.00 per candle	*Offers to Buy Candles,* by buyers competing to acquire candles

Because demand is such a basic force in markets, the market system is sometimes said to be *demand-driven*. And because of the key role played by prices and price changes in adjusting production to demand, the market system is sometimes referred to as the *price system*.

How Is a Market System Organized?

Figure 1-5 illustrates the operation of a market system. The upper flows in Figure 1-5 represent consumers buying goods and services from businesses. These flows represent many thousands of markets for specific goods and services, in which millions of consumers buy these items at the prices and in the quantities determined in each marketplace.

In other words, the upper flows would consist of the market for hamburgers, jeans, apartments, laptop computers, haircuts, and all of the other markets for all of the other goods and services that consumers buy. And in each of these markets, a *price* is determined for the product or service involved.

The lower flows in Figure 1-5 represent a different side of the economy, in which businesses buy the inputs for producing the goods and services shown in the top flows.

So the lower flows would include markets for factory workers, for accountants, for retail clerks, for professional athletes, and for all of the other job skills that the economy needs. And in each of these markets, a price—in the form of a wage rate or salary level for that type of skill—is established.

The operation of a market system such as that shown in Figure 1-5 involves billions of individual decisions by consumers, business firms, and workers about consumer purchases, production levels, prices, the numbers of workers to be employed, wage rates, capital investment, and so on. It is through these innumerable decisions, made in countless markets, that the answers are developed to the three basic questions of what to produce, how to produce it, and how to divide it up.

Figure 1-5
The Operation of a Market Economy

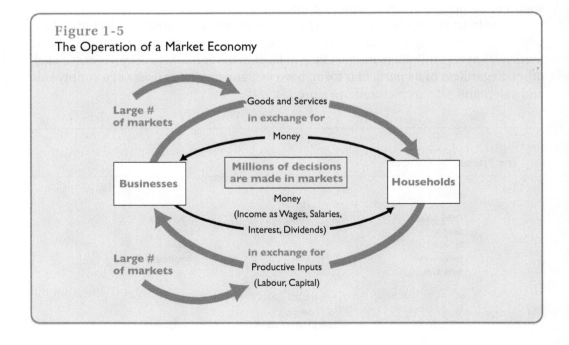

How Does the Market System Answer the Three Questions?

What to Produce?

Consumers play the largest role in deciding what will be produced. Since the basic goal of business is to earn a profit, businesses will produce those goods and services that are in demand. This process is described by the phrases *consumer sovereignty* (meaning that the consumer is viewed as "king of the marketplace") and *dollar votes* (meaning that, by buying a product, a consumer is in effect casting a vote in the marketplace for the production of that product).

Prices provide an important link between what buyers want and what businesses produce. For instance, if the demand for golfing increases, the price of golfing will increase. The increase in price will make operating golf courses more profitable, creating an incentive for businesses to create more golf courses. In the same way, a reduction in the demand for red meat would depress its price, making its production less profitable and creating an incentive to reduce its production. *Price signals* such as these are also transmitted through labour markets, as shown at the bottom of Figure 1-5. For instance, if the higher demand for golfing led to an increase in the demand for greenskeepers, the wages of greenskeepers would rise, attracting more people into working in that field.

How to Produce It?

The decision of how to produce a product is made by producers, or private businesses, who will strive for the most efficient possible production method. Lower production costs not only mean higher profits; in a highly competitive industry, they may be the key to survival.

Prices also help to decide the production methods for producing goods and services. In determining the most efficient production methods, it makes obvious economic sense to minimize the use of the most scarce inputs. Prices help to minimize using scarce inputs because the more scarce an input is, the more costly it will be for producers to buy. For instance, if lumber is scarce, its price will be high. Since it is such a costly input, producers will minimize waste and will substitute other less costly materials. So in order to maximize their profits, businesses have to manage society's scarce economic resources carefully, economizing the most on the use of the scarcest resources.

How to Divide Up the Economic Pie?

A person's share of the economic pie depends on his or her *income*. For instance, if electricians take home (after taxes) five times as much pay as day-care workers, their share of the economic pie will be five times as large as that of day-care workers.

And since your income is really the *price* of your productive skills, prices play a major role in deciding the question of how to divide up the economic pie. Like other prices, people's incomes (or salaries or wages) are mostly determined by the interplay of supply and demand—in this case, the supply of and the demand for your productive skills. For example, if electricians are in short supply but in great demand, their incomes (and their share of the economic pie) will be quite high. On the other hand, if there is a large supply of day-care workers relative to the demand for them, they will have low incomes and a small share of the pie.

When the price of crude oil rose past $50 per barrel in 2005, Suncor Energy announced plans to invest $10 billion in facilities to increase its production of oil from the Alberta Tar Sands. And in 2008-09, when the price of crude oil fell below $40 per barrel, several oil companies suspended plans for investment projects in the Tar Sands.

How Does the Market System Organize the Use of Economic Resources?

As we have seen, organizing the vast and varied economic resources of an economy such as Canada's into the effective and efficient production of millions of goods and services is an enormous task. On the face of it, the market system might appear to be ill-suited to such a complex task. The market system has no central plan, and seems to lack any organizing or coordinating forces; rather, it looks more like an economic "free-for-all" in which people buy whatever they want, produce whatever they want, and work wherever they want. Economic decision-making is spread among millions of consumers and producers in a decentralized and apparently uncoordinated manner. Nevertheless, the market system has in practice proven to be the best system for achieving effective and efficient use of economic resources, and for providing a high standard of living for its people.

What, then, are the forces within the market system that enable it to mobilize economic resources so effectively and efficiently? The two key features of the market system that promote effectiveness and efficiency are the *profit motive* and *competition*.

The Profit Motive

profits

Those funds left from a business's sales revenues after all expenses have been paid; such funds are therefore available (after taxes have been paid) for dividends to shareholders and reinvestment in the business.

Profits are those funds from a business's sales revenues that are left after all expenses and taxes have been paid. Profits are therefore available for reinvestment in the business or to be paid out as dividends to the shareholders who own the business.

The *profit motive* plays two vital roles in the operation of a market system. First, profits provide incentives for businesses to use economic resources both effectively and efficiently. By producing goods and services that consumers will buy—that is, by using economic resources *effectively*—a business will increase its sales and profits. And by producing those goods and services at the lowest possible production cost—that is, by using economic resources *efficiently*—a business will also increase its profits.

The second important role of profits is that they provide funds for the *purchase of capital equipment*. Each business purchases capital equipment to improve its own efficiency and profitability. But when *many* businesses do this, the result is improved productivity across the economy, which is the basic source of higher living standards for society generally. So, reinvestment of profits by business makes an important contribution to a society's economic prosperity.

In addition, many Canadians have a large stake in the profitability of corporations. Nearly half of adult Canadians own shares of corporations, many of these in mutual funds and registered retirement savings plans. In addition, about three dollars of every eight in pension funds in Canada are usually invested in corporate shares, so many people who do not think of themselves as shareholders have a stake in the success of Canadian corporations. Thus, millions of Canadians have billions of dollars invested in shares. These people not only receive part of the corporate profits as dividends, but also they are counting on the prosperity of those corporations for financial security in their retirement.

Nonetheless, there is a great deal of misunderstanding among the public concerning profits. The very word *profit* evokes for many people images of exploitation of workers and consumers. One misconception concerns the *level* of profits. Surveys indicate that the public believes that manufacturers' profits amount to 30 or 40 cents per dollar of sales, whereas before-tax profits are actually about 7 to 10 cents per dollar of sales, and after taxes, most manufacturers' profits amount to only 4 or 5 cents per dollar of sales. Ironically, the public believes 20 cents per dollar of sales to be a "fair" profit, indicating that there is a great deal of confusion regarding the matter of profits.

The public also has misconceptions concerning the *uses* of profits, which are often regarded as being hoarded away in corporate coffers or being paid out in lavish dividends to wealthy shareholders. In fact, roughly 30 percent of corporate profits goes to taxes, and most of the remainder is reinvested by businesses in capital equipment. Dividends to shareholders generally amount to a modest return on their investment, and these "capitalist" shareholders include not only the wealthy, but also many ordinary Canadians who directly or indirectly own shares, as described above.

Competition

Competition, which is the other key element in a market system, plays three vitally important roles in a market economy. First, competition forces businesses to produce what consumers want, in order to increase their sales and profits. In this sense, competition *promotes effectiveness* in the use of economic resources. Second, competition *promotes efficiency* in the use of economic resources. To prosper in a competitive marketplace, a producer must be as efficient as possible. And third, competition forces producers to *keep prices as low as possible*, in order to compete successfully for business. So, competition ensures that the advantages of higher efficiency and lower production costs are passed along to the consumer, allowing the maximum possible number of people to enjoy them.

Competition is closely linked with *information* in the effective functioning of markets. A free marketplace provides a wide variety of goods and services, of various qualities and at different prices. If consumers are well-informed about what items are available and at what prices, they will be better able to take advantage of the opportunities offered by a free and competitive marketplace. By contrast, poorly informed consumers will be more likely to get less value for their money.

In summary, a highly competitive marketplace pushes private profit-making producers to serve the interest of consumers by being effective and efficient and by keeping prices down. By contrast, in situations in which there is little or no competition, producers tend to be less responsive to consumers' preferences (less effective), to be less efficient than they could be, and to charge excessive prices to consumers.

Together, the two incentives of profits and competition tend to push producers to use economic resources both effectively and efficiently. The ability of the market system to automatically coordinate the decisions of millions of businesses and individuals in response to changes in consumer demand has been referred to as "the miracle of the market."

Figure 1-6 on page 16 summarizes the market system's powerful incentives for efficiency and effectiveness, which contribute greatly to productivity and prosperity. Figure 1-6 also shows how the basic concepts of effectiveness and efficiency relate to the income statement and profits of a business. A business that is *effective* in the sense of producing what buyers want will enjoy a *high sales income*. If that business is also *efficient*, it will have *low production costs* and other expenses. So, the more effective and efficient the business, the more profitable the business.

The Market System in Perspective

About four-fifths of the Canadian economy—the private sector—is organized as a market system. How well does this sector of the economy perform?

Different views of profits

Suppose a corporation has annual sales of $600 million, profits after taxes of $24 million, 4000 employees, and $400 million of shareholders' capital invested in the company.

The *employees* might feel that they are underpaid. If the $24 million of profits were divided among them, each would receive $6000 more ($24 million ÷ 4000).

Consumers might feel that $24 million in profits shows that they are being overcharged by this company. Realistically, though, the total elimination of the manufacturer's profits would only reduce prices by 4 percent ($24 million ÷ $600 million).

From the viewpoint of the *shareholders* of the company, their capital is only earning a rate of return (after tax) of 6 percent ($24 million ÷ $400 million). Compared to other investments, this is not an attractive rate of return.

So, while employees and consumers complain about its high profits, investors might be deciding to sell their shares in the company.

For an indication of the role of information in markets, visit **www.trader.ca** and "shop" for a used car.

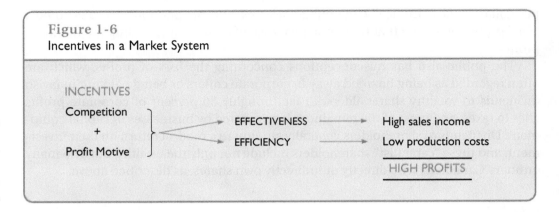

Figure 1-6
Incentives in a Market System

According to the criteria of *effectiveness* and *efficiency*, the market system performs very well. With respect to effectiveness, there is no economic system that is more responsive to consumer demand than the market system, which is marvellously flexible in adjusting its production automatically in response to changes in consumer preferences. And with respect to efficiency, no system provides greater incentives for efficient use of economic resources than the combination of the profit motive and competition.

However, the market system also has certain weaknesses. A basic problem is that the market will tend to produce too little of key *public services* such as health care and education. For instance, if college costs $4000 per year, only 100 000 people will attend college, because they consider the cost of attending college to be justified by the *benefits to them*. However, having more college graduates is of significant *benefit to society*, in the form of more productive and better citizens. So, society would benefit if *more* people attended college, making it logical for the government to *intervene in the market* and reduce the cost of college education, which would encourage more people to attend college. The most common way for governments to do this is to take on the task of operating colleges, and financing them partly with government grants. Reducing the cost of public services also increases the access of citizens to higher education and health care, which many view as an important social policy.

Another problem that can develop in a market system is **market power**, or monopoly-like power in some markets. Sometimes, producers may be able to band together and agree to limit competition among themselves and charge higher prices. In a similar manner, some workers may be able to band together into labour unions that achieve essentially the same result—less competition and higher prices (wages) for their members. In both cases, an organized group (of businesses or workers) reduces competition in the marketplace for its own benefit, at the expense of others.

While free markets for labour provide strong incentives for people to acquire in-demand skills and to work efficiently, it is also true that in a market system there is a tendency for great *inequality in incomes* to develop, as some people enjoy very high incomes while others live in poverty.

While the profit motive provides strong incentives to be effective and efficient, it also provides incentives to do things that are less beneficial to society, including using unfair competitive practices, misleading consumers, unfair treatment of vulnerable employees, and polluting the environment.

On a larger, macroeconomic scale, another fundamental problem with the market system is *economic insecurity*. Market economies tend to slump into periodic **recessions**, during which the economy's output falls and unemployment rises. During a typical recession in Canada, the number of unemployed people rises by more than half a million.

market power
The ability to raise one's price; usually associated with a dominant or monopolistic position in a market.

recession
A period when the economy is producing considerably less than its potential output, and unemployment is high. Commonly defined as two consecutive quarters (a quarter being three months) of declining output.

These weaknesses of the market system have led governments to take corrective action of various sorts, as we will see when we complete our description of Canada's economic system.

The Mixed Economic System of Canada

Canada's economic system can best be described as a *mixed free-enterprise system* because while our economy is basically a market system, it also includes a large government sector and a great deal of government involvement in the private sector.

The Private Sector

As we have seen, about 80 percent of the total annual output of the Canadian economy is produced by the private sector. In this sector, in which the vast majority of Canadians are employed, businesses produce goods and services in response to market demand and for a profit, and economic decisions are made by households (or consumers) and businesses.

The Government Sector

In the government sector, the key economic decisions are made by governments. The government sector accounts for about 22 percent of the annual output of the economy, most of which consists of public services such as health care and education. In broad terms, governments play three major roles in the economy.

First, governments are major *providers of public services*. From health care, education, and law enforcement to traffic control, public transit, and postal service, Canadian governments provide the public with a wide range of services. In most cases, such as health care, police protection, and elementary and secondary education, the public pays for these services with its tax revenues. In effect, then, the government is buying these services collectively on the public's behalf, from the government's own employees (such as teachers) and from others (such as doctors) who provide the services. In some cases, governments *operate enterprises* that provide services, including Crown corporations (such as Canada Post and the Canadian Broadcasting Corporation) and public commissions that provide services (such as public transit and hydroelectricity). In many cases, including public transit and postsecondary education, governments *subsidize public services*. **Subsidies** use tax revenues to pay part of the cost of the service. The grand total of these government-provided services is impressive—when the services of all government employees are counted as government purchases, Canadian governments account for roughly 22 percent of all the goods and services produced by the economy. In 2010, this portion amounted to over $354 billion, or over $10 700 for every Canadian man, woman, and child.

Second, governments *regulate* in many ways the operations and practices of businesses. For example, government laws or agencies set standards for many products, regulate advertising practices, set employment standards such as minimum wage rates and safety standards, set rules for the conduct of employer–union relations, regulate the competitive practices of businesses (including the prohibition of monopolistic practices), and set environmental protection standards. In the case of some farm products, government marketing boards regulate the amount that farmers can produce. In addition, many prices are regulated by government, including electrical rates, tobacco and alcohol prices, some transportation rates, and apartment rents in some areas.

http://canada.gc.ca

subsidies
Government financial assistance to a firm or industry, through grants, loans, or reduced taxes.

The third major area of government involvement in the economy is the *redistribution of income* through programs that transfer income from people with higher incomes to those with lower incomes. Such programs include employment insurance, welfare, old age security allowances, assistance to farmers and other groups, and various features of the income-tax system (tax credits) that reduce the taxes payable by those with lower incomes. In 2010, government transfer payments to persons (mostly through employment insurance, welfare, and pensions) amounted to $174 billion, or roughly $5200 per Canadian. This figure includes only *government payments* to Canadians; it excludes government assistance to lower-income Canadians through *tax credits* that reduce their income taxes and/or entitle them to tax refunds, such as the GST tax credit refunds received by many students.

Taken together, these government programs amount to a great deal of government involvement in the Canadian economy. In 2010, the grand total of spending by Canadian governments (on goods and services, transfer payments to persons, and interest on government debt) amounted to 42 percent of Canada's **gross domestic product (GDP)**, which measures the total of goods and services produced and incomes earned in Canada in any one year. When the many government regulations of economic activity as described earlier are added, the Canadian economy is accurately called a *mixed system*—still mostly *market* in nature, but with a large amount of government involvement.

gross domestic product (GDP)
Total value of goods and services produced (and incomes earned) in a country in one year.

Chapter Summary

1. The fundamental economic problem is *scarcity*: whereas society's economic resources are limited in quantity, people's wants and needs are apparently unlimited; thus, not all wants and needs can be satisfied. (L.O. 1)
2. The opportunity cost of producing something is the foregone opportunity to produce something else with the same inputs. (L.O. 2)
3. Because of the scarcity problem, it is important that economic resources be used both effectively and efficiently. (L.O. 2)
4. The problem of scarcity requires that the following three questions be answered:

    (a) what goods and services to produce,
    (b) how to produce them, and
    (c) how to divide them among people. (L.O. 3)

5. A market system operates through markets. In these markets, what to produce is decided by consumer demand, how to produce it is decided by producers, and the division of the economic pie is decided by people's incomes. (L.O. 4)
6. Profits provide incentives for the efficient and effective use of economic resources and are a major source of funds for capital investment, which contributes to economic prosperity by increasing output per worker. (L.O. 5)
7. Competition keeps prices and profits down and pushes producers to be both efficient and effective (responsive to consumers). (L.O. 6)
8. The main weaknesses of the market system are its tendency toward periodic recessions, a lack of competition in some markets, and a tendency for incomes to be distributed unevenly. (L.O. 7)

9. Canada's economic system is called a *mixed* or *mixed free-enterprise* system: while it is basically a market or free-enterprise system, it includes significant elements of government involvement in the economy. Major aspects of government involvement in the Canadian economy are the provision of various public services, the regulation of economic activity, and the redistribution of income from those with higher incomes to those with lower incomes. (L.O. 8)

Questions

1. The basic economic problem is
   (a) to achieve a more equal distribution of income in order to reduce poverty.
   (b) that economic resources are scarce while human wants are unlimited.
   (c) to establish prices that accurately reflect the relative scarcities of goods.
   (d) to establish a fair system of personal and business taxation.
   (e) to increase your exports so that they exceed your imports.

2. Suppose that in an island mini-economy there are six people working: three people catching a total of six fish per day and three others picking a total of nine baskets of fruit per day. If they decided that they wanted to have two more fish each day, what would be a reasonable estimate of the *opportunity cost* of that decision?

3. Explain how each of the following management decisions would be intended to affect the *effectiveness* and/or *efficiency* of a company:
   (a) A plan whereby the company's sales representatives provide feedback and suggestions to management based on the sales representatives' experience with customers.
   (b) The replacement of an hourly wage rate with an incentive plan under which workers are paid $2 for each of the first 50 products they produce, and $3 for each product beyond 50.
   (c) A quality-control program under which finished products are inspected more thoroughly in order to ensure that they meet quality standards.

4. (a) How could you measure the effectiveness of your school?
   (b) How could you measure the efficiency of your school?
   (c) Explain three ways to increase the efficiency of your school.
   (d) How would these ways of increasing efficiency affect your school's effectiveness?

5. A factory employs 20 workers who work 8 hours per day and produce 800 boxes of candles per day. What is the *productivity* of workers in that factory?
   (a) 800 boxes of candles per day
   (b) 5 boxes of candles per worker per hour
   (c) 40 boxes of candles per worker per hour
   (d) 100 boxes of candles per hour

6. The three basic questions that any economic system must answer are
   (a) what to produce, how to produce it, and how much of it to produce.
   (b) what to produce, how to produce it, and where to produce it.
   (c) what to produce, how much of it to produce, and how to divide it among the people.
   (d) what to produce, how to produce it, and how to divide it among the people.
   (e) what to produce, how much of it to produce, and where to produce it.

7. The market type of economic system would correct a shortage of lumber by
   (a) the government paying a subsidy to lumber producers to encourage them to increase their production of lumber.

(b) lowering the price of lumber and the profits of the lumber producers who are causing the shortage.

(c) government instructions to producers to increase their production of lumber.

(d) increasing the price of lumber and the profits of producers of lumber.

(e) the government establishing a government-owned lumber company.

8. Canada has a mixed economic system, in which both the marketplace and government play a role. For each of the following situations, explain why you think that it would be best dealt with by market forces or by government action.

(a) There are too many restaurants in a town, and several are losing money.

(b) The gap between the rich and the poor is very wide, and the poorest citizens are unable to afford even the bare necessities of life.

(c) The largest supermarket chain in the country is planning to buy the second-largest chain, which would give it a near-monopoly in many communities.

(d) A trend toward healthier eating has driven the price of chicken up so sharply that many consumers are complaining to the government about the high price of chicken.

(e) Several manufacturers are cutting costs by dumping waste into a local river.

9. A common criticism of government departments and agencies is that their operations are *inefficient*.

(a) What might explain why government operations tend to be inefficient?

(b) What is the opportunity cost of any such inefficiency?

10. The internet has brought markets into people's homes as never before. Visit **www.trader.ca** and look for the best price that you can find on a used 2009 Honda Accord. Before the internet, how did people shop for a used car? How has the internet changed the effectiveness and the efficiency of the market for used cars?

Study Guide

Review Questions   (Answers to these Review Questions appear in Appendix B.)

1. "Every society, regardless of the economic system that it has, faces the problem of scarcity." This statement means that

(a) All economies have depressions during which scarcities exist.

(b) There are times when some products can be had only by paying high prices.

(c) There are insufficient productive resources to satisfy all the wants of a society's people.

(d) In the beginning, every society faces shortages, but a mature and prosperous economy such as Canada's has overcome scarcity.

(e) None of the above.

2. Which is the best description of the opportunity cost of a $200 dinner?

(a) It is far too high!

(b) It is not a serious consideration in the decision whether to enjoy the dinner.

(c) It is $200.

(d) It is only a problem if you left your credit card at home.

(e) It is the nice clothes that could have been bought instead of the dinner.

3. The most commonly used definition of *productivity* is
   (a) output per worker per hour.
   (b) the total output (GDP) of a nation.
   (c) profit per unit of output.
   (d) the total number of worker-hours worked per year.
   (e) None of the above.

4. The "what" problem in economics means that
   (a) every society must in some way decide what goods it will produce (and not produce).
   (b) economists should tell us what goods to produce.
   (c) goods and services should be produced as efficiently as possible.
   (d) society should always produce only those goods which it can produce most efficiently with its technology and resources.
   (e) in every society, the government decides what goods will be produced.

5. In economics, the "how to produce" question refers to
   (a) the decision concerning how to go about marketing a product.
   (b) designing products so as to increase their appeal to consumers.
   (c) how much of each product to produce.
   (d) the decision concerning the production methods to be used to produce goods and services.
   (e) None of the above.

6. In economics, the question of for whom to produce goods and services means
   (a) how much should be exported and how much should be kept inside the country.
   (b) how should society divide up its total output of goods and services among the population.
   (c) businesses must research the market for particular products before they produce and market them.
   (d) poor people buy bicycles; rich people buy big cars.
   (e) the more society produces of one product, the less it can produce of other products.

7. In a *market* type of economic system, the questions of what to produce, how to produce it, and how to divide up the economic pie are basically decided by
   (a) the people, working consciously for the social good rather than for their own interests.
   (b) social custom and tradition.
   (c) the free decisions of households and businesses, made out of self-interest.
   (d) the government.
   (e) economists.

8. In a market system type of economy, which of the following best describes how the question of what to produce is decided?
   (a) Government makes most of the decisions regarding what to produce.
   (b) The most important factor is consumer demand, which increases and decreases prices and profits, and so creates incentives for businesses to increase or reduce production.
   (c) Privately owned businesses (producers) make the decisions as to what to produce, in the final analysis.
   (d) This decision is made by the people, as everybody works consciously for the social good rather than for his or her own self-interest.
   (e) None of the above.

9. A market system type of economy would correct a surplus (oversupply) of running shoes by
   (a) government instructing running shoe manufacturers to reduce their production of running shoes.
   (b) raising the price of running shoes and the profits of manufacturers of running shoes.
   (c) reducing taxes on running shoes, to encourage people to purchase them.
   (d) lowering the price of running shoes and the profits of their manufacturers.
   (e) None of the above.

10. In a market system type of economy, which of the following best describes how the question of how to produce goods and services is decided?
   (a) Those productive inputs that are scarcer will be used more efficiently, because they will cost producers more.
   (b) The decisions regarding the production methods to be used are made by producers (businesses).
   (c) The major factor influencing this decision is the government.
   (d) The consumer decides this question, through the demand for goods and services.
   (e) Answers (a) and (b).

11. In a market system type of economy, the question of how to divide up the economic pie is basically decided by
   (a) the social status of individuals and groups.
   (b) the marketing departments of businesses.
   (c) the ways in which total incomes are divided up among individuals and groups.
   (d) the government.
   (e) economists.

12. Everyone knows that medical care is far more important than hockey, yet hockey players are paid far more than nurses. Why is this so?
   (a) Hockey players are really entertainers rather than producers of a service.
   (b) There are fewer professional hockey players than nurses.
   (c) Hockey players are more skilled than persons who get less pay.
   (d) The demand for hockey players is greater than for nurses.
   (e) Compared to the demand for them, good hockey players are more scarce than nurses.

13. State whether each of the following statements regarding business profits is *true* or *false*.
   (a) They provide strong incentives for businesses to produce goods and services as efficiently as possible.
   (b) They provide strong incentives for businesses to produce what consumers want.
   (c) Most profits are paid out as dividends to shareholders.
   (d) They are an important source of funds for capital investment, which increases prosperity.
   (e) They are considerably larger than the general public supposes them to be.

14. State whether each of the following statements regarding competition in a market economy is *true* or *false*.
   (a) It results in higher profits for businesses.
   (b) It promotes the efficient use of economic resources.

(c) It promotes the effective use of economic resources.

(d) It is not considered to be an important element in the operation of a market economy.

(e) It keeps the prices paid by consumers down.

15. Which one of the following is an *inaccurate* criticism of the market type of economic system?

(a) It tends to result in an unequal distribution of income, with a very few rich people and many who are poor.

(b) It suffers from economic instability—the problems of recurrent recessions and inflation.

(c) It fails to produce goods and services efficiently.

(d) Private economic power groups can become established, and enrich themselves at the expense of less powerful groups.

(e) It tends to create economic insecurity, particularly due to periodic increases in unemployment.

Critical Thinking Questions

(Asterisked questions 1 to 5 are answered in Appendix B; the answers to questions 6 to 10 are in the Instructor's Manual that accompanies this text.)

*1. Rupinder wins $1 000 000 in a lottery. Does this mean that Rupinder no longer has to be concerned about the economic problems of scarcity and opportunity cost?

*2. What is the opportunity cost of your attending school this year?

*3. Explain how each of the following management decisions would be intended to affect the effectiveness and/or efficiency of a business.

(a) A business introduces a profit-sharing plan under which a portion of the profits above a certain level will be shared with the employees.

(b) A business invests in industrial robots that are programmed to perform production tasks rapidly and with great precision.

(c) A restaurant reduces the number of servers it employs, so that each server has to serve 10 percent more tables than before.

*4. The market system type of economy is generally regarded as the most successful at providing a high standard of living, *but only if* there is vigorous competition among producers. Why is competition among producers necessary for a market system to operate well?

*5. Explain why you think that each of the following represents a market or government element of Canada's mixed economic system.

(a) Growing demand for goat meat causes its price to increase sharply.

(b) Primary and secondary education is provided at no cost to students and their families.

(c) An oversupply of computers causes their price to decrease considerably.

(d) The federal Competition Bureau stops the largest corporation in an industry from buying its largest competitor.

(e) The poorest Canadians are able to receive welfare benefits.

(f) Following a year-long work stoppage, NHL hockey players accept large pay cuts.

6. Evaluate the accuracy of the following statement. "Profits serve no useful purpose and contribute nothing to society economically. All that profits do is make prices much higher and take vast amounts of money from consumers and give it to businesses and their wealthy shareholders."

7. The sixteenth-century French philosopher Michel de Montaigne asserted that, "No man can profit except by the loss of others, and by this reasoning all manner of profit must be condemned." Do you agree with his argument? Does every economic transaction necessarily involve a winner and a loser?

8. Suppose that a manufacturer is selling two products (product A and product B) for $100 each, and is making a profit (before taxes) of 7 percent of the selling price of each product.
   (a) If strong demand increases the price of product A by just 2 percent, by what percentage will the profits on product A rise?
   (b) If weak demand for product B causes its price to fall by just 1 percent, by what percentage will the profits on product B decrease?
   (c) Given these facts, what would be the logical decision for the management of the company to make?

9. How could having an internet website improve the effectiveness and the efficiency of a business's operations?

10. Explain how a development in communications technology, such as the internet, could improve the way in which some markets function.

Use the Web (Hints for this Use the Web exercise appear in Appendix B.)

1. Visit the website of a news agency such as **www.msn.ca** or a newspaper, and look for news items concerning government policy or business decisions that involve the basic economic concepts of productivity, effectiveness, and efficiency. Write a brief explanation of how the decision that you selected affects productivity, effectiveness, and efficiency.

Introduction to Macroeconomics

After studying this chapter, you should be able to

1. Describe the five key factors on the supply side of the economy and the four components of its demand side.

2. Explain what *capacity output* means, and how the interaction between aggregate demand and capacity output determines whether the economy will be in a condition of recession, boom, or inflation.

3. State three basic macroeconomic goals for the economy.

4. State what the gross domestic product (GDP) measures, list the four major components of GDP, and show how GDP is calculated.

5. Explain the difference between *money GDP* and *real GDP*.

6. State what the consumer price index (CPI) measures, explain how the CPI is constructed to achieve this purpose, and calculate the rate of inflation from the CPI for two consecutive years.

7. State the purpose of the Labour Force Survey, describe the main statistics in this survey (population of working age, participation rate, labour force, employed, unemployed, and unemployment rate), and calculate the unemployment rate from Labour Force Survey data.

8. Describe each of the four basic types of unemployment.

9. Explain how the economic statistics discussed in this chapter can be used to monitor the condition of the economy (boom, inflation, and recession).

Figure 2-1 shows the operation of a market system economy, such as we saw in Chapter 1. The upper flows in Figure 2-1 represent markets for countless goods and services. In most such markets, the products or services are bought by millions of consumers and sold by many producers. Microeconomics studies the market for *each particular* good or service (such as computers, automobiles, or restaurants) that is included in this upper flow, and the price and the amount purchased of each of them. Macroeconomics deals with similar matters, but on a much broader scale—the *grand total* of all goods and services produced in the economy, and the *average level* of the prices of these. In other words, macroeconomics deals with the *total size* of the upper flow of goods and services in Figure 2-1, on an *economy-wide scale*.

Similarly, the lower flows in Figure 2-1 show producers, or businesses, obtaining the productive inputs that they need in order to produce the goods and services in the top flows. The most important of these inputs is labour, ranging from unskilled workers to skilled trades workers to professionals. The lower flows in Figure 2-1 show this wide range of productive skills being "sold" to businesses by the people who possess those skills, in exchange for wages and salaries. Microeconomics examines the market for *each* of these skills, and also the wage rate and the number of workers employed in each market. For instance, in microeconomics, we might study the market for part-time student labour, for accountants, or for NHL hockey players. Again, in macroeconomics, we are concerned with similar matters, but on a much wider scale—the levels of *total employment (and unemployment) and total incomes* in the economy as a whole, or the *total size* of these flows in the lower loop, on an *economy-wide scale*.

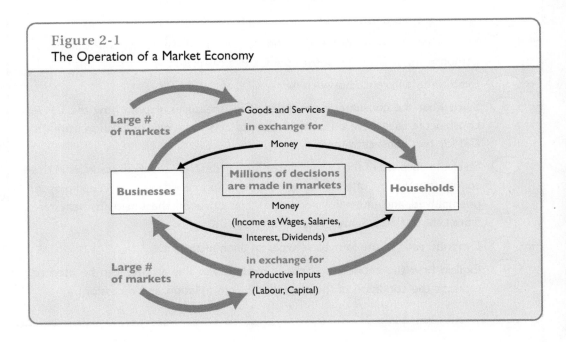

Figure 2-1
The Operation of a Market Economy

Large # of markets

Goods and Services in exchange for Money

Millions of decisions are made in markets

Businesses

Households

Money (Income as Wages, Salaries, Interest, Dividends)

Large # of markets

in exchange for Productive Inputs (Labour, Capital)

demand side
The purchasers of society's output of goods and services.

supply side
The producers of society's output of goods and services.

Markets on a Microeconomic Scale

Before considering these larger macroeconomic matters, let's review how markets operate on a microeconomic scale, as shown in Figure 2-2. Chapter 1 described markets for individual goods and services as consisting of

- a **demand side**, or offers by buyers to purchase a good or service, and
- a **supply side**, or offers by sellers to sell the good or service.

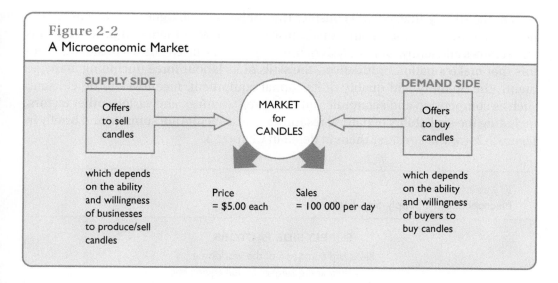

Figure 2-2
A Microeconomic Market

SUPPLY SIDE

Offers to sell candles

which depends on the ability and willingness of businesses to produce/sell candles

MARKET for CANDLES

Price = $5.00 each   Sales = 100 000 per day

DEMAND SIDE

Offers to buy candles

which depends on the ability and willingness of buyers to buy candles

Let's use the market for candles as an example. The key to the demand side of this market is *the ability and willingness of buyers to purchase candles,* and the key to the supply side of this market is *the ability and willingness of businesses to produce candles and offer them for sale.* And it is the interaction of the demand side and the supply side of the market that determines the price and the sales of candles, or any other good or service.

In one sense, the most basic factor is the supply side's ability and willingness to *produce* candles. If society is to *have* the volume of candles that it needs or wants, the candle industry must be able to *produce* this volume of candles at a price per candle that will allow the industry to pay the production costs and earn a profit. This ability to produce will depend upon the labour, capital equipment, and other inputs available to the candle industry.

On the other hand, the demand side of the market is equally important—candles will only be produced if there is a demand for them. The key on the demand side is the ability and willingness of people to *buy* candles. If the demand for candles is low, production and prices will be low, with the result that candle workers will be laid off. Higher demand for candles would cause higher production, and more workers would be employed. And, if the demand for candles were so high that the producers could not keep up with it, the price of candles would rise rapidly.

Markets on a Macroeconomic Scale

Macroeconomics is concerned with how the economy operates on a much larger scale—that is, the *grand total* of all the goods and services produced in the whole economy. However, the general approach to analyzing macroeconomic matters is the same as that used in analyzing markets on a microeconomic scale. In both cases, the basic economic forces are supply and demand.

As with microeconomic markets, we can divide the economy on a macroeconomic scale into a *supply side,* in which the key is the ability and willingness of all the producers in the nation to produce goods and services and offer them for sale, and a *demand side,* in which the key is the ability and willingness of all of the buyers of the nation's output to purchase goods and services. These are the same supply side and demand side forces that we saw in our microeconomic analysis, but on a much larger, economy-wide scale.

On the supply side, we will consider the ability and willingness of the entire economy—*all* producers, large and small, private and government—to produce goods and services efficiently. Our analysis of the supply side will lead us to consider the factors that make a nation productive—the skills of its labour force (including management), the quantity and quality of its capital equipment, incentives to be efficient, such as competition and economic gain (the *profit motive*), and various other factors, including the availability of natural resources. These factors are summarized briefly in Figure 2-3; we will consider them in detail in Chapter 3.

Figure 2-3
Macroeconomic Supply-Side Factors

SUPPLY-SIDE FACTORS

Skills and education of the workforce
+ Quantity and quality of capital equipment
+ Natural resources
+ Incentive of economic gain
+ Incentive of competition

**POTENTIAL OF THE ECONOMY
TO PRODUCE
GOODS AND SERVICES
EFFICIENTLY**

And on the demand side, on a macroeconomic scale we have to take into account the total of *all* spending on goods and services in the entire economy by *all* buyers. We can divide these buyers into four basic groups: consumers, businesses, governments, and foreign buyers. The total spending on goods and services by all of these groups is known as **aggregate demand**. The components of aggregate demand are summarized in Figure 2-4; we will consider these factors in detail in Chapter 4.

aggregate demand
Total spending on goods and services by all buyers of the economy's output.

Figure 2-4
Macroeconomic Demand-Side Factors

DEMAND-SIDE FACTORS

Consumer spending on goods and services
+ Business investment spending on capital goods
+ Government spending on goods and services
+ Foreign spending on Canadian goods and services

**TOTAL SPENDING ON
(AGGREGATE DEMAND FOR)
GOODS AND SERVICES**

The Operation of the Economy on a Macroeconomic Scale

Figure 2-5 shows these supply-side and demand-side factors as the key parts of a model of the economy.

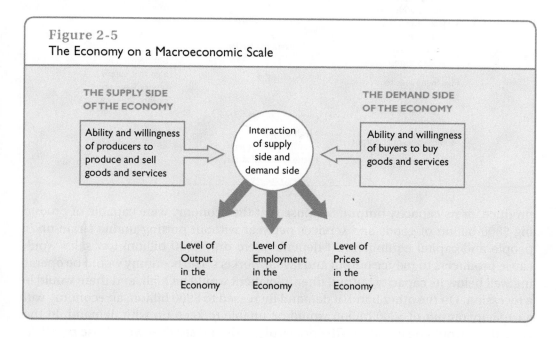

Figure 2-5
The Economy on a Macroeconomic Scale

While it is much larger and considerably more complex than the market for a single item, the macroeconomic model of the economy shown in Figure 2-5 operates in the same way that the microeconomic markets covered earlier do. For instance, if demand in the economy were low, output and employment would be low, and there would be a recession. If demand were to increase, output and employment would rise to higher levels, and there would be an **economic boom**. Finally, if demand were to rise to such high levels that output could not keep up with demand, prices would rise rapidly and there would be **inflation**. Each of these situations is covered in much more detail in the chapters that follow.

An Illustration of a Smoothly Functioning Market System

Figure 2-6 shows a market system that is operating ideally on a macroeconomic scale. On the supply side of the economy, there is a strong ability to produce efficiently the goods and services that are in demand. The economy possesses all of the productive inputs needed to produce goods and services efficiently: a capable labour force, good capital equipment, and ample natural resources or raw materials. In addition, the economy provides producers with strong incentives to use these inputs as efficiently as possible, in the form of the "carrot" of profits (after taxes) and the "stick" of competition. In short, the supply side of the economy is capable of efficient and effective production. However, for the supply side to be able to achieve its potential, there has to be an appropriate level of demand.

On the demand side of the economy, what is a healthy level of demand? This level depends on the volume of goods and services that the supply side is readily able to

economic boom
High levels of output and employment in the economy as a whole.

inflation
An increase in the general level of the prices of goods and services.

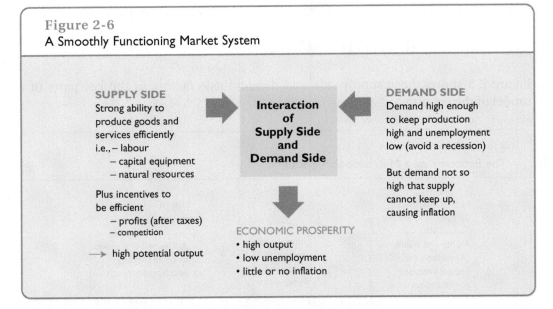

Figure 2-6
A Smoothly Functioning Market System

SUPPLY SIDE
Strong ability to
produce goods and
services efficiently
i.e., – labour
    – capital equipment
    – natural resources

Plus incentives to
be efficient
    – profits (after taxes)
    – competition

→ high potential output

**Interaction
of
Supply Side
and
Demand Side**

DEMAND SIDE
Demand high enough
to keep production
high and unemployment
low (avoid a recession)

But demand not so
high that supply
cannot keep up,
causing inflation

ECONOMIC PROSPERITY
• high output
• low unemployment
• little or no inflation

capacity output

The maximum amount of output the economy can produce without generating excessively rapid increases in production costs and prices.

produce, or its **capacity output**. Suppose that the economy were capable of producing $800 billion of goods and services per year without putting undue strain on its people and capital equipment. If demand were only $700 billion, low sales would cause producers to reduce output and lay off workers. The economy would be operating well below its capacity output, unemployment would be high, and there would be a recession. On the other hand, if demand increased to $900 billion, an economy with a capacity output of $800 billion would be unable to keep up with demand. In that case, there would be inflation—the prices of goods and services would rise rapidly as the economy was pushed beyond its capacity output.

In summary, the economy's capacity output is not a *physical limit* on how much the economy can produce; rather, it is the *economic limit* beyond which costs and prices start to rise rapidly. Reaching the economy's capacity output can be compared to reaching the red line on the tachometer of a car—the car *could* go faster, but it will begin to overheat. In fact, inflation is often explained in similar terms—the economy *could* produce more, but it would "overheat" as production costs and prices increased rapidly. In Chapter 3, we will look at the economic factors that actually impose the limits that establish an economy's capacity output.

We have learned through experience that both recession and inflation can cause economic hardship. Ideally, then, the level of demand would be neither too low nor too high relative to the ability of the supply side to produce goods and services. In other words, the demand side would generate high enough spending to prompt the supply side to produce as much output as it readily could, but not so much spending that the supply side could not keep up with demand, which would result in rapid inflation.

If the economy has a strong ability to produce goods and services, and demand is neither too low nor too high relative to capacity output, the results will be as shown at the bottom of Figure 2-6:
• high output of goods and services (i.e., at or near the economy's capacity, or potential output),
• high levels of employment (and low unemployment), and
• little or no inflation.

Of course, market economies do not always perform as well as in the ideal situation portrayed in Figure 2-6. There are three basic types of problems that a market economy can develop on a grand macroeconomic scale (excluding international problems, which are covered later):

- *weaknesses on the supply side* that prevent it from producing goods and services efficiently, such as a poorly trained labour force or inadequate capital equipment,
- *inadequate demand for goods and services* on the demand side, which will cause unemployment and a recession, and
- *excessive demand for goods and services* on the demand side, which will cause inflation, or rapid increases in prices.

Supply-side problems are covered in Chapter 3. The problems of inadequate demand and recessions and those of excessive demand and inflation are dealt with in Chapter 6.

Our Macroeconomic Goals and How We Measure Them

Figure 2-6 shows a smoothly operating economic system that generates prosperity as measured by three criteria—high output, low unemployment, and little or no inflation. In the following sections, let's take a closer look at each of these performance standards, and see just what each involves. Then, in the remainder of this chapter, we will see how to track the performance of the economy in these areas.

High Output of Goods and Services

As we saw in Chapter 1, the most basic task of any economic system is to provide its people with a *high standard of living*, by producing a high volume of goods and services. One key to reaching this goal is to achieve high levels of *productivity*, or output per worker. A related goal is a *stable* level of output, in the sense of avoiding downturns in output, or recessions, which threaten both living standards and jobs.

Low Unemployment

Another fundamental economic objective is the lowest possible level of unemployment. High unemployment means economic hardship for many people, and that a significant proportion of the economy's most important economic resource—its people—is being left unused. Ever since the Great Depression of the 1930s, minimizing unemployment has been an important economic objective of governments. This goal is called **full employment**, which is considered to be the lowest rate of unemployment that can be achieved without aggregate demand being so high that it generates excessively rapid inflation.

full employment
The lowest rate of unemployment that can be achieved without generating unacceptable inflation in the economy.

Little or No Inflation

If the 1930s established low unemployment as a basic economic objective, the experience of the 1970s and 1980s established the dangers of allowing inflation to become too rapid. Since this experience, the goal of restraining inflation, or keeping prices as stable as possible, has become another important goal.

Economic Statistics

Statistics Canada collects economic statistics so that we can track how the economy is performing with respect to output, employment, inflation, and a variety of other criteria. By providing up-to-date information regarding the performance of the economy and economic trends, these statistics can be very helpful to decision-makers in business and policy-makers in government. Many economic statistics (relating to output, employment/unemployment, prices/inflation, money supply and interest rates, productivity and costs, wage rates, government finances, exports and imports, flows of capital between nations, and the value of nations' currencies) are used to monitor the performance of the economy. In subsequent chapters, some of these statistics will be introduced as we look into different aspects of the economy. However, in this chapter, we will consider only those that measure the economy's success in achieving the three broad objectives referred to earlier. These are

- *gross domestic product*, which measures the economy's output of goods and services,
- *the consumer price index* and *the rate of inflation*, which measure the performance of the economy with respect to prices and inflation, and
- *employment statistics* and *the unemployment rate*, which measure the extent of the economy's success in providing jobs.

The Task of Gathering Economic Statistics

We have seen how markets work, as businesses produce the supply of goods and services to meet the demands of consumers. This economic activity produces macro-economic flows of spending, goods, and services between the business sector and the household sector of the economy, as shown by the upper loops in Figure 2-1 on page 26. In addition, this activity generates employment and investment and flows of income (wages, salaries, interest, dividends) that arise from these, as shown in the lower loops in Figure 2-1. Obviously, the more economic activity that is occurring in the economy, the more output will be produced, the more jobs there will be, the more income will be earned (and spent), and the greater the economic prosperity of the society will be. The flows of goods, services, and incomes in Figure 2-1 will grow, and the economic statistics used to keep track of these developments will reflect this growth.

> The three statistics covered in this chapter are so important that *Statistics Canada* displays them on its homepage.

Monitoring the performance of the economy in this way is not a simple task—it involves tracking the production and sale of over $1.6 trillion ($1 600 000 000 000) of goods and services and the prices of these goods and services, as well as the activities of a labour force consisting of over 18 million people. This important function is performed by *Statistics Canada*.

www.statcan.gc.ca

Measuring Output: Gross Domestic Product

Measuring the total flows of output and income in an economy is a massive task. The statistic that measures these total flows is called the **gross domestic product (GDP)**.

> **gross domestic product (GDP)**
>
> The total value of goods and services produced (and incomes earned) in a country in one year.

The gross domestic product measures the grand total of economic activity across Canada. It is an estimate of the annual output of all the sectors of the nation's economy—consumer goods and services, capital goods, government goods and services, and exports. These sectors include a tremendous volume and diversity of goods and services. The only way to take full account of such a variety of goods and services is to add up their values, or prices, expressed in dollars. The grand total figure that results is the gross domestic product, which is defined as *the market value of the total annual output of final goods and services produced in the nation*. A simpler definition of GDP is "the sum of the price tags of all final goods and services produced in the country in that year."

Why are only "final" goods counted? Suppose that

- farmers produce $0.30 of wheat, which
- millers make into flour worth $0.70, which
- bakeries make into $1.20 worth of bread.

At first, it looks as though this process has added $2.20 of production to the GDP ($0.30 + $0.70 + $1.20). But closer examination shows that the real addition to GDP is only $1.20—the value of the bread that is the final good in this process. The wheat and flour are *intermediate* products in the production of the bread. The $1.20 price of the bread *includes* the value of the wheat and flour, as part of the cost of producing the bread. If we had included, or counted, the values of the flour and wheat in the GDP, we would have overstated the GDP, because we had "double-counted" some items. To avoid double-counting, the GDP is calculated in such a way as to include only the final goods and services produced: in our example, only the value of the bread ($1.20) would be included.

Subdivisions of Gross Domestic Product

Gross domestic product consists of a vast number of diverse goods and services—all of the automobiles, televisions, haircuts, entertainment, houses, factories, machinery, roads, military equipment, police services, education, wheat, minerals, lumber, and other goods and services that are produced in one year. To help understand and analyze these statistics, we can classify them according to the four basic types of purchasers: consumers, businesses, governments, and foreign buyers.

Consumption (C)

This category consists of all *consumer goods and services* purchased by households. This includes a wide range of items, from nondurable goods that are used up quickly (such as food and clothing), to durable goods (such as cars and appliances) that last several years, to services (such as travel and entertainment). In recent years, consumption has amounted to about 56 percent of GDP.

Investment (I)

Investment includes all additions to society's stock of privately owned capital equipment, buildings, and inventories of products. The largest part of the investment category is business spending on plant and equipment—factories, offices, stores, machinery, equipment, vehicles, computers, and so on. The investment statistics also include additions to business inventories of products and new housing construction.[1] Together, these types of investment have comprised nearly 20 percent of GDP in recent years.

Government (G)

Governments (federal, provincial, and municipal) constitute another major purchaser of goods and services. Most of what governments purchase consists of services, the two largest of which are health care and education. Some government purchases,

---

[1] If a manufacturer's inventory of finished products increases by $2 million over last year's inventory, this increase represents $2 million of production that must be included somewhere in the GDP statistics. It cannot be counted as *consumption*, since it has not yet been purchased by consumers, so we add it to the *investment* statistics instead. Newly constructed housing will be purchased by households, but its value is included in the investment statistics, mainly because of its nature as a long-term asset.

such as health care, considered to be *current consumption*. Other purchases, such as schools and roads, are really *capital investment*, in that they are assets that provide social benefits over long periods of time. The government sector of the economy, which is also known as the *public sector*, has accounted for roughly 22 percent of GDP recently.

Net Exports (X – M)

So far, we have accounted for all goods and services produced for Canadian households (consumption, or **C**), business firms (investment, or **I**) and governments (government spending, or **G**). Now we must account for two facts arising from Canada's trade with foreign nations:

- Products and services produced in Canada and sold to foreign buyers (Canada's exports) must be added to our figures. These exports have amounted to about 35 percent of GDP in recent years.
- Some of the Canadian purchases (C + I + G) that we have recorded include purchases of imports of foreign-made goods. While these were *purchased* in Canada, they were not *produced* in Canada. So these imports, which have amounted to roughly 33 percent of GDP recently, should not be included in Canada's GDP, which measures Canadian *production*.

To correct our GDP figures to allow for these effects of foreign trade, we must *add* to our C + I + G total the value of all Canadian exports (X) and *deduct* from our C + I + G total the value of all imports (M) purchased by Canadians. By making these adjustments, we ensure that we are measuring what was *produced* in Canada, as distinct from what was *sold* in Canada. The net effect of these adjustments (X – M) is called *net exports*. The net effect of foreign trade will be to increase the GDP if exports are larger than imports and to decrease the GDP if imports are larger than exports.

Calculating GDP Statistics

GDP measures the total amount of economic activity in Canada in any given year, which can be viewed as the *total output* produced or the *total income* received. So there are two different approaches to calculating GDP statistics: the expenditures approach and the incomes approach.

The expenditures approach calculates GDP by adding up all the spending by consumers (C), businesses (I), governments (G), and the net exports (X – M) on goods and services. The result is expressed in the equation

$$GDP = C + I + G + (X - M)$$

This approach is illustrated in Table 2-1.

The incomes approach is based upon the fact that expenditures and incomes are simply two different sides of any transaction. That is, every dollar that is *spent* on goods and services becomes an *income* to someone—mostly the people and businesses involved in the production and distribution of the goods and services. So GDP statistics can be calculated either by adding up all *expenditures* on goods and services, or by adding up all the *incomes* received in any given year. The incomes approach is illustrated in Table 2-2.

Real GDP Versus Money GDP

If your take-home pay increased by 3 percent due to a pay raise, it would *seem* that you were 3 percent better off economically. However, if the prices of consumer goods and

Table 2-1
GDP Statistics—Expenditures Approach, 2010

		Billions of $
Consumption		
Consumer expenditure on goods and services		940.6
Investment		
Business investment in plant and equipment	178.5	
Residential construction	112.7	
Addition to inventories[1]	2.3	
Total investment		293.5
Government		
Government expenditure on goods and services		420.9
Exports and Imports		
Exports of goods and services	478.1	
Imports of goods and services	508.7	
Balance		−30.6
Gross domestic product		1624.6

Note: Totals do not always add up correctly because of statistical discrepancies.

[1] Includes government.

Source: Statistics Canada, CANSIM Table 380-0017.

Table 2-2
GDP Statistics—Incomes Approach, 2010

	Billions of $
Wages, salaries, and supplementary labour income	849.6
Corporation profits before taxes	180.7
Government enterprise profits	15.6
Interest and miscellaneous investment income	70.0
Accrued net income of farm operators from farm production	1.4
Net income of non-farm unincorporated business including rent	103.6
Inventory valuation adjustment	1.9
Indirect taxes less subsidies on products	172.6
Capital consumption allowances	229.3
Gross domestic product	1624.6

Note: Totals do not add up due to statistical discrepancies.

Source: Statistics Canada, CANSIM Table 380-0001.

www.statcan.gc.ca
Search the site for
"Gross domestic prod-
uct, expenditure-based",
then click on "Gross
domestic product,
expenditure-based".
Do the same for
"Gross domestic prod-
uct, income-based".

services had risen by 2 percent, you would *in fact* be only 1 percent better off. Your *money income* (in dollars) would be 3 percent higher, but your **real income** (in terms of purchasing power, after inflation) would be only 1 percent higher.

A similar "money illusion" occurs with GDP figures whenever prices increase. For example, GDP measured in dollars might have increased by 5 percent, but perhaps real production went up by only 3 percent, with higher prices (inflation) accounting for the other 2 percent.

This problem arises because GDP statistics can increase for two very different reasons:

real income

The purchasing power of income (as distinct from its dollar value).

- *Increased production of goods and services (higher real output).* If the economy's *output* of goods and services increases, GDP will increase. This increase is called *real economic growth*, because there is a larger output of goods and services.
- *Higher price levels.* If the *prices* of goods and services rise, GDP will also rise, because it is stated in terms of current market prices. For instance, suppose that real output were exactly the same as last year's, but the prices of all goods and services were 3 percent higher—in such a case, the GDP would register a 3-percent increase over last year. This increase is obviously not real economic growth; in fact, real output has not increased at all. But because the GDP statistics are boosted by higher prices, it *looks like* the economy has grown.

money GDP

GDP in current dollar terms; that is, including any price increases due to inflation.

We call these inflated GDP statistics *GDP at market prices*, or **money GDP**. The problem with such statistics, as we have seen, is that they are not particularly meaningful. For instance, a 6-percent increase in money GDP could mean that

(a) real output has risen by 6 percent and prices have not risen,
(b) prices have risen by 6 percent and real output has not risen, or
(c) *both* real output and prices have risen, with the combined effect of a 6-percent increase.

The key to interpreting money GDP figures is to know how much prices have risen—then we could readily estimate the increase in real output. Suppose that money GDP increased by 6 percent and prices increased by 2 percent. Of the 6-percent increase in money GDP, higher prices would account for 2 percentage points, leaving a 4-percent increase in real output. The 4-percent increase in real output is a much more accurate representation of the growth of the economy than is the 6-percent increase in money GDP.

So, by adjusting money GDP statistics to eliminate the effects of price increases, we can develop a much more accurate statistic that measures how the real output of the economy is changing. This adjusted statistic is known by several names, including **real GDP**, *GDP in constant dollars*, and *GDP in 2002 dollars*, which means that the GDP figures are calculated as if prices were the same as they were in 2002.

real GDP

GDP statistics that have been adjusted to eliminate the effects of price increases, the result being a statistic that measures only changes in real output. Also called *GDP in constant dollars or GDP at 2002 prices.*

Figure 2-7 shows money GDP and real GDP (in 2002 dollars) since 2002. Note how real GDP has increased less rapidly than money GDP, which is inflated by rising prices. From the real GDP line, it can be seen that the economy grew very rapidly from 2002 to 2008, but shrank in 2009 when there was a recession. The real GDP statistics are more useful than the money GDP figures, because the real GDP figures show *what really happened* to the economy's output of goods and services.

In reading and interpreting economic statistics, you should know whether the statistics have been adjusted for the effects of inflation or not. Generally, the adjusted (real) statistics are more useful because they reflect what *really happened* to the economy's output of goods and services.

Other Limitations of GDP Statistics

Even after adjustments for inflation, GDP statistics do not represent the final word on the economic prosperity of a nation's people. Rather, they are only an estimate of one aspect of economic prosperity—the total production of the country's economy.

One limitation of GDP statistics is that they omit a considerable amount of economic activity. For example, housework, volunteer work, and food grown for home consumption are not included in the GDP, because they are not purchased and are therefore not reported as sales. Also not counted are goods and services sold in the *underground economy*, in which people avoid paying income tax and sales taxes by

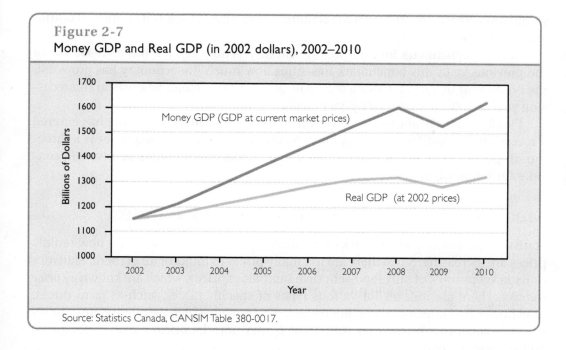

Figure 2-7
Money GDP and Real GDP (in 2002 dollars), 2002–2010

Source: Statistics Canada, CANSIM Table 380-0017.

www.statcan.gc.ca
Search the site for "Real gross domestic product", then click on "Real gross domestic product, expenditure-based".

buying and selling goods and services for cash and not reporting their income. The underground economy is especially active in areas such as residential repairs and food service (tips). The size of the underground economy is unknown, but believed to be considerable—the auditor general of Canada has estimated it to be 4.5 percent of GDP, which would be around $70 billion per year.

GDP does not measure the standard of living of the people of a nation. A better measure of living standards would be personal income per person or consumption per person, rather than the GDP's grand total output of all types of goods and services, many of which are not for the enjoyment of consumers.

GDP does not pretend to measure the quality of life. All that it provides is a measure of the total quantity of goods and services produced; $1000 of health food, $1000 of medical care, $1000 of cigarettes, $1000 of handguns, and even $1000 of economics texts—each counts for $1000 in the GDP.

In fact, sometimes a higher quality of life might mean accepting a *lower* GDP. Consider leisure time. In the twentieth century, the average workweek declined from over 60 hours to less than 40 hours. By working less, Canadians have accepted that they are producing—and consuming—fewer goods and services (real GDP) than they could. However, they willingly choose this increase in leisure because they value it more highly than the higher GDP per person that they could have by working longer hours. In effect, they have decided that higher consumption per person is not everything. So GDP is not a measure—much less *the* measure—of human welfare, but only a useful estimate of material production, which is one part of that welfare.

www.google.ca
Search Google for "underground economy"

For a broader measure of the quality of life, see the United Nations' measure of human welfare at **http://hdr.undp.org.** (Click on *Statistics*.)

Interpreting GDP Statistics

Is a real GDP of $1.6 trillion "good"? That evaluation depends on the size of the economy's *capacity output*, which is an estimate of the economy's maximum potential output. If the economy's capacity output were $1.7 trillion, a real GDP of $1.6 trillion would indicate an economic boom, in which the economy's production is very close to capacity. But if capacity output were $2.0 trillion, the same $1.6 trillion GDP would indicate a recession, with the economy operating far below its potential output and employment.

Another benchmark for interpreting real GDP is how much it has increased from the previous year; this benchmark measures how much the economy has grown. In the boom year of 2006, Canada's real GDP grew by 3.0 percent, whereas in the recession year of 2009, it *decreased* by 2.8 percent.

Finally, real GDP statistics are used to determine when the economy has entered a recession. If real GDP decreases for two consecutive quarters (a quarter is a three-month period), a recession is considered to be underway, a matter that we will consider further in Chapter 6.

Measuring Prices: The Consumer Price Index

Statistics Canada also keeps track of inflation, by monitoring prices and how rapidly prices are increasing. Since there are too many prices to monitor all of them, Statistics Canada keeps track of only representative samples of prices, which are known as *price indexes*. There are indexes for various types of specific prices, such as farm prices, food prices, and housing prices. But the price index with which people are most familiar is the **consumer price index (CPI)**, which measures the prices of consumer goods and services in general.

The consumer price index is an average of the prices of some 600 goods and services bought by representative or typical urban households. The CPI is also described as the cost of a "basket" of goods and services bought by a typical household. As the prices of these goods and services rise, so does the CPI.

To determine the CPI for each month, Statistics Canada actually records the prices of the 600 goods and services in the basket in various centres across Canada. Then the average of these prices is calculated, and this average becomes the CPI for that month, for Canada as a whole, for each province, and for various cities.

The calculation of the CPI takes into account that consumers spend more on some items in the basket than on others. For instance, consumers spend much more on rent than on milk. To recognize this reality, each item in the basket is given a *weight* in the CPI, based upon the proportion of the typical household's income that is spent on it. So if a typical household spends 50 times as much on rent as it does on milk, rent would be given a weight in the index 50 times as large as the weight given to milk. As an example, a 10-percent increase in rents would have 50 times the impact on the CPI as a 10-percent increase in the price of milk. Figure 2-8 shows the weights assigned to each broad category of items in the CPI, such as housing, transportation, food, and so on. However, it is important to remember that *within* each of these categories, there are dozens of individual goods and services, each with its own weight. For instance, the transportation component of the CPI includes car prices, gasoline prices, insurance rates, public transit fares, airline and train fares, and so on.

The CPI does not express the cost of the basket of goods and services in terms of dollars and cents. Instead, the CPI is expressed in terms of how much it has changed from a *base year* (2002 at the time of writing) in which the CPI was 100.0. This is illustrated in Table 2-3, which shows not only the CPI in general, but also the various major components of the CPI. In the base year of 2002, the CPI and each of its components are 100.0. By following each column down, you can track how rapidly prices have risen, both in general ("all items") and for each component. For instance, the fastest-rising component of the CPI from 2002 to 2010 was alcohol and tobacco products, with a 33.1 percent increase from 100.0 in 2002 to 133.1 in 2010.

In most years, an increase of about 3.0 percent in real GDP is considered a healthy rate of growth. We will examine what *healthy* means in Chapter 3.

consumer price index (CPI)

A weighted average of the prices of a "basket" of goods and services purchased by a typical urban family.

Figure 2-8
Weights of the Major Components of the CPI, 2009

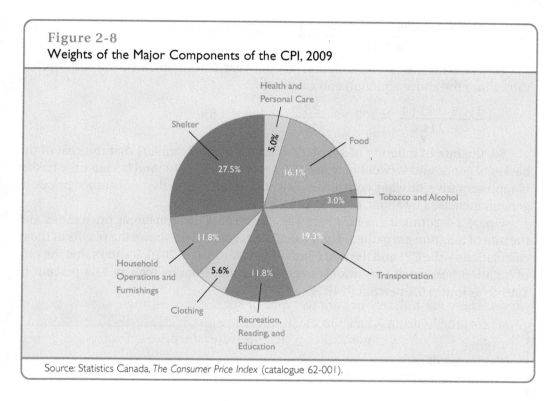

Source: Statistics Canada, *The Consumer Price Index* (catalogue 62-001).

Table 2-3
The Consumer Price Index by Categories, 2002–2010 (2002=100)

(1992 = 100) Year	All items	Food	Shelter	Household operations and furnishings	Clothing and footwear	Trans-portation	Health and personal care	Recreation, education, and reading	Alcohol and tobacco products	Goods	Services
2002	100.0	100.0	100.0	100.0	100.0	100.0	100.0	100.0	100.0	100.0	100.0
2003	102.8	101.7	103.2	100.7	98.2	105.2	101.4	100.8	110.1	101.9	103.6
2004	104.7	103.8	105.8	101.2	98.0	107.7	102.8	101.1	116.0	103.4	105.9
2005	107.0	106.4	109.2	101.7	97.6	112.0	104.6	100.8	119.1	105.8	108.2
2006	109.1	108.9	113.1	102.2	95.8	115.2	105.9	100.6	121.7	107.1	111.1
2007	111.5	111.8	116.9	103.2	95.7	117.1	107.3	101.8	125.5	108.0	114.8
2008	114.1	115.7	122.0	104.6	93.8	119.5	108.8	102.2	127.5	109.4	118.7
2009	114.4	121.4	121.6	107.3	93.4	113.1	112.1	103.1	130.7	107.6	121.2
2010	116.5	123.1	123.3	108.8	91.6	118.0	115.1	104.0	133.1	109.2	123.7

Source: Statistics Canada, *The Consumer Price Index* (catalogue 62-001).

The Rate of Inflation

This brings us to the rate of inflation. The consumer price index measures *how high prices are*, while the rate of inflation tells us *how rapidly prices are rising*. For instance, the CPI was 114.4 in 2009, then increased to 116.5 in 2010, an increase of 1.8 percent over the year, calculated as follows:

$$\frac{\text{This year's CPI} - \text{Last year's CPI}}{\text{Last year's CPI}} \times 100 = \text{Rate of Inflation}$$

To calculate the rate of inflation for the year 2008, substitute the appropriate values into the above equation and calculate.

$$\frac{116.5 - 114.4}{114.4} \times 100 = \frac{2.1}{114.4} \times 100 = 1.8\%$$

So, the rate of inflation of 1.8 percent for 2010 simply means that the cost of the basket of goods and services increased by 1.8 percent in 2010. And because the basket is representative of what consumers buy, the inference is that consumer prices in general increased by about 1.8 percent in 2010.

Figure 2-9 summarizes how statistics concerning the consumer price index and the rate of inflation are gathered and calculated. Figure 2-10 shows the results of those calculations—the CPI and the rate of inflation from 1960 to 2010. It shows that the rate of inflation has varied very widely over this period, from as high as 12.4 percent in 1981 to as low as 0.1 percent in 1994.

A rate of inflation between 1 and 3 percent per year is considered "acceptable." We will discuss this aspect in more detail in Chapter 8.

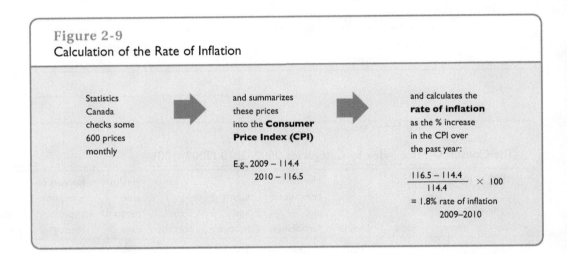

Figure 2-9
Calculation of the Rate of Inflation

Statistics Canada checks some 600 prices monthly

and summarizes these prices into the **Consumer Price Index (CPI)**

E.g., 2009 – 114.4
2010 – 116.5

and calculates the **rate of inflation** as the % increase in the CPI over the past year:

$$\frac{116.5 - 114.4}{114.4} \times 100$$
= 1.8% rate of inflation
2009–2010

These variations reflect major changes in the basic economic forces driving the economy that will be considered in Chapter 6. In this chapter, we have been concerned only with how inflation is measured. In Chapter 8, we will consider what drove inflation to such high rates, the damage that such rapid inflation can do to the economy, and what can be done to control it.

IN THE NEWS

Recent Price Increases

From 2002 to 2010, the Consumer Price Index increased by 16.5 percent. However, behind this *average* rate of increase of 16.5 percent was a very wide range of changes *for individual components* of the CPI. As the figure shows, the price of cigarettes increased by 50 percent, tuition fees by 38 percent, and transportation by 18 percent. At the other end of the spectrum, the prices of household appliances and clothing and footwear *decreased* over this five-year period, and the cost of computers fell by over 70 percent. ∎

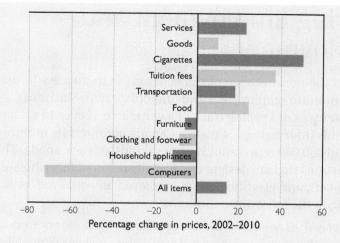

Percentage change in prices, 2002–2010

QUESTIONS

1. Why did the cost of cigarettes, tuition, and transportation increase by so much?

2. What might explain the decreases in the prices of computers, household appliances, and clothing and footwear?

3. Why would the prices of goods in general increase less rapidly than the prices of services in general?

Figure 2-10
The Consumer Price Index and the Rate of Inflation, 1960–2010

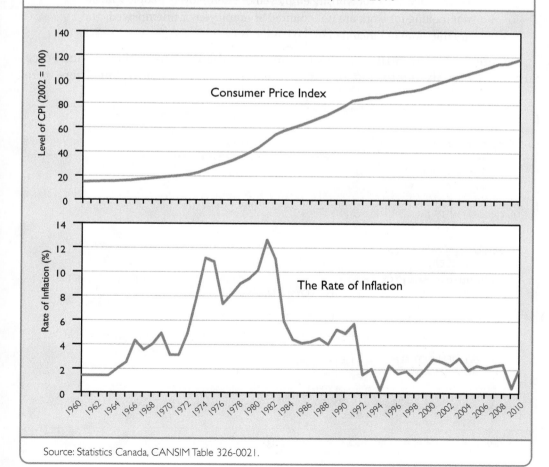

www.statcan.gc.ca
Search the site for
"Consumer price index, historical summary".

Source: Statistics Canada, CANSIM Table 326-0021.

Measuring Employment and Unemployment

A key aspect of the performance of the economy is its success in *providing jobs* for Canadians. To monitor employment and unemployment, Statistics Canada must deal with the complex task of keeping track of a workforce of over 18 million people.

To gather this information, Statistics Canada conducts its monthly Labour Force Survey of roughly 50 000 representative households across Canada. The survey asks a number of questions that are designed to identify respondents who are of working age (15 years and over), and classify them as *employed, unemployed,* or *not in the labour force,* according to the following definitions:

> *Employed:* all persons who, during the survey week, did any work at all or had a job but were not at work due to their own illness or disability, personal or family responsibilities, bad weather, a labour dispute, or vacation.

> *Unemployed:* those persons who, during the survey week,
> (a) were without work, had actively looked for work during the past four weeks, and were available for work,
> (b) had not actively looked for work in the past four weeks but had been on layoff for 26 weeks or less and were available for work,
> (c) had not actively looked for work in the past four weeks but had a new job to start in four weeks and were available for work.

> *Labour Force:* that portion of the civilian non-institutional population 15 years of age and over who are employed or unemployed. People who are not looking for work are not counted as employed or unemployed, and are therefore not included in the labour force.

Figure 2-11 uses 2010 statistics to show how the data from the Labour Force Survey are organized into statistics on employment and unemployment. There were

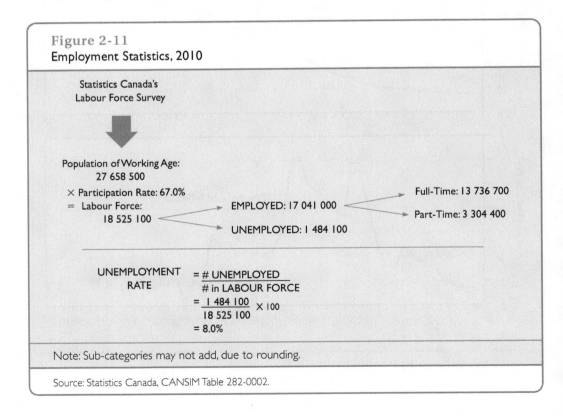

Figure 2-11
Employment Statistics, 2010

Statistics Canada's
Labour Force Survey

Population of Working Age:
27 658 500

× Participation Rate: 67.0%

= Labour Force:
18 525 100

EMPLOYED: 17 041 000

Full-Time: 13 736 700

Part-Time: 3 304 400

UNEMPLOYED: 1 484 100

$$\text{UNEMPLOYMENT RATE} = \frac{\#\ \text{UNEMPLOYED}}{\#\ \text{in LABOUR FORCE}}$$

$$= \frac{1\ 484\ 100}{18\ 525\ 100} \times 100$$

$$= 8.0\%$$

Note: Sub-categories may not add, due to rounding.

Source: Statistics Canada, CANSIM Table 282-0002.

27 658 500 Canadians of working age, of whom 67.0 percent, or 18 525 100, participated in the labour force by either working or seeking work. Economists describe this 67.0 percent as the labour force **participation rate**. Of the **labour force** of 18 525 100, 17 041 000 were employed (13 736 700 full-time and 3 304 400 part-time), leaving 1 484 100 unemployed. This 1 484 100 represented 8.0 percent of the labour force of 18 525 100, making 8.0 percent the **unemployment rate**. By gathering these statistics monthly—not only for Canada as a whole, but also for regions within Canada—Statistics Canada can monitor trends in employment and unemployment across the country.

Figure 2-12 shows Canada's unemployment rate from 1950 to 2010. The recessions of the late 1950s, early 1980s, early 1990s, and 2008–09 are clearly visible. Until the recession of 2008–09, Canada's unemployment rate had generally been trending downward since 1993.

participation rate
The percentage of the population of working age that is working or seeking work.

labour force
Those Canadians of working age who are either employed or are unemployed and both available for work and seeking work.

unemployment rate
The percentage of the labour force that is unemployed.

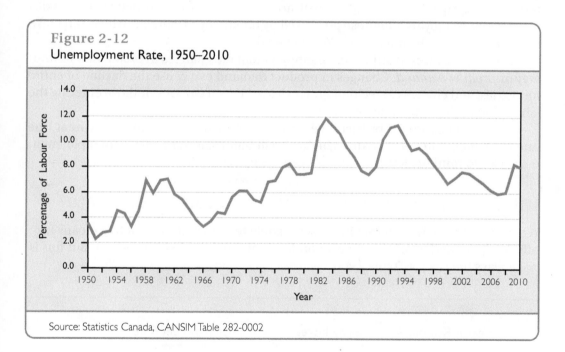

Figure 2-12
Unemployment Rate, 1950–2010

Source: Statistics Canada, CANSIM Table 282-0002

www.statcan.gc.ca
Search the site for "Labour force characteristics", then click on "Labour force characteristics".

Behind the Statistics: Types of Unemployment

One reason for such high unemployment rates is that there are various reasons why people become unemployed, and remain unemployed, even when there is an economic boom.

Cyclical unemployment arises from the periodic recessions associated with economic cycles, when the unemployment rate increases by about 4 percentage points. These recessions cause the periodic peaks in the unemployment rate that are evident in Figure 2-12. And, as Figure 2-12 also shows, when recessions end, the unemployment rate falls as cyclical unemployment decreases. However, there are other types of unemployment, and these keep the unemployment rate relatively high, even in economic booms.

cyclical unemployment
Unemployment that is caused by periodic cyclical weaknesses in aggregate demand associated with recessions.

frictional unemployment

Unemployment arising from people being temporarily out of work because they are in the process of changing jobs.

seasonal unemployment

Unemployment arising from seasonal downturns in employment in some industries.

structural unemployment

Unemployment arising from a mismatch between the skills required by employers and those of unemployed people.

Frictional unemployment is due to people being temporarily out of work because they are changing from one job to another. Most frictional unemployment is quite brief and is considered to be a normal and healthy process in a free and dynamic economy in which people frequently change jobs. In fact, frictional unemployment tends to rise during booms, when there are more job openings and opportunities to switch jobs.

Seasonal unemployment is also short term. In seasonal industries such as agriculture, fishing, forestry, and construction, unemployment will increase in the winter and decrease in the summer. Seasonal unemployment is highest in Eastern Canada, where seasonal industries account for a higher proportion of employment. Like frictional unemployment, seasonal unemployment is an inevitable aspect of Canadian labour markets; however, the extent of seasonal unemployment is lower than it used to be, mainly because the number of jobs in the agricultural sector has decreased.

Structural unemployment is a much more serious problem because of its longer-term nature. Structural unemployment arises from a mismatch between the skills required by employers and those possessed by unemployed workers, which can make it very difficult for the unemployed to find work.

The major causes of structural unemployment are changes in *production technology* or *product demand*. Changes in product demand can cause the decline of entire industries, and changes in technology can leave laid-off workers or those entering the labour force with inadequate or outdated skills.

Due to the existence of frictional, seasonal, and structural unemployment, the unemployment rate remains quite high even in booms, when cyclical unemployment decreases to minimal levels.

Interpreting Changes in the Unemployment Rate

When the unemployment rate increases, people tend to assume that this means lay-offs, lost jobs, and deteriorating economic conditions, such as a recession. But this is not always the case, as Table 2-4 shows.

Table 2-4
Two Different Reasons for the Same Increase in the Unemployment Rate

Year	Labour Force	Unemployed	Employed	Unemployment Rate
20X1	100 000	9000	91 000	9.0%
20X2 (a)	100 000	10 000	90 000	10.0%
20X2 (b)	101 100	10 100	91 000	10.0%

An unemployment rate of about 6.5 percent is considered to be good. The highest monthly unemployment rate since the 1930s was 13.8 percent in January 1983, and the lowest was 5.3 percent in October 2007.

In year 20X1, the labour force is 100 000, 91 000 of whom are employed and 9000 of whom are unemployed, making the unemployment rate 9.0 percent. Suppose that, in year 20X2, the unemployment rate rises to 10.0 percent. This could mean fewer jobs and a recession, as shown in case (a), in which employment has fallen by 1000 to 90 000 and unemployment has risen by 1000 to 10 000. However, as case (b) shows, it could also mean that there are more people looking for work. In case (b), the number of people working is still 91 000, the same as in 20X1; however, 1100 more people are looking for work and not finding it. As a result, the labour force increases to 101 100 and the number of unemployed rises to 10 100, pushing the unemployment rate up to 10.0 percent. In both cases, the unemployment rate increases from 9.0 percent to 10.0 percent; however, in the first case this is due to *fewer jobs*, while in the second case it is due to *more job-seekers*.

When the economy is recovering from a recession, the number of jobs may be increasing quite rapidly, as economic conditions improve. But as the job market improves, more people become interested (again) in working, increasing the number of job-seekers, which keeps the unemployment rate high and makes economic conditions appear to be worse than they are. Conversely, in some months during recessions, the unemployment rate goes down, not because there are more jobs, but because some people give up looking for work.

People who give up looking for work are called *discouraged workers*. These people want to work, but have given up looking because they believe jobs cannot be found. Such people are not counted as *unemployed* because the Labour Force Survey records them as not seeking work. The result is **hidden unemployment**—unemployed people who are not counted in the statistics. It has been estimated that during recessions, when discouraged workers are more numerous, hidden unemployment could amount to as much as 2 or 3 percent of the labour force. Hidden unemployment is higher in regions such as the Atlantic provinces, where chronically high unemployment generates more discouraged workers.

hidden unemployment People who are unemployed but are not counted in the unemployment statistics because they have given up looking for work.

Conclusion: Using the Statistics

The economic statistics described in this chapter allow us to continually "take the pulse" of the Canadian economy. During a typical economic boom, aggregate demand is high and rising, so real GDP and employment will rise more rapidly than usual, and the unemployment rate will decrease. Later, an increase in the rate of inflation might be a sign that the boom is approaching its end, as output is having difficulty keeping up with rising demand. During a recession, aggregate demand is falling. Real GDP actually falls, employment will probably decrease, the unemployment rate will rise, and the rate of inflation will usually decrease. An increase in real GDP, followed by increased employment, would signal the end of a recession. Because they show economic trends, these and other economic statistics are watched closely by the business and financial communities, as well as by government policy-makers.

On its homepage, Statistics Canada shows the most recent updates for the three key statistics covered in this chapter.

In addition, the statistics tell us not only about the performance of the economy as a whole, but also about strengths and weaknesses in particular parts of the economy and regions of the country. GDP statistics provide information about the total output of the economy *and* its *components*: that is, important trends in consumer spending, business investment spending, government spending, exports, and imports. CPI statistics keep track of the overall rate of inflation, and also *which types* of prices (housing, food, transportation, etc.) are rising more or less rapidly. And labour force statistics tell us a great deal about trends in employment and unemployment, not only for the nation as a whole, but also for its various regions and for subgroups of the labour force, such as young people, women, and men. Taken together, these and other statistics can help government and business leaders to gain a clearer picture of not only where the economy has been and currently is, but also where it may be going.

In this chapter, we have looked at *what* economic statistics tell us about the economy. In the next few chapters, we will consider the *reasons why* changes occur in the direction of the economy.

Chapter Summary

1. On a macroeconomic scale, the economy consists of
   (a) a supply side, in which the key is the ability and willingness of producers to produce goods and services and offer them for sale, and
   (b) a demand side, in which the key is the ability and willingness of buyers to purchase goods and services. (L.O. 1)
2. Capacity output is the output of goods and services that the economy can produce without costs and prices rising rapidly. If aggregate demand is too low relative to capacity output, the economy will be in a recession. Aggregate demand approaching capacity output will cause an economic boom, but if aggregate demand exceeds capacity output, it will generate inflation. (L.O. 2)
3. Three basic macroeconomic goals are high output of goods and services, low unemployment, and a low rate of inflation. (L.O. 3)
4. The gross domestic product, which measures the total output of the economy, consists of four components: consumption (C), investment (I), government spending (G), and net exports (X – M). (L.O. 4)
5. The gross domestic product can increase either because the output of goods and services is higher or because their prices have risen. These inflated *money GDP* statistics can be adjusted to eliminate the effects of increased prices, the result being *real GDP* statistics that are more meaningful because they measure only real output. (L.O. 5)
6. The consumer price index is the most common and well-known measure of prices. It is a weighted average of the prices of goods and services bought by a typical urban family. The percentage increase in the CPI from year to year is called the rate of inflation. (L.O. 6)
7. The Labour Force Survey gathers data on the working age population, the size of the labour force, the number of people who are employed and unemployed, and calculates the participation rate and the unemployment rate. (L.O. 7)
8. There are various types of unemployment: cyclical, frictional, seasonal, and structural. (L.O. 8)
9. Statistics on output, employment, and inflation can be used to determine the condition of the economy (recession, boom, or inflation) and the direction in which it is moving. (L.O. 9)

Questions

1. On the left side, list the five supply-side factors that determine how much a country's economy can produce. On the right side, record the four major groups that buy the goods and services that the economy produces.

SUPPLY SIDE		DEMAND SIDE
_____		_____
_____	+	_____
_____	+	_____
_____	+	_____
_____		

= CAPACITY OUTPUT,
or the total amount of goods
and services that the economy
can produce annually

= AGGREGATE DEMAND,
or the total amount of goods and
services purchased by buyers
of the economy's output

2. The *capacity output* of the economy is considered to be
   (a) the amount of goods and services that could be produced if every person of working age were employed.
   (b) the amount of goods and services that could be produced if every business establishment were operating five full days a week for the entire year.
   (c) the amount of goods and services that could be produced if every business establishment were operating six full days a week for the entire year.
   (d) the amount of goods and services that can be produced without aggregate demand being so high that prices start to rise rapidly.
   (e) None of the above.

3. Suppose that the capacity output of the economy were $100 billion of goods and services this year.
   (a) If aggregate demand were $80 billion, the economy would be in a condition of _____, because _____.
   (b) If aggregate demand were $110 billion, the economy would be in a condition of _____, because _____.

4. Chapter 2 describes our three basic macroeconomic goals as
   (a) high output of goods and services, no unemployment, and low interest rates.
   (b) high output of goods and services, low unemployment, and little inflation.
   (c) no unemployment, no inflation, and low interest rates.
   (d) high output of goods and services, no poverty, and little inflation.
   (e) None of the above.

5. The 2008 GDP of $1536 billion was 4.4 percent higher than the 2007 GDP of $1603 billion.
   (a) Does this mean that Canada's economy actually produced 4.4 percent *more output* in 2008 than in 2007? Explain the reason for your answer.
   (b) If your answer to (a) was no, what additional information would you need to have in order to estimate the *actual* increase in output in 2008?

6. Statistics Canada reports that the consumer price index (CPI) for 2008 was 114.1, up from 111.5 in 2007.
   (a) What *is* the consumer price index?
   (b) How does Statistics Canada *gather the data* to determine the CPI?
   (c) Calculate the *rate of inflation* for 2008.
   (d) Explain to someone who has never studied economics exactly what this rate of inflation *means*.

7. Suppose that Statistics Canada reported that the population of working age were 22 000 000, the labour force participation rate were 60 percent, and there were 12 200 000 people employed.
   (a) How does Statistics Canada obtain labour force statistics such as these?
   (b) What is the size of the *labour force*?
   (c) How many people are *unemployed*?
   (d) What is the *unemployment rate*? Show your calculations.

8. To see the recent trends in employment and unemployment, visit the Statistics Canada home page at **www.statcan.gc.ca**, locate the *Latest indicators* section, and click on *Unemployment rate*.
   (a) What have been the recent trends in employment and unemployment?
   (b) Does the most recent release from Statistics Canada identify the reasons for these trends?

Study Guide

Review Questions (Answers to these Review Questions appear in Appendix B.)

1. *Gross domestic product* (GDP) is a statistic that measures _____.

2. If a country's consumption spending is $500 billion, its business investment spending is $100 billion, its government spending on goods and services is $150 billion, its exports of goods and services are $200 billion, and its imports of goods and services are $150 billion, that country's gross domestic product will be
   (a) $600 billion.
   (b) $700 billion.
   (c) $800 billion.
   (d) $1100 billion.
   (e) None of the above.

3. Iron ore is sold to a steel mill for $80 000 to be made into steel. That steel is sold to a metal fabricating plant for $180 000 and is made into filing cabinets that are sold for $300 000. The actual addition to GDP from these transactions is
   (a) $80 000.
   (b) $220 000.
   (c) $260 000.
   (d) $300 000.
   (e) $560 000.

4. Most of the output of Canada's economy is purchased by
   (a) consumers.
   (b) businesses.
   (c) governments.
   (d) foreign buyers.
   (e) speculators.

5. Suppose a country produces exactly the same output of goods and services this year as it produced last year, but the general level of prices this year is 2 percent higher than last year. Which of the following describes this situation?
   (a) Real GDP has increased by 2 percent, but money GDP has not increased.
   (b) Money GDP has increased by 2 percent, but real GDP has not increased.
   (c) Both real GDP and money GDP have increased.
   (d) Neither real GDP nor money GDP has increased.
   (e) None of the above.

6. A 5-percent increase in money GDP could mean that
   (a) real GDP increased by 5 percent and prices did not increase.
   (b) prices increased by 5 percent and real GDP did not increase.
   (c) real GDP increased by 3 percent and prices increased by 2 percent.
   (d) (a) or (b) or (c) could have happened.
   (e) None of the above.

7. Historically, *money GDP* has risen faster than real GDP, because _____.

8. In 2004, Moravia's money GDP (in current dollars) was $500 billion. In 2005, it was $515 billion. Over 2005, the general level of prices in the Moravian economy (as measured by a price index) rose from 130.0 to 135.2. From these facts, we can conclude that in 2005, Moravia's real GDP
   (a) increased.
   (b) decreased.

(c) remained stable.

9. If the consumer price index increases from 120.0 to 123.6 over the course of a year, the rate of inflation for that year is
   (a) 2.9 percent.
   (b) 3.0 percent.
   (c) 3.6 percent.
   (d) 103.0 percent.
   (e) None of the above.

10. If the consumer price index at the beginning of the year is 125.0 and the rate of inflation for that year is 4.0 percent, the CPI at the end of the year will be _____.

11. The difference between the consumer price index and the rate of inflation is that the CPI measures *how high* consumer prices are, while the rate of inflation measures
_____.

12. If the working age population is 10 000 000, the labour force is 5 000 000, and 4 500 000 people are employed,
   (a) the participation rate is ___ percent, and
   (b) the unemployment rate is ___ percent.

13. Identify each of the following as an example of cyclical, frictional, seasonal, or structural unemployment.
   (a) _____ A miner is replaced by new machinery.
   (b) _____ A nurse takes a week to travel from Ontario to her new job in Alberta.
   (c) _____ An auto worker is laid off when car sales fall during a recession.
   (d) _____ A worker is laid off from a fish-processing plant for the winter.
   (e) _____ A worker is laid off because a plant closed due to competition from imports.

14. During an economic boom,
   (a) real GDP is increasing, the unemployment rate is falling, and the rate of inflation is rising.
   (b) real GDP is increasing, the unemployment rate is falling, and the rate of inflation is falling.
   (c) real GDP is decreasing, the unemployment rate is increasing, and the rate of inflation is decreasing.
   (d) real GDP is decreasing, the unemployment rate is increasing, and the rate of inflation is rising.
   (e) None of the above.

15. During a recession,
   (a) real GDP is increasing, the unemployment rate is falling, and the rate of inflation is rising.
   (b) real GDP is increasing, the unemployment rate is falling, and the rate of inflation is falling.
   (c) real GDP is decreasing, the unemployment rate is increasing, and the rate of inflation is decreasing.
   (d) real GDP is decreasing, the unemployment rate is increasing, and the rate of inflation is rising.
   (e) None of the above.

Critical Thinking Questions

(Asterisked questions 1 to 5 are answered in Appendix B; the answers to questions 6 to 10 are in the Instructor's Manual that accompanies this text.)

*1. If real GDP is increasing rapidly, the unemployment rate is low and falling, and the rate of inflation is increasing, the economy is in a _____. What would be the most basic *cause* of these economic conditions?

*2. If real GDP is falling, the unemployment rate is rising, and the rate of inflation is falling, the economy is in a _____. What would be the most basic *cause* of these economic conditions?

*3.

Year	Consumer Price Index	Annual Rate of Inflation
1999	110.5	1.7%
2000	113.5	____%
2001	116.4	____%
2002	119.0	____%

(a) Calculate the rate of inflation for 2000, 2001, and 2002.

(b) In 2001 and 2002, the consumer price index went _____, but the rate of inflation went _____.

(c) Explain the differing trends in the CPI and the rate of inflation in 2001 and 2002.

*4.

Year	Labour Force (000)	Employed (000)	Unemployed (000)	Unemployment Rate
2002	16 580	15 308		
2003	16 954	15 665		

(a) Complete the last two columns in the table.

(b) In 2003, the number of unemployed people _____, while the unemployment rate _____.

(c) Explain why these two measures of unemployment changed as they did.

*5. In 1989, the economy was in the last year of a boom, with the unemployment rate at 7.5 percent. In the recession that followed, the unemployment rate reached a peak of 11.4 percent in 1993.

Year	Population 15 Years and Over (millions)	Partici- pation Rate	Labour Force	Employment Rate	Unemploy- ment	Unemploy- ment Rate
1989	20 901 900	67.2%	14 046 600	12 986 400	1 060 200	7.5%
1993	22 179 700	65.4%	14 504 500	12 857 500	1 647 000	11.4%

As the unemployment rate rose, the participation rate fell, from 67.2 percent in 1989 to 65.4 percent in 1993.

(a) Why do you think the participation rate decreased from 1989 to 1993?

(b) How much did *hidden unemployment* increase from 1989 to 1993?

(That is, if the participation rate had not decreased, how much higher would unemployment and the unemployment rate have been in 1993?)

6. Table 2-3 on page 39 shows that since 2002, the prices of *goods* have risen more slowly than the prices of *services*. Why might such a trend reasonably be expected?

7. What does Table 2-3 in the text tell you happened to the prices of clothing and footwear from 2002 to 2010? What might explain this trend?

8.

Year	Population 15 Years and Over (millions)	Partici- pation Rate	Labour Force (millions)	Employ- ment	Unemploy- ment (millions)	Unemploy- ment Rate
20X1	20.0	60.0%	12.0	10.8	1.2	10.0%
20X2	21.5	61.5%		11.2		

In 20X1, the population of working age is 20.0 million, 60 percent of whom participate in the labour force, making the labour force 12.0 million. Of these, 10.8 million
are employed and 1.2 million, or 10 percent of the labour force, are unemployed.
Suppose that, in 20X2, the following developments occur:

- Employment grows quite rapidly (by 4 percent), to 11.2 million.
- The working age population increases to 21.5 million.
- The participation rate increases to 61.5 percent.

Calculate the unemployment rate for 20X2.

9. Following are the weights of the components of the consumer price index for 1982
and 2009, based on how Canadian consumers spent their money in 1982 and 2009.

	1982	2009
Shelter and household operations	38.1	39.3
Transportation	15.8	19.3
Food	20.0	16.1
Recreation, reading, and education	8.3	11.8
Clothing	8.4	5.6
Health and personal care	4.0	5.0
Tobacco and alcohol	5.4	3.0

What might explain the changes that occurred in the spending patterns of
consumers from 1982 to 2009?

10.

Year	Population 15 Years and Over	Labour Force (millions)	Employment (millions)	Unemploy- ment (millions)	Unemploy- ment Rate
1	100	60	54	6	10.0%
2	101	63	56		

(a) In the economy shown in the table, employment increases by 2 million jobs
from year 1 to year 2. But what happens in year 2 to the number of unemployed people and the unemployment rate?

(b) What explains why *all three* statistics increased in year 2?

Use the Web   (Hints for these Use the Web exercises appear in Appendix B.)

1. To see the recent trends in gross domestic product and the unemployment rate,
visit Statistics Canada at **www.statcan.gc.ca**, and in the *Latest indicators* section,
click on *Gross domestic product* and *Unemployment rate.*
   (a) What are the most recent trends in gross domestic product and the unemployment rate?
   (b) Do these releases from Statistics Canada identify the reasons for these trends?

2. To see the recent trend in the consumer price index, visit the Statistics Canada
home page, locate the *Latest indicators* section, and click on *Consumer price index.*
   (a) What has been the recent trend in the consumer price index?
   (b) What does the most recent release from Statistics Canada say are the main
reasons for this trend?

3

Sources of Economic Prosperity: The Supply Side

LEARNING OBJECTIVES

After studying this chapter, you should be able to

1. Define productivity, calculate productivity from given data, and explain why high productivity is considered to be the basis of a high standard of living.

2. State six factors that influence productivity, and explain how each factor affects productivity.

3. Write an account of possible explanations for the productivity slowdown that occurred in many nations after the late 1970s.

4. Describe Canada's productivity performance, explain two reasons why it is of concern, and explain six possible reasons for this performance.

5. Explain how government policies could improve productivity performance by strengthening each of the six factors alluded to in Learning Objective 2.

6. Explain the concept of *capacity output*, calculate capacity output from given data, state the two key factors underlying increases in capacity output, and state the approximate annual percentage increase in the Canadian economy's capacity output in recent years.

Canadians who lived 100 years ago would be astounded by the high material standard of living enjoyed by today's Canadians—our homes, our cars, our clothes, our shopping malls and entertainment centres, our shorter working hours and longer vacations. How, they would ask, did we do it? Societies that have achieved high *consumption* of goods and services per person are generally able to *produce* goods and services efficiently. Economists describe this as having a strong **supply side** to their economies.

The key to a strong supply side is the ability to make efficient use of economic inputs (labour, capital equipment, and natural resources) in order to achieve high levels of **productivity**, or output per worker. The fact that *output per person* today is about three times as high as in 1961 is the key to our *consumption per person* (standard of living) being so much higher than in the past. And it is because of higher output per hour worked that we are able to enjoy this higher standard of living while *working fewer hours*—on average, about 25 percent fewer hours per year than in 1947. Also, nations that are efficient tend to have lower production costs that enable them to be more successful in international competition. Canada's exports and imports both represent a high proportion of its GDP, so it is important to our prosperity that Canadian producers be able to compete internationally.

supply side
The producers of a nation's output of goods and services.

productivity
Output per worker per hour; one measure of efficiency.

The Nature of Productivity

Productivity is not a word with a single simple meaning. In its broadest sense, it refers to the efficiency with which all three productive inputs (labour, capital equipment, and natural resources) work together to produce goods and services. However, the most common definition of productivity—and one that is easier to understand—is *labour productivity*, or *output per worker per hour.* A less exact measure of productivity (but one that is easier to estimate) is *real GDP per employed person.*

Productivity is the key to the supply side of the economy. As the output of an average worker increases, the economy's *capacity output* (its maximum potential output) grows.

"Labour productivity is probably the most telling measure of economic performance. Unless productivity grows, living standards stagnate."
— *THE ECONOMIST*

www.economist.com

Factors Affecting Productivity

Defining productivity in terms of output per worker (per hour) seems to imply that productivity depends mainly on how hard people work. This is not the case—productivity is more strongly influenced by several other factors, which are summarized in Figure 3-1 on page 54 and explained in the following sections.

As Figure 3-1 shows, the major factors that influence productivity are (a) capital equipment, (b) education and skill levels of the labour force, (c) management, (d) the size of the market and the scale of operations, (e) the incentive of after-tax economic gain, and (f) the incentive of competition. In the sections that follow, we will explain each of these factors. We will then review Canada's performance regarding productivity, and consider government policies that can improve productivity performance.

(a) Capital Investment and the Saving–Investment Process

The amount—and quality—of capital equipment per worker is a key factor in determining workers' productivity. Generally, the more and better capital equipment that workers have to use, the higher output per worker and living standards can be. So, a fundamental factor influencing productivity is the amount of *capital investment* by a society in plants, equipment, and machinery. But a more basic question is this: What does it take for a society to *obtain* this capital equipment?

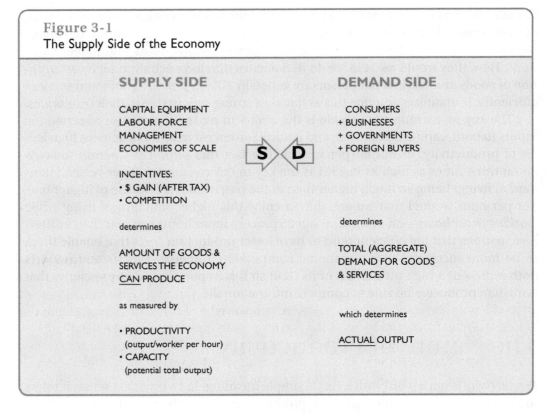

Figure 3-1
The Supply Side of the Economy

SUPPLY SIDE

CAPITAL EQUIPMENT
LABOUR FORCE
MANAGEMENT
ECONOMIES OF SCALE

INCENTIVES:
• $ GAIN (AFTER TAX)
• COMPETITION

determines

AMOUNT OF GOODS &
SERVICES THE ECONOMY
CAN PRODUCE

as measured by

• PRODUCTIVITY
  (output/worker per hour)
• CAPACITY
  (potential total output)

DEMAND SIDE

CONSUMERS
+ BUSINESSES
+ GOVERNMENTS
+ FOREIGN BUYERS

determines

TOTAL (AGGREGATE)
DEMAND FOR GOODS
& SERVICES

which determines

ACTUAL OUTPUT

Building capital equipment: The saving–investment process The process by which a society acquires capital equipment is so fundamentally important that we will examine it in detail. To emphasize the basic economic concepts involved in the process of capital investment, we will use a simple illustration. Suppose you are alone on a deserted island and must find food to survive. The most accessible food is fish from a nearby stream, so you set out to catch some.

You have no capital equipment at all. So you use your hands, with only limited success, and find that you are able to catch two fish per day. This is just enough to feed you for a day, but to catch two fish takes the entire day—all of your available labour. You have no time available for any other productive activities, such as cultivating vegetables or building a shelter. Your low productivity is limiting you to a subsistence-level standard of living.

Before long, you decide that you have to become more efficient at catching fish, so you set out to build a spear. But building a spear has an opportunity cost: the time that you spend building the spear cannot also be spent catching fish. In other words, to obtain the capital good (the spear), you will have to do without, or sacrifice, some consumer goods (fish). It takes an entire day—leaving you very hungry—but you are able to fashion a spear.

Now you have a piece of *capital equipment* to help you produce consumer goods (catch fish). Using the spear, you can now catch six fish per day—a significant improvement. This piece of capital equipment has increased your productivity, and by doing so, it has widened your economic choices considerably. Because you can catch enough fish to feed yourself in less than half a day, you have in effect freed up your time (labour) *to do other things.* You could use your freed-up time to

• produce other *consumer products*, such as shelter or other types of food;
• produce more *capital goods*, such as a net, or a plow, or traps, so as to increase your efficiency further; or
• enjoy some *leisure time.*

Suppose you decide to build a net. This is a more complex two-day project, but because you can now catch all the fish you need in a few hours each day, you can spread the building of the net over a period of four half-days. You could have caught 12 fish in this period of time, but you have decided instead to acquire another piece of capital equipment—a net. Using the net, you are able to catch enough fish to feed yourself for a whole day in about half an hour. Your productivity in fishing is now so high that you have a great deal of free time to do other things. You then use this available time to fashion some primitive tools—a hammer, a saw, a knife, and so on, with which you can construct more capital equipment. After a few weeks, you have a ladder for picking fruit from trees, traps for catching animals, a bow and arrows for hunting, a plow for cultivating vegetables, a house for shelter, and a boat for transportation—not to mention several hours per day of leisure time and a comfortable hammock in which to spend it.

Your standard of living has increased tremendously from its original subsistence level. The key to this process is, of course, the capital equipment that has increased your productivity. But how was this capital equipment obtained? To make the spear, you had to do without one day's consumption of fish—the two fish you could have caught instead of working on the spear. Making the net also involved a sacrifice of consumption: the things you could have produced in the two days' time it took to make the net. Similarly, to acquire all the other pieces of your capital equipment, you had to *forgo consumption*— that is, *forgo present enjoyment*. This is the concept of *opportunity cost* explained in Chapter 1. The opportunity cost of building capital equipment to increase your prosperity in the future is reduced consumption of goods and services in the present.

You were willing to do this because the capital equipment would *increase your future consumption*, by increasing your productivity. So you made the decision to trade off a lower standard of living *in the present* against a higher standard of living *in the future*. Each time you made a piece of capital equipment you were in effect saying, "I'll accept less consumption than I could have had today so that I can have more in the future." At first, this process was quite painful—you had to go a full day without food. Later, as your productivity increased, the sacrifices in the present became less harsh, because you could produce your daily food quite speedily and build more capital equipment in the remaining time each day.

Consumption, saving, and investment These basic ideas are so important that we will define them carefully. **Consumption** refers to consumer goods and services that are produced to be used up by consumers for *present* enjoyment. Consumption includes things such as food, clothing, cars, and entertainment. The production of capital goods, which will make possible greater production of goods and services *in the future*, is called **investment**.

But the basic economic problem of scarcity forces upon us a choice: the *more* of our output we devote to *investment* (for future prosperity), the *less* of our output will be available for *consumption* (for present enjoyment). This basic concept of doing without (forgoing) consumption is known as **saving**. Saving is obviously very important because saving is essential if there is to be the investment necessary for economic progress. Figure 3-2 on page 56 shows this key relationship between consumption, saving, and investment, and how it generates higher productivity.

The saving–investment process in a modern economy The deserted islander scenario has the advantage of illustrating the realities of the saving–investment process as clearly as possible. The islander did without some consumption (fish) in the present in order to build a capital good (spear) to increase productivity and standard of living in the future. This is shown in the top half of Figure 3-3 on page 56.

consumption
Consumer goods and services that are used up by consumers for present enjoyment.

investment
The production of capital goods that make possible increased production in the future.

saving
Doing without (forgoing) consumer goods; disposable income not spent on consumption.

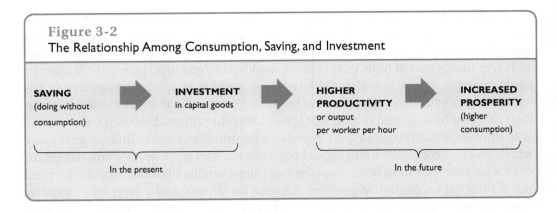

Figure 3-2
The Relationship Among Consumption, Saving, and Investment

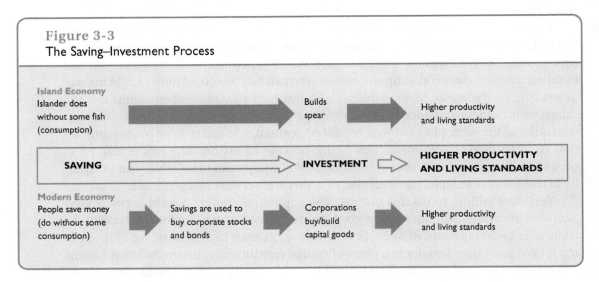

Figure 3-3
The Saving–Investment Process

In a modern economy such as Canada's, the saving–investment process is more complex than on the island, but it is essentially the same process. As the bottom half of Figure 3-3 shows, people save some of their income; that is, they don't spend it on consumption. They *do without some consumption* that they could have had, in the same way that the islander did without fish. These savings can be used to buy shares and bonds issued by businesses. Often, people's savings are put into financial institutions, pension funds, or mutual funds, which invest in stocks and bonds. These decisions are often made by professional financial managers of mutual funds, pension funds, or financial institutions. In any case, the savings can be made available to businesses. The businesses can then use these funds for the purpose of buying or building *capital goods*, which will *increase productivity* in the economy, making higher living standards possible.

In both the deserted island situation and the modern economy, the basic economic realities of the saving–investment process are those shown in the middle of Figure 3-3: saving makes investment possible, which leads to higher living standards.

(b) Education and Skills of the Labour Force

Obviously, the better educated and more highly skilled the nation's labour force is, the more likely it will be that its workers—and the nation—will be highly productive. Over the course of the twentieth century, economic activity shifted steadily away from the physical work associated with agriculture and factories and toward service industries

"If you think education is expensive, try ignorance."
— DEREK BOK, FORMER PRESI-
DENT, HARVARD UNIVERSITY

and high-technology industries that employ large numbers of well-educated and trained "knowledge workers." These changes, which have been accelerated in recent years by advances in computer technology, have made it essential for a modern society to have a well-educated and highly skilled labour force.

In addition to changes in technology, recent changes in the international economic environment have added to the importance of Canada's having a highly qualified labour force. In today's globalized world economy, business investment capital flows more freely than ever among nations, seeking the most attractive location. And given the importance of knowledge workers in modern business, an educated and skilled labour force can attract investment by multinational corporations.

In the past, a nation's prosperity might have depended mainly on its natural resources or its massive investments in facilities to process resources into manufactured goods. In the future, prosperity will be much more dependent upon the education, training, and skills of a nation's labour force, which can in turn attract the business investment needed for prosperity. This is why spending on training and education is regarded as a key strategic investment in the economic future of a nation, and it is often referred to as an "investment in human capital."

> "Increasingly, educated brainpower—along with the roads, airports, computers, and fibre-optic cables linking it up (to the rest of the world)—determines a nation's standard of living."
> — ROBERT B. REICH, "THE REAL ECONOMY," IN *THE ATLANTIC MONTHLY*

www.hrsdc.gc.ca

(c) Management

The quality of management is an important contributor to productivity because management is ultimately responsible for the efficiency with which productive resources are used to produce goods and services. This involves management skills well beyond the traditional skills of planning, organizing, directing, and controlling work activities. In a sophisticated economy that utilizes many knowledge workers, the abilities to communicate effectively, to lead people, and to solve problems are critically important management skills. Furthermore, the quality of employer–employee relations, much of which depends on management, influences employee morale and productivity.

(d) Size of Market and Scale of Operations

Sometimes, as the size of a production operation increases, its production costs per product fall. With larger-scale production, mass-production techniques involving more sophisticated and specialized capital equipment and workers can be used. The increased efficiency is attributable to what economists call **economies of scale**.

Economies of scale are more important in some industries than in others. In many service industries, such as restaurants and barbershops, production methods are labour-intensive, and there are few if any efficiency advantages to huge operations. But in manufacturing and resource industries, large-scale capital equipment and mass-production techniques can bring substantial gains in efficiency and lower production costs per unit.

In many manufacturing industries, firms must be able to produce on a very large scale in order to get production costs per unit low enough to be competitive. To sell such volumes of output, they must have *access to large markets*, either domestically or through international trade. Economists estimate that, in many such industries, producers need access to markets of at least 100 million (three times Canada's population) people in order to operate on a scale that will generate the efficiency that makes their production costs and prices internationally competitive.

Capital equipment, quality of the labour force and management, and size of market are all *physical* factors that *make it possible* for a nation to be efficient. In order to *actually achieve* this potential productivity, there must be *incentives* that push people and businesses to become more efficient. Two basic incentives are *economic gain* and *competition*.

economies of scale
The achievement of increased efficiency as a result of larger-scale productive operations and reductions in production costs per unit made possible by large-scale production and mass-production technology.

(e) The Incentive of After-Tax Economic Gain

Economic gain is a key incentive for both producers and individuals to improve productivity. For businesses, this economic gain is the *profit motive*, which creates incentives for efficiency in at least two ways. First, higher productivity means lower costs and thus higher profits. Second, higher productivity can also make lower prices possible, which can help to increase sales and the growth of the enterprise. On an individual level, managers and employees will be more inclined to improve productivity if there is personal economic gain for themselves in doing so, in the form of pay raises or bonuses based on productivity or profits.

It is important to note that economic gain refers to the *after-tax* gain of the businesses or people involved. If tax rates are too high, the incentive to improve efficiency will be reduced, because the after-tax gains from doing so will be smaller. So government taxation policies can have important effects upon incentives, and upon a nation's productivity and prosperity.

marginal tax rate
The percentage of any *additional* income received that goes to taxes.

The key to economic incentives is the **marginal tax rate**, which is defined as the percentage of any *additional* income (over and above one's present income) that is taken by taxes. If Fred earns a salary of $60 000 per year for working in a library and pays $12 000 in income taxes on this salary, he is paying a 20-percent tax rate on his income. This percentage is his tax rate on his *total* income, whereas his marginal tax rate is the percentage of any *extra* income that he earns that would be taken by taxes. For instance, if Fred earns an *extra* $10 000 as a wrestler in the evenings and he must pay $4000 in income taxes on this $10 000 of additional income, his *marginal tax rate* is 40 percent ($4000 ÷ $10 000). His marginal tax rate will be an important factor affecting Fred's incentive to do such additional work. If the marginal tax rate is too high, Fred's extra work will provide him with so little extra income after taxes that he may decide that the additional work is not worth doing. High marginal tax rates can discourage people from working to earn additional income in various ways such as second jobs, bonuses, profit-sharing plans, overtime, and pay raises for promotions.

High marginal tax rates can also undermine the all-important *saving–investment process*. If high marginal tax rates reduce the after-tax returns to savers/investors on their income from interest, dividends, and capital gains too much, people will be discouraged from saving, and less capital will be available for business investment.

YOU DECIDE

Sally's Taxes

In her regular job, Sally earns $60,000 per year, on which she pays income taxes of $18,000, or 30 percent. Sally works at a second job, at which she earned $20,000 last year, on which she paid taxes of $8,000, or 40 percent. As the table shows, three different tax rates apply to Sally's income: 30 percent on the income from her regular job, 40 percent on the income from her second job, and 32.5 percent on her total income from both jobs.

	Income	Income Taxes	Tax Rate
Regular job	$60,000	$18,000	30.0%
Second job	$20,000	$8,000	40.0%
Both jobs	$80,000	$26,000	32.5%

QUESTIONS

1. Which of the three tax rates shown in the table is Sally's *marginal tax rate*? Explain the reason for your choice.
2. Which of the three tax rates shown in the table is the key to Sally's incentive to do additional work? Explain the reason for your choice.

Similarly, high tax rates on business profits can discourage capital investment—not only by leaving business with less funds for capital investment but also by reducing the profit incentive for businesses to invest in plant and equipment.

Finally, if a nation's tax rates on profits and investment income are too high relative to tax rates in other countries, there is a risk that investment funds will relocate to countries where taxes are lower. This is a particularly important consideration for Canadian tax policy, due to the opportunities for investment in the United States.

In conclusion, in establishing their taxation policies, it is essential that governments take into account not only their need for tax revenue, but also the effect of marginal tax rates on incentives to work, save, and invest.

(f) The Incentive of Competition

The other main incentive in a market system is *competition*. Both theory and experience indicate that strong competition pushes producers to become more efficient. Generally, competition is stronger in industries in which there are many competing producers (including foreign competitors), and it is relatively easy for new producers to start up.

On the other hand, when there are only a few firms in an industry and their government protects them from foreign competition, the lack of competition tends to cause the industry to fall behind in efficiency.

Canada's Productivity Performance

Canada's productivity performance is shown in Figure 3-4. The graph in Figure 3-4(a) below shows output (real GDP) per hour worked since 1961, and the graph in Figure 3-4(b) on page 60 shows the percentage growth in productivity in each year.

There are real difficulties in measuring productivity, and worse problems in trying to compare the productivity statistics and performance of different countries. That said, there is broad agreement concerning certain aspects of the productivity performance of the Canadian economy.

First, the *level* of productivity in Canada is relatively high—Canada is among the higher-productivity nations in the world. Second, there was a significant slowdown in

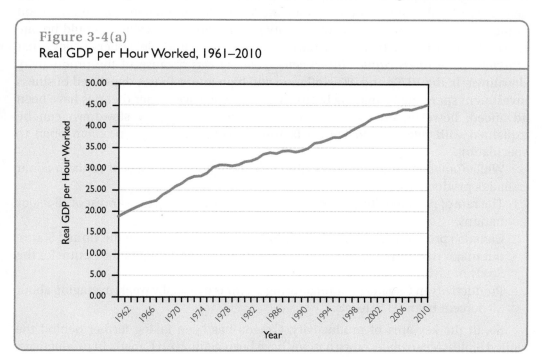

Figure 3-4(a)
Real GDP per Hour Worked, 1961–2010

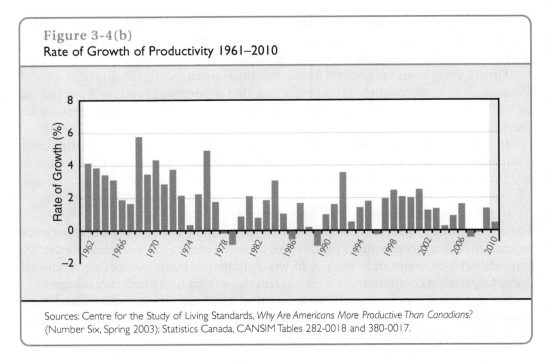

Figure 3-4(b)
Rate of Growth of Productivity 1961–2010

Sources: Centre for the Study of Living Standards, *Why Are Americans More Productive Than Canadians?*
(Number Six, Spring 2003); Statistics Canada, CANSIM Tables 282-0018 and 380-0017.

productivity growth after the late 1970s—after growing at an average rate of 3.2 percent per year from 1960 to 1977, productivity growth averaged only 1.0 percent per year over the next 20 years.

This *productivity slowdown* occurred in most major nations, and is not fully understood. Many observers believe that the *growth of service industries* contributed to slower productivity growth. As economies grow wealthier, a rising proportion of consumer demand—and thus output and employment—is for services, such as restaurants, entertainment, travel, health care, education, and so on. Generally, it is easier to apply productivity-increasing technology to the production of *goods* than to *services*. For instance, mass-production technology can be readily used to produce goods such as appliances, whereas the provision of services such as restaurants, health care, legal counsel, and education are less easily automated. So, the expansion of the service sector, in which productivity growth tends to be slower, could be one cause of slower productivity growth in the economy as a whole. Others believe that *weakness in business capital investment spending* was a cause of the productivity slowdown. In the 1970s and '80s, inflation and high interest rates depressed business investment spending by making borrowing very expensive. Other theories have been advanced; however, only about one-half of the productivity slowdown can be explained with reference to known factors, leaving half of this problem open to speculation.

While Canada's productivity is quite high, there are three areas of concern about Canada's productivity performance:

1. The rate of productivity *growth* in Canada has been among the slowest of all major nations.
2. Canada's productivity is significantly lower than productivity in the United States, our major trading partner—10 to 20 percent lower, according to the Centre for the Study of Living Standards.
3. Productivity in Canada's manufacturing sector is especially weak, averaging about 30 percent below U.S. levels.

So, in the key area of productivity, Canada has been falling farther behind the United States. Meanwhile, other nations have been gaining on Canada in productivity,

www.csls.ca

and passing us. According to the Groningen Growth and Development Centre in terms of GDP per hour worked, Canada has in recent years ranked 18th out of 23 countries in the Organization for Economic Cooperation and Development (OECD), whereas in 1950, Canada ranked fifth.

www.ggdc.nl

Consequences

Such a weak productivity performance can only have negative effects on the living standards of Canadians relative to other nations. For instance, the Conference Board of Canada has warned that if recent productivity growth trends continue, the gap between the standard of living of Americans and Canadians would grow wider in the future. Also, low productivity could limit the ability of Canadian producers to compete internationally—a potentially serious problem for a country that exports and imports as much as Canada does. This concern is especially strong regarding the manufacturing sector, since Canadian productivity there is particularly weak and so much of world trade is in manufactured goods. Furthermore, an economy in which productivity is stagnant is less likely to attract its share of the international business investment and skilled people that are two keys to success in the globalized world economy.

For these reasons, many economists regard poor productivity performance as the most fundamental weakness of the Canadian economy. However, determining the *reasons* for this productivity performance is no simple matter, because productivity depends upon the complex interactions of various factors. While productivity is *measured* in terms of output per worker-hour, the *cause* of high or low productivity is not simply the performance of workers—factors such as capital equipment, management, economies of scale, and incentives are key contributors to productivity. In the following sections, we will look at some of the possible reasons for Canada's weak productivity performance. The discussion of these factors is necessarily in general terms only, which may or may not apply to particular industries or firms.

(a) Capital Investment

In general, Canadian industry uses less capital equipment per worker than U.S. producers. Large Canadian firms, such as the auto companies, often have world-class technology. But many Canadian manufacturers, especially small- and medium-sized ones, have been slower than their foreign competitors to adopt up-to-date production technology, such as robotics and computer-assisted design and manufacturing (CAD/CAM). Canadian manufacturers' use of some technology may be limited by the smaller size of their plants, which is discussed in a subsequent section. And in the 1990s, the sharp decline in the international value of the Canadian dollar limited capital investment by Canadian firms, by making imported capital equipment as much as 25 percent more costly.

A related factor is Canada's low spending on research and development (R&D), which contributes to innovation and productivity growth. Canada usually ranks about 15th among members of the Organisation for Economic Co-operation and Development (OECD) in expenditure on R&D.

www.oecd.org

(b) Education and Skill of the Labour Force

On average, the literacy and numeracy skills of Canada's workforce appear somewhat higher than in the United States. Nonetheless, Canadian employers have often noted shortages of people with middle-level technical, business, and managerial skills—skilled tradespeople, technicians, technologists, and operations managers who contribute to productivity in the day-to-day operations of enterprises of all sorts.

Furthermore, Canadian businesses have failed to fill these gaps with training programs of their own. Canadian employers spend considerably less on training than their foreign counterparts—in fact, Canada ranks only 15th in the world in employee training.

In addition, Canada lags behind the United States in the important area of research universities and the top-quality scientists and engineers associated with them, who are often the originators of productivity-enhancing research.

(c) Management

As noted earlier, management skills are particularly important to the development of high productivity. Canada has sufficient university graduates in business and management to fill *senior* positions, but many observers believe there is a shortage of well-trained, practical, and competent *middle managers* to handle the management of *operations*, which is often a key to efficiency.

Canadian managers have also been criticized for being slow to adapt to the rapid changes in the world economy, particularly the growth of international trade and competition known as *globalization*. According to the Swiss-based World Economic Forum, a weakness in Canada's international competitiveness has been the lack of outward orientation of Canadian management. This may in part be related to Canada's traditional government policy of protecting Canadian manufacturers from foreign competition, as discussed in the next two sections.

www.weforum.org

(d) Size of Market and Scale of Operations

Especially in manufacturing, larger producers enjoy economies of scale that allow them to achieve higher productivity. And, as noted earlier, a market size of 100 million is necessary for many manufacturers to realize the full benefits of economies of scale. But Canada's domestic market is small, and much of Canadian industry has consisted (and still consists) of smaller-scale and less efficient firms. Until recently, these firms were protected from foreign competition by a government policy of tariff protection. While this protection helped Canada's manufacturing sector to survive and grow, it did not help manufacturers to become more efficient. And even after the adoption of free-trade policies, many Canadian firms remained relatively small and oriented to the small Canadian market. We will further examine this issue later in this chapter, and also in Chapter 12, "Canada in the Global Economy."

(e) The Incentive of After-Tax Economic Gain

The role of taxes in the Canada-U.S. productivity gap is unclear. Canadian tax rates on personal income are higher than in the United States; however, when higher payroll taxes on Americans for social security and free medical care in Canada are taken into account, the difference between the two countries is less than is often supposed, and varies from province to province and from state to state. And while tax rates on business profits are higher in the USA than in Canada, various tax exemptions considerably reduce the *actual taxes paid* by many U.S. corporations.

To complicate matter further, several European nations with much higher taxes than the United States have higher productivity than our neighbours to the south. For these reasons, the Centre for the Study of Living Standards (CSLS) says that the evidence showing high taxes as the reason for Canada's low productivity is weak.

(f) The Incentive of Competition

Productivity in the Canadian economy has until recently suffered from a lack of strong competition, for several reasons. First, there has been Canada's *tariff policy*, as discussed earlier, which has protected many Canadian producers from foreign competition. Second, many Canadian industries have been dominated by a few large firms. In such industries, known to economists as **oligopolies**, it is possible that the dominant firms will agree to limit competition among themselves, so as to be able to earn comfortable and secure profits. Obviously, such a situation reduces the competitive pressure to continually improve productivity. Finally, many Canadian industries have historically been subjected to a variety of *government regulations*. Some of these regulations restrict how many firms can operate in a particular field (such as the taxi business and airline industry), and some restrict how much producers can produce (such as egg and poultry marketing boards) or establish prices, often in a way that guarantees producers a certain rate of profit (such as cable television). Many of these government restrictions have the side effect of restricting competition and the incentive to improve productivity in parts of the Canadian economy.

oligopoly
An industry that is dominated by a few firms.

Recent Productivity Performance

Figure 3-4(b) on page 60 shows not only the productivity slowdown of the 1978–96 period, but also that productivity growth *sped up* after 1996. From 1978 to 1996, productivity increased at an average rate of only 1.0 percent per year, but from 1997 to 2003 it grew by 2.0 percent per year. As with the productivity slowdown, different explanations were advanced for this improvement. One prominent explanation was that Canadian industry had invested considerably in new capital equipment in the second half of the 1990s. Another theory was that the faster productivity growth was the time-lagged effect of Canada's moves toward free trade during the 1990s.

However, Figure 3-4 also shows that after 2003, productivity growth slowed down again, and that in 2004 it actually *decreased* slightly. The reasons for this trend are unclear, but perhaps the most interesting theory is that Canadian firms generally enjoyed high profits during this period, which placed management under less pressure to increase productivity and cut costs. By contrast, U.S. firms' profits over this period were much lower, which might have forced them to reduce employment levels in order to increase productivity and cut costs.

While Canada's productivity growth did improve after 1996, it was still less rapid than productivity increases in the United States, so Canada continued to fall farther behind its southern neighbour. This meant that productivity continued to be a basic concern of Canadian government policy-makers, as did policies that could increase productivity.

Government Policies to Strengthen Productivity and the Supply Side of the Economy

While government policies sometimes weaken productivity, they can also help to improve productivity, prosperity, and the international competitiveness of a nation's industries. In the following sections, we will consider some policy directions that have been taken and could be taken to improve the productivity and competitiveness of Canadian industry regarding the factors that influence productivity.

(a) Saving and Investment

By providing tax incentives that make it financially attractive for people to save and invest money—such as Registered Retirement Savings Plans (RRSPs)—and for businesses to invest in capital equipment, governments can promote the *saving–investment process* that is the key to capital formation. Additional support for technological improvements can come from government support for *research and development* (R&D), in the form of tax allowances or other financial support.

(b) Education and Skills of the Labour Force

Given the importance of human capital in a modern economy, governmental education and training policies have become very important to a society's economic prosperity. Most observers believe that the education system should place more emphasis on basic skills and should be linked more closely to the needs of the workplace in which graduates must function. In addition, there should be more emphasis on science programs and the development of middle-level technical, business, and management skills and on apprenticeship programs. Employers should devote more resources to employee training and retraining. Finally, governments have shown increased interest in reforming social welfare programs by linking unemployment and welfare benefits to training or retraining, either by requiring benefit recipients to undertake training or by providing financial incentives for them to do so.

(c) Management

At the strategic level, government export programs can help managers to shift their focus toward the global economy, and to understand how trends and developments in the international economy provide both opportunities and challenges for their firms. At the operational level, Canada's educational system and business community need to develop more well-trained middle managers who are capable of managing for the increased productivity that is needed by both businesses and the economy at large.

(d) Market Size and Scale of Operations

Without access to larger foreign markets, many Canadian producers would be unable to achieve the economies of scale needed to be competitive internationally. From this perspective, Canada's signing of the Canada–U.S. Free Trade Agreement of 1989 and the North American Free Trade Agreement of 1994 (NAFTA) is very important. In the 15 years following the signing of the Canada–U.S. Free Trade Agreement, Canada's exports in real terms increased by 134 percent, as compared to 48 percent growth for the economy as a whole.

(e) The Incentive of After-Tax Economic Gain

capital taxes
Taxes levied on the amount of a corporation's assets, or its capital.

As noted earlier, by the late 1990s, it was believed that high taxes were undermining Canada's economic growth. Over the 2001–2005 period, the federal government made a series of cuts to personal and corporate income taxes that totalled roughly $100 billion. There were also proposals to reduce **capital taxes**, which are levied on the assets of large corporations and are believed to discourage business investment.

(f) The Incentive of Competition

Probably the most important steps taken by the federal government to increase competition in the Canadian economy were the signing of the above-mentioned Canada–U.S. Free Trade Agreement and NAFTA. Under these agreements, the degree of import competition has increased substantially: during the 15 years following the signing of the Canada–U.S. Free Trade Agreement, imports into Canada in real terms increased by 114 percent.

Another step toward promoting competition had been taken in 1986, with the passage of new competition legislation (the Competition Act) that provided stronger measures against anticompetitive practices by corporations, such as price-fixing and mergers of firms in order to dominate a market or an industry.

Finally, as noted earlier, government regulation of industries often has the effect of reducing competition. In recent years, governments have *deregulated* (to varying degrees) different sectors of the economy, including oil and gas, airlines, communications, and financial services, thus promoting increased competition, higher productivity, and lower prices.

The Supply Side of the Economy in Review

We have discussed six factors that influence the productivity, or the production potential—the *supply side*—of the economy:

a) Capital equipment and the saving–investment process
b) The labour force (size, education, and skills)
c) Management
d) Size of market and scale of operations
e) The incentive of after-tax economic gain
f) The incentive of competition

Together, these factors determine not only the efficiency with which the economy can produce goods and services but also its potential total output, or the *capacity output* of the economy. As we saw in Chapter 2, capacity output is the fastest pace of production that the economy can maintain without excessive inflation being generated because aggregate demand has become so high that output (the supply side) cannot keep up with demand.

Growth of the Supply Side (of Capacity Output)

Ultimately, the capacity output of the economy depends on two factors:

• the size of the labour force (the *number of workers* available), and
• productivity (average *output per worker*)

Both of these factors increase gradually over time. The size of the labour force grows due to population growth and immigration. Output per worker increases due to various factors such as improvements in technology and skills. Over the longer term, the size of the labour force has grown by about 1.6 percent per year, and output per worker has increased by about 1.4 percent per year. The combined result of these factors has been that the potential output of the economy has risen by roughly 3 percent per year, as reflected in Figure 3-5. These are average figures, and they vary from year to year. For instance, if productivity growth were to become faster, the

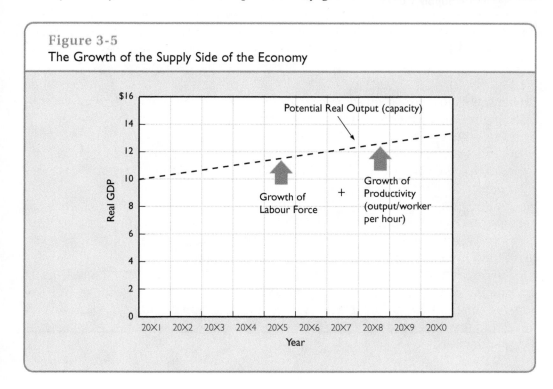

Figure 3-5
The Growth of the Supply Side of the Economy

potential output line in Figure 3-5 would rise more rapidly, and vice versa. Notwithstanding this, the impression conveyed by Figure 3-5—that the supply side of the economy grows at a fairly slow and steady pace—is reasonably accurate.

But what actually *determines* the *capacity* output of the economy as shown in Figure 3-5? What is it that prevents output from increasing beyond the level shown by the dotted line in the figure? In practical experience, the factor that limits the growth of output tends to be *the availability of qualified labour*. We saw in Chapter 2 that the unemployment rate seldom goes below 6.5 percent of the labour force, even in a strong economic boom. So, in a boom the obstacle that producers encounter when they seek to increase output further is a shortage of labour in general, and of skilled labour in particular. This obstacle also helps to explain why in the later stages of a boom, wage rates and labour costs per unit produced often increase, as employers compete for the limited number of qualified workers available. This brings us to the last section of this chapter—the aggregate supply curve.

The Concept of Aggregate Supply

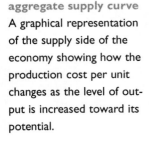

aggregate supply curve
A graphical representation of the supply side of the economy showing how the production cost per unit changes as the level of output is increased toward its potential.

The supply side of the economy can be represented by an **aggregate supply curve**, as shown in Figure 3-6, which illustrates how the level of total output (aggregate supply) is related to the cost per unit of producing that output.

When operating at its highest possible production level, this economy is *physically* capable of producing 100 units of output per week. The farther we move to the right on the aggregate supply (AS) curve, the closer we get to this maximum possible output. But the higher the curve goes, the more costly it is to produce goods and services. Up to about 80 or 90 units of volume, we can increase output without experiencing large increases in production costs per unit because the economy has plenty of inputs (labour, capital, and resources) available or unemployed. It should, therefore,

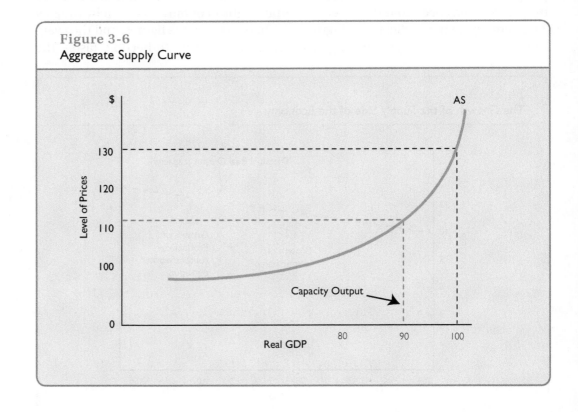

Figure 3-6
Aggregate Supply Curve

be possible to obtain more inputs without having to pay higher wage rates or prices to attract them. Beyond this level, however, it is no longer possible to increase output further without some increases in production costs per unit.

In some industries, production *bottlenecks* will occur due to shortages of labour, production capacity, or other inputs. Output can be increased, but only by means that will also increase production costs per unit: higher wages for overtime, extra shifts, higher prices for increasingly scarce materials or other inputs, and so on. In Figure 3-6, this relationship means that we can move to higher levels of production, but only by accepting higher costs per unit, as shown by the AS curve sloping upward.

The closer we get to the economy's maximum output, the more severe these problems of shortages and production bottlenecks become, and the faster the AS curve rises. By the time output has reached 90 units per week, production costs are rising so rapidly that the economy is considered to have reached its *capacity output*, and is now *overheating*. Finally, at output of 100 units per week, the economy is simply not capable of producing at a faster pace, and the AS curve becomes vertical.

Changes in the AS Curve

Figure 3-6 represents the AS curve at a particular point in time. If the economy's *potential to produce* were to increase next year as its labour force and stock of capital equipment grew, the AS curve would shift to the right, as shown by AS_1 in Figure 3-7.

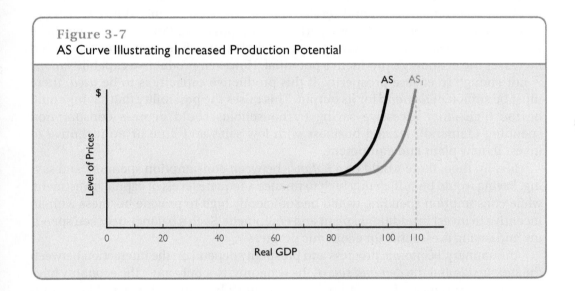

Figure 3-7
AS Curve Illustrating Increased Production Potential

AS_1 reflects the fact that the economy is now capable of producing a higher volume of output (110 units) than last year, at about the same cost per unit. Efficiency (productivity) has not improved, as shown by the fact that production costs per unit are the same as last year, but the greater volume of inputs available makes possible a higher volume of total output.

If *overall productivity* in the economy were to improve so that it was using its inputs more efficiently, not only would its potential (capacity) output rise, but production costs per unit would also fall. This relationship is shown in Figure 3-8 on page 68, in which AS_2 represents the new situation, with production costs per unit lower than before and capacity output higher than before.

When combined with the aggregate demand curve that we will introduce in Chapter 4, the aggregate supply curve will be a useful tool for analysis.

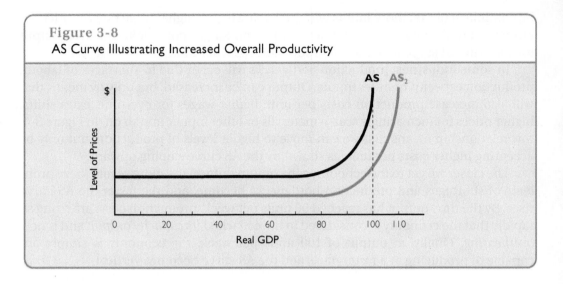

Figure 3-8
AS Curve Illustrating Increased Overall Productivity

Can Saving Be *Too* High? A Preview of the Demand Side of the Economy

In this chapter, we have stressed the importance of the *supply side* of the economy—its ability to produce goods and services efficiently. Without this ability to achieve high productivity, economic prosperity is not possible. Furthermore, we have stressed the desirability of saving, which makes possible the investment that increases the economy's productive potential. However, productive capability *alone* is not enough to ensure prosperity. If this productive capacity is to be *used*, there must be sufficient *demand* for its output. This raises the possibility that saving could be too high—that excessive saving by households could depress consumption spending (demand), leaving business with low sales and little or no incentive to invest in new plant and equipment.

Ideally, then, there would be a *balance* between consumption spending and saving. Saving would be sufficiently high to finance adequate levels of capital investment, while consumption spending would be sufficiently high to provide business with an incentive to invest in additional plant and equipment. Such a balance between spending and saving is essential for economic progress.

In summary, economic progress and prosperity depend on the interaction between the *supply side* and the *demand side* of the economy. Not only must the economy have the ability to produce efficiently, but also there must be sufficient demand for its output to ensure that the economy will actually produce to its fullest possible capabilities. In Chapter 4, we will consider the demand side of the economy more fully.

Chapter Summary

1. A key to economic prosperity is high productivity or output per worker per hour. (L.O. 1)

2. The main factors affecting productivity are

   (a) capital equipment and the saving–investment process that builds it; this requires forgoing current consumption in order to build the capital goods that will increase productivity (and consumption) in the future,

  (b) the education and skills of the labour force,

  (c) management,

  (d) size of market and scale of operations,

  (e) the incentive of after-tax economic gain, and

  (f) the incentive of competition. (L.O. 2)

3. Like most nations, Canada experienced a slowdown in productivity growth after the late 1970s. The reasons for this are believed to include a shift in output and employment from goods-producing industries to service industries, and a slow-down in business capital investment. (L.O. 3)

4. After the late 1970s, productivity growth in Canada was slower than in its major trading partners, with productivity in the manufacturing sector a particular concern. This caused concerns about Canadians' future living standards and the international competitiveness of Canadian producers. (L.O. 4)

5. Canada's weak productivity performance is attributed to various factors, including relatively low amounts of capital per worker, weak R&D, shortages of skills, small plants lacking economies of scale, and various government regulations that limit competition. (L.O. 4)

6. Government policies that could help to improve productivity include policies to encourage saving, investment, and R&D; education more attuned to the needs of the economy; agreements to gain/secure access to larger markets, such as the Canada–U.S. Free Trade Agreement and NAFTA; reducing marginal tax rates on business and personal income; and policies to strengthen competition, such as freer trade, stronger competition legislation, and less government regulation of business. (L.O. 5)

7. In recent years, the capacity output of the Canadian economy has been growing at about 3 percent per year. This is the result of a combination of labour-force growth and productivity growth. (L.O. 6)

Questions

1. In a (very) simple island mini-economy, only one product is produced—breadfruit. There are 10 people working, and each worker toils 8 hours per day. In a day, they produce 400 kilograms of breadfruit. From this, we can conclude that *productivity* in this economy is

  (a) 400 kilograms of breadfruit.

  (b) 5 kilograms of breadfruit per worker per hour.

  (c) 4000 kilograms of breadfruit.

  (d) 50 kilograms of breadfruit per hour.

  (e) None of the above.

2. From the information in the previous question, a reasonable estimate of this economy's *capacity output* would be _____ kilograms of breadfruit per day.

3. In Figure 3-6, it is clear from the graph that the economy has sufficient economic inputs to produce as much as 100 units per week. Why, then, is the economy's *capacity output* considered to be only 90 units per week?

4. The basic contribution that capital goods make to the economy and to society is

  (a) that they increase the profits of business.

  (b) that producing capital goods creates jobs for people.

  (c) that they prevent excessive production of consumer goods by diverting productive resources away from consumer-goods production.

(d) that they increase output per worker per hour (the productivity of labour), and thus the material standard of living of society.

(e) nothing—capital goods are of no special value to the economy or to society.

5. Donna teaches accounting in a community college for a salary of $60 000 per year, and she pays income tax of $15 000.

(a) Donna's *average tax rate* is _____ percent.

(b) If Donna teaches night school, her income will increase to $62 000, and her income taxes will increase to $15 840. The marginal tax rate paid by Donna is _____ percent.

(c) Which would have a greater negative effect on Donna's incentive to work—a significant increase in her average tax rate or a significant increase in her marginal tax rate? Why?

6. Would economies of scale be more important in the house-painting industry or the automobile-manufacturing industry? Explain the reason for your answer.

7. Write a concise argument that lower tax rates on business profits would increase productivity in the Canadian economy and would economically benefit Canadians in general.

8. Since the late 1980s, Canada has entered into various free trade agreements with other countries. Do you think that freer trade has increased or decreased productivity growth in the Canadian economy? Give at least two reasons for your answer.

9. For updates and new information on productivity trends in the Canadian economy, visit Statistics Canada at **www.statcan.gc.ca** and search the website for *Canadian productivity review*. Summarize any new information in the *Review* concerning productivity trends in the Canadian economy, and the reasons for those trends.

Study Guide

Review Questions (Answers to these Review Questions appear in Appendix B.)

1. The most basic source of a higher standard of living for the people of a society is

(a) free services provided by government.

(b) reductions in taxes.

(c) increases in productivity.

(d) Answers (a) and (b) together.

(e) None of the above.

2. *Productivity* is defined as

(a) output per worker per hour.

(b) real gross domestic product

(c) the economy's total output of goods and services.

(d) Answers (b) and (c) together.

(e) None of the above.

3. A factory employs 10 workers who work 8 hours per day and produce 400 fradistats per day. What is the *productivity* of workers in that factory?

   (a) 400 fradistats per day
   (b) 5 fradistats per worker per hour
   (c) 40 fradistats per worker
   (d) 50 fradistats per hour
   (e) None of the above.

4. The basic difference between capital goods and consumer goods is that

   (a) capital goods cost more money than consumer goods.
   (b) capital goods are used to produce more goods, while consumer goods are intended to be used up by consumers.
   (c) the production of capital goods is the end goal of all economic activity.
   (d) capital goods are used up (depreciate) over a period of time.
   (e) capital goods are purchased by governments.

5. The meaning of *investment* as a basic economic concept is

   (a) using society's productive resources to produce capital goods.
   (b) putting money in the bank.
   (c) using money to make money.
   (d) using society's productive resources to produce consumer goods.
   (e) Both (b) and (c).

6. To an economist, the basic meaning of the concept of *saving* is

   (a) putting money in the bank.
   (b) hoarding money.
   (c) doing without consumption so as to make investment possible.
   (d) storing consumer goods (e.g., food) for use in the future.
   (e) hoarding goods.

7. Is it true that a society must *save* if it is to be able to have *investment*?

   (a) No, because capital goods production and consumer goods production are not in any way connected.
   (b) No, because you can borrow money to invest—it need not be saved.
   (c) Yes, because investment involves the accumulation of consumer goods for future use.
   (d) Yes, because the productive resources used to produce capital goods could have been used to produce consumer goods.
   (e) None of the above.

8. *Economies of scale*

   (a) refer to reductions in production costs per unit as a result of higher volumes of output.
   (b) are often achieved by the use of mass-production technology.
   (c) are most readily achieved by firms that produce specialized products for a small-scale market.
   (d) Answers (a) and (b).
   (e) None of the above.

9. Incentives play a key role in increasing productivity. In a market system type of economy, the two main economic incentives that push people and business to become more efficient are

   (a) _____ and
   (b) _____.

10. Under the tax system of socialist British governments of the 1960s, rock and roll's supergroup the Beatles paid a very high marginal tax rate on much of their income. This is the "inspiration" for the lyrics of their song "Taxman," which refers to nineteen pounds of the Beatles' earnings going to the taxman and one pound to the Beatles. The Rolling Stones, like many other higher-income people, left England to escape British taxes.

   (a) According to the lyrics of "Taxman", what was the marginal tax rate paid by the Beatles?
   (b) Did the Beatles pay this tax rate on *all* of their income?
   (c) What lesson should governments learn from this experience?

11. Joan works in an office for a salary of $50 000 per year, and she pays income taxes of $11 000 on her earnings. Joan has been offered some extra work on a special project, for which she would be paid extra.

   (a) The *average tax rate* paid by Joan is _____ percent.
   If Joan agrees to do the extra work that has been offered to her, she will earn an additional $4500 this year. Her friend in the payroll department tells her that the income tax payable on this additional income will be $1500.
   (b) The *marginal tax rate* paid by Joan is _____ percent.

12. Fred works in construction, earns $60 000 per year and pays income taxes of $12 000. If Fred takes a second job as a dancer in a nightclub, his total income will increase to $80 000 per year, and his total income taxes will be $20 000. Fred's marginal tax rate is _____ percent.

13. In an island mini-economy, there are 15 people of working age. Ten of these people are currently working, and each of them produces 10 units of real output per day.

   (a) The real gross domestic product of the island economy is _____ units per day. If the islanders want to increase their real GDP to 150 units per day, the two basic approaches to doing this would be to
   (b) _____, and/or
   (c) _____.

14. In recent years in the Canadian economy, on average,

   (a) the labour force has grown by roughly _____ percent per year, and
   (b) output per worker has grown by roughly _____ percent per year, so
   (c) the capacity output of the economy has grown by roughly _____ percent per year.

15. Slow productivity growth has been a basic weakness of the Canadian economy for many years. Which of the following is considered to be a cause of this weak productivity performance?

   (a) A lack of capital investment by smaller manufacturers.
   (b) The small size of the plants of many manufacturers.
   (c) Low spending on research and development.
   (d) Low spending on employee training.
   (e) All of the above.

Critical Thinking Questions

(Asterisked questions 1 to 5 are answered in Appendix B; the answers to questions 6 to 10 are in the Instructor's Manual that accompanies this text.)

*1. "Societies whose people have a high standard of living tend to have a strong *saving–investment process*."

    (a) Explain how a strong saving–investment process contributes to a high standard of living.

    (b) What could a nation's government do in order to promote the development of a strong saving–investment process?

*2. Suppose Canadian businesses spend $2 billion on capital investment in computers in this year.

    (a) What are the economic benefits of this investment for Canadians?

    (b) What is the opportunity cost of this investment?

*3. People who are working overtime sometimes say that they work the first two hours of overtime for the government, then the next three hours for themselves.

    (a) Use the concept of the *marginal tax rate* to explain what they mean by this.

    (b) What is the marginal tax rate that these workers see themselves as paying?

*4. An island mini-economy has 200 workers. On average, each worker's productivity is 400 units of output per year in 20X1.

    (a) The *capacity output* of this economy in 20X1 is _____ units per year. Suppose that next year (20X2),

      • the workforce grows by 2 percent, and
      • average worker productivity increases by 2 percent.

    (b) The economy's capacity output in 20X2 would become _____ units per year.

    (c) From 20X1 to 20X2, the economy's capacity output grew by _____ percent.

    (d) If productivity had only increased by 1 percent in 20X2, the economy's capacity output in 20X2 would have been only _____ units per year.

*5. Canadians enjoy a relatively high standard of living. Why, then, is it considered so important that the productivity performance of Canada's economy improve?

6. Which do you think would have a more negative effect on productivity in the Canadian economy—an increase in taxes on personal income or higher tax rates on business profits? Explain the reasons for your answer.

7. Capital taxes are taxes on business that are calculated as a small percentage of the assets of a business. In Canada, capital taxes are often four times as high as in the United States. Over the next few years, Canada's federal and provincial governments plan to reduce capital taxes considerably. Why do you think such tax reductions on businesses are planned?

8. Productivity is affected by the condition of the economy. As an illustration of how a recession can affect output per employee, consider the following case.

You are the owner/manager of a small firm that produces candles, with the following labour force:

    • 1 president/manager (you)
    • 2 office staff: your secretary/receptionist and a bookkeeper/clerk
    • 1 sales representative
    • 1 plant supervisor
    • 20 plant workers

The total number of employees is 25, and currently you are producing 5000 boxes of candles per week, for an average productivity of 200 boxes of candles per person employed. (In this question, we will measure productivity by output per worker rather than output per worker per hour.)

Suppose a recession cuts your sales, causing you to reduce output by 20 percent to 4000 boxes per week.

   (a) How many employees will you probably lay off?
   (b) What will *labour productivity* (output per employee) be after the layoffs?
   (c) What is the percentage change in labour productivity, and why has this change occurred?
   (d) When the recession ends and sales and production increase again, what will happen to productivity?

9. The productivity slowdown that occurred since the late 1970s in many countries and especially in Canada is an important problem, but only about half of it has been explained by known factors.

   (a) What are two known factors underlying the productivity slowdown?
   (b) Do you agree with the view of some people who believe that the slower growth of output per worker-hour proves that another factor behind the productivity slowdown is a decline of the *work ethic* or increasing laziness on the part of workers?

10. The graph below shows the aggregate supply curve for an economy that can produce a maximum (capacity) output of 100 units per week. Explain how the AS curve would be changed if

   (a) the economy had 20 percent more of all productive resources, which could be utilized with the same efficiency as its existing resources.
   (b) the efficiency with which the economy's existing productive resources could be utilized increased by 20 percent.
   (c) the economy had 20 percent less of all productive resources.
   (d) the efficiency with which the economy's existing productive resources could be utilized decreased by 20 percent.

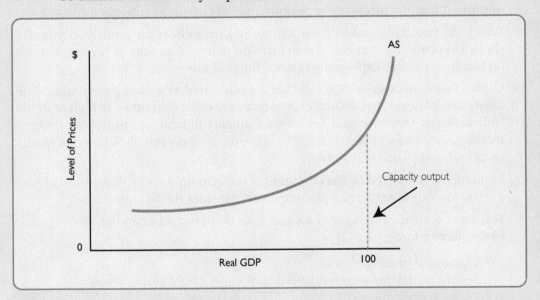

Use the Web   (Hints for this Use the Web exercise appear in Appendix B.)

1. For the most current update on productivity trends in the Canadian economy, visit Statistics Canada at **www.statcan.gc.ca** and search the website for *Labour productivity, hourly compensation and unit labour cost*. Summarize any new information provided by this source concerning productivity trends in the Canadian economy and the reasons for those trends.

4

Sources of Economic Prosperity: The Demand Side

After studying this chapter, you should be able to

1. List the four components of aggregate demand and express each as a percentage of GDP.

2. Explain three factors that have an important influence on the amount of household consumption spending and saving.

3. Explain the two main factors that influence the amount of business investment spending.

4. Explain why saving can be viewed as both an opportunity for economic progress and as a threat to the economy.

5. Using a supply-side/demand-side graph of the economy (or an aggregate demand/aggregate supply graph), explain how and why an increase in aggregate demand would affect output, employment, and the rate of inflation in the economy:

   (a) if output were well below capacity.
   (b) if output were near capacity.
   (c) if output were at capacity.

In Chapter 3, we considered the supply side of the economy, or the factors that determine the economy's ability to produce goods and services. These factors determine the *potential* output (capacity output) of the economy, but they do not decide how much output *actually will* be produced. In a market system, output will only be produced if there is a demand for it. So, the *actual* output of the economy—the gross domestic product—will be decided by the *level of total spending on goods and services* in the economy, or what economists call the **demand side** of the economy.

The level of total spending on goods and services (**aggregate demand**) is critically important to the performance of the economy on a macroeconomic scale. If aggregate demand is too low, there will be a *recession*, with output well below its potential level and high unemployment. Rising aggregate demand will generate higher levels of both output and employment, or an *economic boom*. But if aggregate demand becomes too high, output will be unable to keep up with demand and *inflation* will occur, as prices rise rapidly. Figure 4-1 summarizes the demand side and the supply side of the economy, and shows the need for a reasonable balance between them.

demand side
The purchasers of society's output of goods and services.

aggregate demand
Total spending on goods and services, consisting of consumption spending, investment spending, government spending, and net exports (C + I + G + X − M).

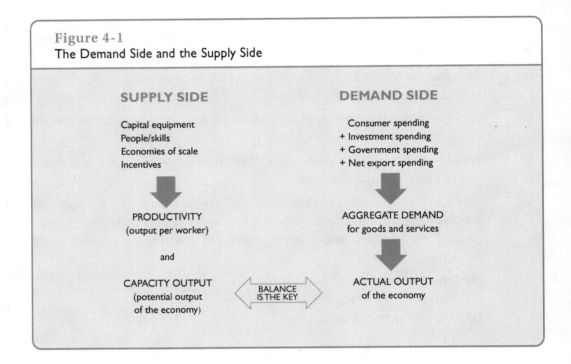

Figure 4-1
The Demand Side and the Supply Side

Aggregate Demand: Purchasers of the Economy's Output

We can divide aggregate demand into the same four categories into which we divided gross domestic product in Chapter 2.

    (a) *Consumption spending.* This is spending by households on consumer goods and services; recently it has bought about 58 percent of the economy's output.

    (b) *Investment spending.* The largest component of this category is business spending on capital goods, which usually purchases 10 to 13 percent of GDP. This category also includes investment by households in new housing, which is generally an additional 5 to 6 percent of GDP.

(c) *Government spending.* Government spending on goods and services has been about 21 percent of GDP in recent years. Current spending on goods and services (such as health care and education) has been about 19 percent of GDP, with spending on capital projects accounting for the rest.

(d) *Net exports (exports minus imports).* Purchases of Canadian exports by foreign buyers adds to aggregate demand in the Canadian economy, while purchases of imports by Canadians reduces demand for Canadian output. So the *net effect* of international trade on demand for Canadian goods and services can be calculated as *exports minus imports*. In recent years, exports have exceeded imports, so the foreign trade sector has boosted demand and output in Canada.

Figure 4-2 illustrates these components of aggregate demand, using statistics from 2010. In the following sections, we will examine each of these components of aggregate demand in more detail in order to better understand the demand side of the economy.

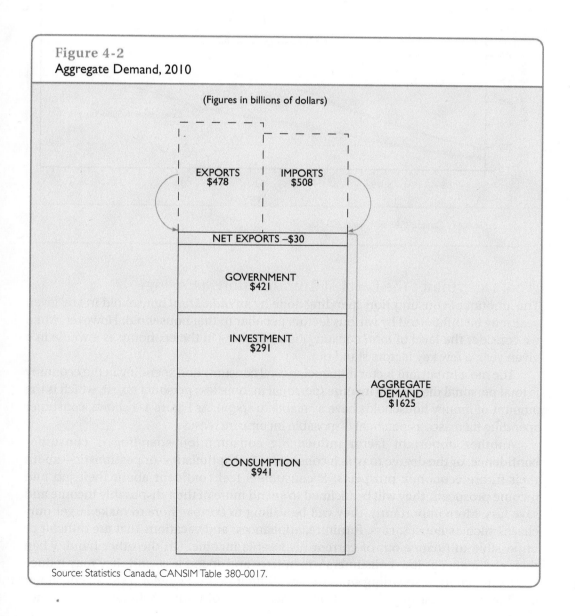

Figure 4-2
Aggregate Demand, 2010

(Figures in billions of dollars)

EXPORTS
$478

IMPORTS
$508

NET EXPORTS –$30

GOVERNMENT
$421

INVESTMENT
$291

AGGREGATE
DEMAND
$1625

CONSUMPTION
$941

Source: Statistics Canada, CANSIM Table 380-0017.

Consumption Spending by Households

consumption spending
Spending by households on consumer goods and services.

Consumption spending is defined as spending by households on consumer goods and services. The goods and services can be divided into three categories: *nondurable goods*, such as food and clothing, which are used up quite quickly; *durable goods*, such as cars and appliances, which last considerably longer; and *services*, such as entertainment, medical services, and travel. Consumption spending is the "workhorse" of the demand side of the economy in the sense that it is by far the largest single purchaser of the economy's output. As Figure 4-3 shows, consumption spending buys nearly three-fifths of the goods and services produced by the economy.

www.statcan.gc.ca
Search the site for "Gross domestic product, expenditure-based", then click on "Gross domestic product, expenditure-based".

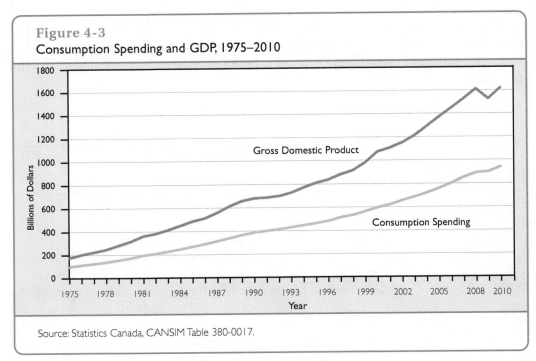

Figure 4-3
Consumption Spending and GDP, 1975–2010

Source: Statistics Canada, CANSIM Table 380-0017.

What Determines the Level of Consumption Spending?

The amount of consumption spending done by an *individual* household in any given year may be influenced by various factors peculiar to that household. However, when we consider the level of *total* consumption spending in the economy as a whole in a given year, a few key factors stand out.

The most important factor influencing total consumption spending in the economy is total **personal disposable income** (personal income less personal taxes), which is the amount of money households have available to spend. As Figure 4-4 shows, consumer spending increases as personal disposable income increases.

Another important factor influencing consumption spending is **consumer confidence**, or the degree to which consumers feel optimistic—or pessimistic—about their future economic prospects. If consumers feel confident about their job and income prospects, they will be inclined to spend more of their disposable income and save less. More importantly, they will be willing to *borrow more* to make larger purchases such as houses, cars, furniture, appliances, and vacations that are difficult or impossible to finance out of current disposable income. On the other hand, when their confidence is low, consumers will borrow and spend less, and they may reduce their consumption spending so as to pay off their debts. Figure 4-5 shows consumer confidence as measured by the Conference Board of Canada's Index of Consumer

personal disposable income
Personal income less personal taxes, or after-tax personal income; may be spent or saved.

consumer confidence
The degree to which consumers feel optimistic (or pessimistic) about their future economic prospects.

Figure 4-4
Consumer Income and Consumer Spending, 1975–2010

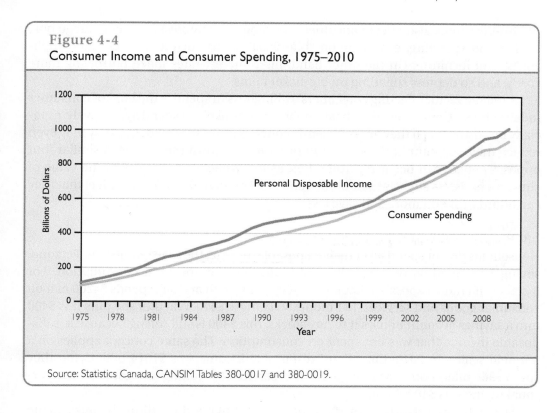

Source: Statistics Canada, CANSIM Tables 380-0017 and 380-0019.

Confidence. The graph illustrates how consumer confidence fluctuates considerably from year to year. During booms, when prospects for jobs and incomes are good, consumers' confidence is high. But during recessions, when unemployment is a concern, confidence falls, as can be seen in late 2008–09, and in the uncertainty in 2010–11.

Figure 4-5
Conference Board of Canada's Index of Consumer Attitudes

www.conferenceboard.ca

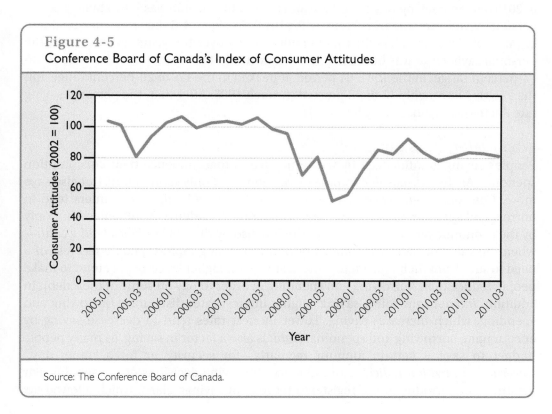

Source: The Conference Board of Canada.

interest rate
Percentage of borrowed money paid by a borrower (and received by a lender) annually.

consumer indebtedness
Consumer debt as a percentage of disposable income.

personal saving
Personal disposable income not spent on consumption.

personal saving rate
The percentage of personal disposable income that is saved.

Interest rates also affect consumer spending. Low interest rates encourage borrowing and spending, especially on "big-ticket" items such as houses, cars, appliances, and furniture. On the other hand, high interest rates make borrowing more costly, and so depress spending on big-ticket items.

A related factor affecting consumers' willingness to spend is the level of **consumer indebtedness**. Consumers with heavy debts are less likely to spend aggressively, especially by borrowing. If they are sufficiently concerned about their debts, they may even reduce their consumption spending in order to pay down their debts. A similar (but opposite) effect can occur regarding *households' assets*—an increase in the value of consumers' assets such as their homes and stocks can make consumers feel that they can afford to spend more and save less.

Saving by Households

Households do not spend all of their disposable income; they save some of it. **Personal saving** is defined as personal disposable income not spent on consumption. For instance, if Fran's disposable income is $4600 per month and she spends $4200 of it on consumer goods and services, her monthly *saving* is $400. Whether she puts this $400 into a savings account or uses it to buy stocks, this $400 is still *saving* because it is disposable income that was not spent on consumption. The same concept applies on a national scale—in 2010, Canadians' disposable income was $1014 billion and they spent $966 billion on consumer goods and services (including interest), so their personal saving was $48 billion.

Saving by households takes many forms. Much of it is done through banks, in the form of savings accounts and guaranteed investment certificates (GICs). Some people prefer bonds or mortgages because they pay higher interest, or corporate stocks or mutual funds because their value may increase.

How much do Canadians save? The best measure of saving is the **personal saving rate**, which is the percentage of personal disposable income that is saved. For example, in 2010 personal saving was $48 billion and disposable income was $1014 billion, so the personal saving rate was 4.8 percent ($48/$1014). As Figure 4-6 shows, the personal saving rate of Canadians has fluctuated considerably over the years. In the 1960s, the personal saving rate was between 5 and 8 percent. In the 1970s, it rose into the 10- to 14-percent range. In the 1981–84 period, it peaked in the 17- to 20-percent range and then settled at roughly 12 or 13 percent through 1993. After that, the personal saving rate decreased again, to very low levels.

What Determines the Level of Personal Saving?

People's saving is influenced by the same factors that influence their consumption spending. As their *disposable income* rises, people not only spend more, but also save more. *Consumer confidence* plays a role—if confidence is high, consumers tend to borrow and spend more, and save less. Consumer confidence is influenced not only by the economic outlook and job security but also by the level of *household wealth*—when the value of their investments or homes is rising rapidly, people feel less of a need to save from their current income. Conversely, higher levels of *debt* tend to make people reduce their borrowing and spending in order to pay off some of their debt. In addition, *interest rates* affect saving. Higher interest rates discourage borrowing and spending, which increases saving. Lower interest rates tend to decrease saving by encouraging borrowing and spending. *Habit* is also a factor in saving, as many people budget to save a certain amount regularly—for security or for a "rainy day." *Government taxation policies* can influence the saving decisions of households. For instance, the introduction of registered retirement savings plans, which allowed tax

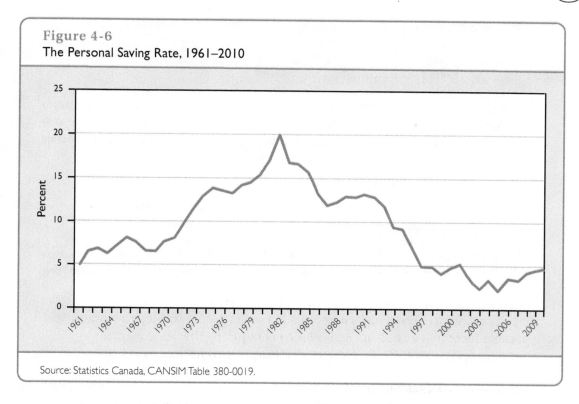

Figure 4-6
The Personal Saving Rate, 1961–2010

Source: Statistics Canada, CANSIM Table 380-0019.

deductions for saving for retirement, contributed to a large increase in the personal saving rate of Canadians in the 1970s. Finally, *demographic factors* can influence the personal saving rate—as the baby boomers approach retirement, their saving is expected to increase, pulling up the saving rate for the country as a whole.

How Do Canadians Invest Their Savings?

Many people think of savings in terms of bank deposits, guaranteed investment certificates, and Canada Savings Bonds (CSBs), or investments in stocks and bonds. However, people save in large amounts in two other ways that are less visible—*pension fund contributions* and *mortgage payments*. People who contribute to a pension fund save for their retirement by having part of each paycheque (often 6 percent) deducted and paid into a pension fund. These savings are invested (mostly in bonds and stocks) for the purpose of providing retirement incomes for members of the pension fund. Repayments of the *principal* [1] on mortgage loans are also counted as saving because they also represent income that is not spent on consumption, but rather is used to pay down the loan that was made to buy a house (i.e., a mortgage). For many people, the major assets later in life consist of their pension entitlements and house, which they obtained by saving in the ways described above.

When Canadians' savings are invested in stocks or bonds, they become available to businesses, which can then invest the funds in capital equipment—the *saving–investment process* that we saw in Chapter 3. This is one of the key economic roles of saving, and brings us to the next component of aggregate demand: investment spending by business.

---

[1] On the other hand, the interest component of mortgage payments is not considered to be saving. It accumulates no assets, and is more like a current consumption item—payment to the lender for the current use of the funds, similar to paying rent for the use of a car or an apartment.

IN THE NEWS

Trends in Saving

Figure 4-6 shows a significant change in the behaviour of Canadian households—the steady decrease in the personal saving rate from over 10 percent of disposable income in the early 1990s to 3 percent or lower from 2001 to 2007, when the U.S. personal saving rate became *negative* for a period. After 2007, the saving rate increased again.

QUESTIONS

1. What might explain the decrease in saving rates from 2001 to 2007?
2. How could the personal saving rate actually become *negative*?
3. Why do you think the saving rate increased again after 2007?
4. How has the personal saving rate changed since 2010, and what might explain these changes? For updates, visit www.statcan.gc.ca, click on *The Daily*, and search for "personal saving rate".

Investment Spending by Business

Investment is defined as spending by business firms on capital goods, which includes all types of capital goods—factories, machinery, equipment and tools, computers and office equipment, and so on. Investment spending includes both additions to society's stock of capital goods and replacements for capital goods that have become obsolete, or worn out or depreciated.

The term *investment* sometimes causes confusion because many people associate the word with purchases of stocks and bonds. The two meanings are obviously related, because companies often finance their purchases of capital goods (investment) by issuing stocks or bonds (in which the public *invests*). However, when the term *investment* is used in this text, it will refer to business spending on capital goods unless otherwise specified.

Business investment spending on plant and equipment amounts in most years to about 10 to 13 percent of GDP—much less than consumption spending. However, business investment spending is a particularly important economic process because capital goods increase output per person, or *productivity*, making possible a higher standard of living and improving the international competitiveness of Canadian producers.

> To forecast investment spending, the federal government twice yearly conducts a survey of business investment intentions. From this survey, the government estimates the future trend of business investment spending.

What Determines the Level of Business Investment Spending?

Two key factors that influence investment spending by business are (1) expectations regarding the profitability of investments, and (2) interest rates.

Expectations regarding the profitability of investment projects Business investment decisions are future-oriented. Since the plant and equipment involved are costly and will typically last for many years, they must be expected to earn a sufficient profit to justify the investment. So the *expectations* of businesses regarding the future financial performance of such investments are very important. If the outlook for the future of investment projects is favourable, investment spending will be high, but if it is uncertain or unfavourable, investment spending can be quite low.

Probably the most important considerations underlying business investment decisions in general are

- how high sales and production are relative to production capacity, and
- whether sales are expected to increase in the future.

If production is at or near capacity levels and sales are expected to rise further, there will be pressure on businesses to expand through capital investment spending projects. On the other hand, if sales are expected to be stagnant or to fall, capital investment spending is likely to be quite low. So *economic forecasts* play a significant role in business investment decisions—if good economic conditions are forecast and rising sales are expected, investment spending tends to increase, and vice versa.

Various other considerations can influence business expectations and investment decisions. Will competition increase or diminish? Will present production facilities have to be upgraded with new equipment in order to remain competitive? Will government trade policy change, bringing new competition from imports or new opportunities in export markets? Will taxes change? Will construction costs increase next year? (If so, maybe it's better to build now.) Will interest rates fall next year? (If so, maybe sit and wait, and borrow money then.) Do government programs provide tax reductions or other incentives that encourage investment?

Because they are specific to firms and industries, expectations are difficult to analyze in detail on a macroeconomic scale. Still, they are the most important factor influencing the level of investment spending. Figure 4-7 shows the Conference Board of Canada's Index of Business Confidence, which is based on surveys of Canadian business firms. The impact of the 2008–09 recession is clear.

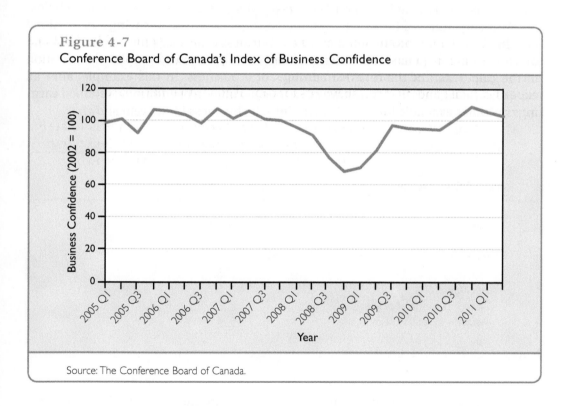

Figure 4-7
Conference Board of Canada's Index of Business Confidence

Source: The Conference Board of Canada.

Interest rates Frequently, capital investment projects are financed with borrowed money, which the company usually raises by selling bonds to the public. To be profitable, an investment project (say, a plant) must *earn* a higher rate of return on the money invested in it than the rate of interest that the business must *pay* on the borrowed funds. For instance, if a company must pay a 6-percent annual interest rate on money borrowed through a bond issue, it would be quite profitable to borrow money to build a plant that earned a 10-percent-per-year rate of return. However, if the company had to pay a 10-percent interest rate, the same investment project would not be profitable. So lower interest rates encourage investment spending by businesses, while higher interest rates discourage borrowing and capital investment.

Financing Capital Investment: The Saving–Investment Process Revisited

In Chapter 3, we used the illustration of fishing on a deserted island to show the saving–investment process that builds capital equipment. We saw that in order to invest in capital goods (spears) that would increase future prosperity, the islander had to "save" in the sense of doing without consumer goods (fish). Investment was the key to economic progress, but it was not possible without *saving*.

This basic economic principle also applies to a modern economy such as Canada's. In recent years, Canadian businesses have invested over $180 billion per year in plant and equipment, which means they must have access to about $180 billion of savings to finance these investment projects. These savings come mainly from three basic sources: *personal savings*, *business savings*, and *foreign savings*.

Personal savings are one source of funds for business investment. These savings can be made available for business investment when they are used to buy stocks and bonds issued by businesses. Some of these stocks and bonds are purchased directly by households, but for the most part this is done on their behalf by pension funds and financial institutions (such as banks and mutual funds), which invest the savings of households.

business savings
Profits retained in a business after taxes have been paid and dividends have been paid to shareholders. (Also known as retained earnings.)

Another source of funds for capital investment is **business savings**, or **retained earnings**. These are profits retained in the business after taxes have been paid and dividends have been paid to the shareholders. Table 4-1 shows a simplified illustration of the calculation of the retained earnings of a business. In this example, after all expenses, taxes, and dividends have been paid, $4 million of additional retained earnings becomes available for reinvestment into the business in the year shown.

Table 4-1
Retained Earnings: An Illustration

	Sales income	$100 million
	Expenses	92
=	Profits before tax	8
−	Taxes	3
=	After-tax profits	5
−	Dividends to shareholders	1
=	Addition to retained earnings	$ 4

As Figure 4-8 shows, profits and retained earnings are a *quite variable* source of savings, rising rapidly in some years but actually falling in others. The most important factor influencing the overall level of profits is the state of the economy itself—in periods of rapid economic growth, profits rise rapidly, while economic slowdowns usually bring declines in profits, such as the recession in 2009.

Canada has traditionally financed considerable amounts of capital investment by "importing" *foreign savings*, mainly from the United States. Foreign investors and firms have historically provided nearly 20 percent of the savings used for capital formation in Canada, if the profits of foreign-owned companies that are reinvested in Canada are included.

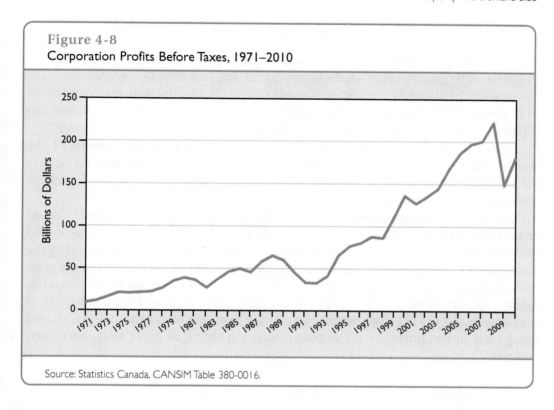

Figure 4-8
Corporation Profits Before Taxes, 1971–2010

Source: Statistics Canada, CANSIM Table 380-0016.

Business Investment in Canada in Recent Years

Figure 4-9 shows business investment spending in Canada in recent years. The graph illustrates that capital investment tends to *fluctuate* considerably more than consumer spending (compare Figure 4-9 with Figure 4-4) as business expectations and interest rates change. The impact of the recession in 2009 is particularly clear.

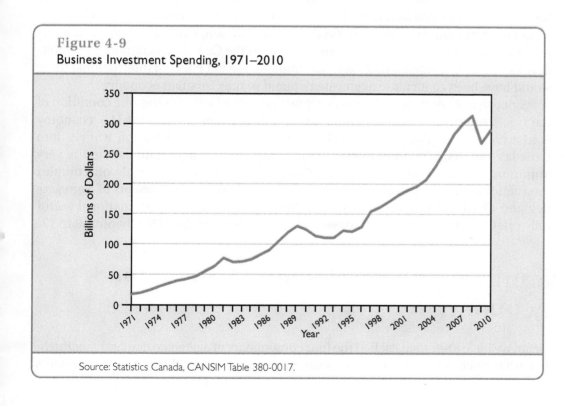

Figure 4-9
Business Investment Spending, 1971–2010

Source: Statistics Canada, CANSIM Table 380-0017.

Government Spending on Goods and Services

Another major purchaser of the economy's output is government. Purchases of goods and services by governments—federal, provincial, and municipal—have amounted in recent years to about 21 percent of Canada's GDP. Of this, the vast majority (about 19 percent of GDP) has consisted of current expenditures, with only a small amount (2 percent of GDP) going to capital expenditures.

Most current government expenditures on goods and services consist of the wages and salaries of government employees, who provide a wide range of services to the public (such as health-care workers, teachers, social workers, law-enforcement workers, civil servants, and the military).

Government spending decisions are made by elected leaders, and therefore could be said to be determined by political factors. However, government spending is limited by the government's tax revenues (and the public's willingness to pay taxes) and by the government's ability and willingness to borrow. Generally, government spending on basic public services such as health care and education tends to be relatively stable, rising gradually as the population grows. An exception was from 1993 to 1998, when very large budget deficits (government spending in excess of revenues) and high and rising debt forced governments to reduce their spending in order to balance their budgets.

Net Exports (Exports Minus Imports)

As we have seen, purchases of Canadian exports by foreign buyers constitute an important component of aggregate demand in the Canadian economy, amounting to about 30 percent of Canada's GDP in recent years. While export spending *adds* strongly to aggregate demand in Canada, Canadian purchases of imported goods and services have the opposite effect—they *reduce* the level of spending within Canada. So, to obtain the net effect of international trade, we must *add* to aggregate demand foreign purchases of Canadian exports and *subtract* Canadian purchases of imports. For instance, in 2010 Canadian exports were $478 billion and imports were $508 billion. So net exports (exports minus imports) were –$30 billion, and the net effect of international trade was to reduce aggregate demand in the Canadian economy by $30 billion. Conversely, if exports had exceeded imports, the net effect of international trade would have been to increase aggregate demand in the Canadian economy.

Since over 70 percent of Canada's exports go to the United States, the condition of the U.S. economy is a key factor affecting Canadian exports. When the U.S. economy is in a boom, Canadian exports will be strong, while a U.S. recession will cut into Canada's exports. While the foreign trade component of aggregate demand is very important to the performance of the Canadian economy, it depends on complex international factors that are quite different from the other components of aggregate demand discussed in this chapter. Therefore, we will cover the international sector only briefly in this chapter, and we will return to it in more detail in Chapters 9 to 12.

Summary of the Demand Side of the Economy

So far, we have examined each of the four components of aggregate demand *separately*. But what really matters on a macroeconomic scale is how these four components

IN THE NEWS

Demand in the Recession

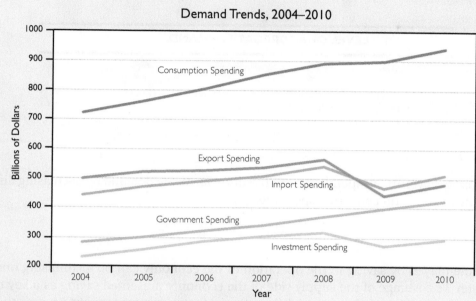

Demand Trends, 2004–2010

Source: *Statistics Canada*, CANSIM Table 380-0017.

The graph shows the trends in the major categories of aggregate demand during the period leading up to and following the recession of 2008–09.

QUESTIONS

1. Which type of spending decreased the most during the recession? Why do you think this happened?
2. How did the behaviour of consumption spending during the recession differ from the behaviour of business investment spending, and what could explain this difference?
3. Which type of spending was least affected by the recession? What might explain why this type of spending continued to increase?

combine to determine the grand total level of spending on goods and services (aggregate demand) in the economy.

Figure 4-10 on page 88 portrays the combined effect of the factors discussed in this chapter on the level of aggregate demand, which is represented by the thick line. The upward-pointing arrows represent factors that *increase* aggregate demand— these are simply the four types of spending discussed earlier in this chapter. The downward-pointing arrows reflect factors that *reduce* demand in the economy. Saving is income that is *not* spent (including profits retained by business), taxes reduce the ability of buyers to spend, and spending on imports removes demand from the Canadian economy.

Anything that changes any of the factors in Figure 4-10 will affect the level of demand in the economy. For instance, if interest rates were to fall, consumer and investment spending would increase, saving would decrease, and aggregate demand would increase. An increase in personal income taxes (assuming no corresponding

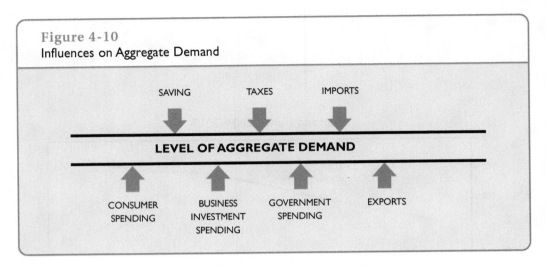

Figure 4-10
Influences on Aggregate Demand

SAVING   TAXES   IMPORTS

LEVEL OF AGGREGATE DEMAND

CONSUMER SPENDING   BUSINESS INVESTMENT SPENDING   GOVERNMENT SPENDING   EXPORTS

increase in government spending) would reduce aggregate demand by decreasing disposable income and consumer spending.

Digression: The Role of Saving in the Economy

The role played by saving in the operation of the economy can be a confusing one. Chapter 3's coverage of the supply side of the economy presented saving as a key to economic progress, as the essential first step in the saving–investment process that generates higher productivity and economic prosperity. On the other hand, Figure 4-10 suggests that saving could lead to problems on the demand side of the economy. Too much saving could mean too little demand in the economy, which could lead to a recession. So does saving represent an opportunity for the economy and living standards to grow, or a threat of reduced aggregate demand that could bring a recession?

Suppose that Canadians increased their saving by $10 billion per year. Would this be beneficial or damaging to their economy? There is no simple answer to this question; the outcome would depend on whether or not the additional savings found their way into investment spending. If they did not, aggregate demand would fall, and the economy would slow down. On the other hand, if these savings did get invested into capital goods, there would be two positive results. First, demand would not fall, and second, with more capital goods, the economy would become more productive, and living standards could rise.

To illustrate the role of saving in the economy, imagine two very different economies—one in which households and businesses saved a very large proportion of their income and another in which they saved none of it. The economy in which saving was very high would suffer from a serious shortage of spending. Without this demand to support current production, producers would have to reduce output and lay off workers. Such a high-saving economy would experience severe *demand-side* problems *in the present.*

The second economy, with no saving, would not have that problem—there would be no shortage of spending with a saving rate of zero! However, without saving, this economy could not invest in capital goods. It would not be able to increase its productive efficiency and total output—in short, it would experience *supply-side* problems that would severely limit its *future* prosperity.

Neither of the two scenarios above will result in good economic performance. What is required for good economic performance is an appropriate *balance* of consumer spending, saving, and investment. Consumer spending should be high enough (and saving low enough) to support output, employment, and prosperity *in the present*, while saving should be high enough to support sufficient capital investment to generate higher productivity and economic prosperity *for the future*.

The Demand Side and the Supply Side

Aggregate demand is the total of spending by the four sectors of the economy: the consumer sector, the business sector, the government sector, and the international (trade) sector. For example, if spending by each of these sectors were as shown in the illustration below, aggregate demand for that year would be $680 billion.

Consumption spending		$400 billion
Business investment spending	80	
Residential construction	40	120
Government spending on goods and services		150
Exports of goods and services	170	
– Imports of goods and services	–160	
= Net exports		10
Aggregate demand		$680

In the illustration above, is $680 billion the "right" level of aggregate demand for the economy in this year? This depends on how much the supply side of the economy is capable of producing—its *capacity output*.

If the economy's capacity output were $850 billion and aggregate demand were only $680 billion, then production would be 20 percent below its potential level—the economy would be in a *recession*, and unemployment would be high.

On the other hand, if the supply side were only capable of producing $600 billion of goods and services, aggregate demand of $680 billion would be *too high*. Supply could not keep up with demand. As a result, prices in general would rise rapidly, generating rapid *inflation*.

From these illustrations, we can see that, ideally, there would be a *rough balance* between the supply side and the demand side of the economy. That is, the level of aggregate demand would be close to the capacity of the supply side to produce goods and services, and not so low as to cause a recession nor so high as to generate serious inflation.

A Supply-Side/Demand-Side Model of the Economy

To understand the economy on a macroeconomic scale, we need to consider both the demand side and the supply side *together*. Figure 4-11 on page 90 shows the two sides of the economy and the key factors that influence each side. But Figure 4-11 is only a *static representation* of the economy. It is the *dynamic interaction* between the supply side and the demand side of the economy that determines the performance of the economy regarding output, real GDP, employment, and prices. This interaction is shown in Figure 4-12 on page 90.

The dotted line in Figure 4-12 represents the economy's *capacity output*—the maximum potential output of the supply side of the economy. As we saw in Chapter 3, the economy's capacity output increases only gradually from year to year as the number of workers in the labour force and output per worker (productivity) both gradually increase. In recent years, capacity output has increased by about 3 percent per year, as reflected by the gradual rising trend of the dotted line.

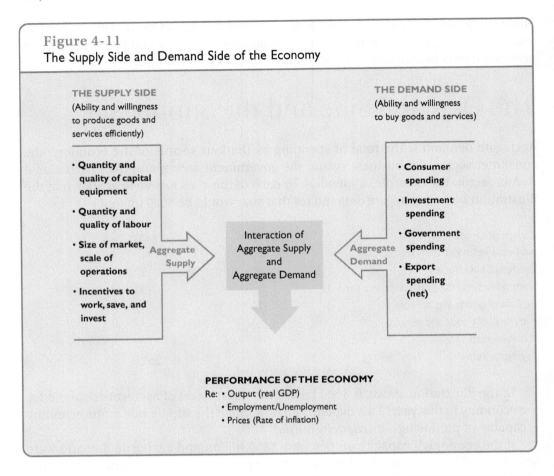

Figure 4-11
The Supply Side and Demand Side of the Economy

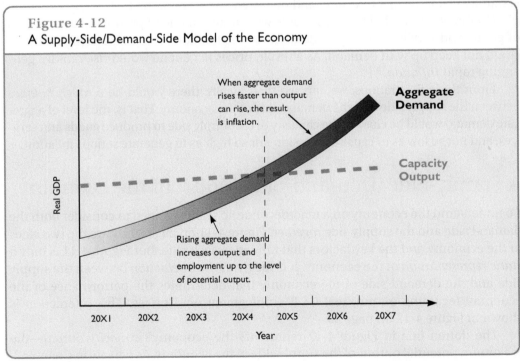

Figure 4-12
A Supply-Side/Demand-Side Model of the Economy

This type of model is useful for illustrating the interaction between the demand side and the supply side of the economy as both sides change over a period of time. The wide solid line shows changes in aggregate demand, from year 20X1 to 20X7.

In 20X1, the economy is in a recession. Aggregate demand for goods and services is well below the economy's capacity production level, leaving production and employment well below their potential levels.

As aggregate demand rises in years 20X1 through 20X4, output increases quite rapidly. Because production has been below capacity levels, it can temporarily rise by more than 3 percent per year, as previously unemployed labour and unused plant capacity are brought into production. In fact, when the economy is recovering from a recession, it is possible for output to rise by as much as 5 or even 6 percent per year.

Such rapid increases in output cannot continue indefinitely, however, because before long the economy's output will reach its capacity level, as shown by the dotted line. From this point forward, output can only increase as rapidly as the productive capacity of the economy increases, which we have seen to be about 3 percent per year. By the end of year 20X4, the economy has reached its potential output, and output cannot increase as rapidly as before. If aggregate demand continues to rise after year 20X4 as it has in the previous three years, output will be physically unable to keep up with demand—and demand will *outrun* supply.

In Figure 4-12, after year 20X4, the output of goods and services (which is limited to the amount shown by the dotted line) is unable to keep up with the rapidly rising demand (as shown by the solid line). As a result, the prices of goods and services in general will rise quite rapidly as they are bid up by the excess of demand over available supply—there will be a growing problem of *inflation* in the economy.

In the real world, the effects of rising aggregate demand on output and prices are not as separate and distinct as this portrayal may suggest. Rising aggregate demand tends to cause *both* output *and* prices to rise, with the effect on prices being stronger the closer the economy gets to its potential output. This relationship is shown by the grey area in year 20X4 in Figure 4-12: the darker the line, the more rapidly prices are rising as higher demand pushes the economy closer to its limits. So a period of economic expansion tends to be characterized not only by rising output and employment but also by inflation, and the closer output gets to capacity, the more rapid inflation is likely to become.

An Aggregate Demand/Aggregate Supply Model of the Economy

Another type of model of the economy uses aggregate demand and aggregate supply curves to illustrate the performance of the economy under different conditions, ranging from severe recession to rapid inflation. In doing so, it illustrates how and why inflation becomes more rapid, the closer the economy moves to its capacity level of output.

Aggregate Demand Graphed

Figure 4-13 shows the relationship between aggregate demand (AD) and the *level of prices* in the economy. At high price levels (in the upper range of the AD curve), the quantity demanded is relatively low, while at low price levels (in the lower range of the AD curve), the quantity demanded is higher. These "opposite" relationships are mainly due to the fact that if the prices of Canadian products are higher, foreigners buy fewer Canadian products and Canadians buy more imports, with the combined effect of depressing the demand for Canadian products. On the other hand, if Canadian prices are lower, both Canadian and foreign buyers will purchase more Canadian goods and services. The level of prices could affect the purchasing behaviour of Canadians in another way: higher prices of goods and services may cause Canadians to postpone their purchases, holding aggregate demand down, while lower prices could have the opposite effect, increasing aggregate demand. The result of these factors is

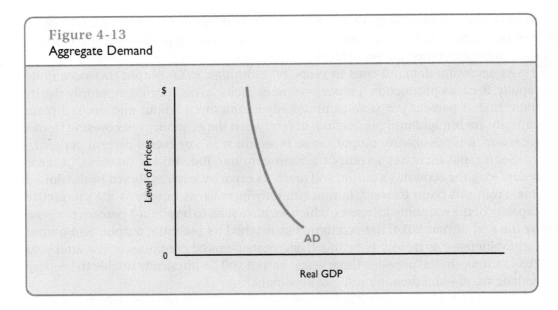

Figure 4-13
Aggregate Demand

that the aggregate demand curve is shaped as it is in Figure 4-13, with the quantity demanded higher at lower levels of prices and lower at higher levels of prices.

We have seen that aggregate demand fluctuates, being low in periods of recession and high during periods of boom and inflation. These fluctuations are shown in Figure 4-14. AD is the same curve as in Figure 4-13, while AD_1 represents the low levels of aggregate demand typical of a recession. Note that, at any given price level, AD_1 indicates a lower quantity demanded than does AD. On the other hand, AD_2 represents a higher level of aggregate demand, with more output being demanded at any given price level.

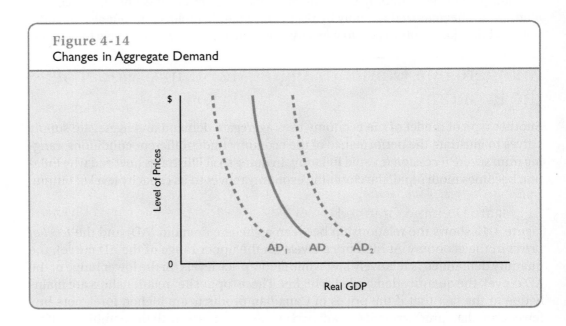

Figure 4-14
Changes in Aggregate Demand

Aggregate Demand and Aggregate Supply Combined

Figure 4-15 adds the aggregate supply curve (AS) from Chapter 3. As we saw in Chapter 3, the AS curve shows that, up to an output of 80 units, output can be increased without significant increases in production costs and prices, because with output so far below the economy's capacity, the plant capacity, labour, and materials needed to increase output are readily available. Businesses wanting to increase production will be able to obtain the labour and materials they need without having to pay higher wages and prices that would increase their production costs per unit and force prices upward.

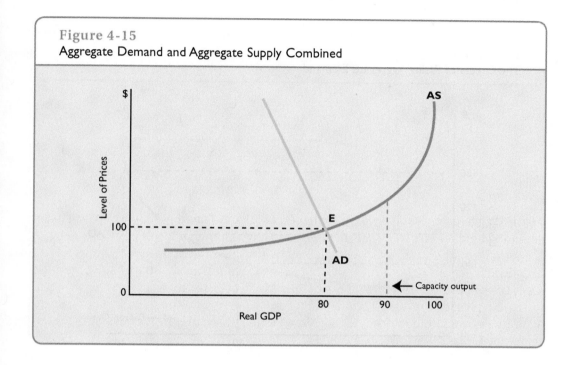

Figure 4-15
Aggregate Demand and Aggregate Supply Combined

However, as output is increased beyond 80 units, *production bottlenecks* begin to appear in the form of shortages of labour, plant capacity, or materials that make it more difficult and costly to increase output. And the closer the economy gets to capacity production, the more severe and costlier these bottlenecks will become. As a result, increases in output beyond 80 units will come at a higher production cost—and price—per unit, and these increases in costs and prices will become greater as capacity output is approached. This relationship is shown by the upward swing in the AS curve beyond 80 units per week. At an output of 90 units per week, production costs and prices are rising so fast that the economy has reached its *capacity output*, and is in danger of *overheating*.

Figure 4-15 shows the interaction of the aggregate supply curve from Chapter 3 and the aggregate demand curve from this chapter. With the AD and AS curves intersecting at E as shown, the level of output will be 80 and the level of prices will be 100: the economy is in a recession, with output well below its capacity level of 90 and unemployment quite high due to inadequate aggregate demand. With aggregate demand so weak, the level of prices is rising very slowly.

If aggregate demand were to increase to the level shown by AD_1 in Figure 4-16, output would rise to its capacity level of 90 units per week, and unemployment would be lower. However, this higher level of demand would also bring *more inflation*, as the price level rises to 110. If aggregate demand were to move still higher, to the level shown by AD_2, demand would have exceeded capacity output. Inflation would become very rapid, as shown by the movement to a price level of 130.

So, increases in aggregate demand can have quite different effects upon the performance of the economy (output, employment, and prices), depending on the circumstances. If the economy is operating well below capacity and unemployment is high, increased aggregate demand (up to the level shown by AD in Figure 4-16) will have mainly *beneficial* effects. Output and employment will increase considerably and prices will increase only slightly, as the summary in Table 4-2 shows.

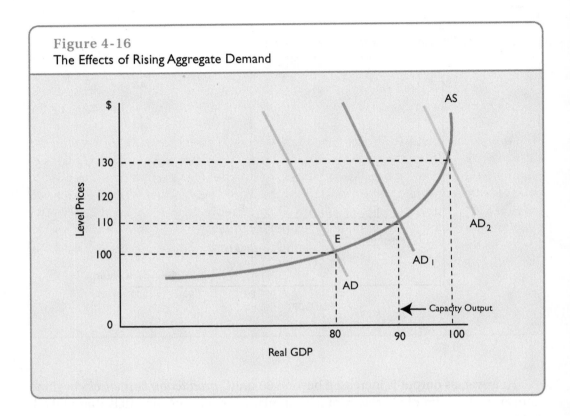

Figure 4-16
The Effects of Rising Aggregate Demand

Table 4-2
The Effect of Increases in Aggregate Demand on the Economy Under Different Conditions

(See Figure 4-16 for graph)		
	Effect upon	
Increase in Aggregate Demand	**Output and Employment**	**Prices**
Up to AD	Major gains	Very small increases
AD to AD$_1$	Lesser gains	More rapid increases
AD$_1$ to AD$_2$	Quite small gains	Quite rapid increases
Beyond AD$_2$	No gains	Very rapid increases

If the economy is closer to its capacity level of output, a similar increase in aggregate demand (from AD to AD$_1$ in Figure 4-16) will have *mixed effects* on the economy. Output and employment will increase, but not as rapidly as before, while prices will rise more rapidly. If aggregate demand were to increase further (from AD$_1$ to AD$_2$ in Figure 4-16), there would be only small gains in output and employment at the cost of rapid increases in prices, as the economy is overheated by aggregate demand that is so high that aggregate supply has difficulty keeping up with it. Beyond AD_2, further increases in aggregate demand cannot boost output and employment any higher and will result only in more severe inflation.

In summary, it is the interaction between aggregate demand and aggregate supply that determines how well the economy functions regarding output, employment, and inflation. Aggregate demand can be too low relative to the economy's productive capacity, causing a recession and high unemployment. Rising levels of aggregate demand can bring worthwhile gains in output and employment, although they will also increase the rate of inflation. But excessively high levels of aggregate demand will generate much more severe inflation and only small gains in output and employment, which makes it desirable to have a balance between aggregate demand and the economy's capacity to produce, or between the demand side and the supply side of the economy.

However, it is not always possible to maintain such a balance between the demand side and the supply side of the economy. In Chapter 6, "Booms, Recessions, and Inflation," we will examine how and why these two sides of the economy can get out of balance with each other, and we will look at the consequences that this imbalance can have on the performance of the economy. But before we do that, we need to consider one more key aspect of the demand side of the economy—the banking system and its effect on the economy, which will be the subject of Chapter 5, "Money and the Economic System."

Chapter Summary

1. Aggregate demand consists of consumption spending, investment spending, government spending on goods and services, and net export spending (exports minus imports). (L.O. 1)
2. Consumption spending, which purchases nearly three-fifths of GDP, depends mainly on the level of personal disposable income. It is also influenced by consumer confidence, household wealth or indebtedness, and interest rates. (L.O. 2)
3. Personal saving increases as disposable income rises. It is also influenced by the same factors as in point 2 above. (L.O. 2)
4. Business investment spending on capital goods is usually 10 to 12 percent of GDP. Business investment, which is vital to prosperity, depends mainly on expectations concerning the future profitability of investment projects and on interest rates. (L.O. 3)
5. Government purchases of goods and services, which consist mainly of the wages and salaries of government employees who provide public services, amount to about 21 percent of Canada's GDP. (L.O. 1)
6. Exports have in recent years accounted for about 30 percent of the GDP; however, when Canadians' purchases of imports are deducted from exports, the net effect of international trade on aggregate demand in Canada is much smaller. (L.O. 1)
7. Saving can pose a threat to the economy because money that is saved by households and businesses does not buy goods and services; however, if savings are used by business for investment spending on capital goods, the economy can grow. (L.O. 4)

8. If aggregate demand is well below capacity output, increases in aggregate demand will cause output and employment to rise quite rapidly, but they will not generate much additional inflation. (L.O. 5)

9. As output approaches its capacity level, higher aggregate demand will still increase output and employment, although less rapidly than before, and will tend to generate more inflation than before. (L.O. 5)

10. If aggregate demand rises above the economy's capacity output, the result will be severe inflation. (L.O. 5)

11. Ideally, there would be a rough balance between the demand side and the supply side of the economy, with aggregate demand close to the economy's capacity to produce goods and services, and neither so low as to cause a recession nor so high as to generate too much inflation. (L.O. 5)

Questions

1. How would each of the following affect total consumption spending in the economy?
   (a) a reduction in personal income taxes
   (b) an increase in the unemployment rate
   (c) forecasts that the economy was heading into a recession
   (d) reductions in interest rates
   (e) very high and rising levels of consumer debt

2. How would each of the following affect total business investment spending in the economy?
   (a) forecasts that the economy was heading into an economic boom
   (b) increases in interest rates
   (c) an election victory by a political party that had campaigned on a promise to increase taxes on business
   (d) reports that consumer confidence was increasing rapidly
   (e) the development of new equipment that significantly reduced labour costs

3. Explain to someone who has never taken an economics course what *aggregate demand* means, and why it is very important.

4. During an economic boom
   (a) prices rise, which causes aggregate demand, output, and employment to fall.
   (b) aggregate demand rises, which causes output and employment to rise, and probably also prices to rise.
   (c) aggregate demand rises, which causes output to rise, which in turn causes prices in general to fall.
   (d) aggregate demand rises, but output falls, with the result that prices rise.
   (e) prices fall, which causes higher aggregate demand, higher output, and higher employment.

5. During a recession
   (a) aggregate demand is depressed, causing output to be depressed, which in turn causes prices to rise more rapidly.
   (b) aggregate demand is depressed and output rises, which in turn causes prices to fall.
   (c) because aggregate demand is depressed, both output and employment are depressed, and there is less inflation.
   (d) output falls, which causes higher unemployment and more inflation.
   (e) interest rates decrease, causing business investment to fall.

6. Suppose there were a significant increase in the personal saving rate of Canadians. Explain how such a development could be viewed as both
   (a) an opportunity for stronger economic growth and high living standards, and
   (b) a threat of slower economic growth and perhaps even a recession.

7. During an economic recession, when output is depressed, why does the depressed supply of goods and services not cause prices to *rise*?

8. Suppose that the economy were operating well below its potential (capacity) output. Suppose also that interest rates fell and there was a general expectation that economic conditions were going to improve.
   (a) Explain how these developments would likely affect aggregate demand in the economy.
   (b) Explain how each of the following would be affected:

   (i) output (real GDP)
   (ii) employment and unemployment
   (iii) the rate of inflation

9. Visit the Statistics Canada website (**www.statcan.gc.ca**) and find the real GDP statistics for the past few years. Search for *Gross domestic product*. Click on *Gross domestic product, expenditure-based*. Calculate the percentage increases over the past year or two for each major demand component of GDP (consumption, investment, government, exports and imports).
   (a) Which components of aggregate demand have been increasing most rapidly?
   (b) Which components of aggregate demand have been increasing most slowly?
   (c) What might explain any trends in (a) and (b)?

Study Guide

Review Questions (The answers to these Review Questions appear in Appendix B.)

1. The four major groups of buyers of the output of the economy are
   (a) consumers, business firms, farmers, and speculators.
   (b) consumers, investors, governments, and business firms.
   (c) consumers, foreign buyers, investment dealers, and business firms.
   (d) consumers, business firms, governments, and foreign buyers.
   (e) None of the above.

2. *Aggregate demand* is a term that means _____.

3. (a) *Consumption spending* by households buys nearly _____ percent of Canada's GDP.

   (b) The main factor that determines the amount of consumption spending is _____.

   (c) Other factors that affect the amount of consumption spending include _____ and _____.

4. If personal disposable income is $500 billion and consumption spending is $480 billion, then *saving* is $_____ billion and the *personal saving rate* is _____ percent.

5. How would each of the following affect the *personal saving rate*?
    (a) a decrease in interest rates: _____
    (b) a decrease in consumer confidence: _____

6. Saving is a possible threat to the stability of the economy because
    (a) too much saving causes inflation.
    (b) it can cause an economic slowdown due to inadequate demand for goods and services.
    (c) the rich people who save a great deal get richer due to their investment income.
    (d) saving leads to speculation in the stock market.
    (e) None of the above.

7. The problem referred to in the previous question will not occur if
    (a) money that is saved is invested in the stock market.
    (b) money that is saved is deposited in banks.
    (c) the government places a tax on savings.
    (d) money that is saved is transferred to businesses and used to purchase capital goods.
    (e) None of the above.

8. (a) *Investment* refers to _____.
    (b) Investment spending by business amounts to roughly _____ percent of GDP.

9. Of the five factors listed below, which is the *most important* factor in deciding the level of investment spending by businesses?
    (a) development of improved technology
    (b) business expectations regarding future profits from investment projects
    (c) trends in consumer spending
    (d) the current level of business profits
    (e) the level of accumulated profits from past years

10. State whether each of the following would cause business investment spending to *increase* or *decrease*.
    (a) an increase in interest rates: _____
    (b) forecasts that the economy will grow rapidly over the next 2–3 years: _____
    (c) an increase in taxes on business profits: _____

11. Investment is a relatively small component of aggregate demand, but it is important to the economy because _____.

12. Classify each of the following as *consumption, saving,* or *investment.*
    (a) Pat buys gasoline for his car. _____
    (b) Pat buys a Government of Canada bond. _____
    (c) Pat buys a stove for his home. _____
    (d) Pat buys a stove for his restaurant. _____
    (e) Pat buys tickets to a Vancouver Canucks hockey game. _____
    (f) Pat buys some shares of Air Canada. _____
    (g) Pat pays his stockbroker $200 in commissions. _____

13. Government spending on goods and services
    (a) amounts to about _____ percent of GDP, and
    (b) consists mostly of _____.

14. The most basic *cause* of economic booms is
    (a) widespread hiring by employers.
    (b) a high and rising level of aggregate demand.
    (c) high interest rates.

  (d) rapid increases in the size of the labour force.

  (e) rapid increases in productivity.

15. The most basic *cause* of economic recessions is

  (a) low interest rates.

  (b) layoffs by employers that cause a rising level of unemployment.

  (c) decreases in the consumer price index (CPI).

  (d) a decrease in the size of the labour force.

  (e) a falling level of aggregate demand.

Critical Thinking Questions

(Asterisked questions 1 to 5 are answered in Appendix B; the answers to questions 6 to 10 are in the Instructor's Manual that accompanies this text.)

*1. State how each of the following would affect aggregate demand in the Canadian economy, and *explain why* this effect would occur.

  (a) consumer confidence improves

  (b) taxes on business profits are reduced

  (c) consumer debt increases to record-high levels

  (d) imports of Chinese goods increase sharply

  (e) interest rates increase

  (f) it is forecast that a recession is likely in a few months

  (g) personal income taxes are reduced

  (h) the U.S. economy enjoys a major economic boom

*2. Suppose that the economy were in a boom and output was very near its potential (capacity) level. Suppose also that interest rates were low and confidence among both consumers and business people was unusually strong.

  (a) What would probably happen to aggregate demand in the economy?

  (b) Explain how each of the following would be affected:

    (i) output (real GDP)

    (ii) employment and unemployment

    (iii) the rate of inflation

*3. Suppose that the economy were in the very early stages of a recession, and consumer and business confidence was reduced by bad economic news and pessimistic economic forecasts.

  (a) Explain what would probably happen to aggregate demand in the economy.

  (b) Explain how each of the following would be affected:

    (i) output (real GDP)

    (ii) employment and unemployment

    (iii) the rate of inflation

*4. One of the most variable components of consumer spending from year to year is spending on durable goods, especially new automobiles. Why do you think this is so?

*5. During an economic boom, when output is rising, why does the rising supply of goods and services not cause the prices of them to *fall*?

6. During the Great Depression of the 1930s, the personal saving rate actually became *negative*—that is, there was *dissaving* by households.

  (a) What would a negative saving rate mean about the behaviour of households?

  (b) Why might dissaving occur during such severe economic conditions?

  (c) What did households probably have to do in order to dissave?

7. During the economic boom and stock market boom around 2000, there was also dissaving in the United States, as the personal saving rate became negative.
   (a) Why might dissaving occur under such favourable economic conditions?
   (b) How were households probably financing their dissaving in 2000?

8. Figure 4-5 on page 79 shows that consumer confidence decreased in the second half of 2008.
   (a) Make an argument that this low confidence was a *cause* of the recession of 2008–09.
   (b) Make an argument that this low confidence was a *result* of the recession.
   (c) How might you be able to tell if the low confidence was a possible cause of the recession, or just a result of the recession?

9. Suppose the economy were slowing down, and was nearly into a recession.
   (a) How would widespread *fear that a severe economic downturn was coming* probably affect the behaviour of consumers?
   (b) How would this change in the behaviour of consumers affect the performance of the economy in terms of output (real GDP), employment, and the rate of inflation?

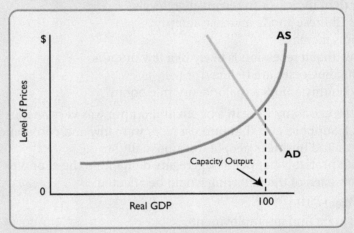

10. Suppose the economy is in the situation shown in the graph above, near its capacity level of output of $100 billion per year.
    Assume that there is a large increase in the price of imported oil that
    (a) reduces the level of aggregate demand by withdrawing large volumes of funds from the economy to pay for the oil, pushing the AD curve to the left, and
    (b) raises production costs throughout the economy by making energy much more expensive, making it costlier to produce any given level of output, thus pushing the AS curve upward to higher levels of cost per unit.

    Draw the new AD and AS curves, and explain the effects of the new situation on the levels of output, employment, and prices in the economy.

Use the Web (Hints for these Use the Web exercises appear in Appendix B.)

1. Visit the Industry Canada website (**www.ic.gc.ca**) and search for the most recent *Consumer Trends Report*. What are the significant recent trends in consumer spending, and what are the reasons for them?

2. Do a Google search for *consumer confidence + Canada* and *business confidence + Canada*. What are the most recent trends in consumer confidence and business confidence, and what are the reasons for these trends?

Money and the Economic System

LEARNING OBJECTIVES

After studying this chapter, you should be able to

1. State the one characteristic that money must have, and four qualities that help to make something acceptable as money.

2. State the three basic functions of money.

3. State the meaning of *money supply*, and explain why the size of the money supply is very important to the performance of the economy.

4. Summarize the historical evolution of the forms that money has taken, and state the three basic types of money in use in Canada today.

5. Write a brief summary of the different definitions of the money supply, and from given data, calculate M1 and M2.

6. Explain how most money is created, and why this process can create money to the extent that it does.

7. Given the cash reserves of a bank and its cash reserve ratio, calculate the potential amount of deposits the bank could support.

8. Explain why the banking industry is subject to a considerable degree of government regulation and influence.

9. Apply the facts and concepts of this chapter to various situations.

In Chapter 4, we emphasized the importance of the level of *aggregate demand*, or total spending in the economy. If aggregate demand is too low, the economy will fall into a recession, while if aggregate demand outruns the economy's capacity to produce goods and services, inflation will result.

money supply

The total volume of money in circulation.

In this chapter, we examine *money* and the **money supply**, which is *the total volume of money in circulation*. The money supply is a very important factor in the performance of the economy. If there were too little money in circulation, the result would be low aggregate demand and a recession. On the other hand, an excessively large money supply would generate excess demand and inflation.

Here, we will deal with two basic questions. First, what *is* money? And second, how is money *created*, or where does money come from? Chapter 6, "Booms, Recessions, and Inflation," will explain why the economy fluctuates from recession to boom to inflation and back to recession again, and the role played by money and the money supply in this process.

In Chapter 7, "Stabilizing the Economy: Government Monetary and Fiscal Policies," we will examine how the government tries to keep the money supply at an appropriate size—neither too high nor too low—in order to avoid the extremes of recession and inflation.

Part A: What Is Money?

Most basically, money is a *medium of exchange*—something that people use to *buy things*. That is, money functions as something that is generally accepted by people in exchange for (as payment for) goods and services.

Without money, transactions would have to be conducted by barter, which is the direct exchange of one product for another. In a barter system, a person who had an extra horse and wanted a cow would have to find another person who had a surplus cow and wanted a horse, making a direct exchange possible. Such a system is so awkward as to be unworkable, except in the most primitive economies where there are few goods for exchange, and few transactions are made. A barter system would be utterly incapable of handling the billions of daily transactions that occur in a modern economy.

Money also serves as a *standard of value*, or the yardstick by which we measure the value of a great number of diverse goods and services. If people were using a barter system instead of money, the value of each product would have to be expressed in terms of every other product for which it might be exchanged: a horse might be worth one cow, or four sheepdogs, or fifty bushels of apples, and so on. With money, the values of all items can be expressed in terms of one simple standard—the unit of currency, or the dollar. So a horse and a cow may each be worth $100, a sheepdog $25, a bushel of apples $2, and so on. Using money makes comparing the values of different goods and services easier.

A third function of money is that it provides us with a *store of value*—a way to save, or store, purchasing power. Under a barter system, you must accept another good at the time you sell something; however, if you receive money, you can save it until some time in the future when you choose to spend it. Sometimes, purchasing power is stored for a very short period of time. For example, you might store enough money in a chequing account for only a few days to cover expenses until next payday. For some reasons, such as a vacation, it may be stored for longer periods of time, perhaps by making regular deposits into a savings account. And for other reasons, such as retirement, purchasing power is stored for very long periods of time, in the form of various longer-term investments.

What Are the Advantages of Money?

We have seen that a barter system is an extremely awkward way of conducting transactions, whereas money is much more convenient. The person with the extra horse can sell one of them, say, for $100, then use the money to buy a cow from someone else. There is no need to find another person who has a cow and wants a horse. Clearly, then, money is a *great convenience* for people who engage in economic transactions.

However, the importance of money goes well beyond being a convenience. As we have seen, the key to a society's economic prosperity is its *productivity*, or output per worker. Generally, people will be more productive if they are *specialized* in a particular kind of work. And when people are specialized in this manner, the number of exchanges of goods and services that take place among them is tremendous, as each person produces only one product or service (or only one part of it) and buys everything else from others. By making it easy for people to exchange (buy and sell) goods and services, money makes such specialization feasible, which in turn makes possible higher levels of productivity and thus economic prosperity. So by serving as a medium of exchange, money actually contributes to our prosperity.

What Can Be Used as Money?

We have seen that the introduction of money into an economy can greatly benefit its people. Now we need to address the question of what people might actually *use* as money.

The short answer to this question is that people can use *anything* as money, provided that other people are prepared to *accept* it as payment for goods and services. Different peoples, in different societies and at different times, have used as money things that seem quite strange to us, including shells, cattle, and heavy stone wheels. In prisoner of war camps in the Second World War, prisoners used cigarettes as money. These examples show that money can be *anything that people agree to use* and accept as a medium of exchange.

The one essential quality that something must have in order to function as money is *acceptability*: people must be prepared to accept it in exchange for goods and services. Four characteristics help to make an item acceptable as money, including *scarcity* (which ensures value), *durability* (money that rots in your pocket is less than ideal), *portability* (so that you can carry it around with you), and *divisibility* (for making change when necessary). However, as some of the above examples show, not all of these characteristics are essential as long as people will accept the item as money—heavy stone wheels, cattle, and cigarettes are not particularly portable, durable, and divisible, yet they have been used as money because people agreed to *accept* them as money.

The Evolution of Money

Most major currencies have developed in a similar manner, originating with precious metals and evolving into the more sophisticated forms of money that we use today.

Precious Metals

Many currency systems originated with gold or silver. Because they are naturally scarce, gold and silver have a naturally high value, which is sometimes referred to as *intrinsic value*, meaning that people intuitively associate such metals with value. It was this value of the precious metal itself that gave the earliest forms of money their acceptability. Someone who was asked to accept money in exchange for something of utilitarian value, such as a horse, had to be confident that the money was as valuable as the horse. In the early days of money, gold and silver provided the necessary confidence.

Gold has always played a special role in people's perceptions of value, and therefore in monetary systems. Gold's most basic quality is, of course, its *scarcity*—all of the gold bullion ever mined in the entire world could be contained in a single cube with edges measuring 20 metres long.[1] In addition, gold is associated with *permanence*—gold is a very stable metal that never tarnishes or corrodes. The gold recovered from a sunken Spanish galleon of the 1500s still shines like new.

At first, pieces of gold and silver of varying sizes were used as money, making it necessary for them to be weighed when used in transactions. Later, gold and silver were made into coins of standard weights and values, which was more convenient.

Gold's scarcity made it very acceptable as money, but it also led to another problem—there was too little gold to provide the growing money supply that was needed as economies grew. This problem was solved (at least in part) by *debasement*—the addition of other or base metals to molten gold or silver. A king, needing money to finance a war or some other endeavour, would recall all of the currency, which consisted of pure gold coins. These would be melted down and re-minted into new coins. During the melting and minting, however, other metals would be added to the gold, so that *more* new coins could be minted. Then, all the pure gold coins that had been taken out of circulation could be replaced with "debased" coins that would be returned to the people who had owned them, *and* there would be surplus coins that the king could keep to pay for his war—a convenient, if not totally straightforward, way of raising revenues for the royal treasury.

The debasement of coinage in this way presents an interesting problem—while the *face value* of each coin remains the same, it contains *less gold* and has lost some of its intrinsic value. What will it now be worth? How much will it buy? The answers to these questions depend on whether people *accept* the coins at their face value in exchange for goods and services. If they do, the new coins will be worth their face value, and they will function as money just as well as the pure gold coins did, because people have faith that they can spend the coinage at its face value. This is the case with our coinage today: the metallic content of the coins that we use is far less than their face value, but they are accepted at their face value in exchange for goods and services. Rather than *possessing* value, they are *representative* of value.

Paper Bills (Bank Notes)

The use of paper bills (bank notes) as money originated with goldsmiths, who performed some of the earliest banking functions. The goldsmith would provide safe-keeping facilities for people who would deposit their money (gold) with him. In return, the goldsmith would issue a receipt, or *bank note*, for the gold, as illustrated in Figure 5-1.

At first, when people wanted to buy things, they would return the receipt to the goldsmith/banker and withdraw their gold in order to make the purchase. However, as they became more familiar with the bank notes, they found it much more convenient simply to use the bank notes for buying goods and services—that is, to use these pieces of paper (bills) as money. Originally, a receipt, or bank note, was made out in the name of the depositor, who would then have to sign the note over to the person to

In England, King Henry VIII and his successor, young Edward VI, tampered with the currency so seriously that by 1551, a penny contained only one-sixth of the silver that it had contained in 1520.

[1]Check www.cupel.com/gold_facts.html for this and many other facts about gold.

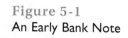

Figure 5-1
An Early Bank Note

J.R. Goldsmith, Banker
will pay to Fred Flintstone
on demand
Twenty Dollars ($20.00)
in gold
(Signed)

JR Goldsmith

J.R. Goldsmith

whom it was being given. Later, however, a goldsmith or a banker would make the note payable "to the bearer" (that is, anyone who held the note). This form was more convenient for bills that would be used as money and exchanged from person to person.

In this way, paper bills, issued by private banks, came to be used as money. These paper bills were special, however, because they involved a *promise to pay* gold to the holder of the notes. It was because of the *gold backing* of bank notes that people would accept these paper bills as money—they were, as the saying went, "as good as gold." But as we will see later in this chapter, the gold backing did *not* mean that there was $1 of gold for *every* $1 of bank notes in circulation.

Later, when governments undertook to regulate currency more systematically, bank notes issued by private banks were replaced by bank notes issued by the government or, more correctly, by government agencies known as *central banks*. Originally, many countries maintained gold backing for the bank notes issued by their central banks in order to ensure the acceptability of their currency.

As time passed, however, this practice became unnecessary, as people became completely confident in the paper bills. As well, gold backing of bank notes became impossible as the volume of money needed by growing economies far outgrew the available stock of gold. Today, there is no gold backing behind the bank notes issued by Canada's central bank, the Bank of Canada.

Bank notes no longer involve a promise to pay but are instead **fiat money**, meaning that the government has simply *declared* them to be legal tender, so that they must be accepted as payment for debts. This fact was officially recognized in the bank note issue of 1971: the new notes issued no longer said, "Will pay to the bearer on demand," but rather simply declared, "This note is legal tender."

Bank Deposits (Book Entries)

In many cases, people use *cheques* to make payments. Are cheques money? At first glance, the answer would appear to be yes. Money is used to buy things, and people do buy things with cheques.

In actual fact, however, cheques are not themselves money. If cheques were money, everyone would be able to write their own money without limit. Also, the cheque shown in Figure 5-2 on page 106 will not stay in Mr. Framish's possession—it will be returned by the bank to Ms. Stuk, for her records. Furthermore, the cheque is valueless if there are not sufficient funds in the account of the cheque writer (which one might suspect to be possible in the case of a cheque writer named U.R. Stuk). So the cheque itself is not money.

In 1996, the Canadian Mint replaced the $2 bill with a $2 coin known as the "toonie" (or, perhaps, "twonie"). The $2 coin cost $0.16 to make compared with $0.06 for the $2 bill; however, the coin's lifespan was projected to be 20 years as compared with only one year for the bill.

www.bankofcanada.ca

fiat money
Money that a government has declared to be legal tender.

Figure 5-2
A Typical Cheque

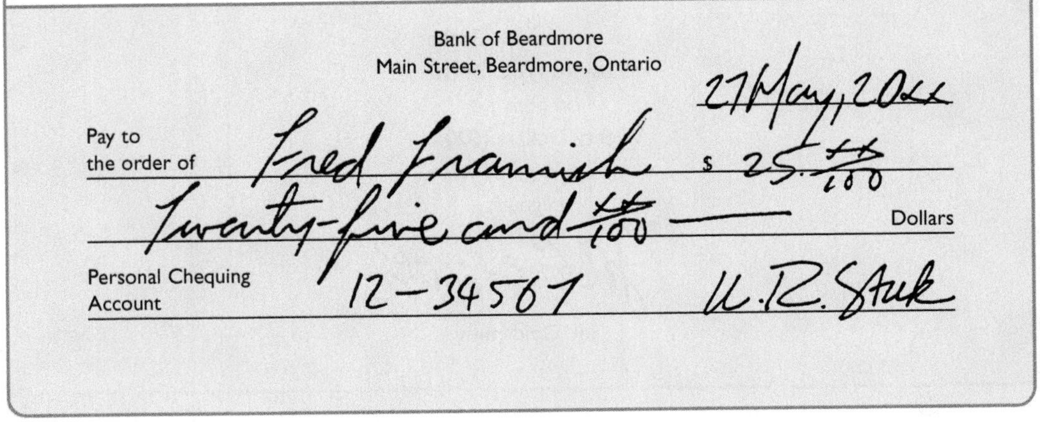

Bank of Beardmore
Main Street, Beardmore, Ontario

27 May, 20XX

Pay to
the order of   *Fred Framish* $ 25.XX/100

Twenty-five and XX/100 —————   Dollars

Personal Chequing
Account   12–34567   U.R. Stuk

If you read the cheque carefully, you will see that it is really simply a *letter to the bank*, instructing the bank to pay $25 to Mr. Framish. Figure 5-3 illustrates this fact by showing the cheque rewritten in the form of a letter.

Figure 5-3
A Cheque Is Really a Letter

Bank of Beardmore
Main Street
Beardmore, Ontario

May 27, 20XX

Dear Banker:
Please pay Mr. Framish $25 of mine. You will
find it in my account #12-34567.

Thank you,

U.R. Stuk
U.R. Stuk

What, then, is the actual money to be paid to Mr. Framish? He may cash the cheque, in which case he receives bank notes and coins, which we have already discussed. The more interesting case is that he might deposit it into his own account—what does he receive then? He will receive a *deposit to his bank account*, in the form of *book entries* on the bank's records. When Mr. Framish deposits the cheque, the book entry in his account will be increased by $25 and the book entry in Ms. Stuk's account will be reduced by $25. There is no cash involved in this transaction at all—just book entries.

Are these book entries in the bank's records money to Mr. Framish? This question can be answered simply by asking if he can *spend* them. Of course he can, by writing cheques on them, as Ms. Stuk did. So these bank deposits (book entries) are money, and banks can transfer this money between people's accounts as instructed by cheques.

Credit cards, like cheques, are used to make purchases, but are not in themselves money. Credit cards give the cardholder access to *instant credit* (or instant loans) for the purchase of goods and services. However, when people *actually pay* their credit card accounts, they almost always do so with bank-deposit money.

Some people think that book entries represent cash deposits (bills and coins) and that bank deposits are not therefore a separate form of money. In fact, this is not true—total bank deposits (book entries) *far exceed* the total amount of bank notes and coins in the economy. Also, these book entries constitute a separate and very important form of money, through which more than 90 percent of the volume of transactions is made. For instance, Sara's cheque for a new cell phone is covered by her deposit of a paycheque written on her employer's account, into which have been deposited other cheques from customers, written on accounts into which people have deposited their paycheques, and so on. In none of these transactions is cash used. In Part B, "How Money Is Created," we will examine the process by which these deposits are actually created.

According to the Canadian Payments Association, the value of transactions cleared through CPA systems in 2010 was $42.8 trillion.

Electronic Banking

The original (and traditional) way of transferring book-entry money between accounts has been through cheques, as described above. However, modern computer and communications technology has provided more convenient alternatives.

Internet banking is the most-used alternative. With a personal computer linked to the bank through the internet, a customer can check account balances, transfer funds between accounts, pay bills, apply for a loan or mortgage, purchase a guaranteed investment certificate, and so on, 24 hours per day, as well as buy stocks and create financial reports for small businesses and professionals. Customers who don't have internet access can perform many of these functions using their telephone.

The other major innovation has been *direct payment (direct debit) cards* such as Interac. With a debit card, a merchant can be paid by electronically withdrawing the money from a customer's account at the point of purchase. In addition, Interac's CashBack program allows customers to obtain cash from participating merchants with high cash balances, such as supermarkets and liquor stores. Canadians are the world's biggest users of electronic banking services.

www.cdnpay.ca

Some Things That Are Not Money

To improve our understanding of what money *is*, we will take a quick look at some things that are *not* money, and why they are not money.

Stocks (corporate shares) and bonds are transferable financial securities, but they are not money because they are not used as a medium of exchange. Because their value fluctuates, using stocks and bonds as money is too inconvenient.

Canada Savings Bonds (CSBs) do not fluctuate in value; they can always be cashed in for their face value (plus the interest that has built up to the time they are cashed). However, Canada Savings Bonds are not legally transferable from one person to another, so they cannot be used as money. Financial assets such as stocks and bonds are not money: they can be converted into money by simply selling them, but the same thing can be done with any asset, even a house or a car. Strictly speaking, *non-chequing bank deposits* (such as savings accounts) are not money, because they cannot be transferred either electronically or to someone else to pay for something. Of course, to use these deposits as money, the funds in this type of account could easily be *transferred into* an account from which they could be transferred by cheque or electronically. Similarly, *term deposits* (which the depositor has agreed to leave on deposit for longer periods, such as from one to five years) can be readily converted into chequable deposits, or money. These non-chequable deposits, which are for obvious reasons known as *near money*, considerably complicate our attempts to define and measure Canada's money supply.

YOU DECIDE

Electronic Cash?

The banks would like to extend the use of electronic banking in ways that *replace cash*. Cash is still the main method of payment for the many small transactions that people make daily; however, for banks, the handling of cash is a labour-intensive and costly function. While automated teller machines (ATMs) reduce the banks' costs by *dispensing* cash, there is also interest in using computer technology to *replace* cash.

This interest has taken the form of experiments with "electronic cash," using what are sometimes called *smart cards* or *stored value cards*. A stored value card is plastic, with a computer chip onto which cardholders can download cash from their accounts at an ATM or a specially equipped telephone. The cardholder could then use the card for small purchases, such as convenience store purchases, from any business or person with the required computer terminal. With each purchase, the balance of cash stored on the card would decrease, just as would the cash in one's pocket or purse.

Some people foresee the final step in the evolution of money as the *cashless society*, in which there would be no cash whatsoever, and all transactions would be handled electronically. Each person would have a card for access to his/her accounts, and would use this card for any purchase. ■

QUESTIONS

1. Would you use an electronic cash card? Why or why not?
2. Would you expect such cards to be used widely by the public? Why or why not?
3. Some people think that the cashless society is *inevitable*, while others think it is *impossible*. Who do you think is right? Why?

Money in Canada Today

Basically, there are three forms of money in Canada today:
- coins
- bank notes
- deposits (book entries)

While many people associate the word *money* with coins and bank notes, these forms of money are only a small proportion of the total amount of money in circulation, or the money supply. Depending on the types of deposits counted, only about 5 to 8 percent of Canada's money supply consists of coins and bank notes, and 92 to 95 percent is deposits (book entries) of various sorts.

Canada's Money Supply Defined and Measured

In defining and measuring the money supply, we must remember that our main concern is that *the size of the money supply* is closely related to *the level of aggregate demand*, which is a major factor in the performance of the economy. The difficulty is that the vast majority of the money supply consists of bank deposits, and there are many different types of these.

At the one extreme are *demand deposits* (current chequing accounts), which will almost certainly be spent very soon, adding to aggregate demand. At the other extreme are *term deposits*, many of which contain long-term savings that are unlikely to be spent soon—some of these, in fact, will be part of people's savings for retirement. Between these extremes lie a variety of types of accounts with different probabilities of being spent soon. If we are trying to develop a definition of money that relates closely to the level of aggregate demand, which types of bank deposits should we include, and which should be excluded?

Table 5-1 shows two of the main measures of Canada's money supply: M1 and M2. **M1** is the narrowest definition of the money supply, including only funds that are very likely to be spent very soon—*currency outside the banks* (that is, bank notes and coins in circulation) plus *chequable* deposits (that is, the sort of funds that are used to pay bills and expenses). **M2** includes all of the funds in M1, plus funds that are less likely to be spent soon—non-chequable (savings) deposits and fixed term deposits.

So Table 5-1 shows three "layers" of the money supply: cash in circulation, which will almost certainly be spent very soon, chequable deposits, which are very likely to be spent quite soon, and savings deposits, which are less likely to be spent soon. Table 5-1 also shows that cash (bank notes and coins) comprise a very small proportion of the money supply. There are other types of deposits and several more refined and complex definitions of the money supply, but M1 and M2 are the major ones.

M1
The narrowest definition of the money supply, including only currency (bank notes and coins) outside the banks plus demand deposits (current chequing account deposits).

M2
A wider definition of the money supply, comprised of M1 plus non-chequable deposits and fixed term deposits.

www.statcan.gc.ca
Search for "Money supply". Click on "Exchange rates, interest rates, money supply and stock prices".

Table 5-1
Canada's Money Supply, November 2008

	Billions of $	Billions of $
Currency Outside Banks	$50	
Chequable deposits	357	
Total: M1		407
Non-chequable deposits and fixed term deposits	431	
Total: M2		838

Source: Statistics Canada, CANSIM Table 176-0020.

The main reason for our interest in these various definitions of the money supply is that the size of the money supply has an important influence on the level of aggregate demand, and therefore on how well the economy performs in terms of output, employment, and inflation. The problem is that these various definitions and measures of the money supply make it difficult to actually *measure* the money supply with any degree of precision.

However, money supply statistics are still useful. We may not be sure of the *level* of the money supply, but by tracking *changes* in the money supply over time, we can gather some useful information—an economy in which the money supply is growing by 12 percent per year reflects a very different situation from one in which the money supply is stagnant, or shrinking. A rapidly rising money supply would provide advance notice that there was a danger of inflation, whereas if the money supply was growing slowly or stagnating, there would be concerns about a possible recession.

The Acceptability and Value of Money in Canada

As we have seen, the vast majority of Canada's money supply is in the form of bank deposits—only a small proportion consists of coins and bank notes.

Until the 1930s, when a uniform national currency was established, Canada's currency consisted of a variety of coins and notes issued by numerous private banks and the federal government.

We have also seen that Canada's money supply is not backed by gold—it functions as money because people have faith in it. People accept money in exchange for goods and services because they believe that they can use the money to buy other goods and services of equivalent value. Ultimately, this confidence in money is really confidence in the monetary authority of the country—that it will not issue an excessive amount of money, causing inflation that will reduce the value of money too rapidly. This monetary authority is the Bank of Canada, an agency of the federal government which will be discussed in Chapter 7.

While faith is what gives money its acceptability, the *actual value* of a dollar—what it is worth—depends on its *purchasing power*, or how much it will buy. The purchasing power of the dollar, in turn, depends on the general level of the prices of goods and services. If prices in general rise due to inflation, the value of the dollar will fall because its purchasing power will be reduced.[2]

Conversely, if prices in general were to fall, the value of the dollar would rise. So the actual value of the dollar is inversely related to the general level of prices—the higher the level of prices, the lower the value of the dollar.

Part B: How Is Money Created?

Where does all the money listed in Table 5-1 *come from*? How is it *created*? Coins are manufactured (minted) and bank notes are printed, under close government supervision. But coins and paper bills are a very small proportion of the money supply. Of much greater importance and interest is the vast majority of the money supply that consists of *bank deposits*. Where do these come from? How are they created? These bank deposits are in fact *created by the banking system, when it makes loans.* This process is more complicated, and it requires some explanation.

The Operation of Early Banks

To illustrate the process by which the banking system creates money, we will use the earliest banks, operating in a simple situation in which money consisted only of gold coins and bank notes (paper bills) issued by privately owned banks—in this economy, book entries were not yet used as money.

These early banks accepted deposits of gold coins, and issued receipts, in the form of bank notes. As we have seen, people eventually found it more convenient to use the bank notes instead of gold coins for transactions. So relatively few holders of bank notes would redeem them for coinage at the banks. A few gold coins were withdrawn and spent, but the people who received them would usually deposit them back into the banks.

So, not much coinage would be withdrawn from the banks, and withdrawals of coinage would tend to be offset by deposits of coinage. These two facts enabled the banks to operate quite smoothly with a relatively *small amount of coins backing up a much larger amount of bank notes.* As an illustration, a bank might receive deposits of $100 000 of gold coins, issue $100 000 of bank notes, but only need $10 000 of gold coins on hand to cover withdrawals of coinage.

---

[2] The value of the dollar referred to here is its value in use *inside Canada*, when used to buy goods and services. The *international value* of the Canadian dollar—its value in terms of other nations' currencies—is a different matter, which will be covered in Chapter 10, "The Canadian Dollar in Foreign Exchange Markets."

But in such a bank, there would be considerable amounts of gold coins sitting around doing nothing—in our example, *$90 000* of idle gold coins. At some point, these early bankers realized that they could use these reserves of coinage to *make loans*, and earn interest income. While borrowers could take loans in the form of coins, they would generally take *bank notes* instead, such as the bank note shown in Figure 5-4, which were the most common form of money.

Figure 5-4
A Typical Early Bank Note

Bank of Beardmore
will pay to the bearer of this note, on demand
Twenty Dollars ($20.00)

Buford McCoy
President

Bank Loans Create Money

The key question is this: *How much* could the bank in our example lend out? The answer lies in the arithmetic of our earlier example, in which $10 000 of gold coins in the bank "covered" $100 000 of bank notes in circulation, meaning that the $90 000 of "idle" gold coins would be able to cover *$900 000* of bank notes, which would be put into circulation when the bank made loans.

So when making loans, banks could put into circulation *far more* bank notes than the amount of coinage, or cash, that the banks had on hand to back their bank notes. And in doing so, the banking system *increased* the volume of bank-note money in circulation—i.e., the banking system *created money* by making loans.

Cash Reserves and the Cash Reserve Ratio

How many bank notes could a bank put into circulation through loans on the basis of a given level of gold coins? Obviously, the process is not unlimited: if a bank made *too many* loans and issued *too many* notes in this way, it would have so many notes in circulation that there would be a high risk that too many note-holders would redeem their notes for gold coins at one time, causing the bank to run out of gold coins and collapse. (It could also prove personally dangerous for the banker.) While this does not mean that *every one* of its notes must be backed by gold coins, the bank must have the gold coins to back *a certain percentage* of its notes, to ensure that it is able to meet withdrawals of coinage by its customers. The coinage kept on hand to cover withdrawals is called the **cash reserves** of a bank. The percentage of its bank notes outstanding kept as cash reserves is called the bank's **cash reserve ratio**. In our example, the bank had $100 000 of bank notes in circulation, backed by cash reserves of $10 000, so the cash reserve ratio would be 10 percent ($10 000 divided by $100 000). Looked at differently, on the basis of $10 000 of cash reserves, the banking system has expanded the money supply to $100 000, creating money in the process of making loans, as shown in Figure 5-5.

cash reserves
That amount of cash kept on hand by a bank to cover day-to-day withdrawals of cash.

cash reserve ratio
The percentage of total deposits that a bank keeps as cash reserves.

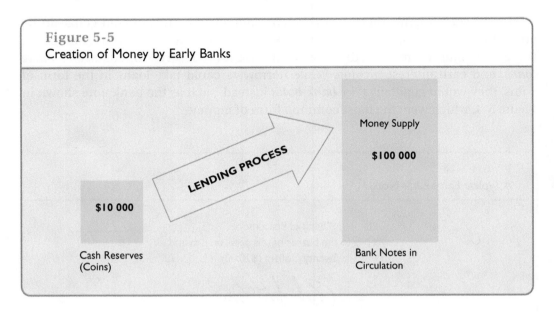

Figure 5-5
Creation of Money by Early Banks

The Creation of Money by a Modern Banking System

In a modern banking system, the nature of money is more sophisticated than in our previous example. Bank notes are no longer issued by the banks, but rather by the government, and, as we have seen, over 90 percent of the money supply consists of bank deposits, or book entries, which are transferred between accounts by cheques or electronically. These bank deposits, however, are created in essentially the same way as bank notes were created by the early banks: through the process of making loans. When a modern bank makes a loan, the borrower does not usually get cash (bank notes or coins). Instead, the bank simply increases the balance in the borrower's account, thus giving the borrower more money (book entries) to spend. Using a small amount of cash (bank notes plus coins) as reserves, a modern banking system is able to create a large amount of money (bank deposits), as illustrated in Figure 5-6. In this

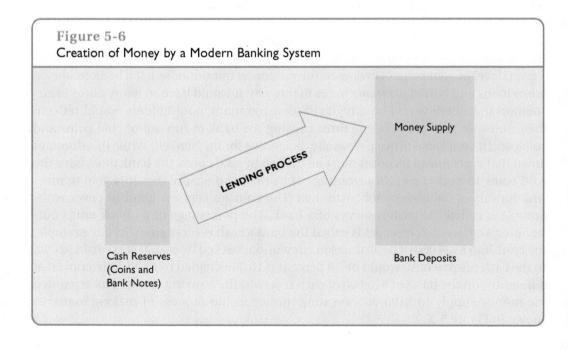

Figure 5-6
Creation of Money by a Modern Banking System

way, the banking system can create a large volume of money on the basis of a small volume of cash reserves.

A Formula for Calculating the Creation of Money

How much money can the banking system create in this way? Money creation depends on two factors:

- the volume of *cash reserves* that the banks have, and
- the *cash reserve ratio* that they maintain.

The extent to which the banking system can create money can be calculated from the following formula:

$$\text{Potential Total Deposits} = \frac{\text{Cash Reserves}}{\text{Cash Reserve Ratio}}$$

So, if the banking system had cash reserves of $18 billion and a cash reserve ratio of 3 percent, total deposits could be as large as

$$\frac{\$18 \text{ billion}}{0.03} = \$600 \text{ billion}$$

Note that $600 billion represents *potential* total deposits: it is not certain that total deposits actually will *reach* $600 billion. In order for the potential to be reached, the banks would have to make every loan that is mathematically possible—they must carry no "excess cash reserves" over and above the 3-percent ratio. Since we cannot know whether this will in fact happen, we must remember that our formula only indicates the *potential* amount of money that can be created by the banking system on the basis of a given amount of cash reserves and a given cash reserve ratio.

The Cash Reserve Ratio and the Money-Creating Process

From our formula, it can be seen that the size of the cash reserve ratio has a large impact on the amount of money that the banking system can create. If the cash reserve ratio had been only 2 percent, total deposits (and therefore the money supply) could have reached $900 billion ($18 billion divided by 0.02)—50 percent larger.

The reason for this relationship is simple: because the banks have to keep *less* cash reserves on hand, they are able to lend *more* money, so that total deposits can rise by more, creating more money.

How Can So Little Cash Back Up So Many Deposits?

How is it possible for banks to operate safely with so little cash to back up their deposits? We have already seen the answer to this question, but it is worth reviewing here. First, in most transactions—over 90 percent by volume—funds are transferred electronically or by cheques so that no cash needs to be taken out of the bank; all that is needed are changes in book entries. This reduces tremendously the need for cash, not only on the part of the public but also on the part of the banks. Second, while people and businesses do make cash withdrawals, they also make cash deposits, and there is a strong tendency for cash deposits to offset cash withdrawals. People take out some cash every payday, and as they spend it over the next two weeks, the stores that receive it deposit it back into the banks.

When a bank has a large number of depositors, it can be confident that while some depositors will be withdrawing cash from the bank at any given time, others will be making deposits of cash that will offset those withdrawals, maintaining the bank's cash on hand.

In one sense, there is an incentive for banks to keep a low level of cash reserves, because the less cash reserves a bank keeps, the more loans it can make, increasing its interest income. On the other hand, banks must not let their reserves get too low because, ultimately, banks rely upon the confidence of their depositors. The worst thing that can happen to a bank is for its depositors to lose confidence in it. The result can be what is known as a *run* on the bank, with many depositors trying to withdraw their deposits in cash at once. In these circumstances, any bank would quickly run out of cash, and would *fail*, a polite term for a bank bankruptcy. So there is also an incentive for banks to be sure to keep sufficient cash on hand to meet depositors' needs and maintain their confidence.

Banks must therefore strike a balance between lower cash reserves for interest income and higher cash reserves for safety. Statisticians have estimated that a large bank can operate quite safely with reserves of about 2 percent of its deposits.

Government Regulation of Banking

All banks are required by law to be members of the *Canada Deposit Insurance Corporation* (CDIC), which provides insurance on depositors' deposits of up to $100 000 per person per institution. The CDIC is financed by contributions by member institutions that are based on the size of their insured deposits.

www.cdic.ca

In 2010 the World Economic Forum ranked Canada's banking system as the soundest in the world for the third consecutive year.

Most people see the CDIC's role as compensating depositors in the event that their bank (or other insured financial institution) fails, as the CDIC has indeed done on several occasions. More basically, though, deposit insurance is intended to help *prevent* financial institutions from failing, and so keeps the financial system stable. The insurance of deposits (or, more properly, the confidence on the part of the public that their deposits are insured) is meant to prevent depositors from panicking and starting a ruinous run on a bank. As we saw earlier, even the soundest bank could not withstand a run because it has deposits far in excess of its cash reserves.

Another safeguard in addition to deposit insurance is that the loans and investments of banks are subject to inspection by audit teams of the Inspector General of Banks. The goal of this inspection process is to ensure that depositors' funds are being invested in an appropriately secure manner.

Finally, banks are required to maintain certain levels of capital relative to their deposits and investments, so that they do not lend excessively.

The Banking System, the Money Supply, and the Economy

We have seen how the banking system, by increasing its lending activities, can cause the nation's money supply to increase. On the other hand, if the banking system were to curtail its lending, the money supply would decrease. As outstanding loans were repaid, a decline in deposits, not offset by new deposit-creating loans, would occur.

This ability of the banking system to create (and destroy) money can greatly affect the money supply and therefore the level of aggregate demand in the economy. Figure 5-7 summarizes how bank lending can affect aggregate demand, and thus output, employment/unemployment, and the rate of inflation.

The economy requires an appropriate money supply in order to generate high levels of output and employment without excessive inflation. Too small a money supply

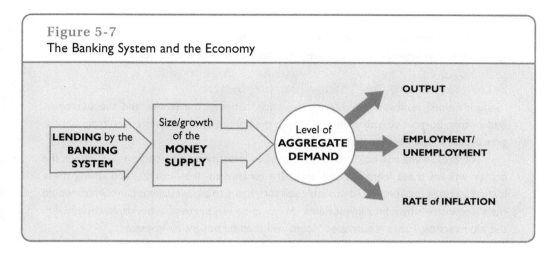

Figure 5-7
The Banking System and the Economy

IN THE NEWS

The American "Shadow Banking" System

Chapter 5 describes the operation of a "conventional" banking system such as Canada's, in which banks accept deposits and make loans to consumers and businesses.

In the United States, a different system evolved alongside the "conventional" banking system, which became known as the "shadow banking system". In this system, lenders do not acquire loanable funds by accepting deposits from the public; rather, they *sell the loans that they have made to investors*, who in effect become the real lenders—a process known as "securitization".

To explain the difference between these systems, let's use mortgage loans as an example and start with a traditional mortgage loan from a bank to people who are buying a home, as shown in the figure.

A Traditional Mortgage

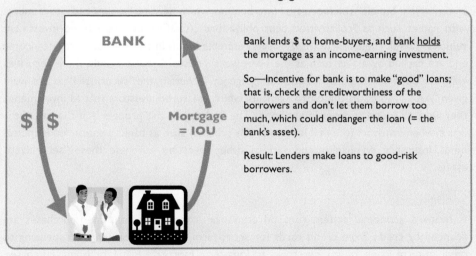

Bank lends $ to home-buyers, and bank holds the mortgage as an income-earning investment.

So—Incentive for bank is to make "good" loans; that is, check the creditworthiness of the borrowers and don't let them borrow too much, which could endanger the loan (= the bank's asset).

Result: Lenders make loans to good-risk borrowers.

After making the loan, the bank *holds the mortgage* as an income-earning investment, or asset. As a result, the bank has an incentive to avoid making risky loans to borrowers who might be unable to make their payments. So the bank will check the creditworthiness

→

→ of all of its borrowers to make sure that it is making "good" loans. The limitation of this approach is that less-qualified borrowers will probably be unable to get loans.

Securitization and the "Shadow Banking System"

"Securitization" removes the direct connection between the lender and the borrower. Rather than borrow directly from the lender, the home-buyer receives a loan from a *mortgage broker*, whose role is to arrange loans.

The broker will not hold these mortgages as investments as a bank would; rather, the broker will *sell* these loans (assets), and earn *commissions* from making and selling these loans. Mortgage brokers would probably sell such loans to an investment bank, which would then "securitize" them into investments that in some ways resemble bonds, as explained in the next section. These "securitized" loans will then be bought by investors.

Securitization

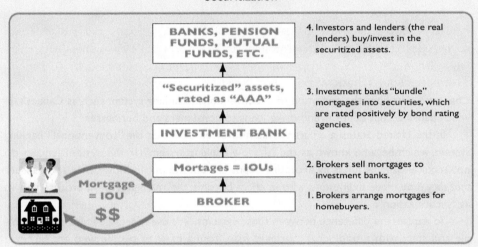

BANKS, PENSION FUNDS, MUTUAL FUNDS, ETC.

4. Investors and lenders (the real lenders) buy/invest in the securitized assets.

"Securitized" assets, rated as "AAA"

3. Investment banks "bundle" mortgages into securities, which are rated positively by bond rating agencies.

INVESTMENT BANK

Mortages = IOUs

2. Brokers sell mortgages to investment banks.

BROKER

1. Brokers arrange mortgages for homebuyers.

Mortgage = IOU

$$

The figure illustrates such a securitization process. Starting at the bottom left, brokers make mortgage loans to homebuyers. The brokers then sell these mortgages to investment banks, which "bundle" the mortgages into batches, which become "securitized" investments with names such as "collaterized debt obligations" (CDOs) and "structured investment vehicles" (SIVs). These "securitized" assets resemble bonds in that they pay interest income and are backed by assets such as the borrowers' houses. And like bonds, these securities will have been evaluated by a bond rating agency. Generally, the "securitized" assets were given "AAA" ratings by the rating agencies, which reassured investors that as investments, they were as sound as government bonds. The final step in this process is at the top of the figure, when investors (the real lenders in this process) such as banks, pension funds, mutual funds, insurance companies, and various other investors purchase these "securitized" assets.

Securitization in Perspective

A modern economic system runs on credit, or loans. Many consumer purchases are financed by credit, from credit cards for short-term loans for consumption spending to medium-term loans for car purchases to long-term mortgage loans for home purchases. Many students' education is financed by loans. In addition, most businesses run on loans that provide the funds to pay their employees and suppliers until the revenues from their sales come in, and much business investment is financed by loans.   →

Securitization, or the bundling of loans into assets that were sold to investors, began in the 1980s and gradually grew to become a key aspect of the American economic system. Because it took place outside of the traditional banking system, this process became known as the "shadow banking system." By the early 2000s, securitized loans (to homebuyers, credit card holders, students, businesses and other borrowers) had become a vital part of the American economy, amounting to **60 percent** of the loans made in the United States.

One of the advantages claimed for securitization was that bundling together large numbers of loans into a single asset made it economical to extend loans to less creditworthy borrowers who would probably not otherwise be able to get a loan. If a few such borrowers were to default on their loans, they would represent only a small proportion of the loans bundled together in the "securitized" asset, which would still be a good investment. And in any event, the risk of such defaults would be covered by the interest rates paid by the mortgage borrowers and by the fact that the lenders could seize the homes of defaulting borrowers and sell them.

The major disadvantage of securitization was that the real lenders (investors) were far removed from the borrowers, and lacked a detailed knowledge of the real quality of the mortgage assets that were bundled into the CDOs and SIVs that they had bought; instead, they relied on the "AAA" rating given to these securitized assets. In the 2003–07 period, these assets included a growing number of "subprime" mortgages that had been made to high-risk borrowers whose income and employment situations made it unlikely that they would be able to repay their loans.

It was this aspect of securitization that would eventually cause serious trouble, because when these borrowers defaulted on their mortgages, lenders/investors (including banks) would be left with billions of dollars of worthless securities, and lenders would foreclose on those properties and put them up for sale, driving home prices in general sharply downwards and leaving millions of Americans with mortgage debts greater than the market value of their properties. This set the stage for the recession of 2008–09.

For a more detailed account of these matters, see the *Lessons from the Recession* supplement to this text.

can slow down spending and economic activity to the point of causing a *recession,* while if too much money is created, excessive demand will generate a problem of *inflation.*

Because the banking system's lending activities can have such strong effects upon the country's economy, the banking industry is subject to an unusual degree of government regulation and influence, as we will see in Chapter 7.

Chapter Summary

1. The one characteristic that money must have is acceptability; other characteristics that help make an item acceptable as money are scarcity, portability, durability, and divisibility. (L.O. 1)
2. Money serves three economic functions: as a medium of exchange, a standard of value, and a store of value. (L.O. 2)
3. The size of the money supply is vitally important to the performance of a nation's economy, since too little money in circulation will cause a recession and too much will cause inflation. (L.O. 3)

4. Money has evolved over the years, from precious metals long ago to bank notes that were backed by gold at first and later not backed by gold, and eventually to electronically stored and transferred book entries today. The forms of money in use in Canada today are coins, bank notes, and bank deposits (book entries). (L.O. 4)

5. The two main definitions of the money supply are M1, which includes only currency outside the banks plus chequable deposits, and M2, which is comprised of M1 plus non-chequable deposits and fixed term deposits.

6. The bank deposits that represent over 90 percent of the money supply are created through the lending activities of the banking system. (L.O. 6)

7. The process of money creation by the banking system is made possible by the fact that banks can operate successfully with cash reserves that represent only a small proportion of their total deposits, which in turn makes it possible to build a large volume of deposits on the basis of relatively small cash reserves. (L.O. 6)

8. The potential level of total deposits, or money, that can be created through the lending activities of the banks is equal to the banks' cash reserves divided by their cash reserve ratio. (L.O. 7)

9. Since the banking system's operations can increase or reduce the nation's money supply, they have a strong influence on the performance of the economy and are therefore subject to various government regulations. (L.O. 8)

Questions

1. For something to function as *money*, the single most basic requirement is that it be

    (a) authorized by the government as legal tender.
    (b) backed by precious metals.
    (c) generally accepted by people as a medium of exchange.
    (d) made of precious metal.
    (e) None of the above.

2. If the money supply were too small, would the economy be pushed in the direction of higher rates of inflation or higher unemployment? Why?

3. Would an excessively large money supply push the economy in the direction of higher rates of inflation or higher unemployment? Why?

4. The banking system has $800 billion of deposits but only $24 billion of cash reserves on hand.

    (a) What is the banking system's *cash reserve ratio*?
    (b) Explain two reasons why the banking system can operate safely and successfully with such a small amount of cash on hand.

5. Explain how the answer to the previous question is a key to the ability of the banking system to *create money*.

6. Suppose that aggregate demand were high and rising, the economy was booming, and the rate of inflation was increasing. How might the business decisions of a privately owned banking system increase the risk that inflation would become more severe?

7. This chapter notes that banks operate with a small amount of cash reserves compared to their deposits.

    (a) How could this situation lead to a crisis for a bank?
    (b) Explain how deposit insurance reduces the risk of such a crisis.

8. Visit the section of the Bank of Canada's website on the history of the Canadian dollar (www.bankofcanada.ca/wp-content/uploads/2010/07/1600-1770.pdf) and read pages 4 to 7 for an account of an unusual period during which playing cards were used as money in New France for most of the period from 1685 to the 1750s.

   (a) Why did the French colonial officials introduce this unusual form of money?
   (b) What does this story show about what can be used as money?
   (c) What risks would the use of playing cards as money involve, and how could the authorities reduce those risks?

Study Guide

Review Questions (The answers to these Review Questions appear in Appendix B.)

1. The term *money supply* refers to
   (a) the total incomes earned by all Canadians in a year.
   (b) the total volume of money in circulation in the economy.
   (c) the total debt of Canadians at any point in time.
   (d) the total amount of government bonds held by Canadians at any point in time.
   (e) None of the above.

2. The size of the money supply is very important to the performance of the economy because
   (a) people need money to survive.
   (b) the more money there is, the better off people will be.
   (c) too much debt can lead to economic problems.
   (d) it strongly influences the level of aggregate demand in the economy.
   (e) None of the above.

3. The three basic functions that money performs are
   (a) _____.
   (b) _____.
   (c) _____.

4. Which of the three functions of money in the previous question is involved in each of the following situations?
   (a) Bobby puts half of his weekly allowance into his piggy bank.
   (b) Jean buys dinner at a restaurant.
   (c) Reza surfs the net comparing the cost of vacations in Mexico with the cost of various skiing holidays in Western Canada.
   (d) M. and Mme. Robert put $2000 into investments in a registered retirement savings plan.

5. Which of the following lists all of the forms of money used in Canada today?

    (a) bank notes, coins, and government bonds

    (b) bank notes, coins, and credit cards

    (c) bank notes, coins, government bonds, and bank deposits

    (d) coins, paper bills, and credit cards

    (e) coins, bank notes, and bank deposits

6. Of the three forms of money in the previous question, the largest one by far is

    _____.

7. The type of money in the previous question is created by

    (a) the Canadian mint.

    (b) the Bank of Canada.

    (c) the lending activities of the banks.

    (d) loans from other countries.

    (e) None of the above.

8. The term *cash reserves* refers to the cash a bank keeps on hand

    (a) to lend.

    (b) to cover against bad cheques.

    (c) as a reserve in case of losses on some of the bank's investments.

    (d) to cover withdrawals of cash by depositors.

    (e) None of the above.

9. If a bank has $500 million of deposits and cash reserves of $25 million, that bank's cash reserve ratio is _____ percent.

10. If the banking system has $12 billion of cash reserves and the cash reserve ratio is 6 percent, the total deposits of the banking system could be as large as $_____ billion.

11. Answer *true* or *false* to each of the following statements concerning bank notes in Canada.

    (a) They are issued by the Bank of Canada, which is a federal government agency.

    (b) They are fully backed by gold.

    (c) They are partially backed by gold.

    (d) They represent a promise by the government to pay money to the holder of the bank note.

    (e) They contain a declaration that each bank note is *legal tender*.

    (f) They comprise more than half of Canada's money supply.

12. State whether each of the following statements concerning bank deposits as money in Canada is *true* or *false*.

    (a) They are not a separate form of money from coins and bank notes; rather, they merely represent deposits of coins and bank notes into depositors' accounts and are held on their behalf by the bank.

    (b) They are transferred between depositors' accounts according to instructions conveyed by cheque, telephone, or electronic means.

    (c) They represent the largest single form of money.

    (d) They are not really money; they are just book entries.

    (e) They are in fact money, but only represent a small proportion of the money supply.

13. Canada's money supply could be said to be *backed*

   (a) dollar for dollar by gold.
   (b) by 8 cents of gold for every dollar.
   (c) by silver as well as gold.
   (d) by Canada's ability to compete in international markets.
   (e) by people's faith in its purchasing power.

14. The banking system is able to operate safely with deposits far in excess of its cash reserves because

   (a) banks are owned by the federal government.
   (b) cash withdrawals from banks tend to be offset by cash deposits.
   (c) most transactions of money involve no cash; rather, they involve transfers of bank-deposit money (book entries) between accounts.
   (d) All of the above.
   (e) Answers (b) and (c).

15. From the data below, calculate

   (a) M1
   (b) M2

Non-chequable deposits	$140 billion
Chequable deposits	$420 billion
Fixed term deposits	$380 billion
Currency outside banks	$60 billion

Critical Thinking Questions

(Asterisked questions 1 to 5 are answered in Appendix B; the answers to questions 6 to 10 are in the Instructor's Manual that accompanies this text.)

*1. Write a reply to the following questions.

   What's so different and so important about the banking system *creating money*? Other businesses make money when they sell goods at a profit, and banks make profits when they lend money and earn interest, so what's so special about what banks do?

*2. A customer buys a dress at a store and pays with cash. Another customer buys a dress and pays with a cheque, and a third customer pays for her dress with a credit card.

   (a) Explain to someone who has never studied economics why in only one of these transactions the store actually received *money* at the time of the transaction.
   (b) Explain what it was that the store received in the other two transactions.

*3. Two key aspects of money are its *acceptability* and its *value*.

   (a) A storekeeper accepts a $20 bank note that says, "This note is legal tender" from a customer. Ultimately, what is it that gives the storekeeper the confidence to *accept* this piece of paper in exchange for valuable goods?
   (b) What determines the actual *value* of a $20 bill? What could increase or decrease its value?

*4. An interesting side effect of the growing use of direct debit cards is that more merchants have been refusing to accept cheques. Why would this be the case?

*5. Suppose that aggregate demand were slowing down, and the economy was in the early stages of a recession. How might the business decisions of a privately owned banking system increase the risk that the recession would become more severe?

6. An important function of money is that it acts as a *store of value*, by allowing people to save their purchasing power for future use.

   (a) What effect would a period of rapid inflation likely have on the role of money as a store of value, and on people's attitudes holding toward money generally? Why?

   (b) If people feared that inflation was going to become more severe, what might they do instead of saving their money? How would this change in their behaviour affect the rate of inflation?

7. The text discusses *barter* as an antiquated system of exchange. However, in recent years there has been an *increase* in barter transactions in Canada. What could explain this?

8. Recent experience has been that automated teller machines were being used extensively by the public for cash *withdrawals*, but relatively little for *deposits*. What could explain this? Have the banks been successful in overcoming this?

9. The text describes *electronic cash*, or the replacement of cash by electronic money that is downloaded onto a *smart card* which is used for all sorts of small purchases.

   (a) Do you currently use a smart card for any transactions?
   (b) Would you use a smart card to replace cash? Why or why not?
   (c) Why are some people concerned about privacy issues related to electronic cash?
   (d) Do you think that cash will ever disappear?

10. In the early 1990s, several trust companies failed, following which the Canada Deposit Insurance Corporation made substantial payments to insured depositors. Following this, *all* financial institutions covered by CDIC were required to make much higher contributions to CDIC. This led to a debate about the possible *negative effects* of deposit insurance on the behaviour of depositors and financial institutions.

   (a) How might the availability of deposit insurance affect the behaviour of depositors in undesirable ways?

   (b) How might the availability of deposit insurance affect the behaviour of financial institutions in undesirable ways?

   (c) In some of the trust company failures, the federal government reimbursed depositors whose deposits were *not* insured. Make an argument that the federal government should *not* have reimbursed depositors in this situation.

Use the Web   (Hints for this Use the Web exercise appear in Appendix B.)

1. Visit the website of the Canada Deposit Insurance Corporation (CIDC) at **www.cdic.ca**.

   (a) When was the CDIC established, how many financial institutions are members of it, and what is the value of deposits insured by CDIC?

   (b) Since CDIC was established, how many of its member institutions have failed?

   (c) Are mutual funds insured by CDIC? Why?

6

Booms, Recessions, and Inflation

LEARNING OBJECTIVES

After studying this chapter, you should be able to

1. Explain the basic reason why business cycles of boom, inflation, and recession occur.

2. Explain how each of the following contributes to the problem of business cycles:

    (a) fluctuations in investment spending
    (b) the multiplier effect
    (c) the accelerator effect
    (d) changes in the confidence of consumers and business people
    (e) inflation psychology

3. Summarize the major economic forces that contribute to each phase of the business cycle, namely,

    (a) the recovery phase
    (b) the expansion (boom) phase
    (c) the inflation phase
    (d) the peak, at which an economic downturn begins
    (e) the recession phase

4. Explain how the Bank of Canada's output gap is used to track the business cycle.

5. Describe the two major techniques used for economic forecasting.

6. Explain how the 2008–09 recession in the United States was unusual.

7. Use aggregate supply and aggregate demand curves to illustrate the business cycle.

8. Apply the facts and concepts of this chapter to various situations.

Since 1950, the Canadian economy has generally grown quite strongly, with real GDP increasing at an average annual rate of over 4 percent. However, this growth has been far from steady. During economic booms, output and employment have increased more rapidly, while in recessions output and employment have actually *decreased*. In fact, one definition of a *recession* is two consecutive quarters of shrinking real GDP (a quarter is a three-month period).

The most infamous economic downturn was, of course, the Great Depression of the 1930s. Since then, there have been several recessions: in 1951, in 1953–54, in 1957–58, in 1960–61, in 1970, in 1974–75, in 1981–82, in 1990–92, and in 2008–09. Most of these have been relatively mild and brief; however, the recessions of the early 1980s and early 1990s, reflected in the graph in Figure 6-1, were the two most severe since the Great Depression. The 1981–82 recession brought the sharpest decline in output and the highest unemployment rate since the 1930s, while the recession of the early 1990s was noteworthy for the slow recovery that followed it. The 2008–09 recession is discussed later in this chapter.

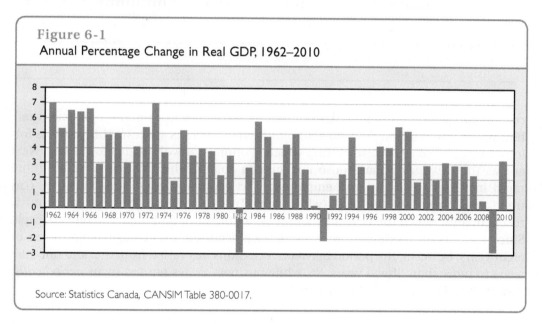

Figure 6-1
Annual Percentage Change in Real GDP, 1962–2010

Source: Statistics Canada, CANSIM Table 380-0017.

All recessions that have occurred since the Great Depression of the 1930s are mild by comparison to it. During the 1930s, real GDP shrank by 30 percent, the unemployment rate soared from 3 percent to over 20 percent, and real GDP did not recover to its 1929 level for 10 years. By comparison, the recession of 2008–09 lasted for less than two years, during which quarterly real GDP fell by 3.6 percent and the unemployment rate rose from 5.9 percent to a peak of 8.7 percent.

And, of course, whenever the economy slips into a recession, the unemployment rate increases, partly because some people are laid off and partly because there are not enough new jobs for those who are entering the labour force. Figure 6-2 shows the fluctuations in the unemployment rate over the years, with the Great Depression of the 1930s included for comparison.

Phases of the Business Cycle

The term **business cycle** describes the fluctuations of the economy between boom and recession. Figure 6-3 portrays a typical business cycle, with its phases labelled. In the

business cycle
The fluctuation of the economy between booms and recessions.

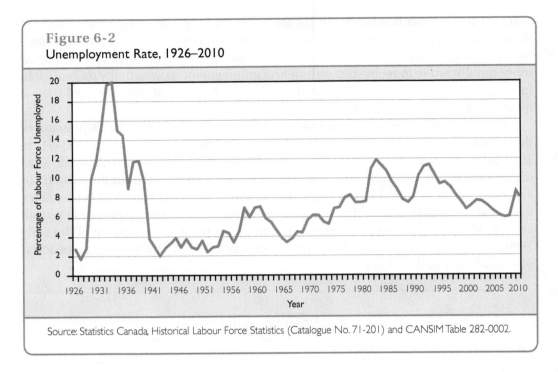

Figure 6-2
Unemployment Rate, 1926–2010

Source: Statistics Canada, Historical Labour Force Statistics (Catalogue No. 71-201) and CANSIM Table 282-0002.

contraction phase (commonly known as a recession), output and employment fall, bottoming out in a *trough* when economic activity is at its slowest. This phase is followed by the *recovery* phase, during which economic growth begins to resume. Next comes the *expansion* phase (also known as a *boom*), which usually involves more rapid increases in output and employment as economic conditions improve. This trend continues until the *peak* (which may involve increasingly rapid inflation) is reached, after which the economy goes into a downturn and the cycle repeats itself. Since the Second World War, recessions have occurred, on average, every seven or eight years; however, the period between recessions has varied from one and one-half years to more than fifteen years. So, while business cycles tend to recur *periodically*, they do not do so in a regular and predictable manner.

"We've had expansions last anywhere from 1 year to 14 years—there's nothing deterministic about these things."
— PHILIP CROSS, STATISTICS CANADA

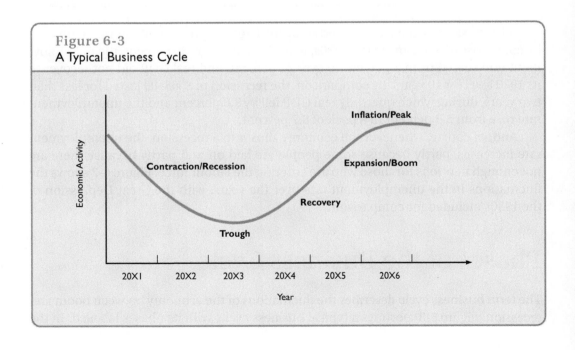

Figure 6-3
A Typical Business Cycle

Our economic system is successful in many respects, but its tendency toward periodic recessions with high unemployment has been one of its traditional weaknesses. This fact makes it important for us to try to understand why business cycles occur, so that we can try to take steps to reduce their severity.

Theories of Business Cycles

Attempts to explain business cycles have brought forward a variety of theories based on various factors that can affect economic activity. Long ago, when gold was used as money, the discovery of *new gold mines* boosted the economy by increasing the money supply. Historically, *wars* have caused high levels of government spending that generated boom-like conditions with high levels of economic activity and low unemployment, although the military output produced did not add to the prosperity of the people as consumer and capital goods do. And certain major *inventions*, such as the railroad, the automobile, and the internet, can stimulate the economy by giving rise to surges of capital investment spending.

While factors such as these affect the economy, they tend to occur at random intervals and therefore are not a convincing explanation for business cycles, which tend to occur repeatedly. For the causes of these economic fluctuations, we will have to look elsewhere.

Fluctuations in Aggregate Demand

Business cycles involve periodic fluctuations of output and employment across the entire economy. From our analysis of the operation of the economy in Chapter 4, the most likely source of such widespread swings in economic activity would be *fluctuations in aggregate demand*, or total spending on goods and services in the economy. An upward surge in aggregate demand would boost virtually all sectors of the economy, while a decrease in aggregate demand would be felt across most of the economy.

However, analyzing fluctuations in aggregate demand is not a simple matter, since aggregate demand is a vast and complex force that consists of various diverse but interconnected elements: consumption spending, business investment spending, government spending, and net export spending. So, untangling the causes of business cycles is a complex task that requires careful analysis.

In addition, the economy sometimes tends to gain *momentum*; that is, booms can feed on themselves and grow stronger, and recessions can deepen and become more severe. Again, the answer to this tendency seems to lie in the dynamics of the economic system itself, and particularly in the complex interactions between consumption spending and investment spending that can generate such momentum, either upward or downward.

This chapter deals with the problem of economic instability in two stages. In the first part of this chapter, we will look at what leads to economic instability, namely,

(a) *fluctuations in business investment spending*, the effects of which spread through the economy due to

(b) *the multiplier effect*, whereby fluctuations in investment spending generate fluctuations in consumption spending, and

(c) *the accelerator effect*, through which changes in consumption spending cause changes in business investment spending, and

(d) *fluctuations in exports*, which are a separate and important source of instability in the Canadian economy.

In the second part of this chapter, we will examine the various stages of a typical business cycle, and how the factors listed above interact in ways that generate business cycles.

The Instability of Investment Spending

Business investment spending fluctuates considerably, rising rapidly in some years and decreasing in others. This fluctuation is reflected in Figure 6-4, which shows investment spending since 1961 in real terms—that is, adjusted for inflation.

Another type of investment that fluctuates considerably is *residential construction*, or the home-building industry. Like business investment, the demand for homes varies widely from year to year—at times, home-builders cannot keep up with soaring demand, while at other times they cannot find buyers for houses they have already built. Figure 6-5 illustrates the fluctuations in housing starts caused by these fluctuations in demand. In both Figures 6-4 and 6-5, the impact of recession in 2009 is clearly visible.

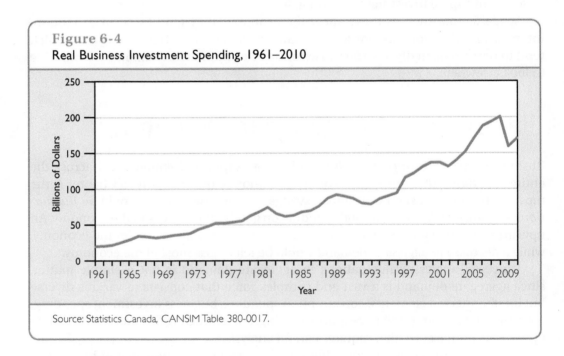

Figure 6-4
Real Business Investment Spending, 1961–2010

Source: Statistics Canada, CANSIM Table 380-0017.

Why Does Investment Spending Fluctuate So Much?

As we saw in Chapter 4, the level of business capital-investment spending depends mainly on two factors: (1) businesses' *expectations* concerning the future profitability of investment projects, and (2) the *rate of interest* that businesses must pay on money borrowed to finance such projects. And, since both expectations and interest rates can change considerably from year to year, business investment spending tends to fluctuate considerably. When the economic outlook is favourable and interest rates are low, business investment tends to rise briskly. At other times, uncertain or poor expectations and/or high interest rates can cause businesses to reduce investment spending, in some cases quite sharply.

Expectations and interest rates also explain most of the fluctuations in the residential housing market. When consumer confidence is high and mortgage interest rates are low, activity in this industry can be frantic—buyers want to buy, and they will pay high prices now because they fear that prices will rise again shortly. Builders and suppliers are barely able to keep up with the demand. But periodically, the situation

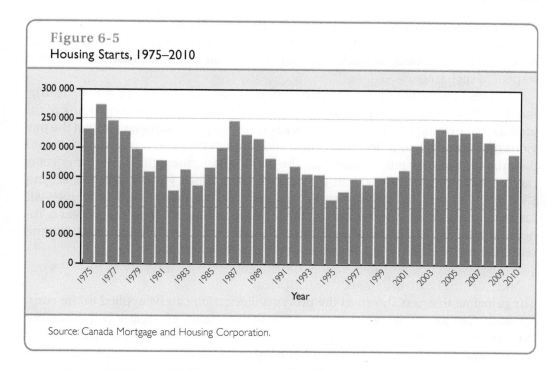

Figure 6-5
Housing Starts, 1975–2010

Year

Source: Canada Mortgage and Housing Corporation.

www.cmhc-schl.gc.ca

reverses itself—mortgage interest rates become high and people expect an economic slowdown in which interest rates and home prices may actually fall. So, the demand for homes falls sharply, and the residential construction industry goes into a slump.

Businesses' investment in inventories also fluctuates a great deal due to expectations. If retailers and wholesalers expect sales to be strong, they will spend heavily to add to their inventories. On the other hand, if sales are slow, retailers may spend little or nothing on inventory.

How Fluctuations in Investment Spending Affect the Economy

Obviously, such fluctuations in business investment spending will strongly affect the capital goods sector of the economy. High business investment spending will bring prosperity to industries such as construction and machinery and equipment, whereas periodic decreases in investment spending will mean hard times and layoffs in these industries.

But business investment spending and the capital-goods industries associated with it seldom amount to more than one-eighth of the nation's GDP, hardly enough to account for booms and recessions that affect most of the economy. For a fuller understanding of these broad economic fluctuations, we will need to go beyond the capital-goods sector, and examine how these variations in investment spending interact with the much larger consumption-spending sector. This brings us to the effects known as the *multiplier* and the *accelerator*, which are discussed in the following sections.

The Multiplier Effect

Suppose that a new family moves into a town and builds a $300 000 house, using local labour and materials. This will add $300 000 to the *incomes* of the townspeople involved. While some of this increase in incomes will go to taxes and some will be saved, much of it will be spent on consumer goods and services, such as clothes, home repairs, restaurant dinners, and so on. To those who receive this money—the tailor, plumber, and restaurant owner and employees—it represents an increase in *their* income. They will respend a large part of it on a variety of goods and services, generating additional income for the suppliers of those items, who, in turn, will increase *their* spending. This *respending effect* will continue as increases in income are respent again and again; however, it will grow weaker at each stage because not all of the increase in incomes is respent at each stage.

The result is similar to the ripples on a pond caused by throwing a stone: the original $300 000 spent on the new house is the initial splash, and the respending of the increases in income at each stage creates a series of ripples, each smaller than the previous one, spreading out from the centre and through the economy. Just as the stone disturbs the pond by much more than the initial splash, the *total* economic effect of the spending of the $300 000 on the house will be much greater than the original $300 000 because as the money is respent, total spending—and incomes—will increase in a series of stages following the initial spending. In effect, the impact of the original $300 000 will be magnified, or *multiplied*, by this respending effect. For this reason, the respending effect is known as the **multiplier effect**.

multiplier effect

The effect whereby fluctuations in spending (for instance, investment spending) spread by means of the respending effect through the economy, with the total impact on GDP and incomes being considerably larger than the initial fluctuations in spending.

A Numerical Example of the Multiplier

The principle that was shown in the previous illustration can be applied to the entire economy. Suppose total investment spending in the economy increases by $100 million over last year's levels, causing the incomes of people in the capital goods industries to be $100 million higher than last year. Not all of this $100 million of additional income will be spent on consumption—part will go to taxes, part will be saved, and part will be diverted to foreign nations through purchases of imports.

Assuming that taxes, saving, and imports absorb one-half of the increase in incomes, consumption spending will rise by $50 million over last year's level. This increase in consumer spending represents a $50-million increase in GDP *and income* to those who receive it. Assuming that they will also respend half of it, this respending will give rise to a further increase in consumption spending of $25 million, which boosts GDP and incomes by another $25 million. Of this $25 million of increased incomes, $12.5 million would be respent as the cycle continues, increasing *both GDP and total incomes* at each stage, as shown in Figure 6-6.

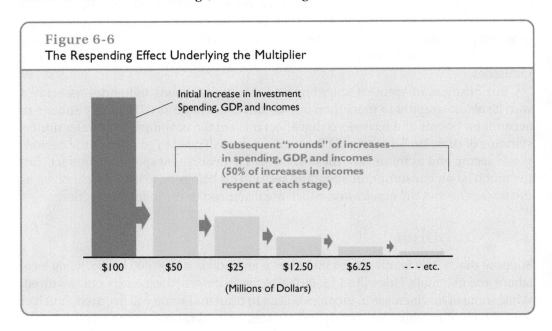

Figure 6-6
The Respending Effect Underlying the Multiplier

Initial Increase in Investment Spending, GDP, and Incomes

Subsequent "rounds" of increases in spending, GDP, and incomes (50% of increases in incomes respent at each stage)

$100 $50 $25 $12.50 $6.25   - - - etc.

(Millions of Dollars)

Obviously, the respending effect means that the initial investment project of $100 million has a much more far-reaching effect on the economy (that is, on GDP and total incomes) than its size suggests. To calculate the total impact of the $100 million of investment spending on the economy, we would have to add together all of the increases in spending, GDP, and incomes at each stage of the process: $100 million + $50 million + $25 million + $12.5 million, etc. And we would find that the $100 million of investment spending caused GDP and total incomes to rise by $200 million, as shown in Figure 6-7. In this example, the size of the multiplier is *2*, because an increase in investment of $100 million caused the GDP to rise by $200 million.

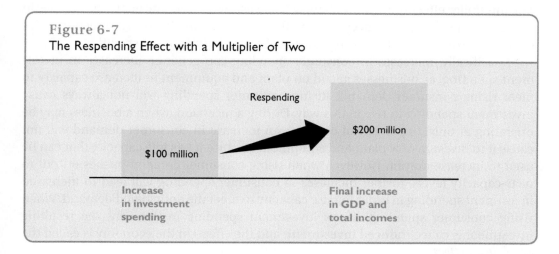

Figure 6-7
The Respending Effect with a Multiplier of Two

Respending

$100 million

$200 million

Increase
in investment
spending

Final increase
in GDP and
total incomes

The Canadian Multiplier

In the Canadian economy, the multiplier tends to be smaller than in the previous example (that is, 2), mostly because the respending effect is diminished by Canadians' high spending on imports. Various economic models and studies, using different assumptions, have developed estimates of the size of the Canadian multiplier. It has been estimated that, for government spending on capital formation (such as public works projects), the size of the multiplier is 1.6 over a one-year period. That is, a $1-million increase in expenditures on public works will boost GDP and total incomes by $1.6 million over the next year. Other studies have estimated the multiplier to be as large as 1.8 and as small as 1.0. These studies agree that the multiplier is higher during economic booms, when people are inclined to respend a greater proportion of any increases in their income, and smaller during recessions, when the opposite is true.

The Downward Multiplier

So far, we have applied the multiplier only to *increases* in investment spending. However, the multiplier also works in reverse. Suppose that investment spending *decreased* by $3.0 billion from the previous year's level. This decrease would *reduce* incomes, with the result that consumer spending would be cut back. These spending cuts would reduce other incomes, which would cause further spending cuts, and so on. This process is known as the *downward multiplier*. Obviously, it can make recessions more severe, by increasing the economic impact of reductions in investment spending. For instance, if the multiplier were 1.6, a reduction in investment of $3.0 billion would lead to a $4.8-billion decline in GDP and total incomes.

The Multiplier and Economic Instability

The multiplier effect contributes to economic instability because it magnifies the impact of any fluctuation in spending on the economy. For instance, with a multiplier of 1.6, fluctuations in investment spending of a magnitude of $5 billion will cause the

GDP and total incomes to fluctuate by roughly $8 billion. The multiplier effect also magnifies the impact of changes in other types of spending besides investment: it is through the multiplier effect that the entire Canadian economy feels the effects of seemingly local developments, such as increased exports of British Columbia resource products, falling wheat sales in the Prairies, or an investment boom in central Canada.

The Accelerator Effect

accelerator effect
The effect whereby rising consumption spending causes rapid increases in induced investment, and a slowing down or levelling off of consumption spending causes sharp declines in induced investment.

induced investment
Capital investment spending undertaken by business in response to increases in sales that have brought production to near-capacity levels and that are expected to continue.

The multiplier effect shows how changes in investment spending generate changes in consumer spending. The **accelerator effect** operates in the other direction, with changes in *consumption spending* causing changes in *investment spending*.

Specifically, increases in consumer spending can generate increases in investment spending, as businesses spend on plant and equipment to increase capacity to meet rising consumer demand. Rising consumer spending will not always cause investment spending to rise in this way. During a recession, when a business may be operating at only 70 percent of capacity, an increase in consumer demand will not cause it to invest in new plant and equipment because it has idle capacity that can be used to increase output. However, when rising consumer demand pushes output to near-capacity levels, further increases in consumer spending will lead to increased investment spending in order to raise capacity to meet the anticipated demand. When rising consumer spending affects investment spending in this way, the resulting investment is called **induced investment**, and the effect on the economy is called the *accelerator effect*.

So, during an economic boom in which many industries are operating near capacity, rising consumer spending can kick off a *surge* of investment spending, which will create a *strong boom* in the capital goods industries (construction, machinery, steel, building materials, and so on). This is illustrated in year 20X2 in Figure 6-8, and can also be seen in the late 1990s in Figure 6-4 on page 126.

However, this boom in the capital goods industries may well prove to be temporary. Soon manufacturers will have enough capital equipment for their present level of sales, and they will not order any more new capital equipment unless consumer spending (that is, their sales) *increases further*. Year 20X3 of Figure 6-8 illustrates this point: the

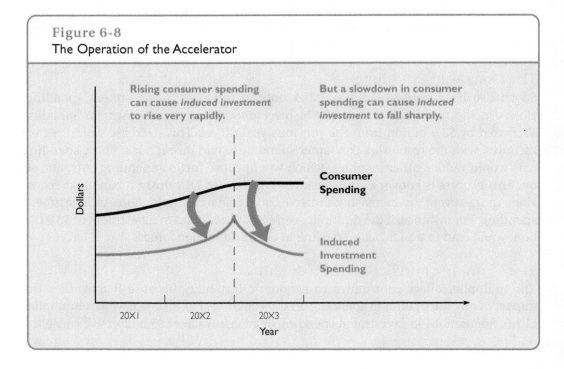

Figure 6-8
The Operation of the Accelerator

Rising consumer spending can cause *induced investment* to rise very rapidly.

But a slowdown in consumer spending can cause *induced investment* to fall sharply.

Consumer Spending

Induced Investment Spending

Dollars

20X1   20X2   20X3

Year

slowdown of consumer spending has a drastic effect on manufacturers' orders for new capital equipment, so that a mere *slowdown* in consumer spending causes a *sharp decline* in induced investment. So, induced investment is a particularly fragile component of investment spending—for induced investment to be *sustained*, consumer spending must *keep rising continuously*. And, when consumer spending merely slows down or levels off, induced investment will fall sharply.

Ironically, in year 20X3 of Figure 6-8, consumer spending, while barely rising, is nonetheless at record-high levels, whereas induced investment has declined sharply from its previous levels. This disparity helps explain why, while the economy in general ("Consumer Spending" on the graph) is prosperous, there can be a slump in the capital goods industries ("Induced Investment Spending" on the graph). So, industries such as construction, steel, and machinery can experience slumps *simply because consumption spending isn't rising fast enough*. As a result, induced investment is very unstable, which helps to explain why capital goods industries tend to experience "feast-or-famine" cycles, and also why the economy tends to experience ups and downs.

To aggravate the situation even further, the decline in induced investment can drag the level of consumption spending down with it through the multiplier effect.

The Multiplier and Accelerator Effects Combined

We have seen how the multiplier and the accelerator operate separately. But when the multiplier and accelerator *combine*, they can add even greater momentum to a boom.

In Figure 6-9, an economic boom is in progress. Rising investment spending is boosting incomes and consumption spending through the respending effect of the multiplier. And if the rising consumption spending pushes production to near-capacity levels, the accelerator effect will cause induced investment to increase. This further increase in investment spending will boost the economy to even higher levels, as the multiplier and accelerator effects are combined.

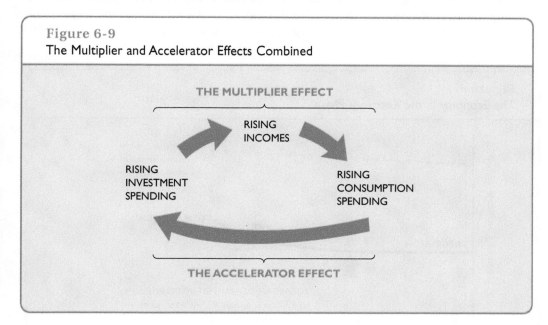

Figure 6-9
The Multiplier and Accelerator Effects Combined

THE MULTIPLIER EFFECT

RISING INCOMES

RISING INVESTMENT SPENDING

RISING CONSUMPTION SPENDING

THE ACCELERATOR EFFECT

Exports as a Source of Economic Instability

With about 30 percent of its GDP sold in export markets (over 70 percent of this to the United States alone), Canada is particularly exposed to international economic fluctuations. When other nations, especially the United States, have economic booms, their demand for Canadian exports adds significantly to aggregate demand in Canada, thus boosting the economy. And, when these nations experience economic slow-downs, their demand for Canadian products slumps significantly, with serious effects on the Canadian economy.

The effects of such fluctuations in exports are not, however, confined to regions and industries linked directly to Canada's export industries. The multiplier effect spreads their effects throughout the economy, and can contribute to a more general economic boom or slowdown.

So economic trends in other countries, especially the United States, are an important source of economic fluctuations in Canada. Unlike the other causes of instability examined earlier in this chapter, the source of this problem lies outside Canada. We will consider the matter of Canada's international trade more fully in Chapters 9 to 12.

The Dynamics of Business Cycles

We have seen how several factors can cause the economy to swing between boom and recession—fluctuations in investment spending, the multiplier effect, the accelerator effect, and fluctuations in exports. Next, we will examine the *actual dynamics* of economic instability—how these and other factors *interact* in order to cause the economy to undergo swings between booms and recessions, and how those swings, once started, can *gain momentum*, making the fluctuations of the economy more severe. No two booms or slumps are the same, but the following will show the typical kinds of interactions that occur in the economy as it swings upward and downward.

To illustrate the dynamics of business cycles, we will use the *supply side–demand side* model from Chapter 4. This model is shown in Figure 6-10, in which the supply side of the economy is represented by the dotted line, which shows potential (capacity) output rising gradually, and the demand side is represented by the solid line showing the level of aggregate demand in the economy. We will start at the stage of the cycle at which the economy is beginning to recover from a recession.

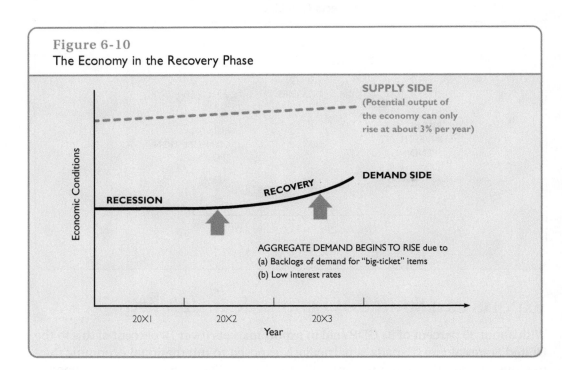

Figure 6-10
The Economy in the Recovery Phase

SUPPLY SIDE
(Potential output of the economy can only rise at about 3% per year)

DEMAND SIDE

RECESSION   RECOVERY

Economic Conditions

AGGREGATE DEMAND BEGINS TO RISE due to
(a) Backlogs of demand for "big-ticket" items
(b) Low interest rates

20X1   20X2   20X3
Year

The Recovery Phase

In year 20X1 in Figure 6-10, aggregate demand is far below the capacity output of the supply side of the economy. Businesses are operating well below their capacity output level, and unemployment is high.

In years 20X2 and 20X3, the economy is in its *recovery* phase from the recession. Aggregate demand has started to rise, causing output and employment to rise slowly. Demand could be rising for various reasons, such as

- *Backlogs of demand* for certain consumer goods probably exist. In particular, during the recession, consumers have probably postponed purchases of "big-ticket" items such as cars and houses, and the appliances and furniture that are often bought with a new house.
- *Low interest rates* could be making it more attractive to borrow money for such purchases. Interest rates tend to be lower during recessions, to encourage borrowing. To finance such purchases, consumers will take out bank loans. This will speed up the money-creation process described in Chapter 5, causing the money supply to begin to increase and contributing to the growth of aggregate demand.

As aggregate demand slowly increases, output and employment will gradually start to recover from the recession. At this point in the recovery, the rising level of aggregate demand will generate little or no additional inflation in the economy. The supply side of the economy can easily increase output to match demand, because firms have excess plant capacity and ready access to labour and materials.

The Expansion (Boom) Phase

In Figure 6-11, the economy is moving into the *expansion* (or *boom*) phase of the business cycle in years 20X3 and 20X4, as rising aggregate demand is driving output and employment toward quite high levels.

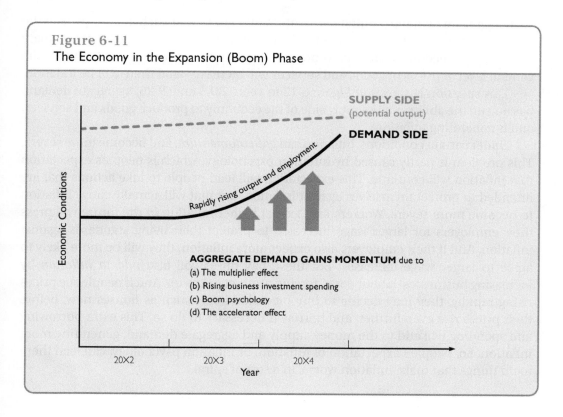

Figure 6-11
The Economy in the Expansion (Boom) Phase

SUPPLY SIDE (potential output)

DEMAND SIDE

Rapidly rising output and employment

AGGREGATE DEMAND GAINS MOMENTUM due to
(a) The multiplier effect
(b) Rising business investment spending
(c) Boom psychology
(d) The accelerator effect

Economic Conditions

20X2   20X3   20X4
Year

During the boom phase, the increases in demand are gaining momentum, pulling output and employment upward at a faster pace. The economy *gains momentum* in this way for various reasons:

(a) *The multiplier effect.* Through the multiplier effect, explained earlier in this chapter, rising spending will generate higher incomes, which will lead to a chain reaction of respending that will boost consumption spending further.

(b) *Rising business investment spending.* As the economic outlook improves, and with interest rates still low, business investment spending can be expected to increase, generating additional increases in employment, incomes, and aggregate demand.

(c) *Boom psychology.* As the economic boom progresses, consumers and business people will feel more confident about the economic future. This **boom psychology** will make them more willing to borrow money to buy houses, and big-ticket consumer durable goods (such as cars, appliances, and furniture) and capital goods for businesses. As bank lending increases to finance these purchases, the money-creation process will speed up further and the money supply will grow at a faster rate, adding momentum to the pace of spending.

(d) *The accelerator effect.* Later in the boom, when rising consumer spending pushes output to near capacity levels, the accelerator effect will add further to demand. At this point, induced investment spending will push aggregate demand, output, employment, and incomes even higher.

The combined effect of these factors can become quite strong. Together, they can cause aggregate demand, output, and employment to rise rapidly in an economic boom, as shown in years 20X3 and 20X4 in Figure 6-11. However, such high levels of aggregate demand can bring not only an economic boom but also a troublesome side effect—*inflation*.

The Inflation Phase

With aggregate demand gaining momentum and growing at such a rapid pace in the boom phase of the cycle, it is quite possible that demand will rise to the point where it exceeds the economy's ability to produce goods and services. If this happens, the general level of prices of goods and services will increase—and there will be inflation.

This situation is shown in Figure 6-12 in years 20X5 and 20X6; aggregate demand has outrun the ability of the supply side of the economy to produce goods and services, and is generating inflation.

Under certain conditions, inflation can *gain momentum*, and become more severe. This problem is partly caused by **inflation psychology**, which is people's expectation that inflation will continue. This expectation will lead people to take actions that are intended to protect themselves against inflation, but that will actually cause inflation to become more severe. Workers who expect higher inflation in the future will press their employers for larger wage increases to protect their living standards against inflation. And if their employers also expect more inflation, they will be more likely to agree to larger wage increases. But these pay raises will also *add to inflation* by increasing businesses' labour costs, forcing product prices up. And if people see prices rising rapidly, they may decide to buy big-ticket items such as houses now, before their prices rise even further, and borrow if necessary to do so. This extra borrowing and spending will add to the money supply and aggregate demand, generating more inflation. So, people's expectation of inflation, or inflation psychology, can lead them to do things that make inflation worse, in a sort of spiral.

boom psychology
People's expectation of a future boom that makes them more willing to borrow to buy big-ticket items and capital goods.

inflation psychology
People's expectation of future inflation that leads them to seek larger wage increases and to make purchases of some big-ticket items quickly, before prices rise further.

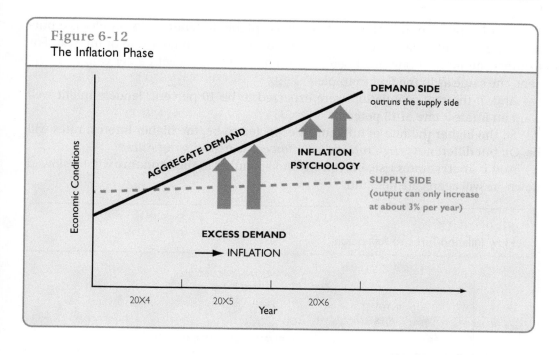

Figure 6-12
The Inflation Phase

The Peak of the Cycle: How a Boom Can Become a Downturn

Once inflation becomes severe, it has a strong tendency to lead toward an economic downturn, or recession. The main reason for this tendency is that *rapid inflation causes high interest rates*.[1]

If lenders fear that inflation will erode the value of their capital, they will insist upon higher interest rates to compensate for this problem. For instance, suppose that someone offers to borrow $100 from you for one year, and to pay you 6-percent interest for the year. Whether this is an attractive investment for you depends on the *rate of inflation* for the next year.

If the rate of inflation were 3 percent,		
you would gain on the interest you receive:	$6	(6% of $100)
while inflation would reduce the purchasing power of your $100 by 3 percent, or $3, causing you to lose:	3	
for a net <u>gain</u> of:	$3	
On the other hand, if the rate of inflation were 7 percent,		
you would gain on the interest you receive:	$6	
while inflation would reduce the purchasing power of your $100 by 7 percent, or $7, causing you to lose:	7	
for a net <u>loss</u> of:	$1	

---

[1]Actually, it is lenders' *expectations* of inflation in the future that leads them to increase interest rates. Usually, however, it is rapid inflation *today* that leads to such fear of inflation *in the future*, so we just say that high rates of inflation cause high interest rates.

Clearly, the second case would be unacceptable to lenders. To protect the purchasing power of their savings, they would insist upon a higher rate of interest. For instance, an interest rate of 10 percent would leave lenders with a net gain of 3 percent, the same as in the first example.

And, if the rate of inflation were expected to be 10 percent, lenders might well want an interest rate of 13 percent.

So the higher the rate of inflation is expected to be, the higher interest rates will be. Or, put differently: *High rates of inflation cause high interest rates.*

And if interest rates rise, borrowing and spending in the economy will be slowed down, as will aggregate demand.

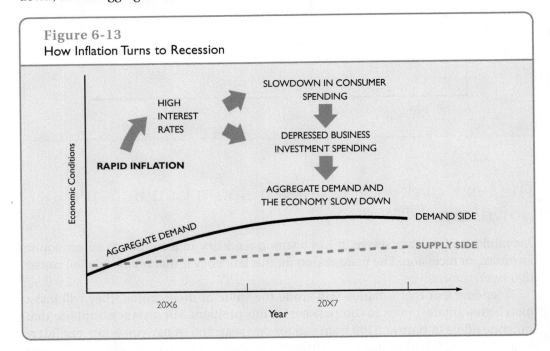

Figure 6-13
How Inflation Turns to Recession

This problem is shown in Figure 6-13, in year 20X7. High interest rates are
(a) depressing (slowing down) consumer spending on big-ticket items such as houses and cars because consumers are reluctant to borrow at such high interest rates to buy these things, and
(b) depressing business investment spending, because

- businesses are reluctant to borrow at high interest rates to finance investment projects, and
- with consumer spending slowing down due to the reason in (a) above, businesses do not need to expand as they had been doing in the previous few years. Note that the point at which a slowdown in consumer spending leads to a cutback in induced investment is where the accelerator effect, described earlier in the chapter, takes place.

As a result, by the end of year 20X7, aggregate demand begins to weaken, the period of boom/inflation comes to an end, and the economy hovers on the edge of a recession.

The Recession Phase

Figure 6-14 shows the economy sliding into recession in years 20X8 and 20X9. Aggregate demand is falling, output is decreasing, and unemployment is rising.

We have seen how inflation and high interest rates will have already slowed down consumer spending and business investment spending. Once the economy *starts* into

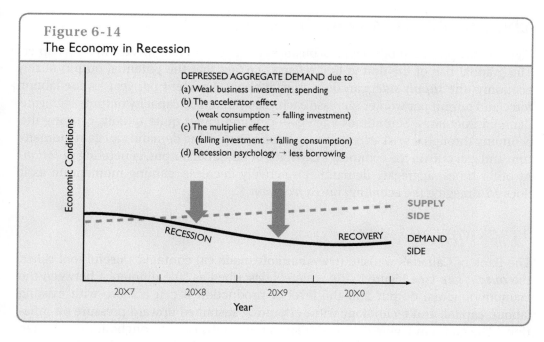

Figure 6-14
The Economy in Recession

DEPRESSED AGGREGATE DEMAND due to
(a) Weak business investment spending
(b) The accelerator effect
     (weak consumption → falling investment)
(c) The multiplier effect
     (falling investment → falling consumption)
(d) Recession psychology → less borrowing

a recession, factors tend to come into play that cause the recession to *gain momentum* and become more severe. These are the same factors that operated during an economic boom, but in a recession, they work in the opposite direction:

(a) *Weak business investment spending.* In a recession, business investment spending tends to fall especially rapidly, because expectations and business confidence tend to be particularly low during recessions.

(b) *The accelerator effect.* With consumer spending levelling off, many businesses will not need to buy as much additional new capital equipment as in the recent past. As a result, their purchases of capital goods will tend to decrease. This behaviour is an example of the accelerator effect operating in reverse—that is, depressing investment spending rather than boosting it.

(c) *The multiplier effect.* In a recession, the multiplier effect also operates in reverse. As business investment spending decreases, incomes in the capital goods sector decrease as workers are laid off, which in turn causes reductions in consumer income and depresses consumer spending. Like a chain reaction, these decreases in consumer spending spread through the economy, dragging down incomes and consumer spending.

(d) *Recession psychology.* Fearing unemployment, consumers tend to borrow and spend less during a recession. Similarly, since businesses expect slow sales, they tend to borrow and spend less because there is no need to expand production capacity or to increase inventory. This **recession psychology** drags aggregate demand down even further, taking with it output, employment, and incomes.

In addition, many consumers and businesses could by now have become concerned about the high levels of debt that they have accumulated over the previous few years. With already heavy debt loads and interest payments, and facing increasingly uncertain prospects for the economy, both consumers and businesses may decide to avoid further borrowing, and concentrate instead on repaying their debts. This decline in borrowing and new stress on debt repayment will create an additional drag on aggregate demand, slowing the economy further.

The factors discussed above will tend to cause the recession to deepen and become more severe. Finally, the recession will "bottom out" and another recovery can begin. This is shown in year 20X0 when a backlog of consumer spending, with the help of low interest rates, marks the beginning of another cycle.

recession psychology
People's concerns regarding recession and unemployment that lead them to curtail their spending, especially on big-ticket items that require borrowing.

The Business Cycle in Review

Figure 6-16 opposite shows a typical business cycle such as that covered in this chapter. The gradual rise of the dotted line reflects the fact that the potential output of the economy (the *supply side*) can only grow at about 3 percent per year, as the labour force and output per worker increase each year. But unlike capacity output, aggregate demand fluctuates. Sometimes aggregate demand grows quite rapidly, carrying the economy through a brisk *expansion*, or boom. Such rising demand can gain momentum and can outrun the economy's capacity, or potential output, generating *inflation*. At other times, aggregate demand can actually decrease, gaining momentum as it does so, dragging the economy into a *recession*.

Tracking the Cycle

The Bank of Canada's website (**www.bankofcanada.ca**) contains a useful tool called the *output gap* (see Figure 6-15), which is described as "the difference between the economy's actual output and the level of production it can achieve with existing labour, capital, and technology without putting sustained upward pressure on inflation." The graph in Figure 6-15 is similar to the graphs used throughout this chapter, with one exception—capacity output is represented by the *horizontal* line at zero, and the graph shows how far actual output (aggregate demand) is below or above capacity, in percentage terms. The graph clearly shows the recession of the early 1990s, when actual output was 3–4 percent below capacity, the strong economic boom of 2005–07, and the sharp decline in economic activity in late 2008–09, as the U.S. recession spread to Canada.

www.bankofcanada.ca/en/
rates/indinf/product_graph_
en.html

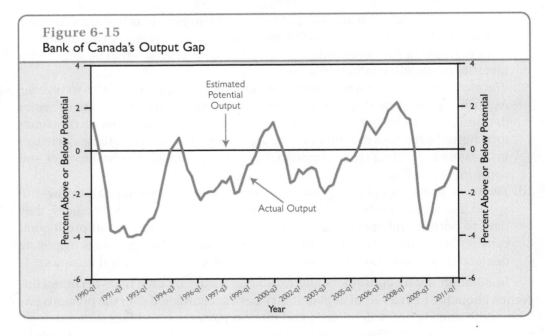

Figure 6-15
Bank of Canada's Output Gap

Economic Forecasting

"The experience of being disastrously wrong is salutary. No economist should be denied it, and not many are."

— JOHN KENNETH GALBRAITH

Obviously, it would be very useful for strategic economic decision-makers in business and government to have advance notice of future economic conditions, so that they could make timely preparations for them. However, it is easier to *appreciate* the value of accurate economic forecasts than it is to actually *prepare* them.

Figure 6-16
The Business Cycle in Review

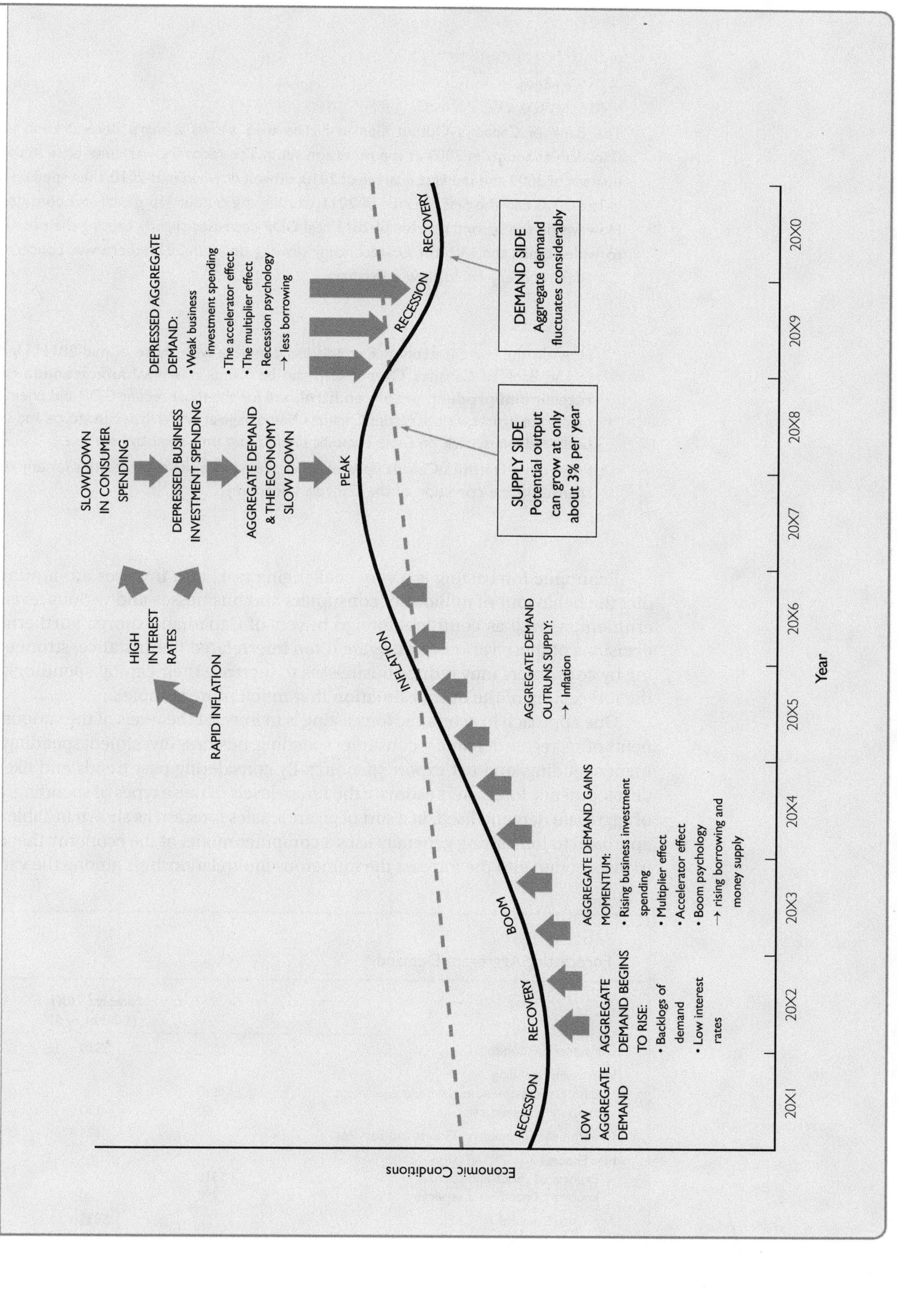

DEPRESSED AGGREGATE DEMAND:
- Weak business investment spending
- The accelerator effect
- The multiplier effect
- Recession psychology
  → less borrowing

SLOWDOWN IN CONSUMER SPENDING

DEPRESSED BUSINESS INVESTMENT SPENDING

AGGREGATE DEMAND & THE ECONOMY SLOW DOWN

PEAK

HIGH INTEREST RATES

RAPID INFLATION

AGGREGATE DEMAND OUTRUNS SUPPLY:
→ Inflation

AGGREGATE DEMAND GAINS MOMENTUM:
- Rising business investment spending
- Multiplier effect
- Accelerator effect
- Boom psychology
  → rising borrowing and money supply

LOW AGGREGATE DEMAND

AGGREGATE DEMAND BEGINS TO RISE:
- Backlogs of demand
- Low interest rates

DEMAND SIDE
Aggregate demand fluctuates considerably

SUPPLY SIDE
Potential output can grow at only about 3% per year

RECESSION   RECOVERY   BOOM   INFLATION   PEAK   RECESSION   RECOVERY

20X1   20X2   20X3   20X4   20X5   20X6   20X7   20X8   20X9   20X0

Year

Economic Conditions

YOU DECIDE

Where Are We Now?

The Bank of Canada's Output Gap in Figure 6-15 shows a sharp deterioration in the Canadian economy in 2009 as the recession set in. The recovery was quite brisk in the last quarter of 2009 and the first quarter of 2010, slowed down in mid-2010, then sped up again in late 2010 and the first quarter of 2011, causing the output gap to narrow considerably. However, in the second quarter of 2011 real GDP *decreased* slightly, causing the output gap to widen again, and with the U.S. economy slowing down in 2011, there was concern that Canada's recovery could slow down, too.

QUESTIONS

1. How do the current economic conditions compare with those of mid-2011? Updates to the Bank of Canada's Output Gap can be found at **www.bankofcanada.ca/en/rates/indinf/product_graph_en.html**, and for the most recent GDP and unemployment rate figures, visit Statistics Canada's home page at **www.statcan.gc.ca** and under *Latest Indicators*, click on *Gross domestic product* and on *Unemployment rate*.

2. From these Statistics Canada updates, what seem to be the main reasons for any recent changes in the condition of the Canadian economy?

Economic forecasting is a very challenging task, as it involves attempting to predict the behaviour of millions of consumers and businesses and various levels of government, as well as countless foreign buyers of Canadian exports. Furthermore, the decisions of these various groups are often interrelated (for instance, stronger spending by consumers may induce businesses to increase their capital spending), making the forecasting of the overall situation that much more complex.

One approach to economic forecasting is to forecast the levels of the various components of aggregate demand—consumer spending, business investment spending, government spending, and net export spending. By considering past trends and likely future developments, forecasters estimate the future levels of these types of spending, and thus of aggregate demand itself, in a sort of gigantic sales forecast, as shown in Table 6-1. This approach to forecasting generally uses a computer model of the economy that attempts to incorporate into the forecast the numerous interrelationships among the variables in

Table 6-1
Forecasting Aggregate Demand

		Forecast 20X1 (Billions of $)
Consumer Expenditure		$510
Investment Spending		
Business investment in plant and equipment	$90	
Housing expenditure	40	130
Government Spending on Goods and Services		175
Net Exports		
Exports of goods and services	$310	
Imports of goods and services	290	20
Aggregate Demand		$835

the forecast. Table 6-1 merely shows the results of such a forecast; it does not reveal the complexity of the process by which such a forecast would be developed.

Another way to gain advance indications of changes in the direction of the economy is through **leading economic indicators**. The values of these economic statistics tend to increase *before* the economy speeds up, and to decrease *before* a downturn begins.

Through a combination of theory and experience, economists have developed several such leading indicators. Some of these are stock prices, money supply data, the average number of hours worked per week, statistics on housing and housing starts, orders for durable goods, and the U.S. leading indicator.

Often, several of these statistics are combined, or averaged, into what is known as a *composite leading indicator*. Because it includes a broader range of data than any one indicator, a composite indicator is considered more reliable. Figure 6-17 shows Statistics Canada's Composite Leading Indicator, which contains 10 components, over the 2005–09 period. Note how the rising leading indicator in 2005 gave early indications of the strong economic boom that would occur in 2006–07, whereas as early as the second half of 2007, the leading indicator was providing advance notice of the economic downturn that would occur in 2008–09. More rapid increases in the indicator after mid-2009 preceded the recovery, while slower increases in mid-2011 raised concerns.

leading economic indicators
Economic statistics that tend to increase or decrease in advance of increases or decreases in the pace of economic activity, thus giving advance notice of changes in economic trends.

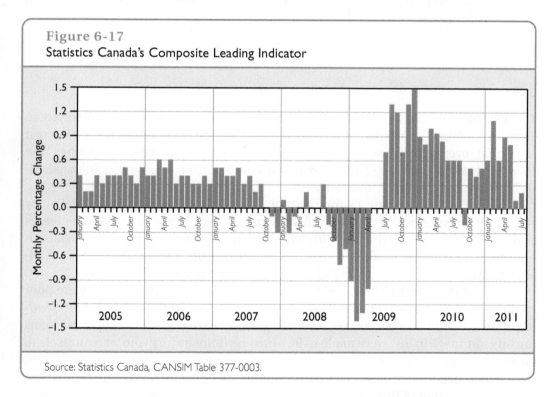

Figure 6-17
Statistics Canada's Composite Leading Indicator

Source: Statistics Canada, CANSIM Table 377-0003.

www.statcan.ca
(published monthly with *The Daily*)

Aggregate Demand and Supply Curves and the Business Cycle

The aggregate supply curve and aggregate demand curve that we saw in Chapters 3 and 4 respectively can be used to illustrate the business cycle. In Figure 6-18, aggregate demand curve AD represents a recession—demand and real GDP are well below capacity, unemployment would be high and the rate of inflation low. Aggregate demand curve AD_1 shows the economy having moved into a boom— higher demand has pulled real GDP up to capacity, and unemployment would be lower but the rate of inflation would be higher. And aggregate demand curve AD_2 shows an overheated economy in which demand has exceeded capacity, output cannot keep up with demand, and prices are rising rapidly.

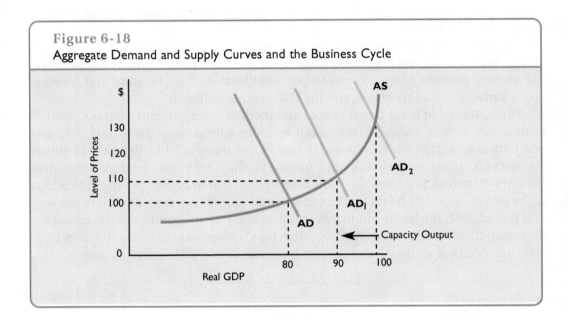

Figure 6-18
Aggregate Demand and Supply Curves and the Business Cycle

The "Balance Sheet Recession" of 2008–09

The recession of 2008–09 was different from the "typical" recession portrayed in Chapter 6, which is preceded by a rising rate of inflation that leads to higher interest rates that eventually slow down borrowing and aggregate demand. Rather, the 2008–09 recession was the result of an unusual event known as a "severe financial crisis" that occurred in the United States.

The 2003–07 period saw a strong economic boom in the United States, fuelled by very low interest rates and readily available loans. This generated very rapid increases in the price of housing, which in turn led to soaring demand for housing (because it seemed like a sure-fire profitable asset to buy, and mortgage loans were readily available at low interest rates), and even faster-rising home prices.

Much of this demand for housing came from low-income buyers who were poor credit risks. At the end of Chapter 5, we saw how in the United States, in the years leading up to the recession of 2008–09, a very large number of high-risk "subprime" loans (mostly mortgage loans) were made to low-income homebuyers who were unlikely to be able to repay those loans. In addition, many people who already owned homes were encouraged to increase their consumption spending by borrowing against the rapidly rising value of their homes; that is, they took out loans using their homes as collateral. Millions of loans of these types worth billions of dollars were then "securitized", that is, bundled together into securities that resembled bonds in that they paid interest and were backed by assets (the borrowers' homes). These securities were then rated by bond rating agencies as very secure ("AAA") investments[1] and were sold to various investors, mostly financial institutions such as banks, insurance companies, and various investment funds, including pension funds.

---

[1]The role of the rating agencies was very important, as their "AAA" ratings reassured many investors that these "securitized" mortgage bonds were as safe as U.S. government bonds.

Beginning in 2006 and accelerating after that, more and more subprime borrowers defaulted on their mortgages[2]. Lenders then foreclosed on their homes, and put them up for sale. This large increase in the supply of homes on the market started a downward spiral in housing prices that continued for several years. In several regions of the United States, home prices fell sharply, including the value of the homes of people who had not borrowed excessively, or at all.

These developments crippled many consumers financially, because they were burdened in either or both of the following ways:

- *very heavy liabilities* due to the heavy borrowing that they had done prior to the recession, plus
- *a sharp reduction in the value of their assets* (mainly homes but also stocks and investments for their retirement)

The result was a sharp deterioration in the balance sheets of many American families—too many liabilities and not enough assets. This made American consumers unwilling (or unable) to borrow more, and forced them to reduce their consumption spending in order to pay down debt.

Lenders had their own balance sheet problems, too. Many banks found themselves holding large amounts of "securitized" assets such as mortgage bonds that had been rated "AAA" but had suddenly lost much of their value. Banks and other financial institutions found themselves saddled with these "toxic assets" on *their* balance sheets, which they could neither sell nor borrow against. This left them unsure of their financial position, and afraid to lend. Lending was also curtailed because the "securitization" process described in Chapter 5 dried up, as investors refused to buy those "securitized" loans. From 2006 to 2008, the amount of securitized investments bought by investors fell from $753 billion to only $139 billion—*a decrease of 82 percent.*

Another problem with balance sheet recessions is a *lack of confidence* on the part of both consumers and lenders. Preoccupied by their debt burden, consumers hold back from borrowing and spending, while banks become more concerned about the risks associated with lending and more cautious about lending to consumers and businesses.

With borrowers unable or unwilling to borrow and lenders unable or unwilling to lend, the level of aggregate demand in the United States fell sharply. The resulting recession was known as a "balance sheet recession" because its origins lay in the balance sheets of consumers, who had heavy liabilities and whose assets had lost much of their value. The balance sheet problems of lenders made the recession worse, because lenders' lack of confidence in the value of the assets on their balance sheets reduced their willingness to make new loans.

The problem with balance sheet recessions is that the recovery from them tends to be long and slow because consumers are so burdened with debt that for several years they are forced to curtail their consumption spending in order to pay down their debts. Whereas the economy can usually recover from a typical recession in one to two years, the recovery from a balance sheet recession can take from five to seven years. In the United States, the recession was *technically* over when real GDP stopped falling in the summer of 2009 and the unemployment rate was 9.7 percent, but by mid-2011, real GDP had risen by only 1.6 percent over the past 12 months, and the unemployment rate was still a high 9.1 percent. Only after U.S. consumers had worked off their debts was economic growth likely to resume, and it was projected that this was not likely until mid-2012 at the earliest.

---

[2]A wave of defaults was inevitable, because many subprime mortgage lenders had lured borrowers with low "teaser" interest rates for the first two years, after which the interest rates would increase to levels that made it impossible for most borrowers to make the payments.

The situation was less severe in Canada; consumer debt was very high, but consumers had not suffered the devastating reduction in the value of their homes and other assets that many Americans did. However, the economic weakness in the United States due to these problems would also affect Canada, through weaker exports to the USA.

For a more detailed account of these matters, see the *Lessons from the Recession* supplement to this text.

Conclusion

Market economies—in which consumers and businesses are free to spend or not spend, as they see fit—have a natural tendency toward instability. At times, consumers and businesses will spend strongly, pushing aggregate demand upward and generating economic booms, while at other times, demand will be weak and the economy will experience recessions. And when these economic fluctuations become severe, they can cause serious problems.

The hardships associated with recessions are well known. In fact, many people have experienced unemployment, or know people who have been unemployed. And, as we will see in Chapter 7, "Stabilizing the Economy: Government Monetary and Fiscal Policies," the experience of the Great Depression of the 1930s left a permanent imprint upon government economic policy, in the form of an undertaking in 1945 to maintain "a high and stable level of employment."

The worst experience with inflation was the Great Inflation of the 1970s and 1980s, when the rate of inflation reached 12 percent per year at one point. This experience showed that high rates of inflation cause serious economic problems:

- Rapidly rising prices can make a nation's products less competitive internationally. This is a serious concern for a country such as Canada, which exports about 30 percent of its GDP.
- Rapid inflation causes hardship for people who cannot increase their incomes as fast as prices are rising.
- Rapid inflation causes very high interest rates, which can lead to an economic downturn and high unemployment.

The experience of the 1970s and 1980s left its own imprint upon government policy, in the form of an undertaking in 1991 that the rate of inflation would be kept below a maximum of 3 percent per year.

The problem of economic instability has historically been one of the most serious weaknesses of the market system economy. In this chapter, we have examined the causes of this problem; in Chapters 7 and 8, we will see what governments have been able to do to try to correct it.

Chapter Summary

1. The basic cause of business cycles is fluctuations in aggregate demand for goods and services. (L.O. 1)
2. Various factors contribute to fluctuations in aggregate demand and business cycles, including
   (a) fluctuations in business investment spending, (L.O. 2a)
   (b) the multiplier effect, whereby fluctuations in investment spending cause fluctuations in consumption spending, (L.O. 2b)

(c) the accelerator effect, through which fluctuations in consumption spending cause much sharper fluctuations in induced investment, (L.O. 2c)

(d) fluctuations in the confidence of consumers and business people (L.O. 2d), and

(e) inflation psychology. (L.O. 2e)

3. In the *recovery phase* of the cycle, the economy is recovering from a recession as aggregate demand is starting to grow, perhaps due to backlogs of demand for big-ticket items and low interest rates. (L.O. 3a)

4. In the *expansion (boom) phase*, aggregate demand is rising and gaining momentum, as consumption spending and investment spending boost each other through the multiplier and accelerator effects, and *boom psychology* encourages higher levels of borrowing and spending. (L.O. 3b)

5. In the *inflation phase*, aggregate demand has begun to outrun the capacity of the economy to produce goods and services, causing the rate of inflation to increase. Inflation psychology may cause inflation to gain momentum. (L.O. 3c)

6. At the peak of the cycle, inflation causes higher interest rates, which depress consumer spending on housing and big-ticket items. Business investment spending is also depressed by higher interest rates and the slowdown in consumer spending, and aggregate demand weakens. (L.O. 3d)

7. In the *recession phase*, aggregate demand falls. The multiplier and accelerator effects operate in reverse, with low consumer spending pulling down investment spending and low investment spending dragging down employment, incomes, and consumer spending. Recession psychology depresses aggregate demand further. (L.O. 3e)

8. The Bank of Canada's output gap tracks the business cycle by estimating the difference between the economy's capacity output and aggregate demand. (L.O. 4)

9. Economists attempt to forecast the future direction of the economy by preparing forecasts of the level of aggregate demand and through using leading economic indicators. (L.O. 5)

10. Aggregate supply and aggregate demand curves can be used to illustrate the business cycle. (L.O. 6)

Questions

1. During a recession,
   (a) aggregate demand is depressed, causing output and employment to be depressed and prices to rise.
   (b) aggregate demand is depressed and output and employment rise, causing prices to fall.
   (c) aggregate demand is depressed, causing output, employment, and prices to be depressed.
   (d) prices fall, causing aggregate demand to rise and output and employment to rise.
   (e) prices rise, causing output, employment, and aggregate demand to fall.

2. Suppose that there were indications that the economy was in the early stages of a recession. Explain three reasons why government economic policy-makers might be concerned that the recession could become more severe in the future.

3. Which *one* of the following would be most likely to experience high unemployment during a recession? Explain the reason for your answer.
   (a) teachers
   (b) managers

(c) employees of insurance companies

(d) bricklayers

(e) employees of Canada Post

4. Explain why each of the following is or is not likely to occur during a typical economic recession.

(a) automobile sales decrease

(b) interest rates decline

(c) housing sales are depressed

(d) the rate of inflation increases

(e) unemployment increases

5. Explain why each of the following is or is not likely to occur during a typical economic boom.

(a) housing sales increase rapidly

(b) capital investment spending by business increases more rapidly

(c) the prices of goods and services in general increase more rapidly

(d) automobile sales increase rapidly

(e) interest rates decrease

6. (a) At what stage of the business cycle does *inflation* tend to become a problem?

(b) Why does inflation tend to become a problem at this stage of the cycle rather than at other stages?

7. (a) Explain why inflation is a problem that, once started, can gain momentum and become an increasingly serious problem.

(b) If the rate of inflation is rising significantly, what will happen to interest rates? Why?

8. In the years before the Great Depression of the 1930s, 5 percent of Americans received 33 percent of all personal income. Explain why such a high concentration of income in the hands of a few people made the U.S. economy more vulnerable to a severe downturn.

9. Visit Statistics Canada at **www.statcan.gc.ca** and find the following statistics for the past three years:

• Unemployment rate: Search the site for "Labour force characteristics", then click on "Labour force characteristics".

• Inflation rate: Search the site for "Consumer price index, historical summary".

• Trends in demand: Search the site for "Gross domestic product, expenditure-based", then click on "Gross domestic product, expenditure-based".

(a) What are the trends over the past three years in the unemployment rate and the rate of inflation?

(b) What recent trends in aggregate demand, and in particular components of demand, might help to explain the trends in (a)? (*Hint: To see the trend in each component of aggregate demand, calculate the percentage change over the period under review.*)

Study Guide

Review Questions (The answers to these Review Questions appear in Appendix B.)

1. The most basic reason why the economy experiences booms, recessions, and inflation is _____.

2. Which one of the following statements best describes the behaviour of investment spending?
   (a) It regularly increases over past levels.
   (b) It is quite variable—although the general long-term trend has been upward, from time to time it actually declines.
   (c) It is very steady—the most dependable component of total spending.
   (d) It is stagnant—it seldom rises much above past levels.
   (e) It generally rises when GDP is falling and falls when GDP is rising.

3. Business investment spending behaves in the way described in the previous question because
   (a) business profits vary considerably from year to year.
   (b) consumer spending often fluctuates considerably from year to year.
   (c) interest rates tend to rise and fall from year to year.
   (d) business expectations of future profits vary considerably from year to year.
   (e) Both (c) and (d).

4. The effect of this behaviour of business investment spending on the economy is
   (a) to contribute to the economy's tendency to undergo swings between booms and recessions.
   (b) to cause the unemployment rate to increase continually.
   (c) to generate steady economic progress.
   (d) to cause continual inflation.
   (e) to smooth out the business cycle.

5. The basic reason why the *multiplier effect* exists is that
   (a) increases in consumption spending always lead to increases in investment spending.
   (b) increases in consumption spending will lead to increases in investment spending if businesses are producing at or near capacity levels.
   (c) governments often tax the same product or transaction more than once.
   (d) increases in income tend to be partially respent, generating further increases in income and spending.
   (e) higher incomes are taxed at higher rates of taxation.

6. Because of the multiplier effect
   (a) upswings and downswings in business activity are made larger.
   (b) the economy grows less rapidly during booms.
   (c) price levels are more stable.
   (d) unemployment is higher.
   (e) None of the above.

7. The *accelerator effect* refers to a situation in which
   (a) a fall in the demand for capital goods will cause the demand for consumer goods to fall.
   (b) an increase in the demand for consumer goods causes an increase in the demand for capital goods.
   (c) increases in income are partially respent, causing larger increases in GDP and total incomes.
   (d) without increased government spending, the economy will collapse.
   (e) None of the above.

8. The condition that must exist if the accelerator effect is to boost aggregate demand is that
   (a) there must be substantial unemployment.
   (b) capital equipment must depreciate rapidly.
   (c) production must be at or near capacity levels.

(d) new types of capital equipment must be available.

(e) None of the above.

9. The effect of the accelerator on the economy is to
    (a) make the demand for capital goods more stable.
    (b) smooth out the economic fluctuations associated with the business cycle
    (c) ensure that the economy will continue to grow steadily.
    (d) make economic booms stronger and recessions more severe.
    (e) Both (a) and (d).

10. During recessions, which *one* of the following is most likely to decline sharply?
    (a) household spending on consumer goods
    (b) government spending on goods and services
    (c) business spending on capital goods
    (d) consumer spending on services
    (e) municipal government spending

11. During an economic boom,
    (a) prices rise, causing aggregate demand, output, and employment to fall.
    (b) aggregate demand rises, causing output, employment, and prices to rise more rapidly than usual.
    (c) aggregate demand rises, causing output and employment to rise, which causes prices to fall.
    (d) aggregate demand rises and output and employment fall, causing prices to rise.
    (e) prices fall, causing output, employment, and aggregate demand to rise.

12. Which of the following most accurately states the relationship between inflation and the general state of the economy?
    (a) Inflation tends to become more rapid when the economy is in a recession.
    (b) When prices rise, this tends to cause unemployment to rise, too.
    (c) Inflation tends to gain speed during economic booms, when unemployment is low.
    (d) Rising prices mean less economic prosperity for society in general.
    (e) There is no relationship between the rate of inflation and the general state of the economy.

13. The relationship referred to in the previous question exists because
    (a) the high levels of aggregate demand which generate economic prosperity also tend to cause inflation.
    (b) during recessions, due to lower sales volumes, businesses must raise prices in order to maintain profits.
    (c) when prices rise rapidly, sales fall and workers are laid off, causing unemployment to rise.
    (d) price increases reduce the purchasing power of the dollar and, thus, the general degree of economic prosperity.
    (e) None of the above.

14. *Inflation psychology* refers to
    (a) the tendency of people to save more money during periods of severe inflation in order to cope with higher prices.
    (b) the tendency of people to seek larger income increases during periods of severe inflation.
    (c) the tendency of people to spend a higher proportion of their disposable income during periods of severe inflation, and save less.
    (d) Both (b) and (c).
    (e) None of the above.

15. The effect of inflation psychology on the economy is to
   (a) slow down aggregate demand and inflation.
   (b) cause interest rates to decrease.
   (c) make inflation more severe.
   (d) increase unemployment.
   (e) None of the above.

Critical Thinking Questions

(Asterisked questions 1 to 5 are answered in Appendix B; the answers to questions 6 to 10 are in the Instructor's Manual that accompanies this text.)

*1. Which one of the following would tend to suffer the greatest decline in sales during recessions? Explain the reason for your answer.
   (a) clothing stores
   (b) breweries (beer)
   (c) building materials manufacturers
   (d) farmers
   (e) exclusive restaurants

*2. In which *one* of the following industries would you expect annual profits to decrease by the most during a recession? Explain the reason for your answer.
   (a) distilling (liquor)
   (b) automobile manufacturing
   (c) life insurance
   (d) cosmetics
   (e) retail food stores

*3. Explain whether or not you would expect unemployment to increase seriously during a recession among each of the following groups.
   (a) assembly line workers in auto manufacturing plants
   (b) servers in exclusive restaurants
   (c) workers 25 years of age and older
   (d) young people (ages 15–24)
   (e) female workers
   (f) young male workers

*4. Suppose that Statistics Canada's *Composite Leading Indicator* decreased each month for several months. Would you expect that over the next few months,
   (a) the unemployment rate would increase or decrease? Why?
   (b) the rate of inflation would increase or decrease? Why?
   (c) interest rates would increase or decrease? Why?

*5. Suppose there were indications that a problem of inflation was developing in the economy. Explain three reasons why government economic policy-makers might be concerned that the rate of inflation could become progressively higher in the future.

6. Suppose that the economy (real GDP) has been growing very rapidly for several years, that the unemployment rate is now the lowest it has been in over a decade and is still falling, and that Statistics Canada's Composite Leading Indicator is continuing to rise.
   (a) What kinds of economic forces would be *causing* such a situation?
   (b) What sort of *problems* would you expect in an economy in this condition?
   (c) Would you expect that the next change in interest rates would be an *increase* or a *decrease*? Why?
   (d) What would you expect to be the direction that the economy described here would take over the next two or three years? Why?

7. Suppose that there was a growing belief among Canadians that the economy was heading into a serious recession. Explain how this expectation would likely affect the future direction of the economy.

8. When total employment in the economy increases, business profits rise. And when total employment decreases, business profits fall. What would explain why employment and profits tend to move in the same direction?

9. Suppose that business inventories increased by $1 billion. How might this statistic be interpreted as an indication
   (a) that economic conditions were deteriorating?
   (b) that economic conditions were improving?

   What might help to determine which of these two possible interpretations of the statistics was correct?

10. Chapter 5 stressed how the lending activities of the banking system create money. Explain how banks' lending and the rate of growth of the money supply would change over the course of the business cycle as portrayed in Figure 6-16 on page 141. Would the banking system's activities tend to smooth out the business cycle, or make it more severe?

Use the Web   (Hints for these Use the Web exercises appear in Appendix B.)

1. On the Statistics Canada website (**www.statcan.gc.ca**), search *The Daily* for the most recent release of the Composite Leading Indicator. What does the leading indicator suggest about the current direction of the Canadian economy?

2. Visit **www.bankofcanada.ca/en/rates/indinf/product_graph_en.html** and see whether the Bank of Canada's output gap has increased or decreased recently. What does the output gap suggest to be the general direction of the economy?

3. Visit the website of TD Bank Financial Group at **www.td.com/economics** and from the *Current Publications* menu, select *Quarterly Economic Forecast*.

   What is the forecast direction of the Canadian economy, and what are the main reasons for this forecast?

Stabilizing the Economy: Government Monetary and Fiscal Policies

After studying this chapter, you should be able to

1. Name the agency that is responsible for monetary policy in Canada and the main policy tools that it uses to influence aggregate demand.

2. State the purpose of an *easy money* policy, describe how the Bank of Canada implements an easy money policy, and explain how an easy money policy affects the economy.

3. State the purpose of a *tight money* policy, describe how the Bank of Canada implements a tight money policy, and explain how a tight money policy affects the economy.

4. Name the body that is responsible for fiscal policy in Canada, and list the two main tools of fiscal policy used to influence aggregate demand.

5. Explain the two main components of fiscal policy for combating a recession.

6. Explain the concept of using fiscal policy to *kick-start* the economy.

7. Define *budget deficit*, and explain the role of deficits in fiscal policy and how deficits are financed.

8. Explain the concept of *countercyclical fiscal policy*, and describe the type of fiscal policy that is appropriate during economic booms and periods of inflation.

9. Use aggregate supply and aggregate demand curves to illustrate the use of monetary and fiscal policies.

10. Apply the facts and concepts of this chapter to various situations.

As we saw in Chapter 6, economic activity in a market economy can fluctuate considerably. During economic booms, output and employment rise rapidly, and inflation can become a concern. And during recessions, output actually falls and unemployment becomes a serious concern.

The most basic cause of these recurrent business cycles is *fluctuations in aggregate demand*. At times, consumers and businesses spend strongly, generating an economic boom, while at other times a decrease in spending will cause declines in output and employment. And the threat of recession or inflation is increased by the tendency of aggregate demand to *gain momentum* at times. During a boom, growing confidence and optimism can cause consumers and businesses to borrow and spend more freely, pushing the money supply and aggregate demand even higher and increasing the danger of inflation. The opposite can happen during recessions, when low confidence and uncertainty reduce borrowing and spending by both consumers and businesses, dragging aggregate demand down further and making the recession worse.

Experience has shown that business cycles can have serious consequences. During the Great Depression of the 1930s, unemployment was very high for a decade. And during the Great Inflation of the 1970s, rapidly rising prices and interest rates brought hardship to many people, and eventually led to the second- and third-most serious recessions of the century.

Because of these problems, a basic goal of government economic policy is to *stabilize the economy*, by smoothing out business cycles. Government policies seek to stabilize the economy by increasing aggregate demand during recessions and by slowing it down when inflation is a concern. This is no small task: aggregate demand exceeds \$1.6 trillion (i.e., 1.6 thousand billion) and, as we saw in Chapter 6, involves complex interactions between the spending decisions of millions of Canadian households and businesses, as well as the countless foreign buyers of Canadian exports who purchase nearly one-third of our GDP.

To influence the direction of the entire economy on such a broad scale requires some very large economic policy tools that are capable of influencing the spending decisions of millions of buyers, both inside and outside Canada. The main such policy levers are *interest rates* and *the money supply* (monetary policy) and *government spending* and *taxes* (fiscal policy). In this chapter, we will consider how these policies can be used in order to smooth out economic fluctuations and reduce their impact on Canadians.

Monetary Policy

monetary policy
The Bank of Canada's use of interest rates and the money supply to influence the level of aggregate demand in the economy.

Monetary policy involves changes in *interest rates* and the *money supply* to influence the level of aggregate demand, and thus the general direction of the economy. In Chapter 5, we saw how the lending activities of the banking system create money, and how this process affects aggregate demand. If borrowing is low, aggregate demand will be low and a recession is likely. On the other hand, high levels of borrowing can boost aggregate demand so high that inflation becomes a problem. During the 1970s and much of the 1980s, inflation was a serious problem in the Canadian economy.

While implementing monetary policy involves operations that can be quite complex (as we will see in the following sections), the goal of monetary policy is quite straightforward—to keep the rate of inflation at a low and stable level. The Bank of Canada seeks to do this by increasing interest rates in order to discourage borrowing and spending when the rate of inflation is becoming too high, and reducing interest rates in order to encourage borrowing and spending when low demand threatens to cause recessions, during which the rate of inflation is typically unusually low.

The Bank of Canada

The Bank of Canada was established in 1935, when the Great Depression caused increased concern regarding economic and monetary management. Unlike the commercial banks, which are corporations owned by shareholders, the Bank of Canada is an agency of the federal government known as a **central bank**. The Bank of Canada does not deal with the general public as the commercial banks do; rather, it has much broader responsibilities relating to government finances and economic policy.

The Bank of Canada is owned by the Government of Canada and managed by a board of directors that consists of the governor, the senior deputy governor, the deputy minister of finance, and 12 directors. The governor is appointed for a seven-year term by the directors, with the approval of the federal cabinet. The governor of the Bank of Canada has been described as "the most powerful unelected official in the country."

The Bank of Canada acts as the sole issuer of Canadian bank notes and as the fiscal agent of the federal government. In this latter capacity, the Bank of Canada operates the deposit account through which government revenues and expenditures flow, handles the sale of government securities, and acts as financial adviser to the federal government. In addition, the Bank of Canada has international responsibilities on behalf of the government, particularly with respect to the international value of the Canadian dollar, as we will see in Chapter 10, "The Canadian Dollar in Foreign Exchange Markets."

Another function of the Bank of Canada is to act as a "bank for banks." Each day, millions of cheques written by businesses and individuals are cleared, requiring funds to be transferred between banks. For instance, if your friend writes you a cheque for $100 on her account at the Royal Bank and you cash or deposit her cheque at your branch of the CIBC, it is the CIBC that provides you with $100 of funds. So the Royal Bank owes the CIBC $100 as a result of this transaction. To facilitate this process of transferring funds between banks, the Bank of Canada holds deposits (**settlement balances**) from chartered banks and other financial institutions, and each day transfers funds between their accounts, thus acting as a means of settling debts between the chartered banks. (Your friend's cheque would cause $100 to be transferred from the Royal Bank's account at the Bank of Canada to the CIBC's account at the Bank of Canada at the end of the day.) The Bank of Canada pays the chartered banks interest on these deposits at a rate known as the **bankers' deposit rate**.

If the clearing of these settlements leaves a bank or other financial institution short of funds, it can borrow funds temporarily from the Bank of Canada, at a rate of interest known as the **bank rate**. More likely, though, it would borrow from another bank or financial institution that has surplus funds. Such short-term loans are known as **overnight loans**, and the interest rate on them is called the **overnight rate.**

The relationship among these three interest rates is as follows:

- The bank rate is the highest (for example, 3.0 percent);
- the overnight rate falls between the bank rate and the bankers' deposit rate; and
- the bankers' deposit rate is a half percentage point below the bank rate (in our example, 2.5 percent).

The gap of a one-half percentage point between the bankers' deposit rate and the bank rate is known as the Bank of Canada's **operating band**.

The Bank of Canada's Monetary Policy

The single most important responsibility of the Bank of Canada is monetary policy, or *controlling the money supply* of the nation, as set out in the preamble of the Bank of

www.bankofcanada.ca

central bank
A government agency with responsibility for monetary policy, as well as other financial functions, on behalf of the government.

settlement balances
Deposits (at the Bank of Canada) of the commercial banks and other financial institutions that are used to settle debts and transactions between them.

bankers' deposit rate
The rate of interest paid by the Bank of Canada on the chartered banks' deposits at the Bank of Canada.

bank rate
The rate of interest charged by the Bank of Canada on loans (advances) it makes to banks and other financial institutions.

overnight loans
Very short-term loans between financial institutions to cover temporary shortfalls in areas such as settlement balances.

overnight rate
The rate of interest on one-day loans made by banks, investment dealers, and other financial institutions to each other.

operating band
The one-half percentage point range established by the Bank of Canada for the overnight rate; the top of the range is the bank rate and the bottom of the range is the bankers' deposit rate.

Canada Act, which states that the central bank's mandate is to

> ... regulate credit and currency in the best interests of the economic
> life of the nation ... and to mitigate by its influence fluctuations in
> the general level of production, trade, prices and employment, so far
> as may be possible within the scope of monetary action ...

The most visible aspect of the Bank of Canada's monetary policy is its announcements regarding interest rates. On eight predetermined dates each year, the Bank of Canada announces its decision concerning its "target" for its key policy interest rate, which is the overnight rate. The Bank of Canada's target for the overnight rate is in the middle of the operating band between the bankers' deposit rate and the bank rate.

Monetary Policy to Combat Recession: An Easy Money Policy

To combat a recession, the Bank of Canada would want to reduce interest rates in order to increase borrowing and spending by consumers and businesses.

A Target for Interest Rates

easy money policy
Monetary policy directed toward making interest rates lower in order to stimulate aggregate demand.

The Bank of Canada would announce that it was *lowering* its target for the overnight rate (and lowering the operating band and the bank rate as well). This announcement would include an explanation for the change in the Bank of Canada's policies, and would be interpreted as a signal to Canadians that the Bank of Canada was shifting toward an **easy money policy** of lower interest rates and greater availability of credit. This announcement of a lower target for the overnight rate would help to build confidence that action was being taken to combat the recession.

Reaching the Target for the Overnight Rate

The next step is to actually push the overnight rate downward toward this new target. The Bank of Canada can do this in different ways. One way is for the Bank of Canada to offer overnight loans to banks and other financial institutions at an interest rate that is below the prevailing market rate, which will push the overnight rate downward in the way that the Bank of Canada wants.

The Bank of Canada can also increase the ability of the banks to make loans by *increasing the banks' cash reserves*. To do this, the Bank of Canada can *buy government bonds* from the banks. When the Bank of Canada pays the banks for the bonds, the banks' cash reserves—and their ability to make loans—will increase. The Bank of Canada can also buy government bonds from the public. When the public deposits the proceeds from the sale of the bonds into the banking system, the banks' cash reserves will increase. And with more funds to lend, the banks will lower their interest rates on loans, following the trend set by the reduction in the overnight rate.

Another approach is for the Bank of Canada to *shift Government of Canada deposits* from the government's account at the Bank of Canada into its accounts at the banks. This will increase the funds on deposit with the banks. If the banks then invest these surplus funds by lending them out as overnight loans, the increased supply of these funds will push the overnight rate lower, toward the Bank of Canada's new target.

The combination of lower interest rates and increased availability of loanable funds sets the stage for increased borrowing and spending by consumers and businesses.

Easy Money Policies, the Canadian Dollar, and Exports

An easy money policy can also increase aggregate demand by increasing *foreign demand for Canadian exports*. When Canadian interest rates decrease, Canadian dollar deposits and securities that pay interest become less attractive to foreign investors. Then, foreign investors will reduce their purchases of Canadian dollars for the purpose of making these investments, causing the international price (value) of the Canadian dollar to decrease.

A lower-priced Canadian dollar makes Canadian products more attractive to foreign buyers. For instance, if the Canadian dollar were to decrease from US$0.80 to US$0.75, Canadian goods and services would become about 6 percent cheaper to U.S. buyers. If Americans then buy more Canadian goods and services, Canadian exports would rise, increasing aggregate demand for goods and services in the Canadian economy.

From 1991 to 2001, the Canadian dollar fell by 26 percent against the U.S. dollar. Over the same period, Canada's exports grew by 107 percent.

The Effects of an Easy Money Policy on the Economy

An easy money policy is intended to stimulate bank lending and spending by consumers and businesses. Consumers will be able to borrow more at lower interest rates to buy houses and cars, and businesses will be better able to handle the cost of loans for working capital, inventories, and equipment. As borrowing increases, the money supply and aggregate demand will increase, causing real output to rise and unemployment to decrease, as shown in Figure 7-1. In addition, the lower Canadian dollar should add to exports, further bolstering aggregate demand.

A reduction in interest rates from, say, 3.00 percent to 2.75 percent may not seem significant. However, this decrease reduces the cost of borrowing *by 8.3 percent* (0.25 divided by 3.00).

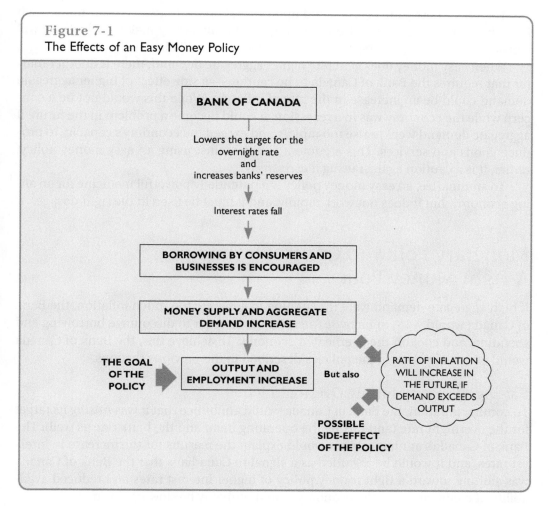

Figure 7-1
The Effects of an Easy Money Policy

BANK OF CANADA

Lowers the target for the
overnight rate
and
increases banks' reserves

Interest rates fall

BORROWING BY CONSUMERS AND
BUSINESSES IS ENCOURAGED

MONEY SUPPLY AND AGGREGATE
DEMAND INCREASE

THE GOAL
OF THE
POLICY

OUTPUT AND
EMPLOYMENT INCREASE

But also

RATE OF INFLATION
WILL INCREASE IN
THE FUTURE, IF
DEMAND EXCEEDS
OUTPUT

POSSIBLE
SIDE-EFFECT
OF THE POLICY

However, lower interest rates are not a sure fix for an ailing economy. If the economy is in quite severe recession and confidence is low, consumers and businesses may be reluctant to borrow and spend money, despite reductions in interest rates.

This problem has been likened to "pushing on a string," which suggests that easy money by itself may not always be sufficient to lift the economy out of a recession.

And even when an easy money policy does work, it is not a quick fix for an ailing economy. In fact, the effects of monetary policy occur with quite long *time lags*. There are three such time lags: the *recognition lag*, the *policy lag*, and the *impact lag*.

(a) The *recognition lag* arises because it takes time for economic policy-makers to be sure that the economic situation requires action. It may take several months before the available economic statistics make it clear to policy-makers that they should take action.

(b) The *policy lag* occurs due to delays in the implementation of policies by the government. In the case of monetary policy, this lag is short, since the Bank of Canada can move quite quickly to reduce short-term interest rates.

(c) The *impact lag* arises because it takes time for government policies to affect the economy. For monetary policy, the impact lag is long. Lower interest rates will not speed up borrowing and spending immediately—consumers and businesses will need time to reassess their borrowing plans. And many will wait to see if economic conditions are in fact changing in ways that justify changing their plans. As a result, it can take a year or more for an easy money policy to generate a significant increase in aggregate demand.

Together, these time lags can add up to a total of one to two years or more. Such long time lags can create real problems for economic policy-makers, which we will consider in Chapter 8, "Perspectives on Macroeconomic Policy."

When easy money does generate higher aggregate demand, there is another matter that requires the Bank of Canada to be cautious—a side effect of higher aggregate demand could be an increase in the rate of inflation. While this would not be a concern while the economy was in a recession, it could become a problem in the future if aggregate demand were to rise too rapidly and exceed the economy's capacity to produce goods and services. This argument is not against using an easy money policy; rather, it is a caution against using it *excessively*.

To summarize, an easy money policy is a potentially powerful medicine for an ailing economy, but it does not work rapidly, and it must be used in the right dosage.

Monetary Policy to Control Inflation: A Tight Money Policy

If high aggregate demand were threatening to generate too much inflation, the Bank of Canada would want to *increase interest rates* in order to discourage borrowing and spending, and cool off the overheated economy. To achieve this, the Bank of Canada would essentially reverse the policies described in the previous sections.

Raising the Target for the Overnight Rate

To combat inflation, the Bank of Canada would announce that it was *raising* its target for the overnight rate (and raising the operating band and the bank rate as well). The Bank of Canada's announcement would explain the reasons for the increase in interest rates, and it would be regarded as a signal to Canadians that the Bank of Canada was shifting toward a **tight money policy** of higher interest rates and reduced availability of credit, and that the economy would probably be slowing down.

Reaching the Target for the Overnight Rate

The next step is to actually *push* the overnight rate upward toward this new target. To do this, the Bank of Canada "mops up" some of the reserves of the banking system.

tight money policy
Monetary policy directed toward making interest rates higher in order to slow the growth of aggregate demand.

One way of reducing bank reserves is for the Bank of Canada to *sell government bonds* to the banks. When the banks pay the Bank of Canada for the bonds, the banks' cash reserves will decrease. If the Bank of Canada sells government bonds to the public, the public will remove funds from the banking system to pay the Bank of Canada, and the banks' cash reserves will decrease.

The Bank of Canada may also *shift Government of Canada deposits* out of the banks and into the government's account at the Bank of Canada. This will reduce the banks' reserves. If the banks then have to borrow from the overnight loans market to replenish the reserves, the increased demand for these funds will push the overnight rate higher, toward the Bank of Canada's new target.

With the banks having less funds available for lending, the interest rates on loans in general will tend to rise, following the trend set by the increase in the overnight rate. And the combination of higher interest rates and reduced availability of loans sets the stage for decreased borrowing and spending by consumers and businesses.

Tight Money Policies, the Canadian Dollar, and Exports

A tight money policy can also dampen aggregate demand by decreasing *foreign purchases of Canadian exports*. Higher Canadian interest rates make Canadian dollar deposits and securities that pay interest more attractive to foreign investors. When foreigners buy more Canadian dollars in order to make these investments, the international price (value) of the Canadian dollar will rise.

A higher-priced Canadian dollar makes Canadian products less attractive to foreign buyers. For instance, if the Canadian dollar were to increase from US$1.00 to US$1.05, stateside buyers would have to pay 5 percent more for Canadian goods and services. The effect of such an increase would be to depress Canadian exports and aggregate demand in the Canadian economy, as the effects of slower exports were spread across the economy by the multiplier effect.

The Effects of a Tight Money Policy on the Economy

The higher interest rates associated with a tight money policy will discourage borrowing by consumers and businesses, causing aggregate demand to grow more slowly. A higher Canadian dollar will also help to slow down demand, by holding down exports. And, as Figure 7-2 shows, with aggregate demand held in check, the rate of inflation will decrease.

However, the rate of inflation may not fall quickly. If people remain optimistic about the future, or if consumers and businesses expect inflation to drive prices even higher, they may continue to borrow and spend, despite the increase in interest rates.

Also, the effects of a tight money policy are delayed by the same time lags that delay the effects of an easy money policy. Because of the *recognition lag*, policy-makers will take some time to decide that a tight money policy should be implemented. The *policy lag* is short because the Bank of Canada can move quickly to increase short-term interest rates, but the *impact lag* is long. Consumers and businesses will complete major purchases that had already been planned, and the spending on these will continue to ripple through the economy for some time, due to the respending effect of the multiplier that we saw in Chapter 6. Even after borrowing is reduced and the growth of the money supply slows down, the rate of inflation will take about a year to decrease. Such long time lags make economic policy-making a difficult task, as we will see in Chapter 8.

Experience has shown that, eventually, tight money policies will depress aggregate demand, and will slow down inflation. However, a tight money policy will also have the unpleasant side effects of *slower economic growth* and *higher unemployment*.

There are other problems associated with tight money policies. High interest rates affect some sectors of the economy particularly severely. *Construction* is probably the

The role of the Bank of Canada has been described as one where it "take[s] away the punch bowl just when the party gets going."

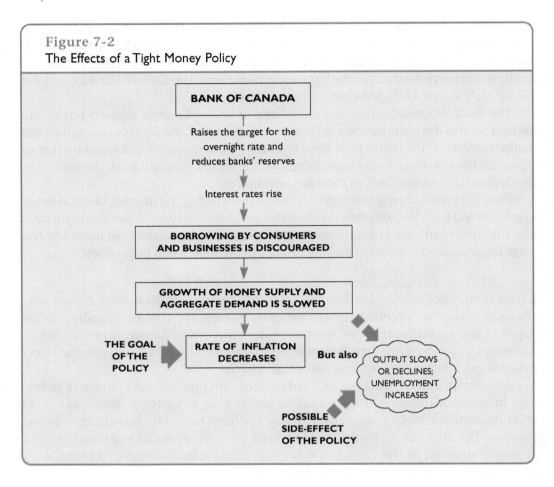

Figure 7-2
The Effects of a Tight Money Policy

industry that is hardest hit by tight money because high mortgage rates discourage the buying of new homes and the building of commercial and industrial complexes. As you can see in Table 7-1, rising mortgage interest rates have a significant effect upon the monthly mortgage payments faced by homeowners.

Table 7-1
Monthly Payments on a 25-Year $100 000 Mortgage at Various Interest Rates

Interest Rate	Monthly Payment[a]
5%	$ 584.59
6%	644.30
7%	706.78
8%	771.82
9%	839.20
10%	908.70
11%	980.11
12%	1053.22
13%	1127.84
14%	1203.76
15%	1280.83
16%	1358.89
17%	1437.80
18%	1517.43
19%	1597.68
20%	1678.45

[a]Assuming interest is compounded monthly.

Because high interest rates will reduce investment spending, tight money also tends to have severe effects on the *capital goods industries*, such as building materials and industrial equipment. In the consumer goods sector, the effects of tight money fall the hardest on the big-ticket items, such as cars and appliances, which involve considerable borrowing to buy and whose sales tend to follow the sales of new houses.

Small businesses are affected more severely by tight money than are big corporations. Because they tend to have smaller profit margins than do large corporations, small businesses tend to be more dependent upon borrowing to finance their operations; also they are less able to afford high interest rates.

So, for various reasons, a tight money policy is a painful policy direction for a government to have to take. Despite these difficulties, a tight money policy is regarded as essential to any successful anti-inflation program. Indeed, most economists believe it to be the *only* really effective anti-inflation policy, because only a tight money policy will attack the most common cause of inflation, which is excessively rapid growth of the money supply generated by high levels of borrowing.

Does the Bank of Canada *Control* Interest Rates?

Sometimes the policy actions of the Bank of Canada are misinterpreted as meaning that the Bank of Canada *controls* interest rates in the Canadian economy. In reality, this is not possible.

Interest rates are a *price*—the price of borrowing money. Interest rates are expressed as a percentage of the loan per annum—for instance, 6 percent per year. Any price must find a middle ground (known to economists as *equilibrium*) between the needs of buyers and sellers. A market interest rate of, say, 6 percent represents a balance between the needs of lenders (suppliers of funds) and borrowers (buyers of loans). If the government were to try to decree that the rate of interest be only 4 percent, lenders might well prove unwilling to make loans at such a low rate.

This reality is made more forceful by the fact that money is an internationally traded item, in the sense that investors lend money around the world, just as wheat and oil are sold globally. If the world price of oil increases, Canada will have to pay the world price for the oil that it imports. For the same reasons, if interest rates in the United States or in the world generally rise, there will be pressure on Canadian interest rates to rise also. If the government tried to hold Canadian rates too low, lenders would take their funds out of Canada to countries where they could earn a higher return.

For these reasons, the Bank of Canada cannot *control* interest rates in Canada. What it can do, however, is *influence* interest rates by using the policies described in the previous sections to nudge interest rates higher when inflation threatens, and lower when recession and unemployment are the larger concerns. And by doing so in a timely manner, the Bank of Canada can influence aggregate demand and the direction of the Canadian economy.

Monetary Policy in Review

Monetary Policy and the Recession of 2008–09

In 2008, a serious recession began in the United States. Over the previous few years, a combination of low interest rates, very lax mortgage lending standards, weak government regulation of lending, and excessive confidence on the part of American consumers and banks and other lenders had generated a sharp increase in mortgage lending and a soaring demand for housing that drove housing prices to unsustainably high levels (a price "bubble"). Many Americans then borrowed heavily against the higher value of their homes in order to increase their consumption spending, going very deeply into debt in the process. This surge in spending by American consumers generated a strong boom in the USA that spread around the world, through U.S. purchases of other countries' products.

But the housing price "bubble" burst as many homebuyers were unable to pay their mortgages and their lenders foreclosed, throwing a large number of homes onto the market. This drove housing prices sharply downward, leaving many American families with homes that were worth less than the mortgage loan(s) against them. With their confidence shocked by these events, and now lacking the collateral to support further borrowing, American consumers cut their spending, causing a recession. The U.S. recession was made worse by the fact that many banks and other lenders that had financed home purchases and consumer loans that used homes as collateral found themselves in serious financial trouble because many of the loans that they had made would never be repaid. In turn, this made U.S. banks and other lenders extremely cautious about making new loans to consumers and to businesses, which only made the U.S. recession worse. And this recession spread around the world as American purchases of foreign products (including Canada's) fell.

So in 2008–09, the recession spread to Canada. The weakness in the Canadian economy began with exports to the USA, but before long spread to business investment and consumer spending, as the confidence of both business leaders and consumers plunged.

This situation presented the Bank of Canada (and central banks in many nations) with an exceptional challenge—how to prevent this sharp downturn from spiraling downward into the worst recession since the Great Depression.

The Bank of Canada and other nations' central banks responded with a series of exceptionally large and rapid reductions in interest rates, as can be seen in Figure 7-3.

In the United States, where the financial crisis was most severe, the government and the Federal Reserve (the U.S. equivalent of the Bank of Canada) took even stronger steps that were unprecedented. Massive "bailout" financial assistance was provided to various banks that owned billions of dollars of "securitized" mortgage bonds that had lost much of their value, and because investors would not buy such mortgage bonds, the Federal Reserve itself provided the funds for more than 80 percent of mortgage lending for a period of time. And to finance government spending for rescuing banks and combating the recession, the Federal Reserve took the unusual step of buying large amounts of federal government bonds itself—a process officially described as "quantitative easing", but more commonly known as "printing money".

Canada did not suffer a U.S.-style financial crisis, and by the fall of 2009, an economic recovery was underway in Canada and the outlook was improving. Consequently, the Bank of Canada raised the overnight rate in June 2010 and again in July, as can be seen in Figure 7-3. However, when slower growth in 2011 raised uncertainties about the economic outlook, the Bank of Canada did not increase the overnight rate further, and left it unchanged at 1.00 percent into the fall of 2011, when the unemployment rate was 7.2 percent. ■

QUESTIONS

1. How has the economic situation changed since the fall of 2011? Current statistics for the unemployment rate and GDP growth rate can be found on Statistics Canada's homepage at www.statcan.gc.ca.
2. Has the Bank of Canada changed the overnight rate since the fall of 2011? The target for the overnight rate can be found on the Bank of Canada's homepage at www.bankofcanada.ca under "Key Indicators".
3. What does the Bank of Canada's most recent interest rate announcement say about the current economic situation? Visit www.bankofcanada.ca and under *Media Room*, click on *Press Releases* and look for a press release involving the overnight rate target.

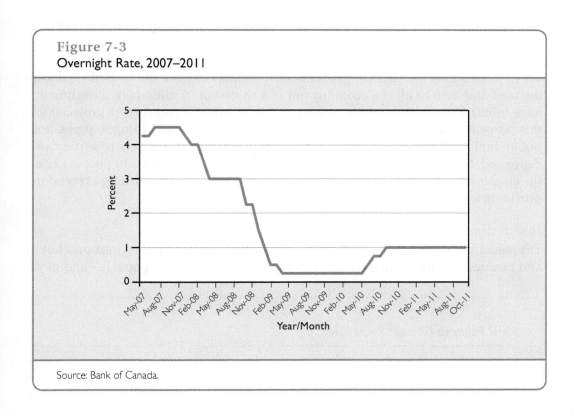

Figure 7-3
Overnight Rate, 2007–2011

Source: Bank of Canada.

Fiscal Policy

Fiscal policy uses changes in *government spending* and *tax revenues* to influence the level of aggregate demand and the direction of the economy. As we saw in Chapter 6, government spending adds to aggregate demand, either by buying goods and services itself or by providing transfer payments to people who will use the funds to buy goods and services. We also saw in Chapter 6 that taxes have the opposite effect—they reduce aggregate demand, by reducing the purchasing power of households and businesses.

fiscal policy
The use of government spending and taxes (the government's budget) to influence the level of aggregate demand and thus the performance of the economy. Also known as *budget policy*.

www.fin.gc.ca

With spending and tax revenues of over $275 billion per year, Canada's federal government is in a position either to boost aggregate demand in the economy by increasing spending and/or cutting taxes, or to decrease demand, by doing the opposite. Since government tax revenues and expenditures are contained in the government's budget, the use of fiscal policy (the government's budget) in these ways is sometimes referred to as *budget policy*. Fiscal policy is the responsibility of the federal Department of Finance, under the direction of the minister of finance and the federal cabinet.

How Fiscal Policy Combats Recession

In Figure 7-4, the economy has slipped into a recession in year 20X1—aggregate demand has been falling, dragging the levels of output and employment down with it. In 20X2, the government's budget is planned so that government *spending* is larger than the government's *tax revenues*. The purpose of this policy is to boost aggregate demand in order to help the economy out of the recession.

The boost to aggregate demand pictured in Figure 7-4 could be achieved by an increase in government spending (on goods and services, or on transfer payments), by tax reductions, or by some combination of these, as discussed in the following sections.

Increases in Government Expenditures

We have seen how increases in government spending can raise the level of aggregate demand and help to lift the economy out of a recession. Traditionally, governments have used *public works projects* (more recently renamed *infrastructure* projects) for this purpose. These projects involve building or repairing roads, bridges, parks, and public buildings during recessions, when the construction industry is particularly depressed. In addition, government spending on transfer payments to people under the employment insurance (EI) and welfare programs will increase during a recession, providing more support to the level of aggregate demand.

Reductions in Taxes

Tax reductions during a recession can boost aggregate demand by leaving households and businesses with more after-tax income to spend. The most popular—and most

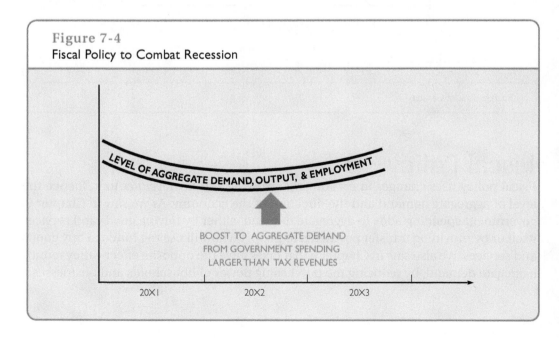

Figure 7-4
Fiscal Policy to Combat Recession

effective—of such policies is a reduction in personal income taxes, because consumers will generally increase their spending when their disposable income rises. Reductions in taxes on business are considered less effective as an anti-recession policy, because in a recession businesses would be less likely than consumers to spend their tax savings.

The operation of fiscal policy to combat recessions is summarized and illustrated in Figure 7-5.

Automatic Stabilizers

Some aspects of fiscal policy, such as public works projects, are described as *discretionary* policies because they require decisions by the government. It takes time for a government to implement discretionary fiscal policies. Other aspects of fiscal policy, however, swing into action *automatically* when the economy slips into a recession. For instance, government expenditures on employment insurance and welfare benefits rise automatically during recessions, as unemployment rises. In addition to this, many government tax revenues, such as those from income taxes, profits taxes, and sales taxes, tend to be depressed by slower economic activity during recessions. This combination of lower government tax revenues and higher expenditures will provide automatic support to the level of aggregate demand during recessions. For this reason, such programs are described as **automatic stabilizers**.

automatic stabilizers
Government spending and taxation programs that have the effect of automatically supporting aggregate demand during recessions and depressing aggregate demand during periods of boom/inflation.

The Multiplier

As we have seen, fiscal policy is used to stabilize the economy in recessions by increasing spending on goods and services by government, consumers, and businesses. The *multiplier effect* will help fiscal policy to work, by spreading increases in spending through the economy as money is respent. For example, a government road-building program will increase the incomes of construction workers, who will spend part of their increased incomes on consumer goods and services, starting a chain of respending that will increase total incomes and GDP by perhaps 1.6 times the original increase

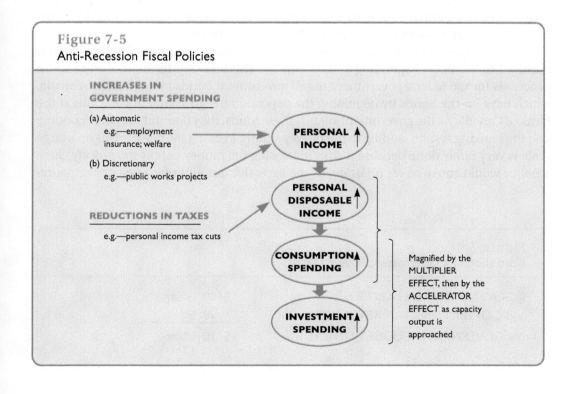

Figure 7-5
Anti-Recession Fiscal Policies

INCREASES IN GOVERNMENT SPENDING

(a) Automatic
e.g.—employment insurance; welfare

(b) Discretionary
e.g.—public works projects

REDUCTIONS IN TAXES

e.g.—personal income tax cuts

PERSONAL INCOME ↑

PERSONAL DISPOSABLE INCOME ↑

CONSUMPTION SPENDING ↑

INVESTMENT SPENDING ↑

Magnified by the MULTIPLIER EFFECT, then by the ACCELERATOR EFFECT as capacity output is approached

in government spending. Similarly, personal income tax cuts that boost consumer spending will initiate a respending effect that will ripple through the economy. The contribution of the multiplier effect to fiscal policy is also shown in Figure 7-5.

Kick-Starting the Economy

Fiscal policy that is used to stimulate the economy can also benefit from the *accelerator effect*. Once the level of consumption spending has risen to the point where it is causing induced investment spending by business, the economy should be able to grow again on its own.

In this way, fiscal policy can be used to *kick-start* the economy out of a recession. Just as a motorcycle needs a kick-start to get it moving, the economy can sometimes benefit from a temporary boost. And just as the motorcycle works on its own once kick-started, the economy should be able to grow on its own once set right on the path to recovery from a recession. Following a *temporary stimulus* from fiscal policy, the multiplier and accelerator effects might be able to carry aggregate demand and the economy into recovery and expansion, as shown at the lower right of Figure 7-5.

Fiscal Policy and Budget Deficits

budget deficit

A government budget in which expenditures exceed tax revenues.

We have said that using fiscal policy to deal with a recession involves *increasing government spending* and *reducing taxes*, which will require the government to spend more than it collects in tax revenues, or run a **budget deficit**. Suppose that the government has a balanced budget, with spending and tax revenues both at $95 billion. Then a recession occurs, causing the government's spending to increase to $100 billion and its tax revenues to fall to $90 billion, as shown in Figure 7-6.

Financing Deficits: Where Will the Money Come From?

In the illustration in Figure 7-6, the government's spending exceeds its tax revenues by $10 billion. Where will the government obtain the $10 billion that it needs?

The federal government can (and does) raise the necessary funds by *borrowing them*—by *selling government bonds*. These bonds are bought as investments by pension funds, investment funds, banks, insurance companies, other financial institutions, and by investment dealers, who sell them to individuals.

The government also has the power to create new money (the popular term is "print money") to finance its spending and its deficits. The first step in the money-creation process is for the federal government to sell government bonds to the Bank of Canada, which pays for the bonds by increasing the deposit in the government's account at the Bank of Canada. As the government spends these funds, they flow out into the economy and the banking system, adding to the money supply. Printing money like this on a large scale is very rarely done because it risks increasing the money supply *too quickly*. Such a policy would cause *severe inflation*, as the excessive amount of money in circulation

---

Figure 7-6
Illustration of a Government Budget Deficit

If GOVERNMENT SPENDING is	$100 billion
and GOVERNMENT TAX REVENUES are	90 billion
the GOVERNMENT BUDGET DEFICIT is	$ 10 billion

pushes aggregate demand up so rapidly that output cannot keep pace. So, while a financially pressed government may find it tempting to print money to finance its budget deficits, this method would usually be inappropriate, and has seldom been used.

But What About Balancing the Government's Budget? And What About Government Debt?

Two concerns that emerge from the situation described here are that the government is *not balancing its budget* and that *government debt will increase.* In each year that the government has a budget deficit, its borrowing will cause its debt to increase.

Both of these are true for the years in which the government is using deficits to combat a recession. However, when the economy has recovered from the recession and is operating at high levels of output and employment, the situation regarding government finances should change considerably, as the next section shows.

Fiscal Policy for Economic Booms and to Control Inflation

As the economy recovers and expands into a boom, the automatic stabilizers described earlier will reduce the government's budget deficits. Government tax revenues will automatically grow as sales, incomes, and profits all increase. In addition, government spending on employment insurance and welfare will automatically fall as unemployment decreases. As other temporary antirecession spending programs and tax cuts are ended, the government would develop a **budget surplus**—an excess of tax revenues over government expenditures. A budget surplus would serve two important purposes:
(a) the excess of taxes over government spending would help to *hold down aggregate demand*, reducing the risk of inflation as a result of the economic boom, and
(b) the funds from the budget surplus could be used to *reduce the government's debt* that it had accumulated while fighting the recession a few years earlier.

> "When prosperity comes, do not use all of it."
> — CONFUCIUS

budget surplus
A government budget in which tax revenues exceed expenditures.

Countercyclical Fiscal Policy

Properly timed, budget deficits and surpluses can help to smooth out the economic fluctuations associated with the business cycle. As Figure 7-7 shows, budget deficits can support aggregate demand, output, and employment during recessions, while budget surpluses can help to ease the pressures of excess aggregate demand during the inflationary peaks of the business cycle.

Figure 7-7 also shows how the government debt that will accumulate while budget deficits are being used to combat a recession can be reduced when the economy recovers and moves into a boom. During a boom, the government will have budget surpluses that can be used to reduce the government's debt.

Economists refer to this as **countercyclical fiscal policy** because the government is deliberately using its budget to offset (or counter) the economic ups and downs of the business cycle, and to smooth out these economic fluctuations.

countercyclical fiscal policy
A policy of using fiscal policy (budget deficits during recessions and surpluses during periods of inflation) to smooth out the economic fluctuations associated with the business cycle.

Should the Government Ever Balance Its Budget, Then?

According to the theory of countercyclical fiscal policy, *in any given year* it is unlikely that a **balanced budget** (with government spending equal to tax revenues) would be appropriate. As we have seen, if the economy were in a recession, a budget deficit would be in order, while a period of boom/inflation would call for a budget surplus. Only if the economy were operating at a near-ideal balance between these conditions (as in the middle of Figure 7-7) would a balanced budget be appropriate. In these circumstances, a budget that neither stimulated nor depressed aggregate demand would be what the economy needed.

Over the longer run, the budget deficits that are incurred during recessions should be more or less offset by budget surpluses during boom periods, creating a more or

balanced budget
A government budget in which tax revenues and expenditures are equal.

less balanced budget *over a period of years*, rather than *in each year*. If this were done, the use of fiscal policy to stabilize the economy would not cause government debt to grow so large as to become a problem.

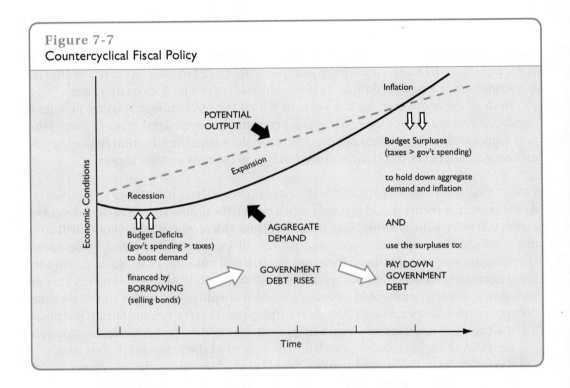

Figure 7-7
Countercyclical Fiscal Policy

IN THE NEWS

Fiscal Policy and the Recession of 2008–09

As described in the *In the News* box on *Monetary Policy and the Recession of 2008–09* earlier in this chapter, in 2008–09 the Canadian economy fell quite suddenly into a recession that was widely considered to be potentially very severe. The Bank of Canada responded with an unprecedentedly sharp decrease in the overnight rate, and the federal government responded with an equally remarkable shift in the federal budget, from budget surpluses to large budget deficits.

In Figure 7-8, the figures up to and including 2009–10 are *actual* (past) budget surpluses, and the deficits for years after that are budget deficits as *projected* by the Federal Department of Finance as part of the government's effort to combat the recession, then bring its budget back out of deficit.

Figure 7-8 illustrates the extent of this change in the government's budget, from a surplus of nearly $10 billion in the boom year 2007–08[1] to a deficit of nearly $56 billion two years later. The 2009–10 deficit of $55.5 billion was the largest ever; however, to place it in perspective, that deficit was about 3.5 percent of GDP, as compared to the deficits of the early 1990s, which amounted to over 5 percent of GDP.

---

[1] 2007–08 is described as a boom year because the government's fiscal year ends on March 31, which means that nine months of the 2007–08 budget related to 2007, when the economy was still booming. The recession started in late 2008.

Figure 7-8 also shows how the federal government was planning for its budget deficits to become smaller and smaller as the economy recovered from the recession, eventually turning to surpluses after 2014. ■

QUESTIONS

1. Did the government appear to be planning for a quick recovery from the recession?

2. Were the federal government's actual budget deficits for 2010–11 and later years significantly different from the projections in Figure 7-8? For actual budget deficits, visit the Department of Finance's website at http://www.fin.gc.ca and search the site for *Fiscal Reference Tables*. Click on the most recent issue listed, and in the Table of Contents, scroll down to *Federal Government Public Accounts*. Click on *Fiscal Transactions (millions of dollars)*, and in the column titled *Budgetary Surplus or Deficit* you will find the budget surplus or deficit for recent years.

3. Are any differences between the actual and projected budget figures apparently related to the speed of Canada's economic recovery? For a reference point, the unemployment rate in the 2009–10 budget year averaged 8.2 percent, and the faster the unemployment rate decreased, the more rapidly the government's budget deficit would decrease, too.

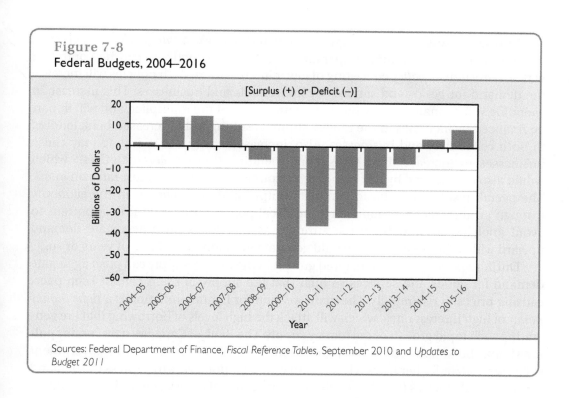

Figure 7-8
Federal Budgets, 2004–2016

Sources: Federal Department of Finance, *Fiscal Reference Tables*, September 2010 and *Updates to Budget 2011*

Monetary and Fiscal Policy in Review

We have seen how the Bank of Canada uses monetary policy and the federal Department of Finance uses fiscal policy to influence the level of aggregate demand in the economy. To conclude this chapter, we should review briefly how monetary and fiscal policies interact to influence the performance of the economy, as shown in Figure 7-9.

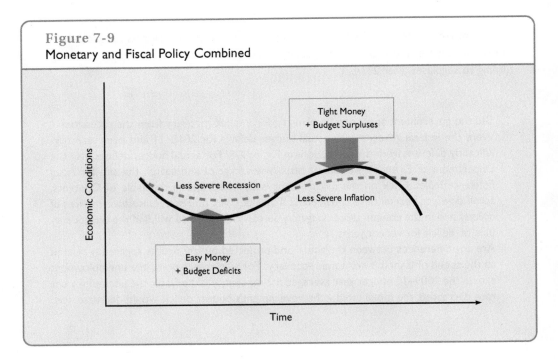

Figure 7-9
Monetary and Fiscal Policy Combined

During a recession, when aggregate demand is weak, a *budget deficit* (achieved through increased government spending and/or tax reductions) can be combined with an *easy money policy* consisting of lower interest rates. Both policies will increase the demand for goods and services by households and businesses. This increase in spending will be magnified by the responding effect of the multiplier, and will in part be financed by increases in the money supply resulting from increased bank lending to both consumers and businesses. Also, increased consumer spending may cause businesses to increase their investment spending (the accelerator effect), which would also be financed by bank lending, encouraged by lower interest rates on loans. The overall result would be to stimulate output and employment in the economy through an interaction of monetary and fiscal policies. However, it is important to avoid applying these policies too strongly, as this could push aggregate demand upward with a momentum that would generate inflation in a couple of years or so.

During a period of inflation, rapid growth in the money supply can push aggregate demand for goods and services so high that the supply of them cannot keep pace, causing prices to rise rapidly. The main weapon for fighting inflation is a *tight money policy* of high interest rates, which will attack the high levels of borrowing that are generating such rapid growth of the money supply. The Bank of Canada's tight money policy should be supported by fiscal policy in the form of reductions in government spending and/or higher taxes. The objective of these policies is to depress the demand for goods and services in order to relieve the pressure of excess demand on the supply and on the prices of goods and services. With total demand depressed in these ways, the rate of inflation will tend to decrease. However, as aggregate demand slows down, unemployment will increase. If these policies are applied too strongly, they could push the economy into a recession.

As Figure 7-9 shows, the fiscal policy of the Department of Finance and the monetary policy of the Bank of Canada can be combined to influence the economy's performance. By coordinating the two types of policy, the effect can be made considerably stronger than if either were used by itself.

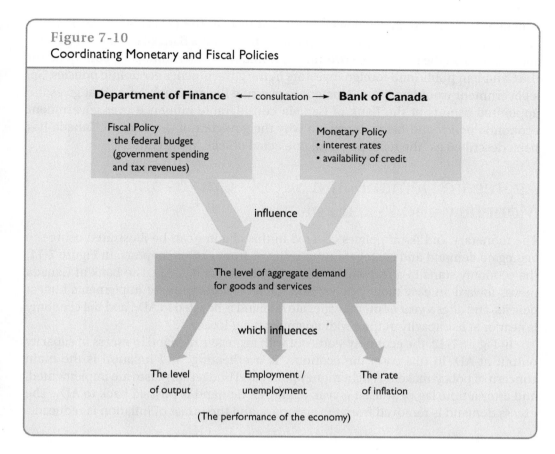

Figure 7-10
Coordinating Monetary and Fiscal Policies

Department of Finance ← consultation → Bank of Canada

Fiscal Policy
• the federal budget
 (government spending
 and tax revenues)

Monetary Policy
• interest rates
• availability of credit

influence

The level of aggregate demand
for goods and services

which influences

The level
of output

Employment /
unemployment

The rate
of inflation

(The performance of the economy)

Coordinating Monetary and Fiscal Policies

Figure 7-10 shows the coordination of fiscal policy, which is conducted by the federal government (the Department of Finance, under the minister of finance), and monetary policy, which is conducted by the Bank of Canada.

The Department of Finance reports to a federal minister who is a key member of the federal government's cabinet. The cabinet represents an elected government that is ultimately accountable to the public in the next election. On the other hand, few members of the cabinet (or other members of Parliament) have the technical expertise in economic and financial matters required for making monetary policy decisions.

The governor of the Bank of Canada and the people on staff at the central bank certainly possess great expertise concerning economic and financial issues. However, they are not elected and accountable to the public; they are appointed. And they are appointed for quite long terms—in the case of the governor and the senior deputy governor, seven years. This enables them to view economic policy from the longer-term perspective.

To provide for coordination between the government and the Bank of Canada, the Bank of Canada Act requires regular consultation between the governor of the Bank of Canada and the minister of finance (on behalf of the government). In addition, the Act provides that in the event of a fundamental disagreement, the federal government can direct the central bank, in writing, as to the monetary policy to be followed; that is, the government can overrule the governor of the Bank of Canada.

However, it would be very difficult for a government to do so. The law requires that any government directive overruling the Bank of Canada be made public. And it is generally understood that following such a directive, the governor of the Bank of Canada would resign. Given the widespread respect for the Bank of Canada's expertise, such actions on the part of the government would risk undermining the confidence of the Canadian public and foreign investors in the government's economic policies. So, a government would be quite reluctant to overrule the governor, a fact that gives the appointed experts at the Bank of Canada considerable influence over government economic policy and helps to explain why the governor of the Bank of Canada has been described as "the most powerful unelected official in the country."

Aggregate Demand and Supply Curves and Monetary and Fiscal Policy

The monetary and fiscal polices covered in this chapter can be illustrated using the aggregate demand and aggregate supply curves from earlier chapters. In Figure 7-11, the economy starts in a recession with aggregate demand at AD. The Bank of Canada moves toward an easy money policy, and the federal government implements budget deficits, and after a year or more, aggregate demand is boosted to AD_1, and the economy is near or at its capacity output, with unemployment lower.

In Figure 7-12, the economy starts out with aggregate demand in excess of capacity output at AD. In this case, the economy is overheating, and inflation is the main concern of policy-makers. A tight money policy and budget surpluses are implemented, and after a time lag of at least a year, aggregate demand is pushed back to AD_1. The excess demand is removed from the economy, and the threat of inflation is reduced.

Looking Ahead

The thoughtful reader will by now be wondering why, if monetary and fiscal policies really work as described in this chapter, Canada has not succeeded in eliminating both unemployment and inflation.

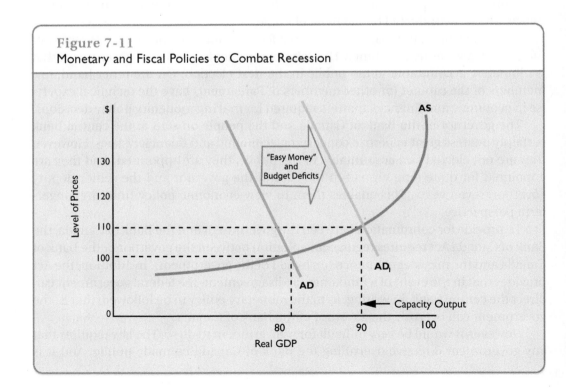

Figure 7-11
Monetary and Fiscal Policies to Combat Recession

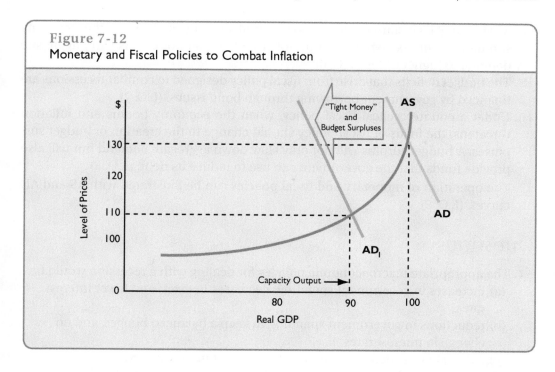

Figure 7-12
Monetary and Fiscal Policies to Combat Inflation

First, there are some real-world obstacles that make it impossible to eradicate *both* unemployment *and* inflation; we will consider these in Chapter 8. And, as we will also see in the next chapter, governments have not always used their economic policies effectively—sometimes their policy decisions have actually caused problems rather than resolved them.

Chapter Summary

1. The Bank of Canada is responsible for monetary policy, which uses changes in interest rates and the money supply to influence the level of aggregate demand. (L.O. 1)

2. To combat a recession, the Bank of Canada would use an *easy money policy*. The Bank of Canada would lower its target for the overnight rate of interest and take actions to increase the reserves of the banking system. (L.O. 2)

3. An easy money policy would reduce interest rates and encourage borrowing and spending by consumers and businesses. It might also reduce the international price of the Canadian dollar, which would stimulate exports and reduce imports. If aggregate demand were increased too rapidly, the rate of inflation could increase in the future. (L.O. 2)

4. To combat inflation, the Bank of Canada would use a *tight money policy*. The Bank of Canada would raise its target for the overnight rate of interest and take actions to reduce the reserves of the banking system. (L.O. 3)

5. A tight money policy would increase interest rates and discourage borrowing and spending by consumers and businesses. It might also increase the international price of the Canadian dollar, which would depress exports and increase imports. As the growth of aggregate demand slowed, unemployment would rise. (L.O. 3)

6. Fiscal policy, which is conducted by the Department of Finance, uses changes in government spending and taxes to influence the level of aggregate demand. (L.O. 4)

7. For combating recessions, fiscal policy involves increased government spending and/or tax reductions, which lead to government budget deficits. (L.O. 5)

8. After being kick-started by temporary budget deficits (L.O. 5), the economy should grow on its own as the multiplier and accelerator effects carry aggregate demand to higher levels. (L.O. 6)

9. The budget deficits that arise from fiscal policy designed to combat recessions are financed by government borrowing through bond issues. (L.O. 7)

10. Under a countercyclical fiscal policy, when the economy booms and inflation threatens, the focus of fiscal policy should change to the creation of budget surpluses. A budget surplus will not only slow down aggregate demand but will also provide funds that the government can use to reduce its debt. (L.O. 8)

11. The operation of monetary and fiscal policies can be illustrated with AS and AD curves. (L.O. 9)

Questions

1. The appropriate macroeconomic policies for dealing with a recession would be
   (a) increases in government spending, decreases in taxes, and lower interest rates.
   (b) reductions in government spending to keep a balanced budget, and no change in interest rates.
   (c) federal budget deficits combined with a tight money policy.
   (d) reductions in both interest rates and the federal government's debt.
   (e) a balanced budget, and increases in interest rates if necessary.

2. "The federal government should never have budget deficits, and should always balance its budget each year." Would this proposal have a beneficial effect on the Canadian economy? Why or why not?

3. Suppose that Canada's economy were in a boom, with real GDP growing by over 3 percent, a very low unemployment rate, and a rising rate of inflation. The federal government's budget surplus is projected to be over $10 billion and opposition parties are insisting that the government increase its spending on various programs and/or reduce taxes.
   (a) In these circumstances, should the federal government boost its spending on programs and/or reduce taxes?
   (b) If the surplus were not used to increase spending or reduce taxes, how should it be used?

4. Suppose that the Bank of Canada has just announced a significant reduction in the overnight rate.
   (a) What would have led the Bank of Canada to make such a change?
   (b) How is the Bank of Canada's policy change intended to influence the economy?
   (c) How soon would you expect to see the results of the Bank of Canada's policy change?
   (d) How might you expect this policy change to affect you personally?

5. Suppose that Statistics Canada's Composite Leading Indicator has been increasing fairly rapidly over the past few months. Does this make it more likely that interest rates will *increase* or *decrease* over the next few months? Explain the reason for your answer fully.

6. Do you think that macroeconomic policy at the present time should be used to increase aggregate demand or slow down the growth of aggregate demand? How would you decide your answer to this question?

7. "Politically, it is much easier for a government to have to fight a recession than it is to have to attack inflation." Do you agree with this statement? Why or why not?

8. Visit the Bank of Canada website (**www.bankofcanada.ca**) and check its most recent press release announcing any change to the overnight rate. How has the Bank of Canada changed its target for the overnight rate recently, and what were the reasons for its change in the target?

9. As the recession deepened in early 2009, one of the gloomier outlooks was provided by Professor Niall Ferguson of Harvard. In his view, the accumulation of excessive debt by consumers in the 2002–07 period meant that neither a quick nor a strong recovery of consumer spending was likely. His opinion was that the recession could easily last for two years, and that any recovery would be quite slow for another two years. Has Professor Ferguson's outlook proven accurate or not?

Study Guide

Review Questions (The answers to these Review Questions appear in Appendix B.)

1. The similarity between monetary policy and fiscal policy is that they both seek to
_____. The difference between them is that in order to achieve this goal, monetary policy uses _____,
while fiscal policy uses _____.

2. The *overnight rate* is
   (a) the rate of interest charged by banks and other financial institutions on very short-term loans to each other.
   (b) the top rate in the Bank of Canada's half-point target range for the overnight interest rate.
   (c) used by the Bank of Canada as a signal of the direction of its monetary policy.
   (d) the rate of interest charged by banks on loans to their more creditworthy customers.
   (e) Answers (a) and (c).

3. The objective of an *easy money policy* is to
   (a) combat recessions.
   (b) reduce unemployment.
   (c) reduce the rate of inflation.
   (d) Answers (a) and (b).
   (e) Answers (a), (b), and (c).

4. The objective of a *tight money policy* is to
    (a) reduce the rate of inflation.
    (b) reduce unemployment.
    (c) combat recessions.
    (d) promote more rapid economic growth.
    (e) Answers (b), (c), and (d).

5. If the Bank of Canada were concerned about rising unemployment and a recession, which of the following would it probably do?
    (a) reduce the overnight rate
    (b) shift government deposits from the banks to the Bank of Canada
    (c) buy government bonds
    (d) All of the above.
    (e) Answers (a) and (c).

6. If the Bank of Canada were concerned that the rate of inflation was becoming too high, which of the following would it probably do?
    (a) shift government deposits from the government's account at the Bank of Canada into the banks
    (b) sell government bonds
    (c) increase the overnight rate
    (d) Answers (b) and (c).
    (e) All of the above.

7. A reduction in the overnight rate is generally considered to be
    (a) an indication that monetary policy is becoming "easier."
    (b) an indication of a trend toward lower interest rates.
    (c) Answers (a) and (b).
    (d) an indication that monetary policy is becoming "tighter."
    (e) None of the above.

8. An increase in the overnight rate is generally considered to be
    (a) an indication that the Bank of Canada is concerned about inflation.
    (b) an indication that monetary policy is becoming easier.
    (c) an indication that interest rates are likely to rise.
    (d) Answers (a) and (c).
    (e) None of the above.

9. A *tight money policy* tends to have a particularly severe effect on the sales of
    (a) the housing industry.
    (b) the entertainment industry.
    (c) the gasoline industry.
    (d) the clothing industry.
    (e) the food industry.

10. If the Bank of Canada reduced interest rates in Canada, the international value of the Canadian dollar would
    (a) increase, which would lead to higher exports and employment in Canada.
    (b) decrease, which would lead to higher exports and employment in Canada.
    (c) increase, which would reduce foreign demand for Canadian exports.
    (d) decrease, which would reduce foreign demand for Canadian exports.
    (e) None of the above.

11. If the Bank of Canada increased interest rates in Canada, the international value of the Canadian dollar would
    (a) increase, which would lead to higher exports and employment in Canada.
    (b) decrease, which would lead to higher exports and employment in Canada.
    (c) increase, which would reduce foreign demand for Canadian exports.
    (d) decrease, which would reduce foreign demand for Canadian exports.
    (e) None of the above.

12. A change in the Bank of Canada's monetary policy will have an effect upon the direction of the economy (output, employment, and the rate of inflation)
    (a) immediately.
    (b) after about 3 months.
    (c) after about 6 months.
    (d) after 1–2 years.
    (e) None of the above.

13. Suppose that government spending were $300 billion and the government's tax revenues were $275 billion.
    (a) The government would have a budget _____ of $25 billion.
    (b) Such a budget would _____ the level of aggregate demand in the economy.
    (c) Such a budget would be helpful in dealing with a problem of _____.

14. The concept of *kick-starting* the economy is that
    (a) continuous annual government budget deficits are required to prevent the economy from falling into recession.
    (b) if the economy is in a recession, it is possible for the government to boost it temporarily with budget deficits, after which the economy can recover and grow without further stimulation from the government.
    (c) taxes should be reduced each year to boost demand.
    (d) the economy will collapse unless government spending is increased each year.
    (e) None of the above.

15. Suppose that government spending were $200 billion and the government's tax revenues were $220 billion.
    (a) The government would have a budget _____ of $20 billion.
    (b) Such a budget would _____ the level of aggregate demand in the economy.
    (c) Such a budget would be helpful in dealing with a problem of _____.

16. *Countercyclical fiscal policy* involves
    (a) regular annual government budget deficits, whether the economy is in a recession or not.
    (b) government budget deficits and increases in government debt to combat recessions.
    (c) government budget surpluses that are used to reduce government debt when the economy is booming.
    (d) the government always having a balanced budget.
    (e) Answers (b) and (c).

17. Which of the following is generally considered to be the most appropriate way to finance federal budget deficits?
    (a) Borrow the money by selling bonds.
    (b) Print as much money as necessary to finance the deficit.
    (c) Borrow the money from the World Bank.
    (d) Borrow from other nations.
    (e) None of the above.

18. If the government finances its budget deficits by printing money too quickly,
    (a) aggregate demand will fall and there will be a recession.
    (b) the economy will benefit greatly.
    (c) the result will be severe inflation.
    (d) prices will fall.
    (e) Answers (a) and (d).

Critical Thinking Questions

(Asterisked questions 1 to 5 are answered in Appendix B; the answers to questions 6 to 10 are in the Instructor's Manual that accompanies this text.)

*1. Suppose that the Bank of Canada has just announced that the overnight rate has been increased significantly.
    (a) What would you conclude is the Bank of Canada's reason for making this change?
    (b) Name two industries and two occupational groups that would probably be negatively affected by this policy change, and explain why they would be so affected.
    (c) How would you expect this announcement to affect the stock market?
    (d) How might you expect this policy change by the Bank of Canada to affect you personally?

*2. Suppose that the capacity GDP were $800 billion and it were forecast that there would be a recession in which aggregate demand would fall to about 2 percent below capacity over the next year. Assuming a multiplier of 1.6, what amount of increased government spending would be required to keep aggregate demand stable and minimize the risk of a recession?

*3. Suppose that the economy is growing sluggishly, and Canadian manufacturers are losing export sales because the international price of the Canadian dollar has increased considerably. In these circumstances, what might the Bank of Canada do that would be helpful to the economy in general and manufacturers in particular?

*4. Suppose that the leading indicator *for the U.S. economy* were decreasing. Would this make it more likely that the Bank of Canada would increase or decrease interest rates? Explain the reason for your answer.

*5. Late in an economic boom, there often occurs a seemingly peculiar and contradictory sequence of events. First, there are reports of the boom becoming stronger— higher output, lower unemployment and so on. This is followed promptly by a *decline* in the stock market. This is apparently not a random event; in fact, it sometimes seems that *the better* the economic news, *the worse* is its effect on stock prices. Can you explain the reason for this phenomenon?

6. Fiscal policy to stimulate the economy can include increases in government spending and/or reductions in taxes.
   (a) Which of the following do you believe would boost aggregate demand *more strongly*—a $1 billion increase in government spending or a $1 billion reduction in personal income taxes? Why?
   (b) Which of the two policies in (a) do you believe would have a *faster* effect on the economy? Why?

7. "Even apparently pointless 'make-work' programs ('digging holes and filling them up again') run by the government can be of economic value under certain conditions."
   (a) What are the "certain conditions" to which the speaker is referring, and what is the speaker's reasoning?
   (b) Make an argument against such make-work programs. (*Hint: think opportunity cost.*)

8. Why is the governor of the Bank of Canada described as "the most powerful unelected official in the country"? Why do you think the governor is appointed for such a long term (seven years)?

9. (a) At the level of aggregate demand represented by AD$_1$ in the graph below, the level of GDP is $600 billion. The economy is in a condition of _____, because _____.
   (b) What would be the appropriate monetary and fiscal policies in these circumstances?
   (c) Draw a new aggregate demand curve (AD$_2$) to represent the new situation that might result from the policies in (b), and show on the graph how this new AD curve would affect
      (i)   the level of GDP, and
      (ii) the level of prices.
   (d) Explain why the effects referred to in (c) will occur.

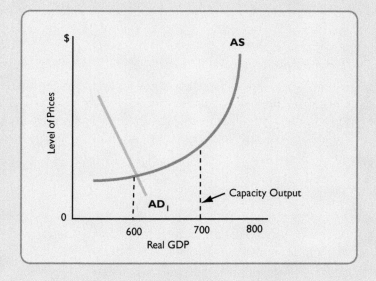

10. (a) At the level of aggregate demand represented by AD_1 in the graph on page 175, the level of GDP is $800 billion. The economy is in a condition of _____, because _____.

(b) What would be the appropriate monetary and fiscal policies in these circumstances?

(c) Draw a new aggregate demand curve (AD_2) to represent the new situation that would result from the policies in (b), and show on the graph how this new AD curve would affect

(i) the level of GDP, and

(ii) the level of prices.

(d) Explain why the effects referred to in (c) will occur.

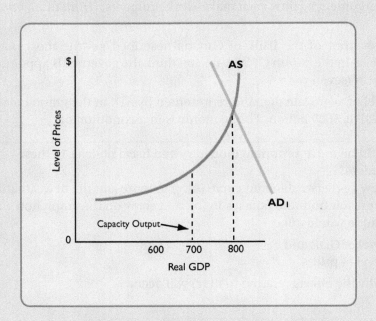

Use the Web (Hints for this Use the Web exercise appear in Appendix B.)

1. On Statistics Canada's website (**www.statcan.gc.ca**), find the following statistics for the past five years:

   - Unemployment rate: Search the site for "Labour force characteristics", then click on "Labour force characteristics".
   - Inflation rate: Search the site for "Consumer price index, historical summary".
   - Interest rates: Search the site for "Interest rates", then click on "Exchange rates, interest rates, money supply, and stock prices".

   (a) What has been the trend in interest rates over the recent past?
   (b) Can you see a logical relationship between the trend in interest rates and the trends in the unemployment and inflation rates?

8

Perspectives on Macroeconomic Policy

After studying this chapter, you should be able to

1. Explain how monetary and fiscal policies that increase aggregate demand will affect output, employment, and the rate of inflation

   (a) during a recession, and
   (b) as the economy approaches its capacity output and full employment.

2. State the unemployment rate that is considered to represent *full employment*, and explain why this rate is as high as it is, with reference to

   (a) the trade-off between unemployment and inflation,
   (b) the different types of unemployment, and
   (c) differences in unemployment rates among regions and age groups.

3. Referring to Canada's experience, explain why it is important for government policy-makers to keep the rate of inflation low and relatively stable.

4. State the target range for inflation that has been established by the Bank of Canada and the federal government, and explain the purposes of this target range.

5. Describe two situations in which government borrowing is economically beneficial.

6. Referring to Canada's experience, explain why it is important for government policy-makers to keep government debt under control.

7. Explain how the time lags involved in implementing monetary and fiscal policies can limit the effectiveness of these policies.

8. Explain three ways in which international factors limit the freedom of Canadian economic policy-makers.

The monetary and fiscal policies described in Chapter 7 are impressive in scope, directed toward speeding up or slowing down the entire economy by influencing the behaviour of millions of consumers and businesses. The impact of these policies is measured in terms of tens of billions of dollars of output and hundreds of thousands of jobs.

If these policies worked ideally, we might expect to have very little unemployment or inflation. However, this has not been the case—in the last quarter of the twentieth century, the average unemployment rate was over 9 percent of the labour force, and the average rate of inflation was nearly 6 percent. Also, as Figure 8-1 shows, economic conditions were far from stable, as the rates of both unemployment and inflation fluctuated widely over the period.

Why have we not been able to do better than this? To a large extent, our less-than-ideal economic performance reflects the fact that when monetary and fiscal policies are implemented in the real world, certain obstacles exist that limit the extent to which unemployment and inflation can be reduced. In addition, governments have sometimes used these policies unwisely, with unfortunate results. To explain the track record in Figure 8-1, we will consider the following five limitations:

1. Obstacles to reducing unemployment.
2. The need to keep inflation under control.
3. The need to keep government debt within limits.
4. Time lags associated with implementing policies.
5. International limitations on Canadian policies.

Finally, Figure 8-1 also shows that after the mid-1990s, Canadians generally enjoyed both lower unemployment rates and lower inflation rates than in the previous two decades. We will conclude the chapter with a review of these improvements.

1. Obstacles to Reducing Unemployment

Figure 8-1 shows that the lowest annual unemployment rate we have achieved since 1974 has been 6.0 percent in 2007, and that the unemployment rate has seldom been below 7 percent. To understand these facts better, we need to consider the matter of unemployment in more detail.

Types of Unemployment

In Chapter 2, we saw that there are various reasons why people become unemployed. An examination of these reasons can provide a better understanding of unemployment and what can be done about it.

Cyclical unemployment, which arises from the periodic recessions associated with the business cycle, is probably the best-known type of unemployment. Cyclical forces account for the periodic peaks in the unemployment rate that are evident in Figure 8-1, during recessions. And when the economy recovers, cyclical unemployment and the unemployment rate decrease.

However, there are several other factors that also affect the unemployment rate, and these considerably complicate the government's task of reducing unemployment.

Frictional unemployment is due to people being temporarily out of work because they are changing from one job to another. Frictional unemployment is considered to be a normal aspect of a free and dynamic economy in which jobs change in response to constant changes in product demand and technology.

cyclical unemployment
Unemployment that is caused by periodic cyclical weaknesses in aggregate demand associated with recessions.

frictional unemployment
Unemployment arising from people being temporarily out of work because they are in the process of changing jobs.

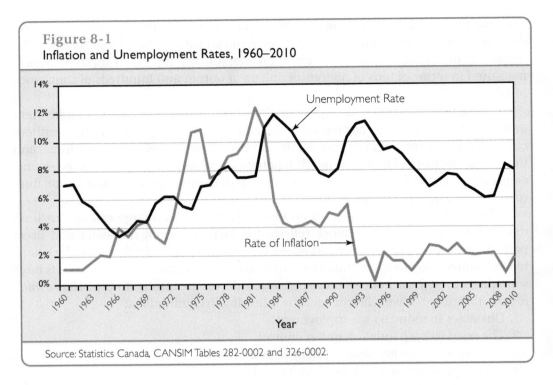

Figure 8-1
Inflation and Unemployment Rates, 1960–2010

Source: Statistics Canada, CANSIM Tables 282-0002 and 326-0002.

seasonal unemployment
Unemployment arising from seasonal downturns in employment in some industries.

Seasonal unemployment is also relatively short term in nature. Because of the seasonal nature of industries such as agriculture, fishing, forestry, and construction, unemployment is higher in the winter. Seasonal unemployment is an inevitable aspect of Canadian labour markets; however, today it affects relatively few people.

structural unemployment
Unemployment arising from a mismatch between the skills required by employers and those of unemployed people.

Structural unemployment is a much more serious problem for affected workers because of its longer-term nature. Structural unemployment arises from a mismatch between the skills required by employers and those possessed by unemployed workers, which can make it very difficult for the unemployed to find work. Structural unemployment can be caused by changes in *production technology* or *product demand*; for instance, the replacement of manufacturing workers by industrial robots and the replacement of coal with natural gas for heating homes. Another factor underlying structural unemployment is the lack of the education and/or skills for employment in a modern economy.

As we will see, the existence of these various types of unemployment complicates the government's task of reducing unemployment considerably.

Regional Differences in Unemployment Rates

As Figure 8-2 on page 179 shows, there are large and persistent differences in unemployment rates in the various regions of Canada. Unemployment rates in the Atlantic provinces and Quebec are persistently higher than the national average, while in Ontario and the Prairies, the unemployment rate has usually been below the average. British Columbia's unemployment rate is sometimes above and sometimes below the national average, depending upon swings in that province's resource export–based economy.

Statistics Canada collects data on 69 different regional labour markets across Canada.

These regional variations in unemployment also complicate the government's efforts to reduce unemployment, because even when an economic boom makes unemployment quite low in Canada as a whole, and very low in some parts of the country, it will still be quite high in other regions.

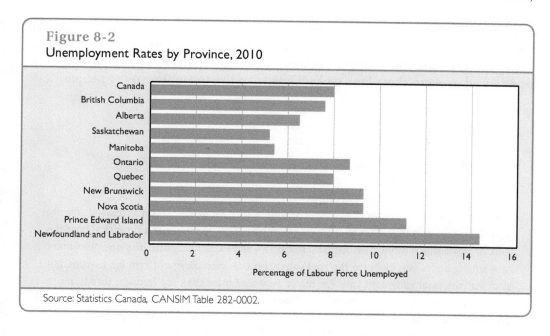

Figure 8-2
Unemployment Rates by Province, 2010

Source: Statistics Canada, CANSIM Table 282-0002.

Age Differences in Unemployment Rates

As Figure 8-3 shows, unemployment rates are particularly high among young people. In 2010, when the unemployment rate for people age 25 and over was only 6.8 percent, 19.9 percent of the 15–19 age group was unemployed.

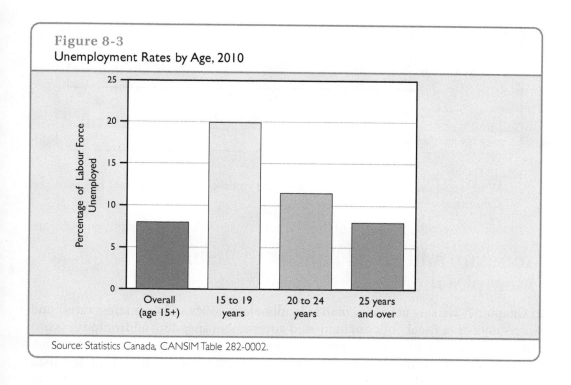

Figure 8-3
Unemployment Rates by Age, 2010

Source: Statistics Canada, CANSIM Table 282-0002.

There are various reasons why unemployment rates for the young are so high. When the economy slows down, employers reduce or cease hiring, leaving many young people who are trying to enter the labour force unable to find work. Also, layoffs are most commonly done by seniority, so the young are generally laid off first. In addition, frictional unemployment is high among the young, because people move more frequently from job to job early in their careers. Also, Canada's minimum wage laws are believed to contribute to Canada's high rate of youth unemployment. By requiring minimum wage rates for younger workers that are not much less than those for more experienced workers, these laws make it less attractive to employ young people.

YOU DECIDE

The 2008–09 Recession and Jobs

During the 2008–09 recession, the unemployment rate for all Canadians increased sharply, from 6.1 percent in May 2008 to 8.5 percent in May 2009. However, the recession hurt the jobs of males much more than females. The figure shows not only that the unemployment rate among males was *higher* in the recession than the unemployment rate for females, but also that the unemployment rate for males *increased more* than for females; that is, more "male" jobs were lost than "female" jobs. The unemployment rate for females increased by 1.5 percentage points, while the increase for males was 3.4 percentage points, and the unemployment rate for males age 15–24 was 4.7 percentage points. ■

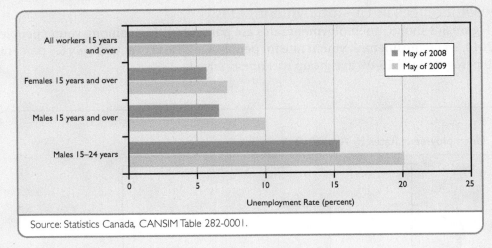

Source: Statistics Canada, CANSIM Table 282-0001.

QUESTION

1. What would explain the different impact of the recession on these different groups of Canadian workers?

Monetary and Fiscal Policies to Reduce Unemployment

In Chapter 7, we saw how *easy money* (a monetary policy of low interest rates) and *budget deficits* (a fiscal policy of increased government spending and/or lower taxes) can be combined to combat unemployment by increasing aggregate demand. However, since 1981, the number of unemployed Canadians has never been less than one million. To see why we have not been able to get the unemployment rate as low as we would like, we will examine how the economy responds to government policies that boost aggregate demand

(a) when unemployment is high, and

(b) when unemployment is low.

First, it is helpful to recall that in any market, an increase in demand can have three effects: it can cause an *increase in output* (and employment), an *increase in*

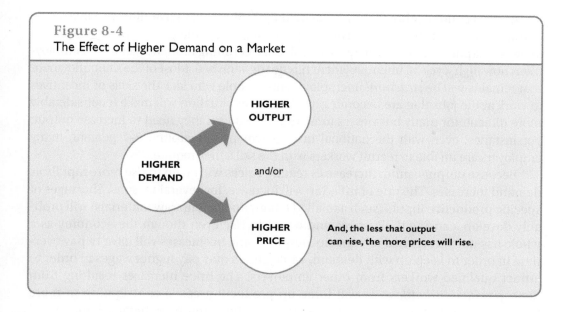

Figure 8-4
The Effect of Higher Demand on a Market

HIGHER DEMAND

HIGHER OUTPUT

and/or

HIGHER PRICE

And, the less that output can rise, the more prices will rise.

prices, or a *combination of these*, as shown in Figure 8-4. And the more that output can rise in response to higher demand, the less prices will rise. On the other hand, if output cannot rise as fast as demand, prices will rise. So, the faster output can increase, the less rapidly prices will rise.

The Effects of Increased Demand When Unemployment Is High

Suppose the economy is in a recession, with cyclical unemployment high and output far below capacity. With aggregate demand this low, the rate of inflation will be very low.

If the government uses its monetary and fiscal policies to increase aggregate demand, the results should be quite favourable. Output and employment will be able to increase, but the rate of inflation will remain low.

First, output and employment can be increased readily in a recession. Businesses will have unused plant capacity and will be able to obtain materials from suppliers who are in a similar position. And with cyclical unemployment high, businesses will be able to recall or hire unemployed workers in order to increase production.

The rate of inflation will remain low for several reasons, the basic one being that output can be increased so readily. Also, with unemployment high, businesses will be able to obtain the workers they need without having to pay higher wages. And as output increases, production costs per unit will actually fall, as production facilities are used more efficiently and fixed costs are spread over more units of output. Furthermore, with the economy still sluggish, businesses and unions will be unlikely to increase prices and wages for fear of jeopardizing their sales and jobs.

In short, when there is a recession, government policies that increase aggregate demand will have *very beneficial effects* on the economy, by causing quite large increases in output without increasing the rate of inflation significantly. And as the economy recovers from the recession, the unemployment rate will decrease as cyclical unemployment falls.

The Effects of Increased Demand When Unemployment Is Low

As these expansionary monetary and fiscal policies bring unemployment down, their effects on the economy will gradually change. As output gets nearer to capacity and unemployment becomes quite low, further increases in aggregate demand will have *mixed effects* on the economy. Output will not be able to rise as rapidly as before, and prices will begin to rise more rapidly.

As the economy approaches capacity output, firms will have difficulty increasing output as rapidly as in the past. They may no longer have the unused plant capacity to increase output, and/or they may have problems recruiting more workers. With employment now high, cyclical unemployment has nearly vanished. Most of the unemployment that remains will be *structural* unemployment—people who lack the skills or incentives to work at the jobs that are becoming available. This situation will make it considerably more difficult for many businesses to recruit the workers they need to increase output. For instance, even with the national unemployment rate around 6–7 percent, many employers are unable to recruit workers with the skills they require.

Because output cannot increase as readily, prices will begin to rise more rapidly as demand increases. The rate of inflation will increase, for several reasons. Shortages of specific productive inputs (such as skilled labour and certain raw materials) will probably develop, causing their prices and wages to rise even though the economy as a whole has not yet reached its capacity output. Some businesses will have to pay overtime in order to keep up with demand, while others may pay higher wages in order to attract qualified workers from other employers. The price increases resulting from these *production bottlenecks* will force up production costs, contributing to more rapid inflation. Furthermore, as economic conditions improve, higher demand will enable more businesses to raise prices, and labour unions will take advantage of the improved bargaining position that low unemployment rates bring, negotiating larger wage increases that add to employers' labour costs and push prices higher.

In summary, as the economy expands into the boom phase of the cycle, government policies that drive aggregate demand higher will encounter more difficulty in pushing output and employment higher, but will drive the rate of inflation up. And the closer the economy gets to its capacity output, the more severe inflation will become.

The Problem of Inflation

And therein lies the problem. Long before monetary and fiscal policies have eradicated unemployment, they will be generating a problem of inflation. With aggregate demand high enough that inflation is threatening to become a serious problem, unemployment will still be high in some regions, such as the Atlantic provinces and Quebec, and among some groups, such as the young and the structurally unemployed. And if the government attacked this unemployment by using its monetary and fiscal policies to push aggregate demand even higher, it would achieve only small improvements in unemployment at the cost of generating a growing problem of inflation that threatens to accelerate. (The next section will explain the dangers of accelerating inflation.)

At this point, the economy would have reached **full employment**; that is, the unemployment rate would be as low as it can go without inflation becoming a problem.

full employment
The lowest rate of unemployment that can be achieved without generating unacceptably rapid inflation.

What Is Full Employment?

How low can the unemployment rate go before inflation becomes a problem? There is no magic number that is the answer to this question. Rather, the evidence is that the answer can change over time.

One way to estimate the unemployment rate that represents full employment is to examine recent economic booms, and see how low the unemployment rate managed to get before the boom ended.

In 1989, at the peak of the boom of the late 1980s, the unemployment rate dipped to 7.5 percent. But in the 1980s, inflation was much more ingrained into the Canadian economy than now, so accelerating inflation killed off that boom relatively early. Since inflation was tamed in the 1990s, we have done better: in the boom of 2000, the unemployment rate bottomed out at 6.4 percent, and the boom of 2006–07 saw the unemployment rate reach 6.0 percent. This has led some observers to conclude (tentatively) that full employment is now in the 6.0 to 6.5 percent range. And if the retirement of the baby boomers generates the labour shortages foreseen by many forecasters, "full employment" could come to represent an unemployment rate below 6 percent in the future.

2. The Need to Keep Inflation in Check

The previous section explains that the need to restrain inflation limits how far government policies can reduce unemployment. Now, let's consider *why* government policy-makers place such emphasis on keeping inflation in check. The experience of the Great Inflation of the 1970s and '80s demonstrated painfully that if the government does not keep the rate of inflation quite low, inflation can *accelerate*, with serious economic consequences. As a result, much more emphasis is placed today on *preventing* inflation from reaching the point at which it begins to gain momentum.

The Great Inflation of the 1970s

The Great Inflation of the 1970s was generated by a very rapid increase in the money supply of Canada and other nations. Subsequently, aggregate demand and the economy also grew rapidly. At first, the increase in the rate of inflation that accompanied these developments seemed to be a small trade-off for the gains in output and employment.

However, after a time lag of about a year, the money-supply growth pushed aggregate demand beyond the economy's capacity, and the rate of inflation soared from less than 3 percent per year in 1971 to nearly 11 percent in 1974.

How Inflation Accelerated

Once inflation got underway, it tended to gather momentum and became more and more rapid, due to *inflation psychology*, or people's behaviour when faced with inflation. As discussed in Chapter 6, in this kind of situation people came to expect that rapid inflation would continue. To protect themselves against this expected rapid inflation, they sought very large wage and salary increases and spent their money before prices rose further, even borrowing to do so. This behaviour made inflation more severe, as higher wages pushed up production costs and prices, and higher spending added to inflationary pressures. As a result, rates of inflation of 9 to 12 percent per year became ingrained in the economy for about a decade after 1972, as Figure 8-5 shows.

The Damage Caused by Severe Inflation

Inflation and Exports

If inflation in Canada is more rapid than in other countries, Canadian goods will become more expensive relative to foreign goods, and Canadian producers will become less competitive internationally. Foreigners will buy fewer Canadian exports, and Canadians will buy more foreign imports, causing output and employment in Canada to fall. Because Canada's exports and imports are such a high proportion of its GDP, the potential loss of output and also of employment in such a situation are a serious concern.

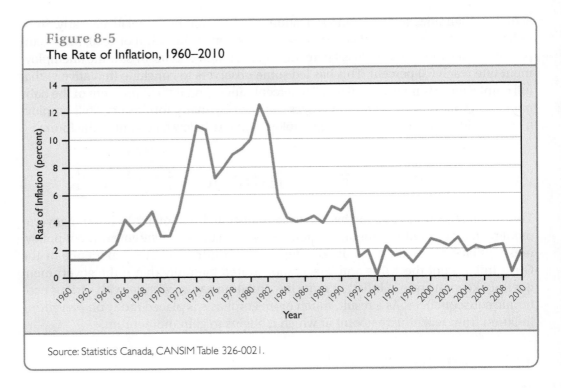

Figure 8-5
The Rate of Inflation, 1960–2010

Source: Statistics Canada, CANSIM Table 326-0021.

Inflation and the Economically Weak

Another concern is the effect of rapid inflation on the economically weak members of society. With prices rising rapidly, people must obtain large wage increases just to stand still economically. For professionals, skilled workers, and members of strong labour unions, this is generally possible. But economically weak groups such as pensioners, the unskilled, and nonunion workers will not be able to increase their incomes as fast as prices are rising. For them, rapid inflation means that their standard of living will fall.

Inflation and the Saving–Investment Process

Inflation *undermines the saving–investment process*, which is the key to higher productivity and prosperity. The main reason for this problem (as we saw in Chapter 6) is that rapid inflation *causes high interest rates* that discourage business investment spending. Fearing that continuing inflation will erode the real value (purchasing power) of the capital that they loan out, savers/lenders will insist on higher interest rates to offset the declining value of their capital. This situation is shown in Table 8-1 on page 185. In the low-inflation scenario in the left column, savers/lenders expect inflation to reduce the value of their capital by 2 percent per year, so they accept an interest rate of 5 percent on any loans they make—after inflation, this would leave them with a **real interest rate**, or after-inflation gain, of 3 percent. But in the high-inflation scenario in the right column, they expect inflation of 10 percent, so they will have to earn an interest rate of *13 percent* to earn the same real (after inflation) interest rate of 3 percent. But if rapid inflation forces interest rates too high, businesses may find borrowing for capital investment to be too costly. And less investment means slower growth of productivity and living standards.

But Table 8-1 also shows a second problem: *rapid inflation reduces the incentive to save*. In the low-inflation scenario in the left column, on an investment of $100 the saver/investor earns a real return of $3 before taxes, and $1 after taxes of $2 (40 percent of the $5 interest income). But in the high-inflation scenario in the right-hand

real interest rate
The rate of return earned by a lender after inflation is taken into account.

Table 8-1
Inflation and Incentives to Save and Invest

$100 invested for one year	With Inflation Expected to Be 2%		With Inflation Expected to Be 10%	
Interest rate	5%		13%	
⟶ Interest income	⟶	$5.00	⟶	$13.00
less:				
Loss of purchasing power on the $100 due to inflation	2%	2.00	10%	10.00
equals:				
"Real" return (after inflation)	3%	$3.00	3%	$3.00
less:				
Taxes on interest income (40%)		−2.00		−5.20
equals:				
Return after inflation and taxes		+1.00		−2.20

column, the saver/investor *loses money*. On the $13 of interest income, the taxes will be $5.20 (40 percent of $13), leaving the investor with a *loss* of $2.20 after inflation and taxes. So the incentive to save and invest is actually lower in the high-inflation/high-interest-rate situation than in the low-inflation/low-interest-rate situation.

In summary, rapid inflation is the enemy of the saving–investment process that is a key to prosperity. Rapid inflation discourages not only capital investment, but also the saving upon which much capital investment depends. By doing so, severe inflation can undermine productivity growth and the supply side of the economy.

Inflation Leads to Recession

Periods of severe inflation tend to end in recessions. Eventually, the problems caused by inflation will force the government to fight inflation with a tight money policy of very *high interest rates* to discourage borrowing. Such policies led to mortgage interest rates of over 20 percent in 1981 and a recession in 1981–82. This unhappy experience was repeated in the early 1990s, when mortgage rates exceeded 13 percent and a recession followed.

So, for a variety of reasons that are summarized in Figure 8-6, we learned in the 1970s and 1980s that rapid inflation will have serious economic consequences. As a result of these experiences, the government decided that keeping inflation under control should be a priority for economic policy in the future.

Inflation Targets

In 1993, the federal government and the Bank of Canada announced the objective of keeping the rate of inflation inside a "target range" of 1 to 3 percent per year. This announcement asserted that in the future, the Bank of Canada's primary goal would be to *prevent* inflation from accelerating as it had done in the 1970s and 1980s. Because monetary policy operates with long time lags, this goal would require that the

" . . . commitment to the targets has helped anchor public expectations for low, stable inflation and has reduced fluctuations in economic activity."
— THE GOVERNMENT OF CANADA AND THE BANK OF CANADA, MAY 2001

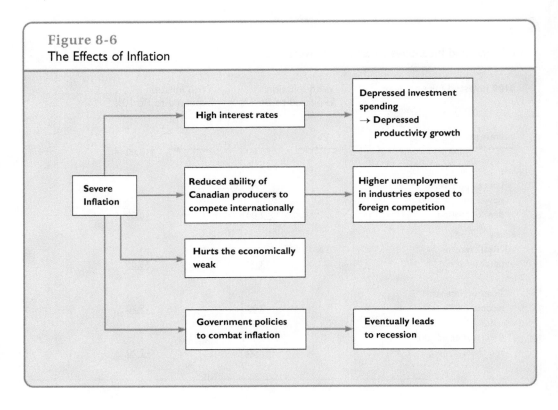

Figure 8-6
The Effects of Inflation

Bank of Canada be ready to take *early action* to increase interest rates if there were signs of inflation accelerating in the economy.

Inflation targets could also help to keep inflation under control by changing expectations concerning inflation. If the public believes that inflation will be kept under control, the public's expectation that causes inflation to accelerate (inflation psychology) will be less likely to develop, making it easier for the Bank of Canada to maintain a low rate of inflation.[1]

3. The Need to Keep Government Deficits and Debt Under Control

The experience of the 1970s and 1980s demonstrated the need not only to keep inflation under control, but also to keep government budget deficits and debt under control.

This is not a simple question of government borrowing and debt being "bad." In the right circumstances, government borrowing can bring economic and social benefits. First, we will consider two situations in which government borrowing can be beneficial, then we will examine the problems that Canada has experienced with government deficits and debt.

---

[1] This does not mean that price stability was to be the *only* goal of the Bank of Canada. When the economy is in a recession and the rate of inflation is very low, the Bank of Canada will reduce short-term interest rates with the intention of stimulating aggregate demand, as described in Chapter 7. This was done in 2001–02 and again in 2008–09, when economic conditions were sufficiently slow that such a policy would not create a danger of inflation.

Countercyclical Budget Deficits

As we saw in Chapter 7, periodic government budget deficits can help to boost aggregate demand during recessions, through a combination of higher government spending and lower taxes. These *countercyclical* deficits will, of course, require the government to borrow and increase its debt during recessions. However, after the recession has ended and the economy is booming again, there is an opportunity for the government to pay down its debt by running budget surpluses, as shown in Figure 8-7(a). Such countercyclical budget deficits are a generally accepted element of government economic policy.

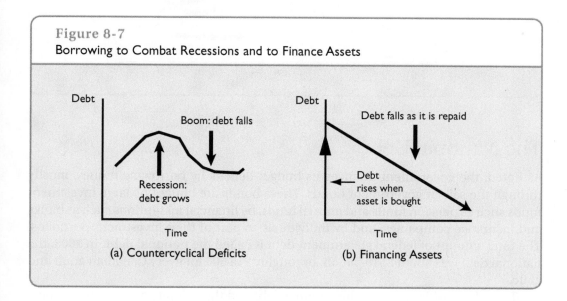

Figure 8-7

Borrowing to Combat Recessions and to Finance Assets

(a) Countercyclical Deficits

(b) Financing Assets

Borrowing to Finance Social Assets

A common reason for borrowing is to *acquire assets,* such as homes and cars for households, and plant and equipment for businesses. Borrowing is necessary because such assets are too costly to purchase out of the current year's income. And since the benefits from the asset will be received over a long period of time, it is quite reasonable to borrow to buy the asset and to pay for it over a period of years, as the loan is repaid, as shown in Figure 8-7(b).

In a similar manner, it is considered reasonable for governments to borrow to build *social assets,* such as hospitals, schools, transportation systems, and so on. Since these assets will provide long-term benefits to the public, governments typically issue long-term bonds to raise the funds to build them.

What Not to Do

While it is considered reasonable to borrow to pay for large *one-time expenditures* such as assets (or combatting a recession), borrowing to pay *ongoing current operating expenses* is a very different matter. These are not one-time expenditures; rather, they recur regularly, month after month. Borrowing to pay expenses such as these will only lead to regular monthly borrowing, and an ever-increasing debt. And after the debt reaches a certain point, the *rising interest costs* on the debt might well eventually become unmanageable, pushing the debt even *higher* in a sort of spiral, as shown in Figure 8-8.

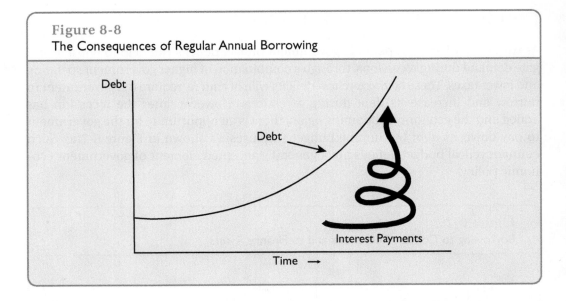

Figure 8-8
The Consequences of Regular Annual Borrowing

The National Debt

As noted, the government finances its budget deficits by borrowing money, mostly through the sale of government bonds. These bonds are bought by large investment funds such as pension funds and mutual funds, by financial institutions such as banks and insurance companies, and by individuals as part of their investment portfolios. The total amount of federal government debt is called the **national debt**. In 2008, the national debt was about $516 billion, or roughly $15 500 for every Canadian adult and child.

national debt (net)
A measure of the indebtedness of the federal government; specifically, the difference between the government's liabilities (mostly outstanding bonds) and its financial assets.

The relationship between the national debt and the federal government's budget deficits is shown in Table 8-2. The national debt is the *total accumulated federal debt* as a result of past budget deficits, while each year's budget deficit represents *that year's addition* to the national debt.

Table 8-2
Federal Budget Deficits and the National Debt

Year	Government Spending	Government Tax Revenues	Budget Deficit	National Debt
		($ Billions)		
20X1	$50	$50	$0	$0
20X2	60	55	5	5
20X3	70	56	14	19
20X4	80	68	12	31
20X5	83	75	8	39

In Table 8-2, it is assumed that the government has no debt at the start of year 20X1, no budget deficit in 20X1, and therefore no debt at the end of 20X1. After that, there are deficits for four years, with the total government debt (national debt) increasing by the amount of each year's deficit. Note that even after the government manages to *reduce its deficits* in 20X4 and 20X5, the national debt continues to grow.

As long as there is *any* budget deficit, the national debt will rise. Only by having budget surpluses (revenues larger than spending) can the government *reduce* its debt.

Canada's Experience with Government Deficits and Debt

Beginning in the mid-1970s, an unusual situation developed concerning the federal government's budget. *In every year* the government had a budget deficit, and these deficits became *very large*—as large as $13 billion in the late 1970s and $37 billion in the 1980s.

During the 1970s, the federal government had made various policy decisions that *increased its expenditure commitments* and *depressed its tax revenues*. The government increased benefits under various social programs, and made commitments to transfer large amounts of federal funds to the provincial governments to help finance provincial government spending on programs such as *health care, welfare,* and *post-secondary education*. At the same time, the government *cut taxes* on both personal and business income, which depressed its tax revenues.

So a built-in imbalance developed between government spending and tax revenues, generating **structural budget deficits**—budget deficits that occur each year, *whether the economy is in a recession or not*. Figure 8-9 shows the budget deficits and the growth of the federal government's debt during the 1970s and '80s.

The recession of the early 1980s increased federal budget deficits sharply, and by 1985 the national debt was nearly seven times its 1975 level. In the second half of the 1980s, the government tried to reduce its deficits by restraining its spending and increasing various taxes. But by this point, *interest payments on the government's massive debt* were keeping the deficits high, and forcing the government to borrow even more.

The recession of the early 1990s drove the federal budget deficit to nearly $40 billion. The federal government's debt was over $500 billion, and was being driven higher by annual interest payments in the $40-billion range.

structural budget deficits

Deficits arising from a built-in imbalance between government expenditures and revenues that results in deficits even when the economy is in a period of boom.

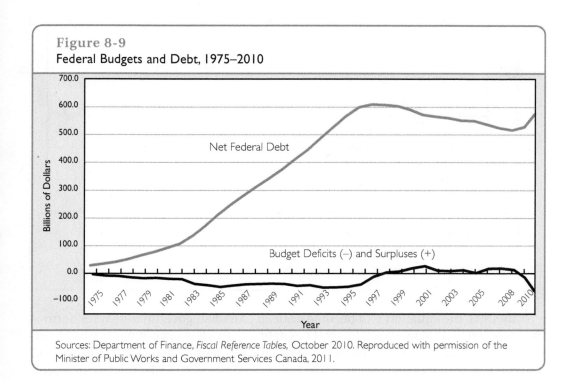

Figure 8-9
Federal Budgets and Debt, 1975–2010

Sources: Department of Finance, *Fiscal Reference Tables*, October 2010. Reproduced with permission of the Minister of Public Works and Government Services Canada, 2011.

The finances of the provincial governments were also deteriorating. To reduce its budget deficits, the federal government had cut its transfer payments to the provinces for health care, welfare, and post-secondary education. This forced the provincial governments into large budget deficits of their own.

Canada's Foreign Debt

While the federal government sold most of its own bonds *within* Canada, its borrowings were so large that they absorbed much of Canadians' savings. So, provincial governments and corporations often had to borrow from *foreign lenders*. The federal government also increasingly borrowed from those same lenders. As a result, Canada's total foreign indebtedness reached roughly 45 percent of GDP, by far the largest of any major nation. (Italy was second highest at about 10 percent of GDP.)

Deficits, Debt, and Interest Rates

Such high government deficits and debt pushed interest rates to very high levels. In part, this was because of governments' high demand for borrowed funds; however, another reason for high interest rates was that foreign lenders were becoming increasingly concerned about the financial condition of Canadian governments. Figure 8-10 shows how the real (after-inflation) interest rate on Government of Canada long-term bonds became very high in the 1990s. By making borrowing very expensive, such high interest rates prolonged the recession of the early 1990s. They also added to governments' interest costs, making their deficits worse.

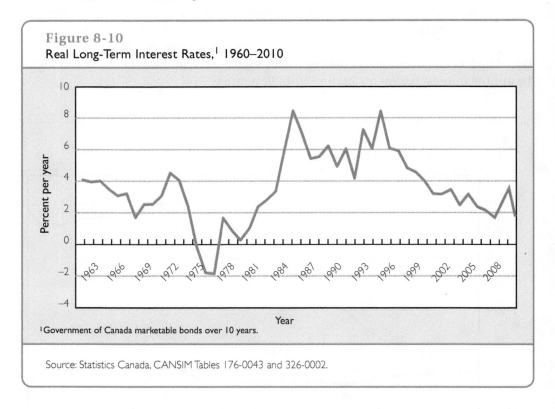

Figure 8-10
Real Long-Term Interest Rates,[1] 1960–2010

Percent per year

Year

[1] Government of Canada marketable bonds over 10 years.

Source: Statistics Canada, CANSIM Tables 176-0043 and 326-0002.

By 1993, the situation had become critical. Canadian governments were borrowing over $66 billion per year. The total net debt of Canadian governments was 95 percent of GDP, and interest payments were driving the debt higher, in an upward spiral. Canada's debt to foreign lenders, about half of which was owed by Canadian governments, was by far the largest in the world and rising rapidly. Foreign lenders were growing concerned about the creditworthiness of Canadian governments, and Canadian real interest rates were the highest in the world. These developments intensified the pressure on Canadian governments to deal with their budget problems.

Fixing the Problem

Finally, the federal government made cuts to its spending, particularly its transfer payments to the provinces. This led to a series of painful budget slashes by provincial governments in the mid-1990s that cut into all of Canada's key social welfare programs— health care, education, and welfare. Welfare benefits were reduced, health-care services were cut back, and cuts in funding for education led to large increases in tuition fees.

In the years following 1997, spending cutbacks (combined with rising tax revenues due to a booming economy) generated federal *budget surpluses*, which can also be seen in Figure 8-9 on page 189. These surpluses provided the federal government with the opportunity to

- pay down the federal debt (see Figure 8-11),
- cut personal and business taxes, and
- begin to restore spending in some of the programs that had been cut during the deficit-elimination period.

So, by the early 2000s Canadian governments had come through their period of excessive deficits and debt, and their respective financial positions were once again relatively sound. The increase in debt in 2009–10 was the result of the 2008–09 anti-recession budget deficits as discussed in Chapter 7.

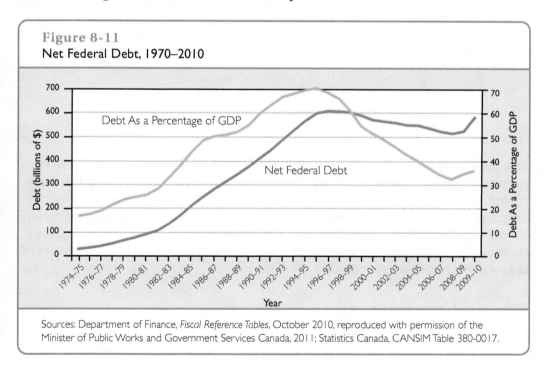

Figure 8-11
Net Federal Debt, 1970–2010

Sources: Department of Finance, *Fiscal Reference Tables*, October 2010, reproduced with permission of the Minister of Public Works and Government Services Canada, 2011; Statistics Canada, CANSIM Table 380-0017.

4. The Problem of Time Lags

Another limitation on the effectiveness of government monetary and fiscal policies is that they work slowly, or with *time lags*.

We first looked at the problem of time lags in Chapter 7. To recap, there are three types of time lags, which are summarized in Figure 8-12. The first is the *recognition lag*, or the time that it takes for policy-makers to clearly recognize that there is a problem of inflation or unemployment that needs to be addressed. Next is the *policy lag*, which occurs because government policies cannot be put in place immediately. The Bank of Canada can move quickly to change short-term interest rates, but changes in fiscal policy involving taxes and government spending take longer, as they may involve budget or legislative changes. Finally, there is the *impact lag*, or the time it takes for the policies to take effect on the economy. Changes in interest rates and government budgets will affect spending by consumers and businesses, but not for six to eighteen months. Monetary policy operates with long time lags, especially policies intended to slow down inflation.

Together, these time lags can add up to a total of *between one and two years*. Such long time lags can create real problems for economic policy-makers. Because of the lags, the problem being attacked (either inflation or recession) can grow considerably more severe and difficult to correct by the time the government's policies take effect.

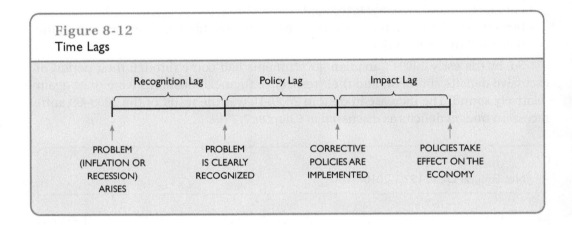

Figure 8-12
Time Lags

Taking Aim Carefully

Since the effects of the government's monetary and fiscal policies will not be felt for a year or two, the government should direct its policies toward correcting economic problems that it *expects will exist* in a year or two. Accurate economic forecasts are particularly helpful to governments in deciding the direction of their policies and in introducing their policies as early as possible. Unfortunately, as we saw in Chapter 6, economic forecasting is an imprecise process at best, adding to the uncertainties of the economic policy-making process.

Driving Carefully

Using monetary and fiscal policies to steer the economy is somewhat like handling an oil supertanker. These massive ships move with such momentum that there are major time lags involved in handling them. For instance, after its rudder has been turned, a supertanker will continue to go in the same direction for several kilometres before even *beginning* to turn. So in handling such ships, one must carefully *plan far ahead* and make only *gradual changes* in direction and speed in order to avoid steering in the wrong direction (and maybe at the wrong speed!) and being unable to make corrections for some time.

Trying to steer a nation's economy involves time lags like those involved in handling a supertanker, but with some additional complications. A supertanker is trying to reach (or avoid) certain *fixed locations*, such as a port (or a reef). But macroeconomic policy-makers must direct their policies toward what is essentially a *moving target*—the economic conditions that they *expect will exist* in a year or two. To return to our analogy, it is somewhat like trying to steer a supertanker past a distant reef that is moving in a direction and at a pace that you can only try to predict.

These problems both complicate the task of economic policy-makers and increase the cost of errors. Like a supertanker, if the economy gets moving in the wrong direction or at the wrong speed, it can get into serious trouble, such as hitting a reef, or its economic equivalent in the form of a recession or inflation. And as with a supertanker, these dangers make it appropriate to take a very *deliberate approach* to economic policy-making—it behooves economists to take a long-term perspective, plan well ahead, get all the facts before acting, be cautious and patient, and not do anything sudden that might get the economy off course and into dangerous waters.

Finally, following all this good advice is much easier for the captain who is in complete command of a supertanker than for an elected government that faces an impending election, unfavourable economic statistics, critical media, and opposition parties gaining in the polls. So, while good economic policy-making requires a long-term perspective, elected governments sometimes have much shorter political time horizons that can influence their decisions.

5. International Limitations on Canadian Policy-Makers

The Canadian economy has an unusually large exposure to international economic forces. Canada sells about 30 percent of its GDP to foreign buyers, of which over 70 percent goes to the United States. And Canada benefits greatly from capital investment by multinational corporations such as automobile manufacturers, which provides not only jobs, but also modern technology. This economic reliance on foreigners as both buyers and investors places certain limitations on the economic policies of Canadian governments.

Monetary Policy and Interest Rates

Probably the major international limitation on Canadian policies relates to monetary policy, particularly *interest rates*. In today's globalized world economy, money flows quite freely from country to country, and from one nation's currency into another's. This has created a virtual world market for money, with interest rates being the "price" of funds. In order to attract foreign funds that are needed and to keep Canadian funds from leaving Canada, Canadian interest rates must be competitive with interest rates elsewhere, particularly in the United States.

These international considerations can limit the freedom of the Bank of Canada in formulating Canadian monetary policy—when considering its interest rate policy, the Bank of Canada must keep one eye on economic conditions in Canada and the other eye on international interest rates and the concerns of foreign investors and lenders.

Canadian authorities are also generally reluctant to allow Canada's *rate of inflation* to significantly exceed U.S. inflation rates for long. If Canada's prices were to rise faster than U.S. prices, Canada's exports to the huge market stateside could decrease and imports could increase, threatening Canadian jobs.

Fiscal Policy

International considerations limit the *tax policies* of Canadian governments. If Canadian taxes on profits or investment income such as interest or dividends become too high relative to U.S. taxes, there is a risk that the flow of investment capital into Canada will be reduced, and that Canadian and foreign businesses will invest in the United States instead of in Canada.

Summary: You Can't Have It All . . .

Canadians want a great deal from their economic system, including the following:

(a) *Full employment.* Since the Great Depression, a basic objective of government economic policy has been full employment, or the lowest possible rate of unemployment.

(b) *Steady economic growth.* Another key objective of economic policy is a steadily growing economy, in which rising production of goods and services will provide both a higher standard of living for Canadians and jobs for a growing labour force.

(c) *Stable prices.* Economic policy-makers seek the lowest possible rate of inflation in order to avoid the problems experienced with inflation during the 1970s and '80s.

Over the long term, Canada's economy has been very good at providing rising output and employment and high living standards. However, its growth tends to be irregular due to business cycles, and when the economy stumbles into periodic recessions, unemployment often rises to quite high levels.

Monetary and fiscal policies can help to moderate business cycles and ease their impact on people. However, they can only do so within limits that are imposed by economic realities. For instance, policies that stimulate aggregate demand will reduce unemployment, but beyond a certain point, the danger of accelerating inflation limits what can be done to reduce unemployment. Also, the implementation of fiscal policy is limited by the need to avoid excessive government debt. In addition, the problem of possibly quite long time lags in implementing government policies limits the potential success of these policies. Finally, the fact that Canada is just one small player in a large international economy limits what can be expected of Canadian economic policies.

. . . But Good Economic Policies Can Help a Lot

In this chapter, we have seen several limitations on government economic policies, and the lessons learned from the negative effects of some past policies. But we have also seen how corrections to these policies have brought significant economic benefits to Canadians.

Look back to Figure 8-1—while it shows past problems regarding unemployment and inflation, it also shows lower and more stable rates of *both* unemployment *and* inflation in recent years. And while Figures 8-9 and 8-11 show some serious past problems with federal budget deficits and debt, they also remind us that those deficits were turned into surpluses, and that federal debt decreased from 72 percent of GDP in 1996 to only 32 percent of GDP in 2008, prior to the recession. And while Figure 8-10 shows how high inflation rates and rising government debt generated exorbitant real interest rates in the first half of the 1990s, it also illustrates how government policies that slowed inflation, eliminated budget deficits, and reduced debt paved the way for a very beneficial decrease in real long-term interest rates, from 8.4 percent in 1994 to 2.7 percent in the 2000–10 period.

These lower real interest rates reflect the more stable macroeconomic environment of Canada since the late 1990s, which has improved the confidence of not only lenders but also consumers and businesses.

Chapter Summary

1. During a recession, monetary and fiscal policies that increase aggregate demand will produce considerable increases in output and employment without increasing inflation significantly. (L.O. 1)

2. As the economy approaches its capacity output and full employment, monetary and fiscal policies that increase aggregate demand will produce smaller increases in output and employment, and will generate more inflation. (L.O. 1)

3. Full employment is considered to be an unemployment rate of 6 to 6.5 percent under the conditions prevailing in the early 2000s, because

    (a) this rate was the lowest unemployment rate that could be sustained without generating a problem of accelerating inflation (L.O. 2),
    (b) government policies that increase aggregate demand can reduce cyclical unemployment, but they are not as effective at reducing other types of unemployment (L.O. 2), and
    (c) it is particularly difficult to reduce unemployment in provinces east of Ontario and among young people. (L.O. 2)

4. It is important to keep the rate of inflation low and stable because inflation can accelerate, and high rates of inflation make Canadian producers less competitive internationally, hurt the economically weak, impair the saving–investment process, and eventually lead to recession. (L.O. 3)

5. In 1993, the federal government and the Bank of Canada established a target range of 1 to 3 percent per year for inflation, to ensure that the Bank of Canada would take timely action to prevent inflation from gaining momentum. The existence of the target could also reduce inflationary expectations that could add to inflation. (L.O. 4)

6. When governments borrow to combat recessions and to build social assets, such government borrowing is considered to be economically beneficial. (L.O. 5)

7. It is important to keep government deficits under control because a series of deficits can lead to the accumulation of a large government debt that can gain momentum due to heavy interest payments. Such heavy debt can generate very high real interest rates and lead to large cutbacks in government social welfare spending in order to eliminate the deficits. (L.O. 6)

8. Time lags involved in implementing monetary and fiscal policies make it difficult for governments to use these policies as effectively as we would like. (L.O. 7)

9. In deciding policies that affect interest rates, taxes, inflation, and government borrowing and debt, Canadian governments are limited by the need to keep

Canada attractive to foreigners, upon whom Canada relies as both buyers of its output and as investors and lenders. (L.O. 8)

Questions

1. Monetary and fiscal policies that push the economy close to full employment tend to
   (a) reduce the rate of inflation.
   (b) take effect only after time lags of one year or more.
   (c) generate higher rates of inflation.
   (d) slow down consumer spending.
   (e) Answers (b) and (c).

2. State whether each of the following is an example of *frictional unemployment, seasonal unemployment, cyclical unemployment,* or *structural unemployment.*
   (a) a construction worker who is laid off due to a recession that started last fall
   (b) a person who has quit her job and is in the process of moving to a new job that begins in two weeks
   (c) a golf course employee who is out of work until the golf courses open next spring
   (d) an assembly worker in an industrial plant who has been unable to find work since being replaced by new computerized equipment
   (e) a high school dropout who lacks the skills needed to find a job

3. Suppose that the following statistics represent economic trends over the past four years.

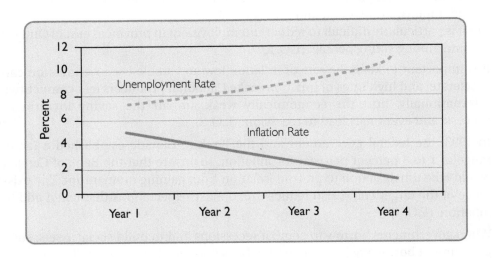

   (a) What is the main *economic problem* as of Year 4?
   (b) What would be the *basic cause* of this problem?
   (c) What type of *monetary policy* should the government use under these conditions, and how could this policy help to deal with the problem?
   (d) What type of *fiscal policy* (budget policy) should the government use under these conditions, and how could this policy help to deal with the problem?
   (e) What undesirable side effects could the policies in (c) and (d) have on the economy, and when and why might these occur?

4. Write a critical analysis of the following statement. "Full employment should mean no unemployment at all—an unemployment rate of zero. There is no reason why a country with Canada's economic resources and potential should tolerate any unemployment at all. The government should do whatever is required to reduce the unemployment rate to zero as quickly as possible."

   In your analysis, explain why full employment is not considered to be an unemployment rate of zero, and state the unemployment rate that is considered to represent full employment in the Canadian economy.

5. Since 1993, the Bank of Canada and the federal government have agreed that the rate of inflation should not exceed 3 percent per year. The intention of this agreement is to stress the importance of *preventing* the rate of inflation from becoming high, as it did in the 1970s.
   (a) Why do you think the federal government has determined that it would rather prevent inflation from becoming a problem than have periods of inflation at the peak of each cycle, followed by monetary and fiscal policies to drive the rate of inflation back down again?
   (b) Has the rate of inflation stayed below 3 percent per year since 1993? To check, visit **www.statcan.gc.ca**. Search for "Consumer price index, historical summary". Click on "Consumer price index, historical summary".

6. Write a critical analysis of the following statement. "It is both unnecessary and bad public policy for governments to have budget deficits and borrow under any circumstances. All that deficits do is pile up government debt that will cause problems in the future."

7. Canada's experience between 1975 and 1993 showed that several years of regular large structural budget deficits
   (a) will increase the long-term economic prosperity of the people of the country by providing them with social welfare benefits and economic security.
   (b) will generate a large and growing government debt.
   (c) will eventually cause lenders to reconsider whether they wish to continue buying bonds issued by the federal government.
   (d) will eventually force the federal government to take painful steps to eliminate the deficit, such as large-scale spending cuts and/or tax increases.
   (e) Answers (b), (c), and (d).

8. Visit Statistics Canada at **www.statcan.gc.ca** and find the following statistics for the past two or three years:
   • Unemployment rate: Search the site for "Labour force characteristics", then click on "Labour force characteristics".
   • Inflation rate: Search the site for "Consumer price index, historical summary".
   • Trends in demand: Search the site for "Gross domestic product, expenditure-based", then click on "Gross domestic product, expenditure-based".

   (a) What are the recent trends in the unemployment rate and the rate of inflation?
   (b) What appear to be the reasons for the present condition of the economy?
   (c) Would you say that the statistics indicate that the government's monetary and fiscal policies should be used to speed up the economy or slow it down? Why?

Study Guide

Review Questions (Answers to these Review Questions appear in Appendix B.)

1. If there is high unemployment in the economy and aggregate demand increases,
   (a) real output, employment, and prices will all rise rapidly.
   (b) real output and employment will rise rapidly, and there will be little or no increase in prices.
   (c) real output and employment will rise, and prices will fall.
   (d) real output, employment, and prices will all fall.
   (e) None of the above.

2. If the economy is near, but not yet at, full employment (or capacity production) and aggregate demand increases,
   (a) real output and employment will rise less rapidly and prices will rise more rapidly than in the previous question.
   (b) real output will rise, employment will fall, and prices will remain stable.
   (c) real output and employment will not rise, but prices will rise rapidly.
   (d) real output will rise more rapidly and employment and prices will rise less rapidly than in the previous question.
   (e) None of the above.

3. "Full employment" refers to
   (a) an unemployment rate of zero.
   (b) the lowest unemployment rate that can be achieved without inflation threatening to accelerate and become a problem.
   (c) an unemployment rate of about 6 to 6.5 percent in recent years.
   (d) Answers (b) and (c).
   (e) None of the above.

4. The unemployment rate referred to in the previous question is considered to be full employment mainly because
   (a) there are no unemployed workers available.
   (b) if unemployment is reduced below this level, inflation tends to gain momentum, making it not feasible to reduce unemployment further.
   (c) those classed as unemployed are really just in the process of changing jobs (i.e., the unemployment is frictional in nature).
   (d) all those classed as unemployed really do not want to work.
   (e) the amount of unemployment referred to in the previous question is seasonal in nature, and nothing can be done about it.

5. Which of the following most accurately states the relationship between inflation and the general state of the economy?
   (a) The rate of inflation tends to increase when the economy is in a condition of recession.
   (b) When prices rise, this tends to cause unemployment to rise, too.
   (c) The rate of inflation tends to increase during periods of economic boom.
   (d) Rising prices mean less economic prosperity for society in general.
   (e) There is no relationship between the rate of inflation and the general state of the economy.

6. The relationship referred to in the previous question exists because
   (a) the high levels of aggregate demand that generate economic booms also tend to cause the rate of inflation to increase.
   (b) during recessions, sales volumes are lower, so businesses must raise prices in order to maintain profits.
   (c) when prices rise rapidly, sales fall and workers are laid off, causing unemployment to rise.
   (d) price increases reduce the purchasing power of the dollar and, thus, the general degree of economic prosperity.
   (e) None of the above.

7. The experience of the 1970s showed that
   (a) rapid increases in the money supply will generate severe inflation.
   (b) inflation is an economic problem that has the potential to accelerate (that is, grow more rapid).
   (c) inflation is an economic problem that is costly and painful to solve.
   (d) Answers (a) and (b).
   (e) Answers (a), (b), and (c).

8. *Inflation psychology* refers to
   (a) the tendency of people to save more money during periods of rapid inflation, in order to cope with higher prices.
   (b) (b)the tendency of people to seek larger income increases during periods of rapid inflation.
   (c) the tendency of people to spend a higher proportion of their disposable income during periods of rapid inflation, and save less.
   (d) Answers (b) and (c).
   (e) None of the above.

9. Inflation psychology tends to
   (a) cause inflation to gain momentum and become more rapid.
   (b) cause the rate of inflation to stop rising.
   (c) have no effect on the rate of inflation.
   (d) cause people to worry about unemployment.
   (e) None of the above.

10. State whether each of the following is *true* or *false*. Rapid inflation
    (a) hurts groups that lack economic power. _____
    (b) causes higher interest rates. _____
    (c) reduces the standard of living of everyone in society. _____
    (d) can make a nation's exports less competitive internationally. _____
    (e) damages the saving–investment process that is a key to higher productivity and prosperity. _____

11. Policies that fight inflation will cause the unemployment rate to _____, because _____.

12. In the table below, fill in the empty boxes.

Year	Government Spending	Tax Revenues	Budget Deficit (−) or Surplus (+)	National Debt
1	$20	$20	$0	$100
2	24	21		
3	29	24		
4	27	28		

13. State whether it would be considered economically reasonable for governments to borrow money (that is, issue bonds) for each of the following purposes.
   (a) to build a college _____
   (b) to pay the monthly wages and salaries of employees of the college _____
   (c) to finance a government spending program to combat a recession _____
   (d) to finance transfer payments to the provinces for the purpose of health care and post-secondary education spending _____
   (e) to finance tax cuts during a recession _____

14. A *structural budget deficit* refers to
   (a) deficits for the purpose of combating periodic recessions.
   (b) deficits that occur regularly, whether there is a recession or not, because they are built into the government's budget through a regular tendency for government spending to exceed tax revenues.
   (c) deficits that the government has incurred for the purpose of financing the construction of public buildings and other structures that could be called social assets.
   (d) deficits that are unplanned; that is, they occur due to unexpected weakness of tax revenues or unforeseen expenditures by the government.
   (e) None of the above.

15. Government policies can help to attract investment by multinational companies to Canada by
   (a) keeping the rate of inflation and interest rates low.
   (b) keeping government budget deficits and debt under control.
   (c) making taxes reasonable relative to those in other countries.
   (d) pushing wages down and keeping minimum wage rates low.
   (e) Answers (a), (b), and (c).

Critical Thinking Questions

(Asterisked questions 1 to 5 are answered in Appendix B; the answers to questions 6 to 10 are in the Instructor's Manual that accompanies this text.)

*1. In a boom, would you expect frictional unemployment to decrease? Why or why not?

*2. Suppose that the following statistics represent economic trends over the past four years.

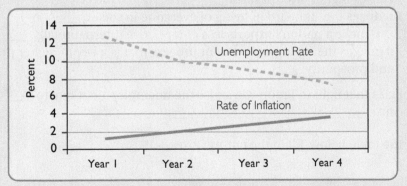

   (a) What is the main *economic problem* as of Year 4?
   (b) What would be the *basic cause* of this problem?
   (c) What type of *monetary policy* should the government use under these conditions, and how could this policy help to deal with the problem?

(d) What type of *fiscal policy* (budget policy) should the government use under these conditions, and how could this policy help to deal with the problem?

(e) What undesirable side effects would the policies in (c) and (d) have on the economy, and why would these effects occur?

*3. In 2007–08, the federal government had a budget surplus of $9.6 billion.

(a) What are the three basic types of ways in which the government could use such a surplus?

(b) In 2008, the population of Canada was 33 million people.

(i) How much *per Canadian* would a budget surplus of $9.6 billion represent for that year?

(ii) How much would it represent per Canadian per day?

*4. It was expected that as inflation was brought under control and the federal government's budget deficits were reduced and finally eliminated, long-term interest rates would *decrease*. Why was this expectation a logical one?

5. The financial crisis and recession of 2008–09 caused very large government budget deficits that left many countries' governments with sharp increases in their debt. By 2011, there were proposals in some countries that laws be passed requiring the government to balance its budgets each year, so as to prevent government debt from rising further.

Make an argument that such laws would have the effect of making recessions more severe.

6. Try your skill at getting into, and then out of, a budget deficit and debt problem.

(a) Fill in the columns in the following table for budget deficit/surplus and government debt for each year from year 1 through year 4.

Billions of Dollars

Year	Government Revenues	Government Spending	Budget Deficit (–) or Surplus (+)	Government Debt
1	$100	$100	$0	$300
2	105	117		
3	110	125		
4	114	136		
5				
6				

(b) By year 4, the budget deficit is $_____ billion and government debt is $____ billion.

(c) Develop a combination of spending reductions and/or tax increases for year 5 and year 6 that eliminates the deficit (balances the budget) by year 6. Would eliminating the deficit be an easy task for government? Why or why not?

(d) If the budget were to remain balanced in each year after year 6, what would happen to the level of government debt over time
(i) in dollars?
(ii) as a percentage of GDP?

7. There are an estimated 325 000 seasonal workers in Canada, and in the winter, seasonal factors probably add some 200 000 people to the ranks of the unemployed.

(a) Can you explain the difference between these numbers?

(b) What might account for the decrease in seasonal unemployment over the past 20 years or so?

8. In 1973–75, real long-term interest rates were actually *negative*.
   (a) What would a negative real interest rate mean?
   (b) What could explain such an unusual development?

9. "The reason for Canada's so-called 'unemployment problem' is the laziness of so many people, especially the young. The solution is to make welfare benefits so low that people can barely survive on them. That would get these people off the backs of the taxpayers and out working where they belong, and unemployment will cease to be a problem."

   Comment on this viewpoint in light of the material in this chapter.

10. Suppose you are the minister of finance. Prepare a statement explaining
   (a) to a group of unemployed young people why the government has decided to implement anti-inflation policies that will have the side effect of increasing unemployment, especially among young Canadians.
   (b) to a group of senior citizens why the government has decided to stimulate aggregate demand to reduce unemployment, when the pensioners fear that these policies will cause more inflation that will reduce the purchasing power of their fixed pensions.

Use the Web   (Hints for these Use the Web exercises appear in Appendix B.)

1. Visit Statistics Canada at **www.statcan.gc.ca** and find the *employment rate* and the *unemployment rate* for the past four or five years. Under "Find statistics", click on "Summary tables" and search "Labour force characteristics", then click on "Labour force characteristics". In this table, the employment rate is called the "Employment to population ratio".
   (a) What are the recent trends in the employment rate and the unemployment rate?
   (b) What might explain these trends?

2. By mid-2011 there was growing concern that the American and European economies would slip into another recession, which would spread to Canada.
   (a) How would this affect the federal government's budget and debt, as shown in Figure 8-9?
   (b) To see what has happened in recent years regarding the federal government's debt in terms of both dollars and as a percentage of GDP, visit Statistics Canada at **www.statcan.gc.ca** and find recent figures for:

   • Net federal debt: Search the site for "Net federal debt", then click on "Federal government net financial debt".
   • Gross domestic product: Search the site for "Gross domestic product, expenditure-based", then click on "Gross domestic product, expenditure-based".

   Over the time period in the tables of statistics, what has happened to
   (a) net federal government debt expressed in dollars?
   (b) net federal government debt expressed as a percent of GDP?

International Trade

LEARNING OBJECTIVES

After studying this chapter, you should be able to

1. Describe the importance of international trade to the economic prosperity of Canadians.

2. Describe how the composition of Canada's exports (the proportion represented by resources and resource-related products and by manufactured goods) has changed since the early 1970s.

3. Explain three ways in which trade between nations helps to generate higher productivity and living standards.

4. Explain how tariffs and other restrictions on trade affect prices, productivity, living standards, and employment.

5. Explain why lower wages do not necessarily give a country a competitive advantage over higher-wage countries.

6. Summarize the effects of freer trade and technological change on employment in the Canadian economy, and on the pay gap between more- and less-skilled workers.

7. Describe the *infant industry* argument for imposing tariffs, and explain the problems associated with such a strategy.

8. Explain the meaning of *globalization*, and state four reasons for the world economy's trend in this direction.

9. Explain the implications of globalization for the Canadian economy.

10. Apply the facts and concepts of this chapter to various situations.

International trade is tremendously important to the economic prosperity of Canadians. Despite its impressive geographic size, Canada is a small country economically, with about one-half of one percent of the world's population and less than 3 percent of total world output of goods and services. The state of California represents a larger market than all of Canada.

Because its domestic market is small, international trade is much more important to Canada than it is to most major nations. The United States exports more than three times as much merchandise as Canada, but Canada's exports represent about 30 percent of its gross domestic product, compared to less than 13 percent for the USA. And while Japan is a major exporter, its exports as a percentage of GDP amount to about half of Canada's.

These figures show that much of Canada's economic prosperity comes from its relationship with—especially exports to—larger nations. In recent years, about one in five Canadian jobs has been directly dependent upon exports, and exports of goods and services have amounted to nearly $17 000 for every Canadian.

But despite Canada's export success, there are continuing concerns about the ability of many Canadian producers to compete internationally, as we will see later in this chapter and again in Chapter 12.

Patterns of Canadian Trade

In 2010, the value of Canada's exports of wheat was $4.4 billion. The value of exports of automotive products was $54.5 billion in the same year.

Canada's traditional image is that of a major exporter of natural resources and importer of manufactured goods. Indeed, as Table 9-1 shows, resources and resource-related products do comprise a large share of Canada's merchandise exports.

On the other hand, Canada's exports of manufactured goods have grown strongly over the past fifteen years or so, which means that the economic benefits of export-

Table 9-1
Canadian Exports, 2010

	Billions of Dollars
Passenger automobiles and chassis and motor vehicle parts	54,474
Crude petroleum	50,111
Food, feed, beverages and tobacco	29,210
Industrial machinery	16,199
Natural gas	15,619
Aircraft, aircraft engines and parts	13,836
Chemicals	10,827
Television, telecommunications and related equipment	7,739
Lumber	5,019
Meat and meat preparations	4,705
Iron ores, concentrates and scrap	4,645
Wheat	4,413
Office machines and equipment	4,276
Newsprint paper	3,759
Trucks, truck tractors and chassis	2,310
Electricity	2,019

Source: Statistics Canada, CANSIM Table 228-0003.

ing have become spread quite widely across Canada rather than concentrated in resource-producing regions. As recently as 2005, manufactured goods represented nearly half of Canada's merchandise exports. However, after 2007 the recession of 2008–09 caused a reduction in exports of manufactured goods (mostly to the United States), and rising resource prices increased the value of Canada's resource exports, especially crude oil. Notwithstanding these factors, Table 9-1 presents a snapshot of Canada's exports in 2010 in which manufactured goods such as automobiles, industrial machinery, aircraft, and industrial equipment are strongly represented, as well as the traditional exports of resources and resource-based products.

Roughly 200 000 Mexican workers come to Canada annually on temporary work permits, mostly as unskilled labourers on farms and in orchards.

Canada's exports have grown strongly, from 18 percent of GDP in 1971 to 30 percent in 2010, and reached 35 percent during the 2004–07 boom. Much of this growth has come from exports of manufactured goods, which increased faster than exports of resource-related products. And in addition to the merchandise exports shown in Table 9-1, Canada exported $73 billion worth of services in 2010.

As Table 9-2 shows, the vast majority of Canada's trade is conducted with one nation—the United States. The importance of the U.S. market to Canada has grown in recent years—in 2010, about 74 percent of Canada's merchandise exports went to the United States. The strong link between the two economies was enhanced by the Canada–U.S. Free Trade Agreement of 1989, which evolved five years later into the North American Free Trade Agreement (NAFTA) with the addition of Mexico. In 2010, the value of merchandise trade between Canada and the United States amounted to nearly *$1.4 billion per day.*

Table 9-2
Canada's Merchandise Exports and Imports by Country, 2010

	Billions of Dollars		
	Canadian Exports to	Canadian Imports from	Total Merchandise Trade
United States	$299.0	$203.4	$502.4
China	13.2	44.5	57.7
United Kingdom	16.4	10.7	27.1
Mexico	5.0	22.1	27.1
Japan	9.2	13.5	22.7
Germany	3.9	11.3	15.2

Source: Industry Canada, *Trade Data Online* (www.ic.gc.ca/tdo).

After rapid increases for most of the 1990s, the growth of both Canada's exports and imports slowed considerably after 2000, with the notable exception of trade with China. From 2000 to 2010, the surge in trade between the two nations shown in Figure 9-1 made China Canada's second-largest trading partner (see Table 9-2, in which trading partners are ranked according to the total of exports plus imports between them and Canada).

In a six-day period, Canada exports more to the United States than it exports to Mexico in an entire year.

Imports from China have increased very rapidly, rising from only 3.2 percent of total merchandise imports into Canada in 2000 to 11.0 percent in 2010. The $45 billion of Chinese imports in 2010 represented nearly $1,400 per Canadian. The most visible

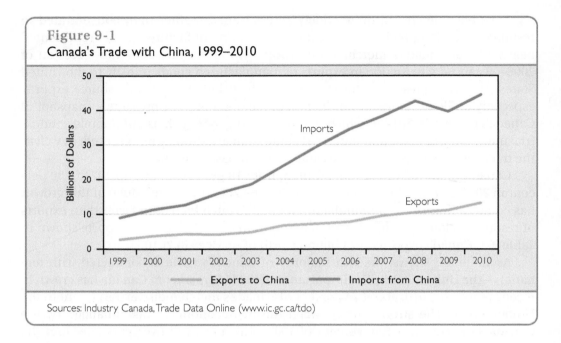

Figure 9-1
Canada's Trade with China, 1999–2010

Sources: Industry Canada, Trade Data Online (www.ic.gc.ca/tdo)

of these Chinese imports are the *consumer goods* that have quickly become familiar in Canadian stores; however, a large proportion of Canada's imports from China are now purchases by Canadian businesses of *capital goods* such as machinery and equipment. Many of these are computers and telecommunications equipment, although imports of auto parts have grown rapidly, as have imports of industrial goods such as pipes and tubes used in Canada's oil and gas industry.

But trade is a two-way street. While Canadian exports to China are still not very large (only about 3 percent of Canada's total exports), they nearly quadrupled from 2000 to 2010, much faster than the 17 percent growth rate for Canada's total exports over the same period. Canada has been well positioned to take advantage of the export opportunities arising from China's program of industrial development. Canada's exports to China have been led by goods that contribute to economic development, such as machinery (especially for construction and mining) and transportation equipment. China has also been a large purchaser of Canadian wheat, and Canadian exporters see future opportunities in China in areas such as power generation, transportation, mining, water purification, and waste treatment.

In Chapter 11, "The Global Economy," we will see more about China's rapid industrialization and entry into world trade, which rank among the more important international economic developments of recent years.

How Does International Trade Contribute to Prosperity?

The period since the end of the Second World War has seen a remarkable increase in the economic prosperity of many nations. Much of this improvement in living standards is attributed to the great expansion of world trade that occurred during that period, and to the trend toward freer trade among nations. Nonetheless, the matter of international trade involves many misunderstandings, myths, misconceptions, and fears. In order to work through these, our examination of this topic will take the form of a discussion between a curious citizen and an economist.

Citizen: Why do economists see international trade as such a major contributor to economic prosperity?

Economist: The key to high living standards is high *productivity*, or output per worker. Nations with high output per worker can enjoy high consumption per person, or high living standards. Trade between nations contributes to higher productivity in three ways: through increased *competition*, *economies of scale*, and *specialization*.

Citizen: It's easy to see how international trade would increase competition, and how competition from foreign firms would push producers everywhere to become more efficient. But what do you mean by "economies of scale"?

Economist: Economies of scale refer to the fact that in some industries, the most efficient production methods involve mass-production technology that generates high productivity. As a result, world-class plants in these industries tend to be very large, and produce a high volume of output.

For instance, a modern automobile manufacturing plant can produce 75 vehicles per hour. In turn, these industries must have a *large market* into which to sell all that output. In some mass-production industries, it has been estimated that the minimum market size needed for fully efficient production is about 100 million people. International trade can provide access to the very large markets that can support such plants and the economies of scale that they deliver. This is particularly important for a small country like Canada, with its domestic market of only 33 million people. As an example, Canada's "showpiece" producers such as automobile companies and resource companies export most of their output.

Citizen: So, international trade improves productivity through economies of scale as well as through competition. But you also mentioned specialization. How does that work?

Economist: The competition of international trade pushes nations to specialize their production. Instead of trying to be self-sufficient and produce all sorts of products, many of them inefficiently, nations will specialize in what they produce most efficiently, in order to be competitive. And by increasing efficiency throughout the world, specialization makes possible higher living standards.

Citizen: But wouldn't that make us dependent upon other nations for products that are important to us? Wouldn't it be better to be independent, or self-sufficient?

Economist: Trade doesn't make nations so much dependent as *interdependent*—nations depend upon each other, and all can gain in the process. The idea of being independent has a certain superficial appeal, but it doesn't stand up well to the test of logic. If you believe that Canada should keep out foreign goods, then why shouldn't Ontario or Alberta seek to shut the door on out-of-province goods, too? But then where do you stop with this "us versus them" line of thought? Should British Columbia or Montreal keep out goods produced by "outsiders"? Should your family isolate itself from the rest of the world in a quest for self-sufficiency? Families that actually do this are considered to be eccentric survivalists at best, whereas government policies of the same sort are seen by some people as patriotic.

The answer lies, of course, in the fact that it is *economically beneficial* for people—and regions, and nations—to specialize in things that they do well, to sell those things to others, and to buy from others those things that the others produce more efficiently.

Citizen: It's easy to find examples of this. Alberta is best suited to oil production, and Southern Ontario specializes in manufacturing—obviously the most efficient

"It is the maxim of every prudent master of a family, never to attempt to make at home what it will cost him more to make than to buy. The tailor does not attempt to make his own shoes, but buys them of the shoemaker. The shoemaker does not make his own clothes, but employs a tailor.... What is prudence in the conduct of every private family, can scarcely be folly in that of a great kingdom."
— ADAM SMITH, 1776

arrangement at present. And it's obviously best for both Canada and Brazil to specialize in wheat and coffee, respectively, and to trade their products.

Economist: Those examples are accurate enough, but international specialization goes much further than that, and is often much more subtle. Surprisingly, a great deal of trade is not between countries that are dissimilar, but rather between countries that are quite similar—the highly developed and industrialized nations such as the United States, Japan, Canada, Britain, Germany, France, Italy, and others.

Citizen: That seems rather odd. How do you explain that?

Economist: These industrially advanced economies have in many cases pushed specialization to the *n*th degree. For example, the United States exports large, long-range aircraft to Europe but imports smaller, short-range planes from Europe. These high degrees of specialization create even greater opportunities to benefit from trade.

Citizen: I'm having trouble with this. Suppose a nation has the highest productivity in the world—it's so advanced technologically that it is more efficient than most other countries in the production of most products. So how can such a nation *gain anything* through trade with other nations?

theory of comparative advantage

The theory that even if one nation is more efficient in the production of all items than another nation, it can still be to the economic advantage of both nations to specialize in what they produce most efficiently (items in which each has a "comparative advantage"), and trade with each other.

Economist: This can be explained by something economists call the **theory of comparative advantage**. It can be illustrated by a simple example on a personal level. Suppose the best lawyer in town is the best typist in town—should she do her own typing?

Citizen: I don't think so. She may be a faster and better typist than her secretary, but her greatest gains come from doing legal work. For every hour she spends typing, she might save $15 on secretarial costs, but she would lose maybe $150 by not using the time for legal work.

Economist: In other words, she can increase her efficiency and her income by specializing in what she does *best of all*?

Citizen: Right. If she does something else, she will lose more than she will gain. She just has better uses for her time. It's that idea of opportunity cost from Chapter 1.

Economist: And the same principle applies to the way nations use *their* productive resources such as labour and capital equipment. Suppose a nation is 30 percent more efficient than other nations at producing machinery, and 3 percent more efficient at producing shirts. Then that nation would be economically better off to concentrate on producing machinery—it would not make sense to divert scarce productive resources away from producing machinery, where they are most efficiently used, and into producing shirts, where they are less efficiently used. It's the same principle as the lawyer and the typist, but on a much larger scale. And with all nations specializing in products that they produce best of all, there is an opportunity to increase overall productivity and living standards. And the international competition that we discussed earlier will push nations' economies toward such specialization, because the most efficient producers will be successful and will grow.

Citizen: To summarize what you have said, international trade increases productivity and prosperity through competition, economies of scale, and specialization. (See Figure 9-2.)

Economist: That's right.

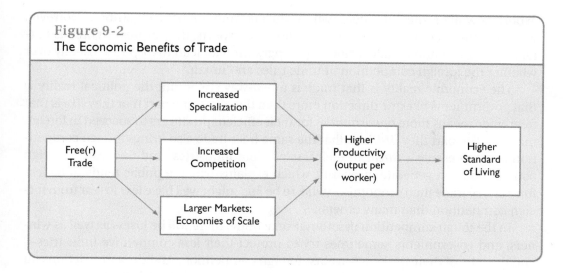

Figure 9-2
The Economic Benefits of Trade

Citizen: Okay—I can see how, *in theory*, international trade increases economic prosperity. But what I see *in the real world* is foreign imports causing trouble for Canadian producers and workers in areas such as appliances, clothing, toys, footwear, and so on.

Economist: The problem with that line of thought is that it only looks at *one part* of the total picture—the import competition. The broader picture takes into account that we have more exports, increased efficiency, more competition, and lower prices and higher living standards for people.

And what's wrong with competition? Isn't that what free enterprise is supposed to be all about? It's interesting how many people instinctively favour competition between firms *within* their country, but also instinctively oppose competition from *outside* it. Sure, it causes problems for some producers, but it also keeps them on their toes, and benefits consumers through lower prices.

Also, international competition works both ways—Canadian producers sell a great deal abroad, you know. In recent years, about 30 percent of Canada's gross domestic product has been exported, and in those markets, *we* are the "foreign competitors," and rather successful ones at that.

Citizen: If free trade is as wonderful as you say it is, then why are there so many trade disputes between nations?

Trade Disputes

Economist: That point is too true to be good. Governments everywhere declare themselves to be in favour of free trade, and sign trade agreements pledging to reduce barriers to trade. The next thing you know, there's a bitter trade dispute between the governments of these "trading partners," accompanied by accusations and threats of restrictions on imports and retaliation in kind. All too often, we hear reports that these trade skirmishes might escalate into a trade war, in which nations increase tariffs against more and more of each others' goods, in retaliation against each other. In a trade war, no one wins—trade wars hurt both consumers and workers in all countries that are involved.

Citizen: So it seems that in the area of trade, there is often a wide gap between what governments *preach* and what they *practise*.

Economist: That's often true. While officially favouring free trade, many governments act as though their real goal is to gain access to foreign markets for their

"Governments commit themselves ad nauseam to defend and protect the liberal trading order (free trade). Often, in the same breath, they criticize the 'unfair' practices of their trading partners and threaten to raise barriers in retaliation."

— THE ECONOMIST

exporters while protecting their own producers from import competition. However, when another nation places restrictions on their exports, they express righteous outrage and threaten to retaliate. Not surprisingly, this can lead to disputes, usually over whether the foreign competition or trade rules are "unfair."

The economic reality is that trade is a two-way street, but the political reality is that governments like one direction more than the other. The part that they *like* is that freer trade means more *opportunities* for their efficient producers to succeed in foreign markets. The part they *dislike* is that the same freer trade also brings foreign competition that represents a *threat* to their less efficient industries. And this fear of foreign competition can generate insecurity, which explains why the public tends to be less fond of free trade than economists (who, to be fair, might well have less to fear from foreign competition than many others).

In the tough competition of international trade, there will be losers as well as winners, and governments sometimes try to protect their less competitive industries—and the jobs of their workers—against foreign competition. And these restrictions on imports can lead to retaliation by other nations, and to economic hostilities. This is the next matter that we must consider.

Tariffs and Other Barriers to Trade

Citizen: How do governments try to protect their domestic producers from imports?

Economist: The traditional, and most visible, restriction on trade is **tariffs** (or customs duties), which are taxes levied on goods imported into a country. The effect of a tariff is to increase the price of the imports, making it more difficult for them to compete. For instance, Japanese automobiles imported into Canada are subject to a tariff of about 6 percent, and certain Canadian agricultural products such as dairy products and poultry are protected by extremely high tariffs.

Another way to protect domestic producers is through **import quotas**, which limit the amount of a product that can be imported into Canada in any one year. Quotas have the effect of reserving the rest of the market for domestic producers.

Citizen: It sounds as though if a government wanted to keep out import competition, tariffs and quotas should be able to do the job.

Economist: They would, except for the fact that most nations have signed trade agreements in which they specifically agree *not* to increase tariffs and quotas (more on this in Chapter 11). Largely because of this, governments that want to restrict imports have in recent years turned to more subtle trade barriers, known loosely as **nontariff barriers**.

Nontariff barriers obstruct imports in various ways, often through the use of rules. Sometimes these are overt, as when governments practise *preferential purchasing policies* by buying only from domestic suppliers, or when they give *subsidies* (financial assistance) that give domestic companies an unfair advantage. However, sometimes nontariff barriers are subtler. For instance, some nations impose so many bureaucratic *rules and procedures* (red tape) on would-be importers that they give up trying to do business in those countries. Sometimes nations adopt *product standards* that coincidentally "happen to" exclude certain imported products. For instance, for years the European Union has effectively kept Canadian and U.S. beef out of the European market by refusing to allow imports of meat from livestock treated with growth hormones that were used in North America but not in Europe.

Trade agreements between nations can outlaw tariffs and quotas, but nontariff barriers such as these are more difficult to regulate. When the Canadians and

tariffs

Taxes, or import duties, levied by a nation on products imported from foreign countries.

import quotas

Legal limits on the volume of particular goods that may be imported into a nation.

nontariff barriers

Other methods (besides tariffs) of restricting imports, including quotas and licences for imports, preferential purchasing policies, and subsidies for domestic producers.

Americans complained that Europe was restricting their sales, the Europeans argued that the hormone ban was purely a health concern that had nothing to do with obstructing imports. And when international trade authorities ruled that they were in fact violating trade rules, the Europeans kept the ban in place pending further scientific study of the long-term effects of the hormones on humans, which would take many years.

So despite general agreement that trade is economically beneficial, governments sometimes protect their domestic producers by restricting imports, even when doing this circumvents trade agreements and rules. And disagreements over such trade restrictions periodically lead to threats of retaliation and trade wars, a far cry indeed from the ideals of harmonious free trade preached by those same governments.

What About Jobs?

Citizen: But wouldn't keeping out imports protect Canadian jobs from foreign competition? Unemployment is an ongoing concern in Canada, and maybe tariffs could help to reduce unemployment.

Economist: Let's do a reality check on this idea. If raising tariffs would reduce unemployment, wouldn't we have solved our unemployment problems long ago? So we need to look into this a little further. Suppose Canada tried to reduce unemployment by increasing tariffs on imports from other countries. What would *those nations* probably do about this?

Citizen: I see—they would retaliate, by increasing their tariffs on our exports to them. Then Canada's exports would fall and jobs would be lost in *our* export industries.

Economist: Exactly. What we might gain in employment in some industries by raising tariffs, we would lose in our export industries when our trading partners retaliate. What many people forget is that Canada is a small nation that counts upon selling 35 percent of its output to other countries. For us, getting into avoidable trade disputes with our trading partners is not a good idea. In the words of Edward Carmichael of the C.D. Howe Institute,

www.cdhowe.org

> For a country as dependent on trade as Canada, matching foreign trade restrictions with domestic ones is not a winning strategy. Canadians would be denied access to an international market large enough to sustain efficient scale production, and an important source of improved productivity and living standards would be foreclosed.

Citizen: Does this explain why Canadian government officials are so frustratingly *patient* so much of the time when dealing with irritating trade matters?

Economist: It's probably one reason—we do have more to lose in trade disputes than most nations. They may also be remembering some lessons from history. During recessions, when people are especially concerned about unemployment, public opinion in all countries can create pressure to raise tariffs. However, governments need to remember that raising tariffs is a dangerous course of action that can actually make unemployment worse. During the Great Depression of the 1930s, governments tried to "export unemployment" by raising tariffs. By the time that everyone had retaliated against everyone else in what became a trade war, tariffs had gone so high that international trade had been severely reduced, with large job losses in all nations.

Citizen: The whole matter of tariffs and trade restrictions seems both important and pretty complex. Can we sort it out?

Economist: Let's summarize, using as an illustration tariffs on bicycle imports into Canada. The conclusions we will reach would apply equally to any type of restriction on imports of any product.

Suppose the Canadian government places a tariff on imported bicycles in order to protect Canadian bicycle producers and workers' jobs against competition from more efficient producers in Europe. By sheltering them from foreign competition, this tariff will benefit the Canadian bicycle industry and its workers. Their sales and output will be higher than they would have been, producers' profits will be higher, and there will be more jobs and quite possibly higher wages for workers in the bicycle industry.

However, Canadian consumers will have to pay for this through higher prices for bicycles. Obviously, the tariff will increase the price of imported bicycles; however, the effects will not stop there. With competition reduced in the Canadian market, Canadian producers will also be able to charge higher prices. So bicycle prices in general will be higher as a result of the tariff. And if Canadians shop outside Canada for bicycle bargains, they will be stopped at the border and required to pay the tariff (duty) at that point.

In addition, the tariff on bicycles could have a third important effect, and one that is not so readily seen and understood by the public. The tariff could become part of a trade dispute in which the Europeans retaliate with tariffs on Canadian products such as lumber or steel. To make matters worse, if such retaliation against Canadian exporters became widespread, they could be denied access to the larger international markets that they need in order to achieve economies of scale. And confined to the small Canadian market, they would be less efficient, making their prices in Canada higher.

Citizen: So tariffs protect inefficient and uncompetitive producers, and penalize efficient industries that are internationally competitive.

Economist: Yes, which explains why some of our industries (such as resources and large and efficient agricultural and manufacturing industries) are strongly in favour of free trade, while others (such as clothing, footwear, and some small manufacturers and farmers) want protection against imports. To some, free trade is an *opportunity,* while to others it represents a *threat.*

Citizen: In summary, then, tariffs and other barriers to trade benefit a few of us, but at the cost of lower living standards for the general public.

Economist: Yes, as a general rule that is true. If you were to summarize what we have said, it would be as follows (see Figure 9-3):

(a) Tariffs do benefit the protected industry and its workers. Their sales, employment, profits, and wages will be higher than they would have been if imports were not restricted.

(b) Tariffs reduce the standard of living of the public as a whole, by increasing prices.

(c) Tariffs reduce productivity and prosperity generally, by limiting both competition and the economies of scale available to Canadian producers.

(d) Tariffs also hurt Canadian exporters, who will probably face retaliatory tariffs.

Citizen: It looks like the gains in point (a) are more or less offset by the losses in point (d), leaving on balance points (b) and (c)—a lower standard of living—as the net effect of tariffs.

Economist: Yes, on balance their effect is higher prices, or, if you prefer, lower efficiency and a lower standard of living than we could have had. It's really just two differ-

> "Trade blockades are something our enemies do to us in wartime and we do to ourselves in peacetime."
> —HENRY GEORGE

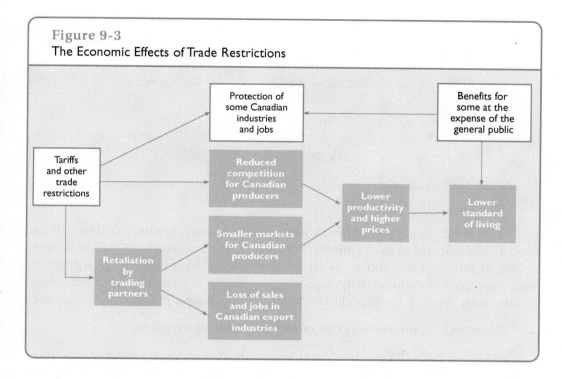

Figure 9-3
The Economic Effects of Trade Restrictions

ent ways of looking at the same thing. Lower productivity means higher costs and prices, and both mean lower living standards.

What About Low-Wage Foreign Competition?

Citizen: You said that trade policy should be in the best interests of the country as a whole. But Canada is a high-wage nation, so wouldn't it be in the best interests of Canadians to have tariffs to protect their jobs against imports from low-wage countries such as Mexico and Taiwan? How can Canadian producers possibly compete against foreign producers who use low-wage labour, such as Mexico?

Economist: That's a common viewpoint, but it's not supported by the facts. Let's subject it to a reality check. First, many high-wage Canadian firms such as auto manufacturers *actually do* compete successfully internationally, so we know that this can be done. Second, if low wage rates were the key to being internationally competitive, you would expect the lowest-wage industries in any country to be its most successful exporters. In actual fact, the opposite tends to be true—it is usually the higher-wage industries such as automobile manufacturing that export the most. And third, if low wage rates were the key to being competitive, nations such as the Dominican Republic would be major manufacturing centres. So low wage rates do not necessarily provide a competitive advantage, nor do high wage rates necessarily mean that an industry or nation cannot compete internationally. The situation is more complex than that.

Citizen: Those facts are interesting. What explains them?

Economist: The key is efficiency, or the productivity of labour—*output per worker per hour*. Suppose a foreign worker receives $5.00 per hour for making pencils and, using simple hand tools, produces 100 pencils per hour. As Table 9-3 shows, the labour cost per pencil is obviously $0.05 ($5.00 divided by 100). Now suppose a Canadian

Table 9-3
Productivity and Labour Costs

	Canadian Worker	Foreign Worker
Hourly Wage	$25.00	$5.00
Hourly Output	500 pencils	100 pencils
Labour Cost per Unit	$0.05	$0.05

worker earns $25.00 per hour, but using modern machinery, produces 500 pencils per hour. The labour cost of each Canadian-made pencil will also be $0.05 ($25.00 divided by 500, as Table 9-3 also shows). What this example shows is that you must consider *both* wage rates *and* productivity: high wage rates can be offset by high productivity, and low wage rates do not provide a competitive advantage if productivity is also low.

Citizen: So high productivity can more than offset high wage rates.

Economist: Right. It's ironic—North American workers worry about competition from low-wage foreign workers, but those same foreign workers also protest against free trade because they fear that they will be unable to compete with North American workers made very efficient by their capital equipment. For example, it has been estimated that while Mexican workers' wages are on average only about one-fifth of those in North America, the average hourly output of a North American worker is roughly five times that of a Mexican worker.

Citizen: Your example of the pencils was rigged to come out in a tie, with the labour cost of the pencils being the same in both cases. Your example of Mexico and North America looked much the same. But in the real world, *who does* have the competitive advantage?

Economist: It depends on the product. So far, we have talked in terms of averages—average wage rates and average productivity. But international competition is on a product-by-product basis, so we have to look at particular products, or at least types of products.

Where production lends itself to mechanization or automation, high-technology/high-productivity nations such as the United States or Canada usually have an advantage. For more manual (or labour-intensive) production tasks such as making clothing or footwear, the lower-wage labour of Third World countries is often more cost-efficient. For some products, companies produce *the parts* in the United States using mass-production technology, then ship the parts to Mexico to be *assembled* by low-wage Mexican labour, then bring back the assembled product to be sold in North America. Similarly, Japan now ships parts of its industrial products to China, where they are assembled into final products by low-wage workers.

Citizen: So, the bottom line is that some nations are better at some things, and others are better at other things.

Economist: Yes, which is why it pays economically to specialize at what you do best, and then trade. Then, it's possible for everyone to be better off. The cheap foreign labour argument is misleading—if it were valid, it would prevent *any* trade from happening, since one nation or the other would fear that it could not compete. And generally, nations with higher wage rates also have higher technology and productivity.

Citizen: But what if third-world nations get our modern production technology—wouldn't they then have *both* high productivity *and* low wages, making it impossible to compete with them? And wouldn't corporations just shift jobs by the millions to those economies, creating massive unemployment in the developed nations?

Economist: I was waiting for that one. That's a more sophisticated concern that requires a more detailed explanation. First, try a reality check on it—if this is so attractive, why hasn't it already been done on a large scale? Next, let's look at *why* it's not been done as much as one might expect.

One reason is that the potential for labour-cost savings is often much smaller than people think it is. In industries that use high-technology (capital-intensive) production methods, direct labour costs (that is, of production workers) are often already quite low. For instance, in industries such as automobile manufacturing and machinery, direct labour costs are often only about 10 percent of total production costs. So saving on labour costs would not be a good reason for relocating this type of industrial firm to a low-wage country. Another reason is that such production methods require a highly skilled workforce and sophisticated transportation and communications infrastructure, which are often not available in low-wage nations. Also, modern manufacturing operations usually rely on outsourcing various parts and service functions to a network of suppliers, which would not likely be available in low-wage regions of the world.

Furthermore, major manufacturing businesses know that any labour-cost savings that they did achieve would be short-lived, for two reasons. First, experience has shown that as the skills and productivity of workforces increase, so do their wages. And second, experience has also shown that if a nation's exports increase a great deal, the international price of its currency will increase, as foreigners buy lots of it in order to buy that nation's products (more on this in Chapter 10, "The Canadian Dollar in Foreign Exchange Markets"). But as the price of that nation's currency rises, so will the cost of its exports to foreign buyers, reducing the advantage of locating there.

In addition, such a corporate strategy might well invite trouble from governments in the industrialized nations. Most international trade agreements permit nations to take emergency measures against a surge of imports that threatens to seriously disrupt their domestic markets, and corporations know this. Together, these considerations reduce the probability that major corporations would risk moving extremely costly high-technology production facilities into low-wage countries on a large scale.

Finally, most modern manufacturing facilities (such as automobiles) in less-developed countries have been focused primarily on producing products for their own domestic markets.

www.tatamotors.com

Citizen: So, just what *is* the overall effect of freer trade on jobs and unemployment?

Economist: To answer that question, we should refer to *both* of the major forces that affect jobs—technological change and freer trade. By increasing labour productivity, technological change can reduce the number of workers needed. Also, competition from imports can reduce employment. The combined effects of these forces are summarized in Figure 9-4.

It cannot be denied that freer trade and technological change have displaced workers from jobs in some industries, such as clothing, footwear, and agriculture. However, trade and technology have also helped to *create new jobs*. First, by lowering

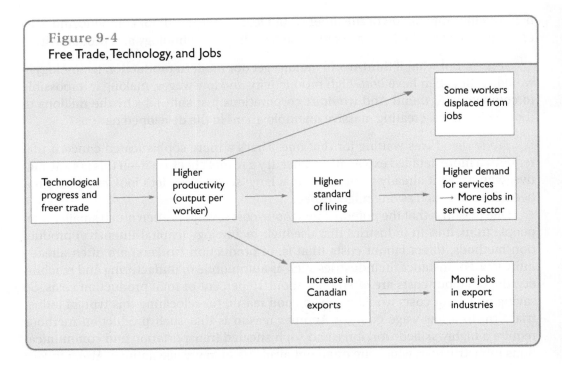

Figure 9-4
Free Trade, Technology, and Jobs

the cost of goods, freer trade and technological progress have increased Canadians' living standards. As families' standard of living has risen, their consumption of services has increased greatly, generating many more jobs in the *service sector* of the economy. And by opening up foreign markets to Canadian products, freer trade has boosted employment in the *export sector* of the economy.

Citizen: So, there have been both job-destroying and job-creating effects. Which is the greater?

Economist: There's no theoretically "right" answer to that question; all we can do is look at the results. Despite people's fears concerning free trade and technological change, Canada's unemployment rate in 2000–08 was lower than it had been since the mid-1970s. So, the indications are that at least so far, free trade and technology have resulted in *different* jobs rather than *fewer* jobs.

Adjusting to Change

Citizen: That may be true about the *total number* of jobs, but the fact remains that many people see free trade and foreign competition as a threat to *their* jobs *now*. Do trade agreements take their concerns into account?

Economist: That's a good question. Free trade brings significant changes to economies, and if the pace of change is too fast, people (and businesses) have trouble adjusting. Almost all trade agreements contain provisions that provide some protection against such problems. The most basic such protection is that tariffs are reduced gradually—for example, a 20-percent tariff might be reduced by 2 percentage points each year for 10 years. Another common provision is that if there is a "surge" of imports into a country, it can impose temporary restrictions on those imports to prevent its markets from being unduly disrupted.

Citizen: So all the concerns about free trade are unfounded, then? Everyone benefits?

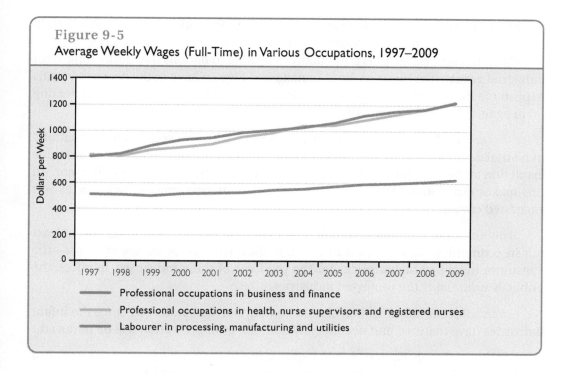

Figure 9-5
Average Weekly Wages (Full-Time) in Various Occupations, 1997–2009

Professional occupations in business and finance
Professional occupations in health, nurse supervisors and registered nurses
Labourer in processing, manufacturing and utilities

Economist: Not quite. There are some legitimate concerns about the effects of free trade, although these are subtler than the simplistic ones we have been discussing.

In labour-intensive industries such as clothing and footwear, where labour costs may be one-third or more of total production costs, there certainly is an incentive to shift production to lower-wage countries. Not only are the prospective labour-cost savings greater, but also the skills required are usually lower, making it easier to find the workers needed. This process has been going on for decades, and is really only one aspect of the specialization we discussed earlier. Nonetheless, it does result in reduced employment opportunities for low-skilled workers in the industrialized nations, and the reduced demand for these workers seems to have held down their wages. In recent years, the gap between the incomes of lower-skilled and higher-skilled people has been widening, as can be seen in Figure 9-5. In fact, the incomes of labourers have not kept up with inflation, so their real incomes (standard of living) have been falling.

Most economists believe that the main reason for this is technology that replaces less-skilled jobs; however, imports would have a similar effect. Two of the most fundamental economic forces in recent years have been technological change and freer trade, and it seems that the combined effect of these forces has been twofold: productivity and the *average* level of living standards have increased, but the *distribution* of income has been shifting in favour of the skilled and away from the less skilled. The impact of these trends is most severe for uneducated young males, who in the past worked in unskilled or semi-skilled jobs in goods-producing industries and who are not qualified for the new and more skilled jobs in service industries and high-technology industries.

Citizen: If tariffs are so bad, why are there so many of them?

Economist: Sometimes, governments impose tariffs for political reasons, to attract votes from citizens who fear import competition. However, many tariffs have their origin in an economic theory known as the *infant industry argument*. This argument is based on the idea that newly established industries (**infant industries**) could grow to become efficient and internationally competitive, *but only if* they were protected by tariffs during their early years. This protection from well-established foreign competitors

infant industries
Industries protected by government from foreign competition until they have matured to the point of becoming internationally competitive without protection.

would give them a chance to become established, in the same way as an infant child gradually matures into an independent adult.

This argument for tariffs is particularly appealing to nations that desire long-term industrial growth. For instance, both Canada and Mexico have in the past used tariffs to promote the growth of the manufacturing sectors of their economies by protecting them against American competition.

Citizen: So, by protecting domestic producers, tariffs can contribute to a nation's industrial development, diversifying its economy away from dependence on resource extraction and agricultural products, and boosting productivity and employment. All this makes tariffs look like a good policy, rather than economically negative as you suggested earlier.

Economist: But it's not that simple—you don't get something for nothing, at least not in economics. Such support of the manufacturing sector comes at a cost—the consumer must pay higher prices for the products of these industries. In effect, the public is *subsidizing* the protected industries.

Citizen: But the subsidization should be temporary, shouldn't it? Once the infant industries have matured and become efficient, the tariff protection will be removed.

Economist: In theory, that should happen, but in reality, it often doesn't work out that way. Because they are sheltered from competition, such industries tend to *remain* inefficient, and dependent upon continued tariff protection. And reduction of tariff protection is often made more difficult by the politics of the situation. Once protected industries become established and employers of significant numbers of people, they can become effective lobbyists for continued tariff protection.

Citizen: So how does the government know when it's time to eliminate the tariff protection of these "infants"?

Economist: There's no simple answer to that question; it's a matter of trade-offs, or benefits versus costs. The benefits are obviously the industrial development and the jobs associated with it. There are two types of costs to consider, the first being the costs to consumers, in terms of higher prices. These costs are often quite high—before free trade, the cost to consumers per job saved by trade barriers was often estimated at $100 000 to $200 000 per year.

In addition to the cost to consumers, there's another type of cost that has to be considered. Other nations may retaliate against your tariffs with tariffs of their own that hurt your export industries and jobs in them. And your export industries are likely to be your most efficient and effective industries, so you could wind up doing harm to your best industries in order to "save" your *least efficient* industries—not a very logical strategy.

Citizen: So, that's why Canada changed to a policy of free trade with the United States in 1989?

Economist: Basically, yes—by then, the infant industry policy had created all the industries that it ever would, and its high tariffs were costing Canadian consumers and exporters too much. And there was another big factor—by 1989, the process known as *globalization* was well under way, and Canada had to get ready for a very different world.

The Globalization of the World's Economy

Citizen: Just what does *globalization* mean? Everybody uses the term, but I'm not at all sure that people really understand it.

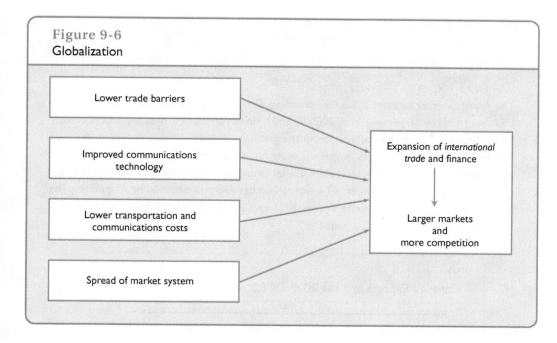

Figure 9-6
Globalization

Lower trade barriers

Improved communications technology

Lower transportation and communications costs

Spread of market system

Expansion of *international trade* and finance

↓

Larger markets and more competition

Economist: Since the early 1980s, the structure of the world's economy has undergone a major transformation. Increasingly, more trade and investment is being conducted *between* countries, rather than *within* countries' borders. This extremely important economic development, which is known as **globalization**, has been the result of several factors, which are summarized in Figure 9-6.

Probably the most important cause has been *tariff reductions* negotiated by nations over the years through various trade agreements (which are covered in more detail in Chapter 11, "The Global Economy"). Another key factor has been improved *communications technology* that facilitates communications between buyers and sellers around the globe. As an illustration, years ago a buyer of fashion clothing for a Vancouver department store might have sought bids on an order of dresses from a list of a limited number of designers/suppliers in Canada and perhaps the United States. Today, the same buyer can use computer and telecommunications technology to scan the offerings of many more designers and to communicate with them anywhere around the world. Within an hour of the order being placed, the designer can send the drawings and specifications for making the garments via satellite to a fibre-optic link in, say, Hong Kong, where they appear on a high-resolution computer monitor, ready for a manufacturing engineer to transform them into prototype garments. The prototypes might then be reproduced in a Chinese factory, with the factory supervisor, the engineer, and the designer working out the details via a videoconference. The finished garments could arrive in Vancouver less than six weeks after the order was placed.

The economic implications of this combination of freer trade and communications technology are tremendous. By allowing buyers and sellers to communicate quickly and effectively all around the world, the very concept of a *market* is expanded dramatically, from your local area to the entire globe. The number of sellers that buyers can choose from (and buyers to whom sellers can sell) are also greatly increased, extending markets to a global basis and intensifying competition.

In addition to freer trade and improved communications technology, *falling transportation and communications costs* have also contributed to globalization. In particular, transporting goods in "containers" and lower prices for oil and fuel from 1986 to 2005 made it more economical for producers to compete from greater

globalization
The trend toward more international trade and investment that has characterized the world economy since the early 1980s.

IN THE NEWS

Canada's Exports in the 2008–09 Recession

The American recession of 2008–09 spread to Canada through Canada's exports to the USA, which fell by 16 percent from 2008 to 2009. However, exports of some products were hit particularly hard, as can be seen from the graph.

Exports of food products in general were not significantly affected; however, exports of manufactured goods were severely impacted, most notably exports of automobiles and parts, which fell by $17 billion, or 43 percent. Lumber exports declined by 47 percent. The loss of jobs associated with these decreases in exports had devastating effects on particular Canadian industries and communities.

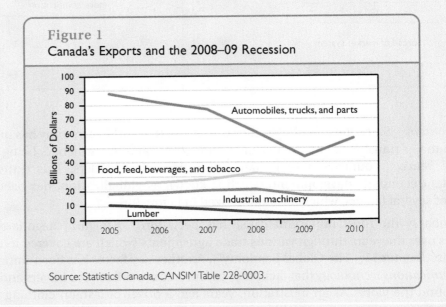

Figure 1
Canada's Exports and the 2008–09 Recession

Source: Statistics Canada, CANSIM Table 228-0003.

QUESTIONS

1. Have Canadian exports fully recovered since 2010? Visit Statistics Canada at www.statcan.gc.ca, and search for "Exports", then click on "Exports of goods on a balance-of-payments basis, by product".
2. Can you determine the causes of any significant changes in the trends of these exports? Recent information can be found at www.statcan.gc.ca; click on *The Daily* and search for "Canadian international merchandise trade", then click on "Canadian international merchandise trade".

distances than in the past. Finally, in recent years more countries have entered into world trade, such as Mexico, China, and former Eastern bloc countries, following the collapse of the Soviet Union at the start of the 1990s.

Globalization has tremendous implications for a nation such as Canada, which is small and widely exposed to international economic forces. Many Canadian producers faced *stronger competition* as globalization brought more players into the marketplace. On the one side, Canada faced strong competition in high-technology industries from the advanced Western economies such as the United States, Japan, and Western Europe. On the other side, the newly industrialized countries such as Mexico, Brazil, and various Asian countries such as Taiwan, Hong Kong, Singapore, Korea, Indonesia,

Malaysia, the Philippines, and Thailand provided strong competition in labour-intensive industries such as footwear and clothing and in assembly activities such as electronics.

However, globalization means not only *more competition*, but also *larger markets* for Canadian producers. As noted earlier, Canada is a small country economically and the rich, advanced economies of the United States and Europe provide very large markets for a wide variety of Canadian exports. In addition, the emerging nations provide smaller but growing markets for the infrastructure and capital goods they need to build. As a world leader in some of these fields (such as telecommunications, engineering services, transportation equipment, and mining), Canada's opportunities for exports to these countries will grow considerably as these nations develop.

Globalization is considered to have been one of the most powerful economic forces in the world over the last two decades of the twentieth century. The globalization of the world's economy, and its implications for Canada, will be considered more fully in Chapters 11 and 12.

Conclusion

The second half of the twentieth century saw major improvements in living standards, for which the growth of international trade has received much of the credit. On the other hand, with the growth of world trade, disputes over trade between nations take on added importance, as such disputes are potentially disastrous in a world grown so dependent upon trade. This makes it more important than ever that nations establish and maintain a stable environment for trade, through *trade agreements* that provide rules for international trade that will be followed by all concerned. This will be one of the two main topics of Chapter 11, where we return to the matter of globalization.

Chapter Summary

1. International trade is very important to Canada, which exports about 30 percent of its GDP, almost 75 percent of which goes to the United States. (L.O. 1)

2. Canada is a major exporter of resource products; however, exports of manufactured goods have increased considerably in importance over the past quarter century. (L.O. 2)

3. Trade between nations promotes economies of scale, international specialization, and competition, all of which increase productivity, making higher living standards possible. (L.O. 3)

4. The results of tariffs and other barriers to trade are: reduced economies of scale; specialization and competition; lower productivity; higher prices; and lower living standards. (L.O. 4)

5. Low wage rates may not give a country or industry a competitive advantage, if labour productivity is also low. (L.O. 5)

6. The combined effects of freer trade and technological change have been to reduce employment in some industries, but to increase employment in service industries and export industries. (L.O. 6)

7. Infant industry tariffs are meant to protect new industries from competition while they develop. However, such industries often remain inefficient and uncompetitive. (L.O. 7)

8. *Globalization* refers to the increasingly international character of business (trade) and investment. It is the result of freer trade, improved communications technology, lower transportation and communications costs, and the entry into world markets of more countries. (L.O. 8)

9. Globalization has great implications for Canada, which is a small country with much international exposure. These implications include both increased foreign competition and increased opportunities in export markets for Canadian producers. (L.O. 9)

Questions

1. The basic economic benefit that international trade brings is
   (a) more economic prosperity for those nations whose exports exceed their imports.
   (b) an opportunity for increased prosperity, due to higher productivity.
   (c) the business profits earned on exports to other nations.
   (d) the taxes that governments collect from tariffs on imported goods.
   (e) None of the above.

2. Explain three basic ways in which international trade contributes to the economic benefits in the previous question.

3. "Free trade can never work for a small economy such as Canada's, because there is no way that Canadian industry can compete with foreign industries that use low-wage labour. Canada needs to place high tariffs on imported manufactured goods in order to protect the jobs of Canadian manufacturing workers, and to preserve the high standard of living of Canadians." Write a critical analysis of this statement.

4. It is generally believed by trade experts that as a result of a free trade agreement between a small country and a large country, the people of *both* countries benefit economically, but the people of the smaller country *benefit more*. Explain why it would be logical to believe that free trade brings greater economic benefits to smaller countries than to larger countries.

5. State whether each of the following statements is *true* or *false*. A tariff on Indonesian shirts imported into Canada
   (a) is an effective policy for increasing employment in Canada.
   (b) will increase the standard of living of the Canadian public.
   (c) could result in fewer exports of other Canadian products to Indonesia.
   (d) will result in higher shirt prices in Canada.
   (e) will benefit Canadian shirt producers and their workers.
   (f) will increase the competition faced by Canadian shirt manufacturers.

6. State whether you think each of the following products are more likely to be produced in a low-wage country, and which might be produced in North America.
   (a) running shoes
   (b) moulded plastic slip-on summer shoes
   (c) acrylic patio furniture
   (d) wooden furniture
   Explain the reasons for your answers.

7. State whether each of the following statements is true or false. In Canada, free trade and technological progress have so far resulted in
   (a) fewer jobs and higher unemployment.
   (b) different jobs, but not fewer jobs.

(c) a higher average standard of living.

(d) a narrowing of the pay gap between more- and less-skilled workers.
Explain the reasons for your answers.

8. For updates on trends in Canada's trade with China, visit Industry Canada's website at **www.ic.gc.ca/tdo** and click on *Search by Product*. On the left side under *Trader*, select "Canada", and for *Trade Type*, select "Total Exports" or "Total Imports". On the right side, for *Trading Partner*, scroll down to "China".

(a) Have Canada's imports from China been growing faster or more slowly recently?

(b) Have Canada's exports to China been growing faster or more slowly recently?

(c) Can you think of any reasons for these trends?

Study Guide

Review Questions (Answers to these Review Questions appear in Appendix B.)

1. Canada's gross domestic product amounts to about
   (a) 1 percent of world output.
   (b) 3 percent of world output.
   (c) 9 percent of world output.
   (d) 14 percent of world output.
   (e) 20 percent of world output.

2. In recent years, Canada's exports have amounted to about
   (a) 20 percent of GDP.
   (b) 25 percent of GDP.
   (c) 30 percent of GDP.
   (d) 48 percent of GDP.
   (e) 60 percent of GDP.

3. The percentage of Canada's GDP that is exported is
   (a) much higher than most nations.
   (b) a little higher than most nations.
   (c) about average for major trading nations.
   (d) a little lower than most nations.
   (e) much lower than most nations.

4. Canada's exports
   (a) increased slowly during most of the 1990s, but rapidly after 2000.
   (b) increased slowly both during the 1990s and after 2000.
   (c) increased rapidly both during the 1990s, and after 2000.
   (d) increased rapidly during most of the 1990s, but slowly after 2000.
   (e) increased slowly during most of the 1990s, then fell each year after 2000.

5. The proportion of total Canadian exports that goes to the United States has in recent years been nearly
   (a) 85 percent.
   (b) 75 percent
   (c) 60 percent.

    (d) 50 percent.

    (e) None of the above.

6. Since 2000,

    (a) Canada's trade with China has increased faster than Canada's trade in general.

    (b) Canada's imports from China have increased faster than Canada's exports to China.

    (c) Canada's exports to China have increased faster than Canada's imports from China.

    (d) (a) and (b)

    (e) (a) and (c)

7. If Moravia were 30 percent more efficient than Grand Fenwick in producing kadiddles and 15 percent more efficient than Grand Fenwick in producing fradistats, Moravia could benefit economically by

    (a) producing both kadiddles and fradistats itself, and importing neither from Grand Fenwick.

    (b) concentrating on producing kadiddles, and importing fradistats from Grand Fenwick.

    (c) restricting the importation of Grand Fenwickian products into Moravia.

    (d) subsidizing exports of fradistats.

    (e) Answers (a) and (c).

8. A tariff on foreign automobiles imported into Canada will

    (a) increase sales of Canadian-produced cars.

    (b) increase the price of cars in Canada.

    (c) decrease sales of imported cars.

    (d) increase the standard of living of Canadians.

    (e) Answers (a), (b), and (c).

9. If Moronia requires that imports of Canadian Christmas decorations be subjected to lengthy inspection procedures that delay the products at the port of entry for months, this would be viewed by Canada as a

    (a) tariff.

    (b) health and safety measure.

    (c) nontariff barrier to imports.

    (d) quota.

    (e) None of the above.

10. "The products of Canadian manufacturers can never compete in price with the products of low-wage nations such as Taiwan and Mexico." The above statement is

    (a) true, because the higher wages in Canada cause production costs per unit of output to be higher than in low-wage nations.

    (b) true only for those products whose production requires a great deal of capital equipment, and relatively little labour.

    (c) false, because technological advancement and higher productivity in some Canadian industries result in lower costs per unit of output despite their higher wage rates.

    (d) false, although production costs per unit are higher in Canada, tariffs on foreign goods bring the price of those goods up to Canadian levels.

    (e) None of the above.

11. "Those manufacturers who successfully compete in international markets by exporting goods generally pay their workers below-average wages." This statement is

    (a) true, because the only way to compete with low-wage foreign manufacturers is to pay low wages too.

(b) false, because low-wage workers produce low-quality products.

(c) false—the minimum wage laws prevent them from doing so.

(d) false—manufacturers who are strong exporters generally pay above-average wages, but are able to keep production costs down by using efficient production methods.

(e) None of the above.

12. The purpose of *infant industry* tariffs is to

(a) protect jobs against competition from cheap foreign labour.

(b) provide newly developing industries with temporary protection from foreign competition.

(c) reduce prices for consumers.

(d) ensure that imported children's products meet health and safety standards.

(e) None of the above.

13. Industries protected by infant industry tariffs

(a) usually mature quite quickly and become sufficiently competitive that they no longer require tariff protection.

(b) often develop slowly, and require continuing tariff protection for much longer than was intended.

(c) often develop into leading exporters.

(d) Answers (a) and (c).

(e) None of the above.

14. Four reasons for the *globalization* of the world economy over the past 25 years are

(a) _____.

(b) _____.

(c) _____.

(d) _____.

15. The globalization of the world economy

(a) represented a great economic opportunity for Canada.

(b) presented serious economic challenges to Canada.

(c) was expected to have little effect on Canada's economy.

(d) Answers (a) and (b).

(e) None of the above.

Critical Thinking Questions

(Asterisked questions 1 to 5 are answered in Appendix B; the answers to questions 6 to 10 are in the Instructor's Manual that accompanies this text.)

*1. Suppose that you are the minister of trade, and an industry that has had tariff protection for more than 50 years holds a press conference at which it states that unless you increase its tariff protection, low-wage foreign competition is likely to result in the loss of thousands of Canadian jobs within two years. Write a response to this statement that explains fully to the industry and the public why you will *not* agree to their request.

*2. "To reduce unemployment in Canada, the government should increase tariffs on imported products. Canadians would then buy more Canadian-produced goods, creating more jobs for Canadians."

Write a critical analysis of this statement.

*3. "A trade war is a war with no winners."

Explain the reasoning behind this statement.

*4. The text in Chapter 9 notes that many people seem to instinctively favour competition between businesses *within* their own country, but oppose competition from foreign producers *outside* their country. What might explain this apparent inconsistency?

*5. "Many people fear that the combined effect of freer trade and technological change will be to increase unemployment. In fact, the evidence so far is that freer trade and technological change do not result in *fewer* jobs, but rather *different* jobs. However, it seems likely that freer trade and technological change are causing a widening of the pay gap between workers with more education and skills and those with less education and skills."

Write a critical analysis of this statement.

6. Everyone sees that one possible economic benefit of free trade is that Canadian firms gain new opportunities to *increase their sales*. But not many people understand that there is another large potential gain for Canadian firms from free trade—the opportunity to *reduce their production costs per product*, and so increase their profits per product.

Explain the reasoning behind this statement.

7. What could Canada's labour-intensive industries such as footwear and furniture do in order to compete more successfully with imported goods?

8. "Most trade is in goods, such as manufactured products. Since 1989, when Canada signed the Free Trade Agreement with the United States, less than 6 percent of the growth of jobs in Canada has been in the manufacturing sector. This shows how free trade has not benefited Canadians."

Write a critical analysis of this statement.

9. Opposition to free trade is far from a new phenomenon. In England in 1824, Lord Macaulay observed that, "Free trade, one of the great blessings which a government can confer on a people, is in almost every country unpopular." And today, politicians still avoid talking about free trade during an election year. What do you think explains the public's generally negative attitude toward free trade?

10. Since 1989, Canada has reduced its tariffs considerably under two trade agreements—the Canada–US Free Trade Agreement of 1989 (which became the North American Free Trade Agreement, or NAFTA, with the addition of Mexico in 1994), and the World Trade Organization's 1995 agreement. Following the signing of these pacts, both Canada's exports and its imports increased sharply. What do you think would have been the consequences for Canadians if Canada had *not* been part of these agreements to reduce tariffs?

Use the Web   (Hints for this Use the Web exercise appear in Appendix B.)

1. The graph shows the rapid increase in exports that led Canada into an economic boom in the 1990s, then the slump in exports caused by the U.S. recession in 2001. Following that slump, more rapid growth of Canadian exports contributed to the economic boom of 2005–08. However, when the U.S. recession of 2008–09 struck, Canada's exports fell sharply, by nearly 16 percent in 2009. They recovered somewhat in 2010, but were still 7 percent below their 2008 level.

Canada's Merchandise Exports and Imports, 2001–10

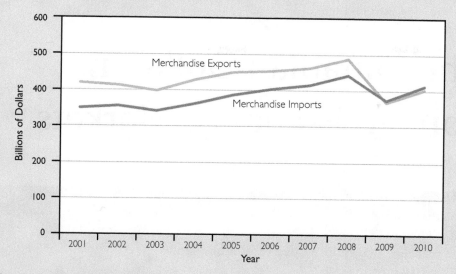

Source: Statistics Canada, CANSIM Table 228-0003.

To see the changes in exports and imports since 2010, visit Statistics Canada at
www.statcan.gc.ca. Search for "Exports of goods on a balance of payments
basis, by product".

(a) Have exports and imports been growing more or less rapidly in recent years?
(Use year-to-year percentage changes to determine this.)

(b) Which types of exports have been growing the fastest, and what might
explain these trends?

(c) Which types of imports have been growing the fastest, and what might
explain these trends?

The Canadian Dollar in Foreign Exchange Markets

LEARNING OBJECTIVES

After studying this chapter, you should be able to

1. Explain how the international value of the Canadian dollar is determined in foreign exchange markets, and how changes in the international value of the Canadian dollar affect Canadians.

2. Define the term *balance of payments deficit*, and explain how, under a floating exchange rate system, a balance of payments deficit will affect the exchange rate, and how this change in the exchange rate will affect the nation's balance of payments.

3. Define the term *balance of payments surplus*, and explain how, under a floating exchange rate system, a balance of payments surplus will affect the exchange rate, and how this change in the exchange rate will affect the nation's balance of payments.

4. Explain the economic problems for a nation that could be caused by a rapid increase or a rapid decrease in its exchange rate, and how the activities of foreign currency speculators can add to these problems.

5. Describe two ways in which a government operating under a *dirty float* system can try to prevent its exchange rate from increasing or decreasing too rapidly.

6. Explain how the Bank of Canada's exchange rate policy interacts with monetary and fiscal policies to influence the direction of the economy.

7. Apply the facts and concepts of this chapter to various situations.

As we have seen, Canada's ability to compete internationally is extremely important to the prosperity of Canadians. One key to Canada's international competitiveness is *productivity*, or efficiency, since this affects the price that foreign buyers must pay for Canadian goods and services. But before they buy Canadian *exports*, foreign buyers must buy *Canadian dollars*. So Canada's international competitiveness is also affected by the price that foreigners must pay for Canadian dollars. This is the international value of the Canadian dollar, also known as Canada's **exchange rate**. For instance, it was easy for Canadian exporters to sell to U.S. buyers between 1998 and 2002, when it often cost Americans only about 65 cents U.S. to buy a Canadian dollar. But in 2010, Americans had to pay over $1.00 U.S. for Canadian dollars, making it considerably more difficult for Canadian exporters.

exchange rate
The international price, or value, of a currency in foreign exchange markets.

Why does the international value of the Canadian dollar fluctuate so much, and what do these fluctuations mean to Canadians? These matters are obviously important, but to many people they seem mysterious. In fact, they can be readily explained and understood in terms of the economic basics involved. In this chapter, we will examine the basic economic forces that determine the international value of the Canadian dollar. In the following two chapters, we will expand our examination of these international matters to a global scale.

Markets for Currencies

International transactions, such as trade, investment, and tourism between nations, require that there be some mechanism for exchanging various nations' currencies. For example, a Canadian importer of French wine must be able to exchange Canadian dollars for euros to pay for the wine, and a Japanese firm buying Canadian pork must be able to convert its Japanese yen into Canadian dollars to complete the purchase.

These transactions take place in **foreign exchange markets** in which various currencies can be bought and sold. For instance, the Japanese importer of Canadian pork is in fact *buying Canadian dollars* and selling Japanese yen, and the Canadian importer of French wine is really *selling Canadian dollars* and buying euros. On any given day, vast amounts of various currencies are bought and sold for a wide number of reasons, including imports and exports, investment, tourism, and the payment of interest and dividends between nations. These transactions are conducted through banks in each country that have arrangements with banks in other countries for exchanging various nations' currencies.

foreign exchange markets
Markets, conducted through banks, in which currencies of different nations are bought and sold (exchanged for each other).

In short, just as there are markets for goods and services, there are *markets for currencies*. The marketplace for international currency transactions consists of banks, where currencies are bought and sold. Most people have participated in this market at least in some small way at one time or another—for example, by converting Canadian dollars to U.S. dollars before travelling to the United States. While we describe such a transaction in terms of "exchanging" or "converting" currencies, the reality is that we are *selling* Canadian dollars and *buying* U.S. dollars.

On a typical day, about CDN$100 billion is bought and sold on international currency markets.

International Exchange Rates

If currencies are to be bought and sold, there must be *prices* for them. For instance, when the Canadian tourist exchanges Canadian dollars for U.S. dollars, will he or she get 100 U.S. cents for each Canadian dollar? Or 90 U.S. cents? Or 110 U.S. cents? Similarly, how much is a Canadian dollar worth in terms of Japanese yen, British pounds, or euros? There are no fixed answers to these questions—exchange rates, or the international values of currencies, are prices that fluctuate on a day-to-day basis. Table 10-1 shows the international price (or value) of the Canadian dollar on one day, but the price of the Canadian dollar fluctuates considerably, as shown in Figure 10-1.

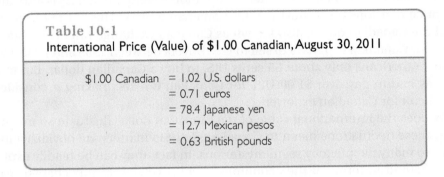

Table 10-1
International Price (Value) of $1.00 Canadian, August 30, 2011

$1.00 Canadian	= 1.02 U.S. dollars
	= 0.71 euros
	= 78.4 Japanese yen
	= 12.7 Mexican pesos
	= 0.63 British pounds

These figures can be interpreted in two ways:

(a) If you were *buying* Canadian dollars on August 30, 2011, the price you had to *pay* for each Canadian dollar was 1.02 U.S. dollars, 0.71 euros, 78.4 Japanese yen, 12.7 Mexican pesos, or 0.63 British pounds.

(b) If you were *selling* Canadian dollars on August 30, 2011, the value you *received* for each Canadian dollar was 1.02 U.S. dollars, 0.71 euros, 78.4 Japanese yen, 12.7 Mexican pesos, or 0.63 British pounds, as shown in Table 10-1.

The lowest-ever international value of the Canadian dollar was US$0.6202, on January 18, 2002.

www.statcan.gc.ca
Search for "Exchange rates", then click on "Exchange rates, interest rates, money supply and stock prices".

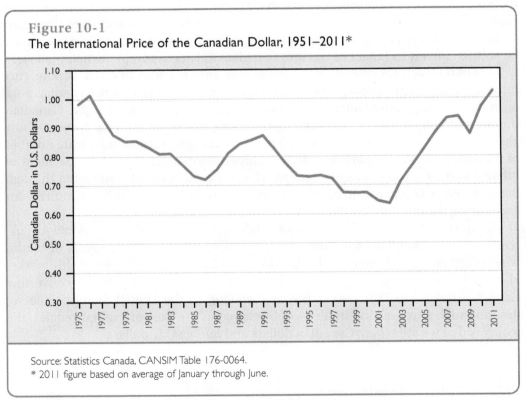

Figure 10-1
The International Price of the Canadian Dollar, 1951–2011*

Source: Statistics Canada, CANSIM Table 176-0064.
* 2011 figure based on average of January through June.

What *Determines* Exchange Rates?

On August 30, 2011, it took US$1.02 to buy $1.00 Canadian (or CDN$1.00). What actually *decided* this value of the Canadian dollar? Why was it not US$1.03, as it had been back in 1976, or US$0.62, as it was in January 2002?

The highest-ever international value of the Canadian dollar was US$1.1030, on November 7, 2007.

Simply stated, the international price of the Canadian dollar, like the price of anything, depends on *supply* and *demand*. In this market, *supply* means the volume of Canadian dollars being offered for sale in foreign exchange markets, and *demand* refers to the volume of offers to purchase Canadian dollars. It is the balance between the supply of, and the demand for, the Canadian dollar in foreign exchange markets that determines its value, or price.

Figure 10-1 shows the ups and downs of the Canadian dollar. In the late 1980s, the Canadian dollar rose as foreign lenders bought large amounts of dollars in order to buy bonds issued by Canadian governments to finance the budget deficits that we discussed in Chapter 8. Then in the 1990s, the dollar moved sharply downward, as Canadian governments sold dollars in order to make interest payments on their foreign debt, and as Canadian investors sold dollars in order to buy U.S. stocks. After 2002, the dollar moved sharply upwards as strong demand for Canadian resource exports generated heavy buying of Canadian dollars. Then in 2008–09, the Canadian dollar moved sharply downward when the global recession sent the volume and prices of Canada's energy and resource exports plummeting, reducing the demand for Canadian dollars. In Chapters 11 and 12, we will see more about the reasons for these recent developments and their importance.

Receipts and Payments

A helpful way to summarize a nation's international transactions (and thus the demand for and supply of its currency) is to classify transactions as either **receipts** or **payments**. For example, Canadian exports of lumber to Japan cause Canada to *receive* foreign currency, so exports are classified as a "receipt" to Canada. Conversely, the winter vacations spent by Canadian tourists in Florida are classified as "payments," because they involve *payments* from Canadians to a foreign nation. Receipts generate a *demand* for the Canadian dollar because foreigners must *buy* Canadian dollars in order to pay Canada, whereas payments generate a *supply* of Canadian dollars, or offers by Canadians to *sell* Canadian dollars in order to pay foreign nations.

In summary, Canada's international transactions can be classified as
- *receipts* (money flowing *into* Canada), which generate *buying* of Canadian dollars that *increases* the international price of the dollar, and
- *payments* (money flowing *out* of Canada), which generate *selling* of Canadian dollars that *decreases* the international price of the dollar.

These receipts and payments generate the forces of demand and supply in the market for the Canadian dollar. Receipts (demand) push the Canadian dollar upward, while payments (supply) push it downward, as shown in Figure 10-2. And it is the balance of these forces of demand and supply that will determine the international value of the Canadian dollar.

A summary of Canada's major receipts and payments is presented in Table 10-2. As the balance between Canada's receipts and payments fluctuates, the international value of the Canadian dollar will rise and fall.

Canada's Balance of Payments

The **balance of payments** is an annual summary of all of Canada's international financial transactions, classed as receipts or payments. These items, as Table 10-3 shows, are divided into **current account** and **capital account** transactions. Current

receipts
International transactions in which a nation receives funds from other countries.

payments
International transactions in which a nation pays funds to other countries.

balance of payments
A summary of all of a nation's receipts and payments for a given year.

current account
Balance of payments items relating to day-to-day transactions in goods and services.

capital account
Balance of payments items involving flows of investment funds (capital) between countries.

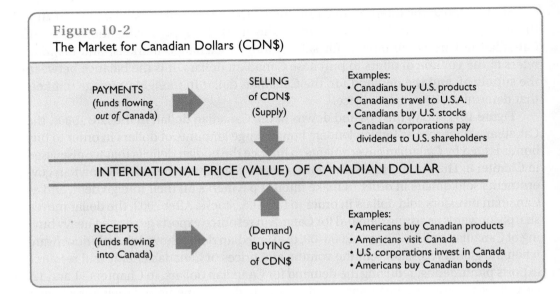

Figure 10-2
The Market for Canadian Dollars (CDN$)

Table 10-2
A Summary of Canada's Major International Receipts and Payments

Canadian Receipts

(Transactions generating *offers to buy* Canadian dollars, and thus increasing the international price of the Canadian dollar.)

1. **Exports of Merchandise**
   (Foreigners must buy Canadian dollars to pay for Canadian goods.)

2. **Foreign Tourists Visiting Canada**
   (Foreigners must buy Canadian dollars to spend while in Canada.)

3. **Interest and Dividends Received**
   (Foreigners must buy Canadian dollars to pay interest and dividends to Canadian lenders and investors.)

4. **Foreign Investment in/Loans to Canada**
   (When foreign funds are invested in or loaned to Canada, they must be converted into—that is, used to buy—Canadian dollars.)

Canadian Payments

(Transactions generating *offers to sell* Canadian dollars, and thus depressing the international price of the Canadian dollar.)

1. **Imports of Merchandise**
   (Canadians must sell Canadian dollars to buy foreign currencies to pay for imports.)

2. **Canadian Tourists Visiting Other Countries**
   (Canadians must sell Canadian dollars to buy foreign currencies to spend abroad.)

3. **Interest and Dividend Payments**
   (Canadian businesses and governments must sell Canadian dollars to buy foreign currencies to pay interest and dividends to foreign lenders and investors.)

4. **Investment by Canadians in Foreign Countries**
   (Canadian citizens and businesses investing in other countries must sell Canadian dollars in order to buy foreign currencies with which to make such investments.)

direct investment
Investments in business enterprises that are sufficiently concentrated to constitute control of the concern.

account transactions include mostly day-to-day transactions in goods and services, and capital account transactions refer to flows of investment funds, both long-term and short-term, into and out of Canada.

The left side of Table 10-3 shows all of Canada's international receipts. These receipts include earnings from the various current account items shown, plus inflows of capital into Canada, including foreign **direct investment**[1] into Canada, foreign

---

[1] *Direct investment* is defined by Statistics Canada as "those investments in business enterprises which are sufficiently concentrated to constitute control of the concern." More specifically, such investments include new plants and equipment built by foreign firms, as well as the provision of working capital for Canadian subsidiaries by foreign parent firms, and mergers in which the assets of Canadian firms are purchased by foreign firms.

> **Table 10-3**
> **Major Categories of Canada's Balance of Payments**
>
> | Receipts | Payments |
> | --- | --- |
> | **Current Account** | **Current Account** |
> | Merchandise Exports | Merchandise Imports |
> | Travel and Tourism | Travel and Tourism |
> | Interest and Dividends | Interest and Dividends |
> | Freight and Shipping | Freight and Shipping |
> | Inheritances and Immigrants' Funds | Inheritances and Emigrants' Funds |
> | **Capital Account** | **Capital Account** |
> | Foreign Direct Investment in Canada | Canadian Direct Investment Abroad |
> | Foreign Purchases of Canadian Stocks and Bonds | Canadian Purchases of Foreign Stocks and Bonds |
> | Foreign Purchases of Canadian Short-Term Deposits and Securities | Canadian Purchases of Foreign Short-Term Deposits and Securities |

purchases of Canadian stocks and bonds (including bonds issued by both corporations and governments), and foreign purchases of Canadian bank deposits and short-term securities. The right side of Table 10-3 shows Canada's payments, which comprise payments for the various current account items, plus outflows of capital from Canada, as Canadian businesses and citizens invest in long-term capital and short-term funds of other nations.

The Balance of Payments and the Exchange Rate

www.statcan.gc.ca
Search for "Canada's balance of international payments".

As we have seen, foreign exchange markets, in which the currencies of various nations are bought and sold, resemble a tug of war between each nation's receipts (which push the international price of its currency up) and its payments (which push the international price of its currency down). There are three possible situations regarding a nation's balance of payments and the international value of its currency:

(a) a **balance of payments deficit**, when payments exceed receipts,
(b) a **balance of payments surplus**, when receipts exceed payments, and
(c) **balance of payments equilibrium** with payments equal to receipts.

Using Canada as our example, we will examine the results of each of these situations.

A Balance of Payments Deficit

If Canada has a balance of payments *deficit*, Canada's payments (offers to sell Canadian dollars) exceed its receipts (offers to buy Canadian dollars). So the supply of Canadian dollars in foreign exchange markets will exceed the demand for Canadian dollars, and the international price of the Canadian dollar will *fall*, as shown in Figure 10-3. An example of such a situation is the 1990s, when outflows of investment funds and interest payments contributed to a considerable decline in the exchange rate.

balance of payments deficit
A situation in which a nation's payments exceed its receipts.

balance of payments surplus
A situation in which a nation's receipts exceed its payments.

balance of payments equilibrium
A situation in which a nation's receipts and payments are equal to each other.

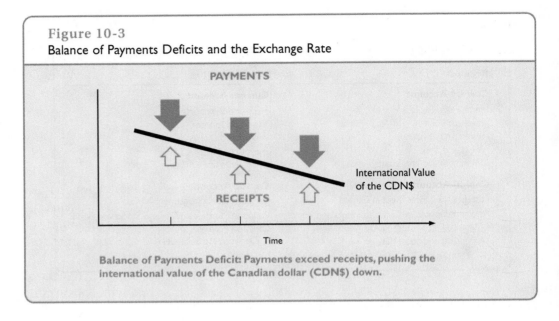

Figure 10-3
Balance of Payments Deficits and the Exchange Rate

Balance of Payments Deficit: Payments exceed receipts, pushing the international value of the Canadian dollar (CDN$) down.

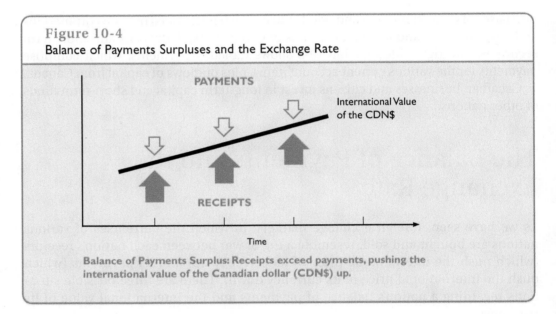

Figure 10-4
Balance of Payments Surpluses and the Exchange Rate

Balance of Payments Surplus: Receipts exceed payments, pushing the international value of the Canadian dollar (CDN$) up.

A Balance of Payments Surplus

If Canada has a balance of payments *surplus*, Canada's receipts will exceed its payments, and the demand for the Canadian dollar will exceed the supply of it. This will cause the international price of the Canadian dollar to rise, as shown in Figure 10-4. Such a situation occurred in 2005–2008, when the world economic boom caused rapid increases in both the volume and the prices of Canada's resource exports, generating strong inflows of funds into Canada and a high demand for Canadian dollars.

Equilibrium in the Balance of Payments

If Canada's balance of payments were *in equilibrium*, with receipts equal to payments, the supply of and demand for the Canadian dollar would be in balance, and the international value of the Canadian dollar would tend to remain stable at its present level.

It is important to appreciate, however, that this does not mean that the Canadian dollar has found its "proper" value, at which it will remain—this stability would last only until receipts and/or payments changed, causing a balance of payments surplus or deficit to develop. Given the dynamic nature of international trade and investment flows, such stability is rare and short-lived. In fact, minute-to-minute fluctuations in currency values in response to market fluctuations are normal.

A Floating Exchange Rate System

We have been examining how the international prices (values) of currencies can rise and fall in response to changes in international receipts and payments. When a nation permits the international value of its currency to move up and down as the supply of and demand for it change, it is said to be operating on a **floating exchange rate** system. Canada has a floating exchange rate.

    In the following sections, we will examine how a system of floating exchange rates, or currency prices, operates under conditions of (a) a balance of payments surplus, and (b) a balance of payments deficit.

floating exchange rate
A situation in which the international value of a currency is allowed to fluctuate freely with the supply of and demand for it.

How a Floating Exchange Rate Operates with a Balance of Payments Surplus

Suppose Canada is operating on a floating exchange rate system, with the international value of the Canadian dollar at US$0.80, when Canada develops a balance of payments surplus (say, due to increased exports). As noted earlier, the balance of payments surplus will cause the international price of the Canadian dollar to rise, say, to US$0.90.

    The increase in the price of the Canadian dollar will set into motion an *automatic adjustment mechanism*, which will work to eliminate the balance of payments surplus. Because the Canadian dollar is more costly to foreigners, Canada's receipts will fall as foreigners buy fewer Canadian goods and travel less to Canada. Also, because the international value of the Canadian dollar has risen, it will be less costly for Canadians to buy imports and travel to other nations. As Canadians increase their purchases of foreign goods and services, Canada's payments will rise. With receipts falling and payments rising, the original balance of payments surplus will tend to disappear, with the international value of the Canadian dollar having moved to a new higher equilibrium level that is more consistent with the high demand for Canadian exports. Such changes in exchange rates help to keep imports and exports in balance.

    This tendency to move automatically toward equilibrium is illustrated in Figure 10-5. It shows a balance of payments surplus causing an increase in the price of the Canadian dollar, which in turn tends to eliminate the surplus.

How a Floating Exchange Rate Operates with a Balance of Payments Deficit

In the case of a balance of payments deficit, the adjustments are the opposite of those described above. Suppose Canada develops a balance of payments deficit, due to increased imports of foreign goods. The deficit will cause the international value of the Canadian dollar to fall from its original level of US$0.80, say, to US$0.75.

    This decrease in the price of the Canadian dollar will cause the automatic adjustment mechanism described earlier to operate in the opposite direction, as shown in Figure 10-6. With the Canadian dollar less costly to them, foreigners will buy more

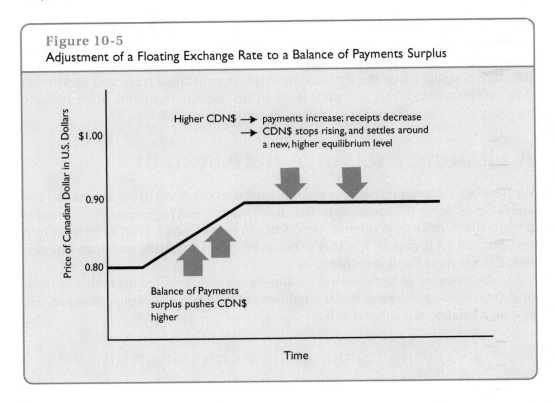

Figure 10-5
Adjustment of a Floating Exchange Rate to a Balance of Payments Surplus

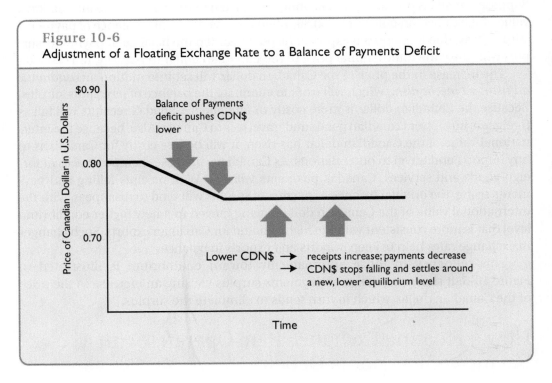

Figure 10-6
Adjustment of a Floating Exchange Rate to a Balance of Payments Deficit

Canadian goods and travel to Canada more, so Canada's receipts will rise. And with other nations' currencies now costing Canadians more, they will buy fewer foreign goods and services, causing Canada's international payments to decline. As a result of the increased receipts and reduced payments, Canada's balance of payments deficit will tend to disappear, and the balance of payments will move toward an equilibrium situation with the Canadian dollar at a new, lower equilibrium level.

IN THE NEWS

Exchange Rate Changes and Competitive Balance

When China burst onto the world trade scene after 2001, a surge of low-cost Chinese goods penetrated North American markets. China's export success was attributed to two key factors: its low-cost *labour* and the low cost of the Chinese *currency* (the yuan), and fears were expressed that cheap Chinese imports would flood other nations' markets, wiping out entire industries and millions of jobs. ■

QUESTION

1. Under a system of floating exchange rates, would it be possible for China to flood other nations' markets to the extent that these people fear?

So, a balance of payments deficit will cause the international price of the Canadian dollar to fall, which will increase receipts and reduce payments, moving the balance of payments toward equilibrium, but at a lower exchange rate.

Summary

Under a system of floating exchange rates, a nation's balance of payments will tend to move toward equilibrium because of the relationship between the balance of payments and the exchange rate (or international price of the currency). This is a two-way street—the balance of payments affects the exchange rate, but the exchange rate also affects the balance of payments.

If a balance of payments deficit develops, it will tend to be removed by a reduction in the exchange rate, which will increase receipts and reduce payments. Conversely, a balance of payments surplus tends to be eliminated by an increase in the exchange rate, which reduces receipts and increases payments. In both cases, the balance of payments tends to return to equilibrium through changes in the international price of the currency.

But there is no single level that represents *the* equilibrium price for the Canadian dollar, toward which the exchange rate will always move. Nor, having reached its equilibrium level, will the price of the Canadian dollar *stay* at that level. As international trade and investment patterns change, causing shifts in payments and receipts, the supply of and demand for the Canadian dollar—and its equilibrium value—constantly change. The equilibrium price of the Canadian dollar is a moving target, toward which the value of the dollar will tend to move under a floating exchange rate system. Table 10-4 presents a summary of the operation of a floating exchange rate in the three contexts that we have discussed.

Exchange Rate Changes and Trade Balances

Changes in exchange rates such as we have been discussing have played a very important and valuable role in maintaining balanced trade among nations. This can

Table 10-4
Summary of the Operation of a Floating Exchange Rate

Situation	Effect on Foreign Exchange Markets	Effect on the Balance of Payments
1. Canada's PAYMENTS exceed RECEIPTS (a Balance of Payments deficit)	The supply of CDN$ exceeds the demand for CDN$; the price of the CDN$ falls.	As the CDN$ falls, receipts will increase and payments will decrease until they are equal and the CDN$ stabilizes at a new, lower equilibrium level.
2. Canada's RECEIPTS exceed PAYMENTS (a Balance of Payments surplus)	The demand for CDN$ exceeds the supply of CDN$; the price of the CDN$ rises.	As the CDN$ rises, payments will increase and receipts will decrease until they are equal and the CDN$ stabilizes at a new, higher level.
3. Canada's PAYMENTS and RECEIPTS are equal (the Balance of Payments is in equilibrium)	The supply of and demand for CDN$ are equal; the price of the CDN$ remains stable.	Payments and receipts remain equal; CDN$ remains at equilibrium level until payments or receipts change.

be illustrated by two of the more dramatic adjustments to exchange rates over the past few decades—the Japanese yen and the British pound.

After 1970, Japanese exports became very successful in world markets. This generated such a high demand for Japanese yen that by 1995 the yen was nearly *four times* its value in 1970 in terms of U.S. dollars. Such a dramatic adjustment of the yen's value had major economic consequences for the Japanese. First, their currency's purchasing power in foreign markets was dramatically greater, giving the Japanese a higher standard of living that amounted to an international *economic reward* for being so successful at building and exporting their products. (The Japanese enjoy their strong international purchasing power more through travel and tourism than through buying imports of foreign products.) On the other hand, the higher value of the yen made Japanese exports more expensive to foreigners. This served as a *limiting factor* on Japanese success, since it had the effect of limiting the further growth of Japanese exports, and prevented Japan from dominating world markets, as some people had feared it would. From another perspective, the higher yen made it possible for other nations to compete with Japan, and so "saved" some manufacturers and many jobs in other countries from Japanese competition.

An example of the opposite situation is provided by Great Britain, which found itself relatively uncompetitive after the Second World War ended in 1945. A combination of low exports and high imports gave Britain large annual balance of payments deficits. With the supply of pounds on currency markets outweighing the demand, the pound lost more than half of its value in terms of the U.S. dollar. This large-scale depreciation of the pound made import prices in Britain much higher, reducing the standard of living of the British—a sort of *economic penalty* for not keeping up with the international competition. On the other hand, the decrease in the pound's international value also served as a *protective factor* for British industry and jobs. With the pound much cheaper for foreigners to buy, the ability of many British industries to compete in international markets was protected, as were some British jobs. For the British, it was similar to a nation taking a pay cut (a lower standard of living) in order to protect jobs.

Exchange rate adjustments such as those of the yen and the pound reflect basic economic forces such as the changing competitiveness of nations. They take effect over long periods of time and to help maintain a competitive balance among nations, as noted above. And because they occur gradually, nations and their industries have time to adjust to the changes they create in international competitiveness.

A quite different situation is presented, however, by *rapid short-term fluctuations* in exchange rates as discussed in the next two sections. When these occur, their effects on a nation's economy can be more disruptive.

Foreign Exchange Speculation

The international values of currencies, including the Canadian dollar, fluctuate considerably over time, sometimes quite suddenly and dramatically.

These fluctuations introduce the possibility of making profits through **speculation** in currencies—that is, buying a currency when its value is low and selling it after its value has risen. For instance, a brilliant (or lucky!) person could have bought a thousand Canadian dollars for about US$620 in January 2002 and sold them for over US$1103 in November 2007, for a profit of $483, or 78 percent.

speculation
The buying of an asset (here, a currency) with the objective of reselling it for a higher price in the future.

Of course, hindsight makes this all seem so easy. At the time that such decisions have to be made, however, the outcome is not at all certain. And, while quick gains can be made through foreign exchange speculation, equally quick losses can be incurred if the currency does not move as the speculator anticipated it would. In spite of these risks, speculators will often move considerable volumes of short-term capital out of currencies seen as weak (likely to fall in value) and into currencies believed to be strong (likely to rise), hoping to make a quick profit by anticipating exchange rate fluctuations arising from economic or political developments.

As a result, there exists a considerable volume of speculative short-term funds, known as **hot money**, that are capable of moving very rapidly from currency to currency. Such speculative purchases and sales of currencies can cause their values to fluctuate more dramatically, by forcing strong currencies higher and weak currencies lower. And such rapid exchange rate fluctuations can cause difficulties for the economies of the nations involved, as we will see in the next section.

hot money
Short-term funds that can be moved readily from one currency to another.

Problems Concerning Currency Fluctuations

If the international value of a nation's currency changes *excessively rapidly*, that nation's economy can be adversely affected. A rapid increase in the international value of the Canadian dollar could threaten the competitive position of Canadian producers (and jobs) by suddenly making Canadian exports more expensive and foreign imports cheaper. On the other hand, a sharp decline in the value of the Canadian dollar would cause import prices to rise quickly, which would reduce Canadians' living standards.

appreciation of a currency

Increases in the international value of a currency.

depreciation of a currency

Decreases in the international value of a currency.

dirty float

A situation in which a government influences the exchange rate.

exchange rate management

Government policies to moderate fluctuations in exchange rates. See **dirty float**.

foreign exchange reserves

Holdings of foreign currencies and gold maintained by governments for the purpose of stabilizing their exchange rates through purchases and sales of their currencies.

As a result, governments prefer that the international value of their currencies not change too rapidly, either upward (known as **appreciation of a currency**) or downward (called **depreciation of a currency**). So governments sometimes seek to *moderate* the currency fluctuations associated with floating exchange rates. When they do so, the situation is referred to as a **dirty float**, because while the exchange rate is floating, it is also being influenced by the government. Government policies that influence the exchange rate are also known as **exchange rate management**.

Exchange Rate Management

Purchases and Sales of Currencies

To influence the international value of currencies, governments can *buy and sell currencies* in foreign exchange markets. By buying a weak currency, governments can hold its price up, or support it. And governments can hold down the value of a strong currency by selling it in foreign exchange markets.

In Canada, exchange rate management is the responsibility of the Bank of Canada. If the Canadian dollar is rising too rapidly as a result of heavy foreign demand, the Bank of Canada could slow down the rise of the dollar by *selling Canadian dollars* to foreign buyers in foreign exchange markets. In the process of selling Canadian dollars to foreign buyers, the Bank of Canada would also *buy foreign currencies*, mostly U.S. dollars. The Bank of Canada holds these foreign currencies as part of Canada's **foreign exchange reserves**, or official international reserves.

These official international reserves are useful when the Bank of Canada wishes to prevent an excessively rapid decline in the exchange rate. If the exchange rate falls too rapidly, the Bank of Canada can *buy Canadian dollars* in foreign exchange markets in order to support its price. Buying Canadian dollars requires that the Bank of Canada *sell foreign currencies* from its official international reserves, which will reduce its reserves. In 2011, the Bank of Canada had about $63 billion of official international reserves.

By selling and buying Canadian dollars (and adding to and decreasing its official international reserves in the process), the Bank of Canada can, within limits, prevent excessive fluctuations in the exchange rate and their possibly disruptive effects on the economy.

Changes in Interest Rates

The Bank of Canada can also influence the exchange rate through its *interest rate policies*. If the exchange rate of the Canadian dollar were falling too rapidly, the Bank of Canada could increase interest rates in Canada. Higher interest rates make Canadian dollar deposits and securities more attractive to foreign investors. And when foreign investors buy Canadian dollars in order to obtain Canadian dollar deposits and securities, the international value of the Canadian dollar is supported. This interest rate policy can also be used in the other direction: if the Canadian dollar were rising rapidly, the Bank of Canada could hold the Canadian dollar down by reducing Canadian interest rates.

Governments tend to be cautious in raising or lowering interest rates to stabilize the values of their currencies because changes in interest rates can have significant effects upon not just the exchange rate, but also the entire economy. An increase in interest rates will support the Canadian dollar, but it will also depress borrowing and aggregate demand in the economy. In a period of high demand and inflation, this

IN THE NEWS

The Floating Canadian Dollar as a "Shock Absorber"

Having a floating exchange rate can be important for a country such as Canada, which exports so much of its GDP that it is vulnerable to "demand shocks" from other economies. For instance if a recession in the United States were causing a downturn in the Canadian economy, a decrease in the international price of the Canadian dollar could act as a sort of "shock absorber", by making Canadian products less costly to American buyers, which would reduce the economic damage to Canada.

The 2008–09 period provides a good example of this "shock absorber" effect. After mid-2008, aggregate demand in the Canadian economy turned sharply downward, as the graph shows. The main source of this problem was a sharp downturn in exports to the United States, which was sinking into a recession.

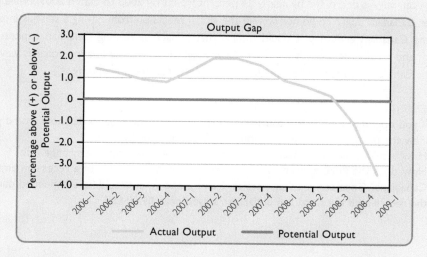

The downturn in Canadian exports reduced the demand for Canadian dollars, which began a downward trend in the exchange rate of the Canadian dollar. This trend gained momentum as the deepening recession in the world economy drove the prices of Canadian resource exports (most notably crude oil) very sharply downwards, further reducing the demand for and the international price of the Canadian dollar.

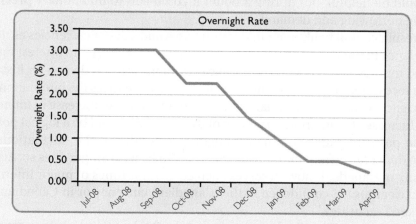

At the same time, the Bank of Canada was reducing the overnight rate at a rapid pace, adding to the downward pressure on the exchange rate.

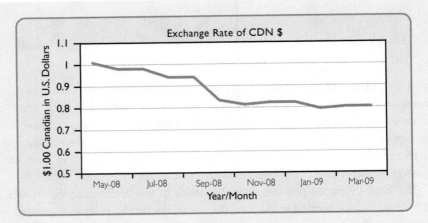

As a result of these recession-related developments, the cost of Canadian dollars to American buyers decreased by nearly 24 percent from May 2008 to March 2009. While the lower Canadian dollar could not *prevent* the global recession from having a serious impact on the Canadian economy, it could *cushion* that impact by making Canadian exports of goods and services less costly to foreign buyers, which is why the floating dollar is viewed by the Bank of Canada as a "shock absorber" for the Canadian economy. ■

QUESTIONS

1. If you operated a Canadian tourism business close to the U.S. border, how would you view the decrease in the international price of the Canadian dollar?
2. How would Canadian consumers view the same decrease in the exchange rate?
3. How does the floating exchange rate help to "spread the pain" of a recession among Canadians? Consider your answers to 1 and 2, and what would have happened during the recession if the Canadian dollar had stayed near $1.00 U.S.

effect may be welcome, but at other times it could tilt the economy toward a recession. Conversely, a reduction in interest rates will hold the Canadian dollar down, but it will also increase borrowing and demand in the economy. During a recession, this effect would be helpful, but during a boom it could add to inflationary pressures by increasing borrowing and demand.

As a result, central banks tend to use purchases and sales of currencies as their first line of defence in their efforts to stabilize exchange rates. Changes to interest rates tend to be used more rarely, and when economic conditions warrant these—for instance, to combat a recession, a decrease in interest rates that also reduces the international price of the currency would be appropriate, and to curb inflation, an increase in interest rates that also increases the international price of the currency would be a logical policy.

In the past, the Bank of Canada sought to smooth out the fluctuations of the Canadian dollar fairly frequently; however, since 1998, it no longer does so. According to the Bank of Canada, it now "reserves such actions for times of major international crisis or a clear loss of confidence in the (Canadian) currency or in Canadian-dollar-denominated securities."

However, as we will see in the next section, the Bank of Canada's changes to interest rates in the normal conduct of its monetary policy also affect the international price of the Canadian dollar.

Objectives of Exchange Rate Policy—More Trade-offs

What is better for Canadians—a high or low international value of the Canadian dollar? While a higher international value of their currency sounds better to many Canadians, the situation is not nearly so simple. Rather, the answer to this question depends on *one's perspective* and on *economic conditions*.

In part, the answer to this question also depends on whether one is a consumer or a producer exposed to international competition. To Canadian consumers, an increase in the international value of their dollar is good news. Because the Canadian dollar buys more foreign currencies, imported goods and trips outside Canada will cost less. But to Canadian businesses that export or compete with imports, an increase in the exchange rate is bad news. The higher-priced Canadian dollar will make Canadian exports more expensive, and the relatively lower value of foreign currencies will encourage Canadians to buy imports instead of Canadian products. Conversely, a reduction in the exchange rate would be welcomed by businesses that export or compete with imports, but it would mean higher prices for consumers. As a result, exchange rate policy involves a degree of balancing trade-offs between the interests of consumers and the interests of producers.

The answer also depends on the *economic conditions in Canada* at the time. If Canada is in a recession, a lower international value of the Canadian dollar will help to boost the demand for Canadian exports, and so help to reduce unemployment. On the other hand, if inflation were the main problem in the economy, a falling exchange rate would only make matters worse, by increasing the price of imports. Instead, a rising Canadian dollar would help contain inflation by keeping import prices down.

Exchange Rate Policy and Monetary and Fiscal Policies

From the foregoing, it can be seen that the Bank of Canada's exchange rate policy is linked to its monetary policy and interest rate policy, and to the whole question of *demand management* that we saw in Chapters 7 and 8. As Figure 10-7 shows, government policies to combat recession could include a government budget deficit and lower interest rates to boost spending by Canadian consumers and businesses, with lower interest rates contributing to a lower exchange rate that could also boost foreign demand for Canadian exports. In 2008–09, this was the direction of Canadian policy.

Figure 10-8 shows the same policies operating in the opposite direction, to slow down inflation. Budget surpluses, and higher interest rates can depress spending by Canadian consumers and businesses, and higher interest rates could push the price of the Canadian dollar higher, depressing both export demand and the price of imports. In 2005–06, this was the general thrust of Canadian policy.

Limits on Exchange Rate Policy

In determining its exchange rate policy, a government cannot ignore the fact that there is at any point in time an *equilibrium international value* for its currency. If a

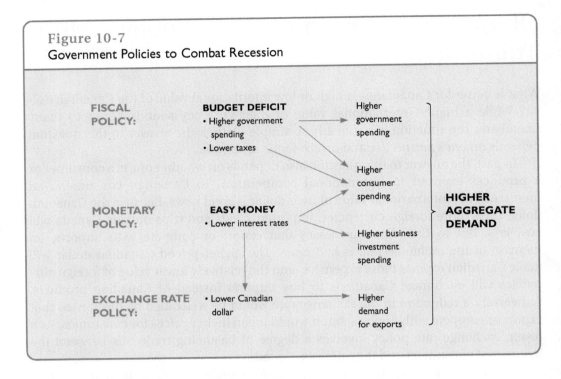

Figure 10-7
Government Policies to Combat Recession

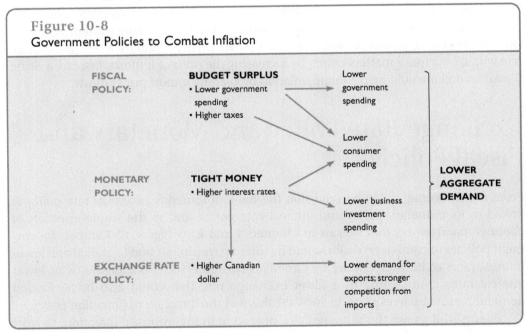

Figure 10-8
Government Policies to Combat Inflation

government tries to maintain the value of its currency *too far* below its equilibrium level to assist its exporters, it would have to sell vast amounts of its own currency in foreign exchange markets. To sell such quantities of its currency, it would have to borrow (or even print) such large volumes of money that it would damage its own economy through severe inflation.

Similarly, a nation that seeks to keep its exchange rate too far above its equilibrium level will encounter difficulties. To achieve excessive upward movement, the government would have to continually purchase its own currency on a large scale, using its foreign exchange reserves to do so. Such a policy would eventually deplete its reserves, and force the government to allow the value of its currency to decrease. The only other

IN THE NEWS

Tar Sands Oil and the Canadian Dollar as a "Petro-Currency"

The Athabasca Tar Sands of northern Alberta are a massive economic resource that is considered to be the world's second-largest deposit of crude oil. However, the oil is embedded in the ground, so it has to be extracted by a huge open-pit mining operation. Extracting the raw product and processing it into usable crude oil requires very large investments in capital equipment and is very costly. The result is that while the Tar Sands contain plentiful oil, it is oil that costly to produce.

If the price of crude oil is high enough, producing Tar Sands oil can be very profitable. In 2005, high ($50 US per barrel) and rising oil prices led two companies to plan investments of $21 billion in Tar Sands facilities, and when the price of oil passed the $100 per barrel mark, was projected that the Tar Sands would attract over $100 billion of investment over the next 20 years. The surge in the value of Canadian oil exports from 2005 to 2008 helped to push the exchange rate of the Canadian dollar past $1.00 US at times, leading some to describe the Canadian dollar as a "petro-currency".

Then the recession of 2008–09 struck, and the price of crude oil plunged to around $40 US per barrel. At this price, oil from previously-built Tar Sands plants was still profitable to produce. However, the much higher costs of building new oil mining and processing facilities meant that for them to be profitable, the price of oil would have to be around $90 US per barrel. As a result, many planned Tar Sands investment projects were put on hold. ■

QUESTIONS

1. If the price of oil were to rise considerably, how would such Tar Sands projects affect the international value of the Canadian dollar? Explain two reasons for your answer.
2. How would the change in the international value of the Canadian dollar in the previous question affect the standard of living of Canadians in general?
3. Why would the prospect of massive development of the Tar Sands cause concern for much of central Canada's manufacturing sector?

way to keep a currency at a level well above its equilibrium would be through making interest rates so high that they would depress the nation's entire economy.

So, when we speak of a government "managing" its exchange rate, we do not mean that the government *controls* the international value of its currency. A government can *influence* its exchange rate, but only to prevent excessively rapid fluctuations around its equilibrium level—it cannot succeed for long in keeping its exchange rate much above or below its equilibrium level.

Summary

In summary, the international value of the Canadian dollar is determined in foreign exchange markets by the buying and selling of the Canadian dollar that is generated by
- regular day-to-day international transactions such as those in the current account of the balance of payments,
- flows of investment funds such as those in the capital account of the balance of payments,

- flows of short-term funds (*hot money*, often speculative in nature) into and out of Canadian dollars, and
- very occasional purchases and sales of Canadian dollars by the Bank of Canada, seeking to moderate the fluctuations in the exchange rate.

Fluctuations in the Canadian dollar can have major effects upon Canadians. When the Canadian dollar was as high as US$0.89 in the late 1980s, Canadian consumers benefited from cheap imports, but many Canadian exporters had difficulty competing internationally, and jobs were lost. On the other hand, when the Canadian dollar plunged to below US$0.63 in 2002, Canadian exporters enjoyed great success, but consumers had to pay more for U.S. dollars and imported goods and services. And the dollar's rapid rise in 2004–2008 and 2010–11 pleased consumers, but concerned many Canadian businesses (employers) that export and compete with imports.

Looking Ahead

This chapter has stressed the importance of the exchange rate of the Canadian dollar to the international competitiveness of Canadian businesses and to the economic prosperity of Canadians. It also emphasized that rapid changes in the exchange rate can have negative effects upon an economy that is as exposed to international economic forces as Canada's is.

On a broader scale, a reasonably stable system of worldwide exchange rates is also economically beneficial. Excessive fluctuations in the prices of nations' currencies create an uncertain climate that discourages international trade and investment. On the other hand, a reasonably stable world exchange rate system can contribute to world economic prosperity by encouraging international trade and investment. For this reason, governments generally try to maintain reasonably stable currency prices, partly by using the exchange rate management policies described in this chapter.

Sometimes these efforts are successful, while at other times exchange rates fluctuate suddenly and sharply, with disruptive effects. In Chapters 11 and 12, we will examine these matters further.

Chapter Summary

1. The international value of the Canadian dollar is determined by the supply of and demand for it in foreign exchange markets, with Canadian receipts from other nations generating a demand for Canadian dollars, and Canadian payments to other nations generating a supply of Canadian dollars. (L.O. 1)

2. The balance of payments summarizes Canada's international receipts and payments for a given year, classifying them into current and capital accounts. If receipts exceed payments, there is a balance of payments *surplus*, and if payments exceed receipts, there is a balance of payments *deficit*. (L.O. 2)

3. Under a *floating* exchange rate such as Canada's, a balance of payments deficit will cause the exchange rate to fall, and a surplus will cause the exchange rate to rise. These adjustments will bring the balance of payments and the exchange rate automatically toward equilibrium. (L.O. 2, 3)

4. A rapidly rising exchange rate can increase unemployment by making a nation's goods and services less competitive internationally, while a rapid decline in its

exchange rate can make inflation worse by generating increases in import prices. (L.O. 4)

5. Foreign currency speculation can add to these problems, as speculators buy currencies that are *strong*, forcing their values even higher, and sell currencies that are *weak*, driving their values down farther and faster. (L.O. 4)

6. Under a *dirty float* system, the government influences the exchange rate so as to prevent excessively rapid fluctuations. To support a weak currency the government can buy its own currency and/or increase interest rates, and to hold down a strong currency the government can do the opposite. (L.O. 5)

7. To combat a recession, a monetary policy of lower interest rates and a fiscal policy of budget deficits can be combined with an exchange rate policy of a lower international value of the Canadian dollar to stimulate aggregate demand. (L.O. 6)

8. To combat inflation, a monetary policy of higher interest rates and a fiscal policy of budget surpluses can be combined with an exchange rate policy of a higher international value of the Canadian dollar to slow down aggregate demand. (L.O. 6)

Questions

1. State how each of the following events would tend to affect the international price of the Canadian dollar, and explain why the dollar would be affected in this way.
   (a) Increasing numbers of retired Canadians travel to warmer countries for the winter.
   (b) Canadian natural gas exports to the United States increase.
   (c) Canadian interest rates increase.
   (d) Poor harvests in Canada cause imports of U.S. fruits and vegetables to increase sharply.
   (e) Foreign investors increase their purchases of shares of Canadian companies.

2. An increase in the international price of the Canadian dollar would
   (a) benefit Canadian exporters, but harm Canadian consumers.
   (b) benefit both Canadian consumers and Canadian exporters.
   (c) benefit Canadian consumers but harm Canadian exporters.
   (d) harm both Canadian consumers and Canadian exporters.
   (e) None of the above.

3. If Canada were operating on a floating exchange rate and had a balance of payments *deficit*, which of the following best describes the adjustments that would take place?
   (a) The international value of the Canadian dollar would fall, Canada's receipts would fall, and its payments would rise until receipts and payments were in equilibrium, at which point the price of the Canadian dollar would stabilize but at a lower price than formerly.
   (b) The international value of the Canadian dollar would fall, Canada's receipts would rise, and its payments would fall until receipts and payments were in equilibrium, at which point the value of the Canadian dollar would stabilize, but at a lower level than formerly.
   (c) The international value of the Canadian dollar would fall, Canada's receipts would rise, and its payments would fall until the balance of payments was in equilibrium, after which the price of the Canadian dollar would stabilize at the same value as formerly.

(d) The international value of the Canadian dollar would rise, Canada's receipts would fall, and its payments would rise, until the balance of payments was in equilibrium, at which point the price of the Canadian dollar would stabilize, but at a higher value than formerly.

(e) None of the above.

4. If the international value of the Canadian dollar were to *increase* rapidly, there would be a risk of

(a) more severe inflation in Canada.

(b) lower-cost imports taking sales from Canadian firms.

(c) an increase in unemployment in Canada.

(d) Both (b) and (c).

(e) None of the above.

5. If the government of Canada were operating on a *dirty float* in the circumstances described in the previous question, it could

(a) sell Canadian dollars in foreign exchange markets.

(b) decrease Canadian interest rates.

(c) Both (a) and (b).

(d) increase tariffs on imported products.

(e) buy Canadian dollars in foreign exchange markets.

6. In 2005, the Canadian economy was in a boom and was operating at, or very near to, its capacity output. During 2005, the international value of the Canadian dollar increased strongly, reaching its highest level in many years.

(a) Manufacturers in Eastern Canada wanted action by the Bank of Canada to stop the international value of the Canadian dollar from rising. Why did they recommend this policy?

(b) Why do you think the Bank of Canada did *not* take steps to hold the international value of the Canadian dollar down in 2005?

7. (a) Visit Statistics Canada at www.statcan.gc.ca. Search for "Exchange rates, interest rates, money supply and stock prices".
   What has been the trend in the international price (value) of the Canadian dollar over the past few years?

(b) On Statistics Canada's website search for "Canada's balance of international payments".

   (i) What have been the trends in Canada's trade in goods and services over the past few years?

   (ii) What have been the trends in spending on travel (and tourism) into and out of Canada over the past few years?

(c) Do the trends in part (b) seem related to any changes in the international price of the Canadian dollar in part (a), or do they seem to be the result of other factors?

Study Guide

Review Questions (Answers to these Review Questions appear in Appendix B.)

1. Explain how each of the following events would affect the international price of the Canadian dollar.
   (a) The Canadian subsidiary of a U.S. corporation pays dividends to its parent company.
   (b) Canadians playing hockey for U.S.–based professional teams send funds back to their families in Canada.
   (c) Canadians buy large amounts of shares of U.S. companies.
   (d) Home Depot in the United States buys a large shipment of plywood from Canada.

2. Which group in Canada benefits economically from a *higher* international price of the Canadian dollar?
   (a) exporters
   (b) farmers
   (c) all Canadians
   (d) consumers
   (e) speculators

3. Which group in Canada benefits economically from a *lower* international price of the Canadian dollar?
   (a) exporters
   (b) consumers
   (c) speculators
   (d) all Canadians
   (e) no Canadians

4. If Canada is operating on a *floating exchange rate system*, the international value of the Canadian dollar will
   (a) remain stable (at one fixed level as decided by international agreement).
   (b) float steadily upward in relation to other currencies.
   (c) rise and fall as the supply of and demand for Canadian dollars in international money markets change.
   (d) gradually decrease in relation to other currencies.
   (e) None of the above.

5. If Canada were operating on a floating exchange rate and had a balance of payment *surplus*, the international value of the Canadian dollar would _____, which would cause Canada's *payments* to _____ and Canada's *receipts* to _____.

6. As a result of the effects referred to in the previous questions, Canada's
   (a) receipts and payments would become equal, and the international value of the Canadian dollar would tend to stabilize at the same level as formerly.
   (b) receipts and payments would become equal, and the international value of the Canadian dollar would tend to stabilize, but at a lower value than formerly.
   (c) receipts and payments would become equal, and the international value of the Canadian dollar would tend to stabilize, but at a higher value than formerly.

(d) receipts and payments would become equal, and the international value of the Canadian dollar would continue to rise.

(e) receipts would exceed payments, and the international value of the Canadian dollar would continue to fall.

7.

Canada's Balance of Payments, Year 200X
(Millions of Dollars)

	Receipts	Payments	Balance
Current Account			
Merchandise	$900	1200	– $300
Travel	150	50	+ 100
Interest and Dividends	150	350	– 200
Balance on Current Account			– $400
Capital Account			
Capital Movements	$500	$ 200	+$300
Balance on Capital Account			+$300
Overall Balance (Current and Capital Accounts)			– $100

(a) State whether each of the following statements is *true* or *false*. In Year 200X,
  (i) Canada sold more merchandise internationally than it bought.
  (ii) foreign tourists spent more money in Canada than Canadian tourists spent in other countries.
  (iii) Canada received more in interest and dividends than were paid out of Canada.
  (iv) more investment funds flowed out of Canada than into Canada.

(b) In Year 200X, did Canada have a balance of payments *surplus* or *deficit*?

(c) In Year 200X, the international price of the Canadian dollar would tend to _____.

(d) One group within Canada that would benefit economically from the change in the price of the Canadian dollar in (c) would be _____, because_____.

(e) One group within Canada that would be hurt economically by this change in the price of the Canadian dollar would be _____, because _____.

(f) Explain how this change in the price of the Canadian dollar will affect Canada's *receipts* from other nations, Canada's *payments* to other nations, and Canada's *balance of payments* (i.e., the relationship between Canada's receipts and payments).

(g) If the change in the price of the Canadian dollar in (c) were large and rapid, what concerns could this cause for the Canadian government in terms of its economic effects on Canada?

(h) To slow down/moderate the change in the international value of the Canadian dollar, the Bank of Canada could
  (i) _____ and/or
  (ii) _____.

8.

Canada's Balance of Payments, Year 200X
(Millions of Dollars)

	Receipts	Payments	Balance
Current Account			
Merchandise	$900	700	+ $200
Travel	100	200	− 100
Interest and Dividends	150	350	− 200
Balance on Current Account			− $100
Capital Account			
Capital Movements	$600	$200	
Balance on Capital Account			+$400
Overall Balance (Current and Capital Accounts)			+$300

(a) State whether each of the following statements is *true* or *false*. In Year 200X
   (i)   Canada sold more merchandise internationally than it bought.
   (ii) foreign tourists spent more money in Canada than Canadian tourists spent in other countries.
   (iii) Canada received more in interest and dividends than were paid out of Canada.
   (iv) more investment funds flowed out of Canada than into Canada.
(b) In Year 200X, did Canada have a balance of payments *surplus* or *deficit*?
(c) In Year 200X, the international price of the Canadian dollar would tend to
   _____.
(d) One group within Canada that would benefit economically from the change in the price of the Canadian dollar in (c) would be _____, because_____.
(e) One group within Canada that would be hurt economically by this change in the price of the Canadian dollar would be _____, because _____.
(f) Explain how this change in the price of the Canadian dollar will affect Canada's *receipts* from other nations, Canada's *payments* to other nations, and Canada's *balance of payments* (i.e., the relationship between Canada's receipts and payments).
(g) If the change in the price of the Canadian dollar in (c) were large and rapid, what concerns could this cause for the Canadian federal government in terms of its economic effects on Canada?
(h) To slow down/moderate the change in the international value of the Canadian dollar, the Bank of Canada could
   (i)   _____ and/or
   (ii) _____.

9. Under a dirty float exchange rate policy, the government
   (a) allows the international value of its currency to fluctuate freely with supply and demand.
   (b) prevents any fluctuations in the international value of its currency.

    (c) moderates fluctuations in the international value of its currency, usually by buying and selling currencies in foreign exchange markets.

    (d) manipulates the international value of its currency contrary to the wishes of its trading partners.

    (e) permits the international value of its currency to float, but outlaws speculative purchases and sales of the currency, which would cause its value to fluctuate.

10. If the international value of the Canadian dollar were to *decrease* rapidly, there would be a risk of
    (a) an increase in unemployment in Canada.
    (b) more severe inflation in Canada.
    (c) more severe competition from foreign manufacturers.
    (d) Both (a) and (b).
    (e) Both (a) and (c).

11. If the government of Canada were operating on a dirty float in the circumstances described in the previous question, it could
    (a) increase Canadian interest rates.
    (b) increase tariffs on foreign products.
    (c) buy Canadian dollars in foreign exchange markets.
    (d) sell Canadian dollars in foreign exchange markets.
    (e) Both (a) and (c).

12. *Hot money*
    (a) consists of short-term funds.
    (b) mostly originates in Afghanistan and Colombia.
    (c) can move swiftly from one currency to another currency.
    (d) can cause exchange rates to fluctuate considerably.
    (e) Answers (a), (c), and (d).

13. If the Bank of Canada were to increase interest rates, the international price (value) of the Canadian dollar would tend to
    (a) fall.
    (b) remain stable.
    (c) rise.

14. The change in the international price (value) of the Canadian dollar in the previous question would be beneficial to the performance of the economy during a period of
    (a) inflation.
    (b) full employment.
    (c) recession.

15. Which of the following combinations of economic policies would be suitable for dealing with a recession?
    (a) budget deficits, lower interest rates, and an increasing international value of the Canadian dollar
    (b) budget deficits, lower interest rates, and a decreasing international value of the Canadian dollar
    (c) balanced budgets, stable interest rates, and a stable international value of the Canadian dollar
    (d) budget deficits, higher interest rates, and a decreasing international value of the Canadian dollar
    (e) budget surpluses, lower interest rates, and an increasing international value of the Canadian dollar

Critical Thinking Questions

(Asterisked questions 1 to 5 are answered in Appendix B; the answers to questions 6 to 10 are in the Instructor's Manual that accompanies this text.)

*1. (a) In a global recession, would it be more likely that the international value/price of the Canadian dollar would increase or decrease? Why?
   (b) Explain how this change would affect the Canadian economy.

*2. Suppose that energy shortages led to expectations of massive investments by multinational corporations in energy development in the Tar Sands (crude oil) and the Mackenzie Delta (natural gas).
   (a) How might these expectations affect the actions of foreign exchange speculators concerning the Canadian dollar?
   (b) Why might the actions of foreign exchange speculators cause concerns for the Canadian government?
   (c) What could the Bank of Canada do to offset the problems in part (b)?

*3. In 2010, Canadians received $62 billion in investment income (interest, dividends, and other investment income) from other countries, while investors and lenders in other nations received $78 billion of investment income on their Canadian investments.

   Explain how these flows of interest and dividends affected the international price (value) of the Canadian dollar.

*4. Following 2001, China's exports increased greatly, generating large trade surpluses. However, for several years the Chinese government froze the exchange rate of its currency (the yuan) at 8.28 yuan per U.S. dollar.
   (a) If the yuan had been *floating*, what would have happened to the exchange rate? Why?
   (b) *Why* do you think the Chinese government froze the exchange rate?
   (c) *How* would the Chinese government freeze the exchange rate; that is, what would it *do*?

*5. If the exchange rate of the Canadian dollar were rising rapidly, would it become more or less likely that the Bank of Canada would increase interest rates soon? Why?

6. During the early-to-mid-1990s, unemployment in Canada was high. Over this period, the international value of the Canadian dollar decreased considerably, and many Canadians demanded that the Bank of Canada intervene to stop the dollar from falling.
   (a) Why would Canadians want the Bank of Canada to stop the international value of the dollar from falling?
   (b) Why do you think the Bank of Canada decided *not* to stop the dollar from falling at that time?

7. Do you think that the Canadian economy would benefit more from an increase or a decrease in the international value of the Canadian dollar at this time? Explain the reason for your answer.

8. The graph shows spending on tourism by Canadians outside of Canada and by foreign tourists coming into Canada. From 2001 to 2008, spending by foreign tourists visiting Canada decreased slightly, while spending by Canadian tourists abroad increased by 43 percent. Explain how the subject matter of this chapter would help to account for this trend.

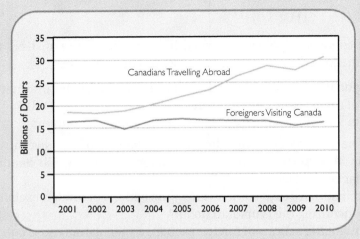

Source: Statistics Canada, CANSIM Table 376-0001.

9. Canadian professional sports teams such as the seven Canadian National Hockey League teams and the Toronto Blue Jays earn much of their income in Canadian dollars, but pay most of their expenses (players' salaries) in U.S. dollars. Since 2002, the value of the Canadian dollar has risen by nearly 65 percent in terms of the U.S. dollar.
   (a) How has this change in the exchange rate of the Canadian dollar affected the ability of Canadian teams to compete with American teams for talented players?
   (b) How might this change in the exchange rate of the Canadian dollar affect the probability of more NHL teams moving from the United States to Canada?

Use the Web   (Hints for these Use the Web exercises appear in Appendix B.)

1. Visit the Bank of Canada website (**www.bankofcanada.ca**) and click on *Media Room* on the top toolbar, then *Press Releases* on the left toolbar. Read recent press releases concerning interest rate announcements (these releases usually refer to the "target for the overnight rate").
   (a) Do these press releases provide any indications as to whether the Bank of Canada is concerned about recent trends in the exchange rate of the Canadian dollar?
   (b) If so, what is the nature of these concerns?

The Global Economy

LEARNING OBJECTIVES

After studying this chapter, you should be able to

1. Explain the lessons learned from two types of destructive economic policies used by governments during the Great Depression.

2. Summarize the goals and achievements of the General Agreement on Tariffs and Trade (GATT, renamed the World Trade Organization (WTO) in 1995).

3. Summarize the main objectives of the Doha Round of WTO trade negotiations, and the progress of these negotiations.

4. Define *trading bloc*, describe three such blocs, and summarize the view that the world might be evolving into three major economic power blocs.

5. Summarize the evolution of the international exchange rate system from 1945 to the present.

6. Describe the recent international economic developments concerning China and the United States

7. Explain the imbalances in the global economy as of 2005-08, and the adjustments that were regarded as necessary to deal with these imbalances.

8. Apply the facts and concepts of this chapter to various situations.

Over the course of the twentieth century, the world changed dramatically. The first half of the century was often characterized by *conflict* between nations in the tradition of the aggressively nationalistic attitudes of the previous century. In the sphere of economic policy as well as foreign policy, these conflicts proved to be mutually destructive for all concerned. Largely as a result of these experiences, the second half of the century saw more attempts to reduce conflict and increase *cooperation* among nations, especially concerning their economic policies.

First, we will review briefly the conflicts of the first half of the century; then we will consider the economic changes since then that have contributed to the *globalization* of the world's economy.

The First Half of the Twentieth Century

In the first half of the twentieth century, the dominant influence was the *nationalism* that had characterized the nineteenth century and often led to conflict between nations. The most dramatic examples of this conflict were of course the two world wars, the first from 1914 to 1918 and the second from 1939 to 1945. However, the nationalism that bred military conflict also extended into economic policy. As a result, much of the period between the two wars was characterized by economic conflict between nations.

This international economic conflict was intensified by the Great Depression of the 1930s, and the weapons used were tariffs and exchange rates—the topics of the previous two chapters. Confronted with high unemployment during the Depression, governments resorted to two types of aggressive economic policies aimed at reducing unemployment in their own countries at the expense of their trading partners. The first such policy involved countries *increasing tariffs* so as to keep out imports and thus "save jobs" of workers in industries facing foreign competition. Unfortunately, this policy merely led to retaliatory tariffs on the part of their trading partners that in turn led to even higher tariffs being imposed by all concerned. The result was a **trade war**, in which tariff barriers became so high that world trade was reduced considerably, forcing layoffs in export industries in all nations and making the Depression even worse.

trade war
Retaliatory escalation of trade barriers by nations against each other's exports.

The second type of aggressive economic policy could be called a **currency war**, and was equally destructive, for the same reasons. Some nations deliberately manipulated the prices of their currencies downward, in an attempt to "export unemployment" by making their products cheaper for foreign buyers. But their intended victims retaliated by taking similar steps to reduce the price of their own currencies. As these actions escalated, currency prices became unstable and unpredictable, thus adding new risks to international business transactions and reducing international trade. From 1929 to 1932, the value of international trade fell *by 63 percent*, throwing millions of people out of work around the globe.

currency war
The deliberate manipulation of the exchange rates of currencies downwards, in attempts to gain a competitive advantage.

The Great Depression was ended by the advent of the Second World War, which forced governments to spend so heavily on the military effort that jobs were created on a massive scale. As the war neared its end in 1945, nations realized that they could not return to the mutually destructive economic policies of the 1930s.

The Second Half of the Twentieth Century

The second half of the twentieth century witnessed the rise of *internationalism* in the area of economic policy. After the Second World War, governments of the world's major nations made substantial changes to their economic policies that were intended to create a more stable environment in which international trade and investment would be encouraged, rather than discouraged as in the 1930s. Specifically, governments agreed to

1. reduce tariffs so as to move in the direction of freer trade, through the *General Agreement on Tariffs and Trade* (GATT), since renamed the World Trade Organization (WTO), and
2. cooperate so as to make exchange rates more stable, through the *International Monetary Fund (IMF).*

Much of the world's economic history since the end of the Second World War has consisted of efforts among nations, through the GATT/WTO and the IMF, to achieve cooperation and stability in the area of international economic relations that would promote international trade, investment, and prosperity. These efforts have met with considerable success—overall, as we will see, much progress has been made. But there have also been setbacks, and threats to the progress of the past half-century.

First, we will consider developments in the area of international trade, and then the efforts of nations to maintain a more stable exchange rate system. Then we will review some of the major trends in the global economy.

Part A: International Trade: The General Agreement on Tariffs and Trade (GATT) and The World Trade Organization (WTO)

The **General Agreement on Tariffs and Trade (GATT)**, which was in 1995 renamed the **World Trade Organization (WTO)**, was one of the most significant international economic developments of the twentieth century.

The half-century following the GATT's establishment in 1947 saw an unprecedented growth of world trade. Indeed, much of the improvement in world economic prosperity in the second half of the twentieth century is attributed to this tremendous expansion of international trade.

The GATT was established when 23 countries, including Canada, signed the original agreement in 1947. The immediate objective of the GATT was to prevent a recurrence of the trade wars of the 1930s. The GATT's longer-term goal was more ambitious—to negotiate reductions in tariffs, with the objective of increasing world trade and prosperity for all concerned. The negotiations are *multilateral*, which means that all parties to the agreement negotiate mutual tariff reductions. The 1947 GATT agreement represented a major change in policy and the start of a long trend toward freer international trade.

Since 1947, the members of the GATT/WTO have met in a series of *rounds* of talks to negotiate tariff reductions, as shown in Table 11-1. The focus of the earlier rounds was reducing tariffs on goods, but in the seventh round (the Tokyo Round, 1973–79), nontariff barriers to trade were also addressed. The eighth round (the Uruguay Round, 1986–93) included 116 nations, a great increase from the original 23. The ambitious agenda of the Uruguay Round included trade in services, which had grown to almost 30 percent of world trade. It was at the conclusion of the Uruguay Round that the GATT was renamed the *World Trade Organization (WTO).* As Figure 11-1 shows, these rounds of negotiations over many years resulted in large reductions in tariffs.

General Agreement on Tariffs and Trade (GATT)
An international agreement under which many nations, following 1947, negotiated reductions in tariffs in order to promote freer trade.

World Trade Organization (WTO)
Successor to the GATT as of 1995.

www.wto.org

Table 11-1
GATT/WTO Rounds of Multilateral Trade Negotiations

Order	Date	Location
1st	1947	Geneva (Switzerland)
2nd	1949	Annecy (France)
3rd	1951	Torquay (England)
4th	1956	Geneva
5th	1960–1962	Geneva
6th	1964–1967	Geneva[a]
7th	1973–1979	Geneva[b]
8th	1986–1993	Geneva[c]
9th	2001–200?	Doha

[a] Kennedy Round
[b] Tokyo Round
[c] Uruguay Round

Figure 11-1
Tariff Levels, 1940–2000

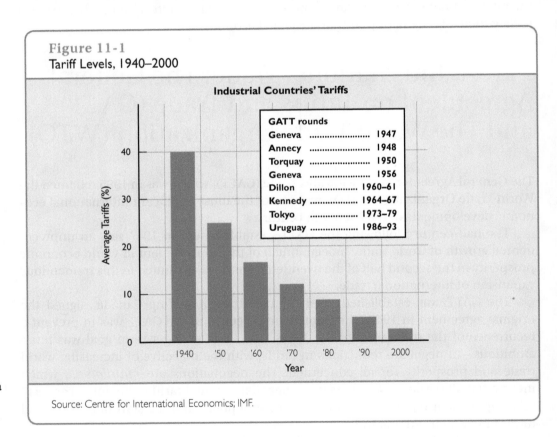

Industrial Countries' Tariffs

GATT rounds	
Geneva	1947
Annecy	1948
Torquay	1950
Geneva	1956
Dillon	1960–61
Kennedy	1964–67
Tokyo	1973–79
Uruguay	1986–93

Source: Centre for International Economics; IMF.

dumping
The practice of exporting a product at a price below the cost of producing it, or below the price charged in the country in which it is produced.

subsidies
Government financial assistance to a firm or industry, through measures such as grants, loans, or special tax treatment.

In addition to reducing tariffs, the GATT/WTO has sought to establish *rules for fair competition* in international trade. For instance, one unfair practice is **dumping**, or exporting a product at a price that is below the cost of producing it or below the price in your home market. It is also considered unfair for a government to give **subsidies**, such as grants or tax breaks, to its industries in order to give them an advantage in international competition by making it possible for them to sell at prices below their real production costs.

Settlement of Trade Disputes

As we saw in Chapter 9, freer trade economically benefits consumers and creates opportunities for efficient producers, but it also threatens less competitive producers due to increased competition from imports. Sometimes foreign competition is alleged to be *unfair*, and these allegations lead to trade disputes between nations. And in trade disputes, there is always the danger that nations will retaliate against each other, escalating the dispute and extending its damaging effects into other industries. So it is important that trade disputes be resolved, rather than allowed to escalate.

The WTO requires that trade disputes between its members be settled in an impartial manner. If the countries involved in a trade dispute (such as whether one country was unfairly restricting imports from the other country) are unable to resolve the problem by themselves, the dispute will ultimately be decided by a panel of experts who are knowledgeable about trade, and neutral with respect to the parties to the dispute.

Successes and Challenges

By many standards, the GATT/WTO has been successful. As noted earlier, in the second half of the twentieth century large reductions in tariffs were achieved, and world trade expanded tremendously.

However, progress toward freer trade has not been smooth and steady. One major problem faced by the GATT since the early 1980s has been renewed *protectionism*. As trade became freer, established industries in the United States and Europe faced strong competition from Japan in high-technology sectors such as automobiles and electronic equipment, and from less developed countries in labour-intensive products such as clothing and footwear. Fear of job losses and allegations that the import competition was "unfair" pushed the U.S. and European governments to restrict imports. Often, these restrictions took the form of *nontariff barriers* to imports. These trade restrictions violated the intent of the GATT, but nations could claim that the restrictions were justified on grounds such as consumer protection, health standards, product standards, and so on.

And these new trade barriers were substantial. While average tariff levels in the 1980s were down to about 10 percent, several of the new *nontariff* barriers were roughly equivalent to a 25-percent tariff—a level of protection that had been common 30 years earlier. These new trade barriers became so controversial that concerns arose that they would breed retaliation that could escalate into a damaging trade war.

The Uruguay Round (1986–93)

The Uruguay Round—the eighth in the series of GATT negotiations that had started in 1947—was intended to reduce trade tensions and to promote the resumption of progress toward freer trade. The Uruguay Round was a very complex and difficult negotiation process. The sheer number of participants (116 by the end of the talks) complicated the negotiation process, making it more difficult to reach agreements. In addition, the negotiations included the complex matter of nontariff barriers, which had become a substitute for tariffs. A third complicating factor was the complex question of trade in services, which had grown to roughly 30 percent of all world trade.

Finally, a new agreement was reached—a 25 000-page document that became effective in 1995, at which time the GATT was renamed the World Trade Organization (WTO). Under this agreement, the developed countries were to reduce tariffs on

"The world would be a dismal place without GATT. The major countries would have made their own deals, and smaller countries like Canada would have been exposed. Certainly there would be less trade. The world would be poorer."
— FRANK STONE, INSTITUTE FOR RESEARCH ON PUBLIC POLICY

industrial goods by 38 percent over six years. For farm products, the troublesome agricultural subsidies and trade barriers were to be reduced. New rules covering trade in services were established, and long-established barriers to trade in textiles were to be phased out over a period of ten years. In addition, clearer definitions of *subsidies* and *dumping* were established, making the rules for international trade clearer.

The Doha Round of WTO Trade Negotiations

Even after all the efforts at the Uruguay Round, the road to freer trade in the years after 1995 was a difficult one. Pushed by concerns about unemployment in its slowing economy, the United States introduced several protectionist measures that led to several major trade disputes, mostly with Europe. It was against this backdrop of protectionist actions and disputes that the ninth round of WTO negotiations was launched in late 2001—the Doha Round, in Doha, Qatar.

One of the basic objectives of the Doha Round was to help developing countries by opening up the markets of the rich countries to their products. In particular, it was hoped that the rich countries would open their markets to developing countries' agricultural products and textiles—two areas in which the rich countries' trade barriers had historically been very high. The developed world pays subsidies of nearly $1 billion US per day to its farmers, which encourages overproduction and results in such low prices that farmers in poor countries cannot compete.

By mid-2011 and nearly ten years after the trade negotiations started, it appeared very likely that the Doha Round would not succeed in reaching an agreement. The major developing countries (including China, India, Brazil, South Korea, and South Africa) rejected demands from the wealthy nations (led by the United States, the European Union, and Japan) that the developing nations lower their tariffs on imports of agricultural and manufactured goods and open their service sectors to more foreign competition. For their part, the wealthy nations were unwilling to give up the extensive subsidies that their governments pay to their politically powerful farmers. In addition, the USA and the EU could not agree between themselves on the contentious issue of agricultural subsidies.

The WTO's director-general told negotiators in mid-2011 that the negotiations were "in paralysis", and urged member countries to use their December 2011 meeting to have a broad conversation about the future of Doha rather than try to make concrete progress. However, many observers believed that the talks would be abandoned, making Doha the first-ever failure of a GATT/WTO negotiating round.

The Future: Globalization or Regionalism?

To some observers, the problems of the Doha Round showed that the WTO's multilateral or global approach to freer trade had gone as far as it could. They believed that the complexities of negotiating worldwide trade agreements among 153 diverse nations, each of which has a veto, had become overwhelming. For them, the future would see more emphasis on *regional* trade agreements, known as **trading blocs**. These are separate trade agreements negotiated outside of the GATT/WTO, usually among nations in a particular region. The most noteworthy trading blocs are the European Union (EU) and the North American Free Trade Agreement (NAFTA). There are several other regional trading arrangements in the Pacific area, Southeast Asia, Australia and New Zealand, Latin America, Africa, the Caribbean, and the Middle East.

The **European Union** (EU; **www.europa.eu**) is the last step in the economic unification of many European countries. From its original six members in 1957

trading blocs
Groups of nations that have a trade agreement among themselves outside of the WTO agreement.

European Union (EU)
A very large trading bloc consisting of 27 European countries.

(Germany, France, Italy, Belgium, The Netherlands, and Luxembourg), the EU expanded to 27 members by 2009, including almost all of the countries in Europe. Expansions in 2004 and 2007 added 8 former Soviet bloc countries, from Estonia in the north to Bulgaria in the south.

The EU is regarded as a major achievement because of the political complexities of creating a free trade agreement among such a large number of nations with such diverse economic, cultural, political, linguistic, and historical characteristics.

A key step in the economic unification of Europe was the introduction of a common currency (the **euro**), which is used by 16 of the 27 members of the EU. Each of these nations has surrendered control of its monetary policy to a supranational institution, the European Central Bank (ECB).

The European Union comprises a very large market with a population of nearly 500 million, with goods, services, and capital moving easily across national borders, and with all of the associated advantages in terms of economies of scale. The euro was intended to make the European market even more integrated, by reducing currency conversion costs and by eliminating uncertainties regarding currency values. In 2010, the EU's output of goods and services of US$16.3 trillion represented about 26 percent of total world output. Supporters of the EU hope that it will challenge, or even surpass, the United States as the world's most powerful economic centre.

The **North American Free Trade Agreement (NAFTA)** is discussed in more detail in Chapter 12, "Canada in the Global Economy," so we will only sketch the outlines of it here. In 1989, Canada and the United States signed the Canada–U.S. Free Trade Agreement, which, with the addition of Mexico in 1994, became NAFTA. In some ways, NAFTA was North America's (and particularly the U.S.'s) response to the European Union—the economic unification of North America into a single vast market, with similar advantages and economic power to those of the European Union.

Asia–Pacific Economic Co-operation (APEC) includes Canada, the United States, Japan, South Korea, China, Australia, and 15 other nations of the Pacific area. It is considerably less fully structured than the other trading blocs that we have discussed. It consists of a very diverse group of nations and, therefore, has much farther to go to become a free trade area. APEC's "action agenda" calls for its members to form a free trade area by 2020; however, APEC is a loosely-affiliated organization that few expect to meet this goal.

Trade, Currencies, and Global Economic Power

Since the Second World War, the degree of international economic cooperation has improved considerably, if not always steadily. Most of this progress was achieved through the two major global institutions of the GATT/WTO and the IMF that operate on a nearly worldwide scale. However, there was growing speculation that the world might evolve into three major trade and currency areas: a western hemisphere bloc centred on the United States, the European Union, and an Asian bloc with Japan and China as its focal points.

For many years, the United States and its currency played an enormous role in the world economy, largely because of the dominance of the U.S. economy internationally. But Europe's plans for its own huge, united market and single currency posed a challenge to U.S. dominance. In response, the United States entered into its own free trade agreements, first with Canada, then with Mexico. The long-term U.S. goal was for a Free Trade Area of the Americas, embracing the entire western hemisphere and matching or surpassing the European Union in size and prosperity. However, progress toward this broader goal had stalled by the late 1990s.

"The single market has given EU companies a large home market to match the domestic markets of the United States and Japan that have enabled their companies to benefit from enormous economies of scale."
— BRUCE BARNARD, BRUSSELS, CORRESPONDENT FOR THE JOURNAL OF COMMERCE

euro
A common currency adopted by 16 of the 27 countries of the European Union.

North American Free Trade Agreement (NAFTA)
Free trade agreement involving Canada, the United States, and Mexico.

Asia–Pacific Economic Co-operation (APEC)
A group of 21 nations that border the Pacific Ocean.

The position of Japan, China, and Asia in this global economic chess match was less clear. While Asia has great potential for economic development, it is not yet a match for the EU or NAFTA blocs. Furthermore, APEC was far from forming a full Asia-Pacific free trade area, and two key players in APEC are the United States and Canada, both of which are members of NAFTA. Only time will tell how the various trading and currency blocs will evolve, and how Asia and APEC will fit into the global picture.

Part B: Exchange Rates: The International Monetary Fund (IMF)

International trade agreements alone are not enough to foster increased international trade and investment. It is also important to have a system of exchange rates that is reasonably stable and predictable, so that trade and investment will not be disrupted by uncertainties concerning exchange rate fluctuations. Such a system will also allow governments and businesses to plan trade agreements, investments, and exports without undue fear of these being damaged or even ruined by sudden and sharp changes in exchange rates.

The Experience of the 1930s

During the 1930s, exchange rates became unstable under the pressure of the Great Depression. Desperately seeking to reduce unemployment, some nations deliberately reduced the international value of their currencies in order to increase employment in their export industries, at the expense of their trading partners. But other nations retaliated by reducing their own exchange rates, the result being a period of unstable exchange rates and uncertainty that further reduced international trade and investment, and made the Depression even worse. The 1930s showed the nations of the world that concerning exchange rates, it would be beneficial for countries to be cooperative rather than combative.

Following the Second World War, nations took steps to prevent a recurrence of the problems of the 1930s. We have seen how in the area of trade and tariffs they established an international organization (GATT, later the WTO), which was intended to promote the expansion of trade. In the area of exchange rates, there were similar developments: an international organization—the **International Monetary Fund (IMF)**—was established, with the goal of stabilizing countries' exchange rates and so creating a better environment for international trade and investment.

International Monetary Fund (IMF)
An international agency established to oversee and maintain the system of pegged exchange rates set up in 1945.

The International Monetary Fund (IMF)

In 1944, 39 nations founded the International Monetary Fund. The IMF is a large international organization with many responsibilities, a key one of which involved stabilizing the exchange rates of nations.

The Post-War System of Pegged Exchange Rates
After the Second World War, the nations of the world resolved to avoid a recurrence of the exchange rate chaos of the 1930s. In 1945, they set up a system of **pegged exchange**

www.imf.org

rates, in which each nation would establish a *par value* for its currency and its government would keep the currency's price within 1 percent of this par value. The U.S. dollar stood at the centre of the system, with the value of each currency *pegged* to the U.S. dollar; the value of each currency was pegged relative to the value of other currencies in a rigid system.

To keep exchange rates at their pegged levels, governments would *buy and sell currencies* in foreign exchange markets. For instance, if the British pound was losing value relative to the French franc, the British and French governments would buy pounds and sell francs in foreign exchange markets in order to support the price of the pound relative to the franc within 1 percent of its pegged level. To enable them to buy their own currencies, governments held deposits of foreign currencies and gold (*foreign exchange reserves*).

In effect, this system was a sort of extreme *dirty float* as described in Chapter 10, but with the objective of not merely moderating fluctuations in exchange rates, but rather of almost *preventing them altogether.* In reaction to the exchange rate instability of the 1930s, IMF members went to the opposite extreme of establishing a very rigid exchange rate system.

Role of the IMF

It was the IMF's task to help preserve the system of pegged exchange rates established in 1945. The IMF conducted *annual consultations* with member nations to encourage them to follow stable economic policies, and to keep IMF members informed of developments in each others' countries. In addition, the IMF could *lend foreign exchange reserves* to member nations that needed them to maintain their exchange rates at their pegged level. Member nations contribute funds to the IMF, which form a pool of money that the IMF can use to make loans to members in financial difficulty.

Strains on the Pegged Exchange Rate System

Despite the efforts of the IMF, it proved impossible to freeze the international prices of currencies indefinitely. Economic conditions changed in ways that made it inevitable that some nations would have balance of payments surpluses (which pushed their exchange rates up) and others would have deficits (which pushed their exchange rates down). Governments could offset small, short-term surpluses and deficits by buying or selling currencies, with IMF help if needed. But in the case of large and persistent deficits or surpluses, it proved impossible to peg the currency values for long, because doing so would have required buying or selling impossibly large amounts of currencies in foreign exchange markets.

Upward pressures on currencies were experienced by nations whose strong internationally competitive positions put their currencies in high demand on foreign exchange markets. For example, West German and Japanese exports grew strongly as these nations benefited from a combination of rising industrial efficiency, low inflation rates, and currency values that were pegged at low levels in 1945. So there was upward pressure on the prices of the Japanese yen and the West German Deutschmark.

A different problem was posed by the downward pressures on the currencies of nations whose weak competitive positions caused their currencies to be in relatively low demand and high supply in foreign exchange markets. For example, Great Britain suffered from a combination of high inflation rates, lagging industrial efficiency, and a currency that was pegged at an unrealistically high value.

pegged exchange rates
Exchange rates that are prevented by their respective governments from moving from their fixed levels in relation to others.

devaluation

A reduction in the level of a pegged exchange rate.

These factors combined to make Britain's goods uncompetitive in both domestic markets and export markets, generating large trade deficits that continually pushed the price of the pound downward. To maintain the pound at its pegged level, Britain had to buy large volumes of pounds, selling off its reserves of foreign currencies to do so. Eventually, Britain ran out of foreign currencies, and the pound fell suddenly and sharply in value relative to other currencies—a process known as **devaluation** of a currency.

The Canadian dollar was part of the pegged system only from 1962 to 1969, when it was fixed at U.S. 93 cents. Like many other currencies, the Canadian dollar was pegged unrealistically low relative to the U.S. dollar, so after being floated, it quickly appreciated to around US$1.00.

By the 1960s, the U.S. dollar—the key currency in the system—was pegged at a price about 25 percent higher than would have occurred under a floating exchange rate system. This over-valuation of its currency made it even more difficult for the United States to compete with Japan, Germany, and other nations in world trade. Finally, in 1973, the United States floated its dollar, effectively bringing the system of pegged exchange rates to an end.

The Pegged Exchange Rate System in Perspective

In one sense, the pegged exchange rate system represented an effort to *attempt the necessary*—that is, to stabilize currencies in order to avoid a repetition of the problems of the 1930s. In another sense, it represented an attempt to *achieve the impossible*—that is, to freeze the prices of nations' currencies despite major changes in the economic circumstances of those nations. By buying and selling currencies, governments were able to hold currencies at their pegged values, but only for so long. At that point, there would be a major change in the relative values of currencies, usually occasioned by the devaluation of one or more of them. So it could be said that the actual effect of the pegged exchange rate system was to *postpone* exchange rate changes rather than to *prevent* them. However, it can also be said that between these periodic adjustments, the pegged system did succeed in creating periods when exchange rates were stable.

After the Pegged Exchange Rate System

In 1973, the pegged system of exchange rates was dismantled. In its place there emerged no single exchange rate system; rather, each IMF member could choose its own approach. Today, probably the most common is the *dirty float* system as described in Chapter 10, in which exchange rates can move up and down with market forces, but with governments intervening (usually by buying or selling their own currency) to prevent such fluctuations from occurring too rapidly. Other nations allow their currencies to float freely, while some currencies are pegged to another currency or group of currencies, or only allowed to change in price to a certain extent from a group of other currencies. As mentioned in Chapter 10, Canada now operates on a floating exchange rate, with the Bank of Canada intervening to influence the exchange rate only rarely, in times of crisis.

There had been fears that the end of the pegged exchange rate system would lead to a return to the exchange rate instability of the 1930s. But this did not happen—nations generally managed their exchange rates quite responsibly, resisting the temptation to manipulate their currency values downward to gain a quick (but almost certainly temporary) competitive advantage.

Part C: Recent Developments in the Global Economy

The "globalization" of the world's economy described at the end of Chapter 9 has provided many interesting and newsworthy events in recent years. The remainder of this chapter will focus on major developments that involve both China and the United States, and which have interacted in ways that have affected Canada and the rest of the world.

China

China's arrival on the world economic stage is one of the most important developments of recent years. China's opening to trade with the world economy and its entry into the World Trade Organization in 2001 was followed by such rapid growth of its exports that by 2009, China had risen from seventh place among the world's merchandise exporters to first place, surpassing both the United States and Japan in the process. As Table 11-2 shows, China's exports amounted to 9.6 percent of world exports in 2009, up from 3.9 percent in 2000.

"What you cannot avoid, welcome."
—CHINESE PROVERB

It is rightly said that China both frightens and attracts foreign business leaders, depending on whether they see China as a low-cost competitor, a cheap source of supply, or a potentially vast market.

China's impact on the global economy has been magnified by two factors:

1. China has a huge, cheap labour force.
2. The Chinese economy is unusually open to trade. Together, exports and imports amount to about 70 percent of China's GDP, as compared to about 25 percent for Japan and the United States.

"Remember, in China, when you are one in a million, there are 1,300 other people just like you."
— MICROSOFT'S SAYING ABOUT THEIR ASIA CENTRE

Table 11-2		
The World's Largest Merchandise Exporters, 2009		
	2009 Exports (US$ billions)	Share of World Exports, 2009
1 China	$1202	9.6%
2 Germany	1126	9.0
3 United States	1056	8.5
4 Japan	581	4.6
5 Netherlands	498	4.0
6 France	485	3.9
7 Italy	406	3.2
8 Belgium	370	3.0
9 Korea, South	364	2.9
10 United Kingdom	352	2.8
11 Canada	317	2.5
12 Russian Federation	303	2.4
13 Mexico	230	1.8

Source: World Trade Organization, *World Trade Developments in 2009.*

For most people, the most visible result of China's entry into the world economy has been store shelves full of imports of lower priced goods, often manufactured by Asian or American firms that have invested in China. However, China's impact on the global economy is considerably broader and more complex than merely providing low-cost goods to western consumers.

Investment in China—China's Economic Development Agenda

The government of China has aggressively promoted industrial development by means of huge investments by state enterprises, concentrated in heavy industries such as steel, aluminum, cement, and car manufacturing. Under the guidance of government, the very high household savings of the Chinese people have been channeled into countless large-scale industrial projects.

Investment by foreign firms has also played a large role in China's economic development, as China became one of the world's largest recipients of foreign direct investment. In the 1980s, most foreign direct investment in manufacturing was concentrated in labour-intensive industries such as clothing and textiles. But in the 1990s, foreign investment shifted to investment goods such as machinery and transportation, electronics, and communications equipment. And since the second half of the 1990s, there has been considerable foreign direct investment in China's information technology sector.

In the auto sector, China's production increased sharply after it abolished a 50 percent limit on foreign participation in local business ventures in order to conform to WTO regulations on foreign investment. Volkswagen became a big investor, and by 2003, China ranked sixth in the world in auto output, after the United States, Japan, Germany, France, and South Korea.

Saving in China

Such high investment requires high saving, and the saving rate for Chinese households is remarkably high for a poor country—in the range of 25 percent of disposable income. Various theories have been advanced to explain such high saving. One explanation is that Chinese people lack access to consumer credit, so they must save in order to buy assets. Another is that because China lacks social welfare programs, people must save for the education of their children (which is costly), for health care, and for old age. It is also believed that the consumption spending of Chinese families has not yet caught up with the rapid growth of incomes. In addition, much of the increase in income in recent years has gone to a relatively small proportion of the population living in coastal areas, whose high incomes allow them to save considerably.

In 2005, there was one car for every 70 people in China, as compared to one car for every two North Americans, and China's oil consumption per person was 1/15 of North America's.

China Joins the World Economy

As noted earlier, one key result of China's economic development program was a dramatic increase in exports. From Table 11-3 it can be seen that while Europe was the single largest destination for Chinese exports (21 percent in 2008), followed by the United States (18 percent), about 37 percent of China's exports went to other Asian nations.

Such rapid growth of exports led to large-scale buying of the Chinese currency, the yuan. In addition, China has in recent years received large inflows of foreign capital. Heavy direct investment by foreign corporations generated additional buying of the yuan. The demand for the yuan was increased further by inflows of speculative capital ("hot money" as described in Chapter 10) from investors who hoped to profit from increases in the international value of the yuan.

China's Exchange Rate

And it was logical to expect that the international price of the yuan would increase. Usually, the currencies of rapidly-developing economies appreciate over time; as their rising exports generate higher demand for their currencies. A classic example is pro-

Table 11-3

China's Exports by Country, 2008

1	European Union	20.5%
2	United States	17.7%
3	Hong Kong	13.4%
4	ASEAN[1]	8.0%
5	Japan	8.0%
6	Korea	5.3%
7	India	2.2%
8	Russia	2.2%
9	Taiwan	1.9%
10	United Arab Emirates	1.6%

[1] Association of Southeast Asian Nations (www.aseansec.org)

Source: Ministry of Commerce of the People's Republic of China.
http://english.wofcom.gov.cu/aarticle/statistic/ie/200901/20090105999708.html

Figure 11-2

Value of the Japanese Yen in U.S. Cents, 1960–2010

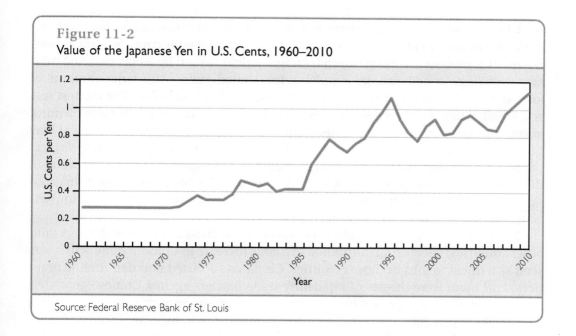

Source: Federal Reserve Bank of St. Louis

vided by Japan, whose great success in export markets in the 1970s and 1980s was followed by a large increase in the exchange rate of its currency (the yen), as shown in Figure 11-2. And as the yen rose in value, Japan's competitive advantage was diminished as its exports became more costly to foreign buyers.

A similar upward movement of the yuan would have reduced the competitive advantage enjoyed by China (and by western corporations that had invested in China). But from 1994 to 2005, this did not happen, because the Chinese government *pegged* its currency at 8.28 yuan to the U.S. dollar[1]. To keep the yuan from rising against the U.S. dollar, the Chinese central bank sold large volumes of its currency and bought large amounts of dollars, *by buying American government bonds*.

China's policy of pegging the yuan had various effects on the world economy. First, by keeping the cost of the yuan to foreigners low, it contributed to the *rapid growth of Chinese exports* that was described earlier.

---

[1] Interestingly, Japan also pegged its exchange rate against the U.S. dollar until 1971, as part of the system of pegged exchange rates at that time. This can be seen in Figure 11-2.

YOU DECIDE

The Bond Price–Interest Rate Connection

Suppose a United States government bond that pays interest of $60 per year is presently selling for $1000. If you bought that bond for $1000, you would be earning a rate of interest of 6 percent on that investment. ($60/$1000 × 100 = 6 percent).

Now suppose that in order to keep the yuan from rising, the Bank of China buys large amounts of U.S. government bonds, which bids the price of those bonds up to $1070. ■

QUESTIONS

1. How will the Chinese purchases of those U.S. government bonds affect the interest rate on those bonds?
2. In general terms, what is the relationship between interest rates and bond prices?

China's buying of U.S. government bonds had another remarkable effect. By lending large volumes of funds to the United States, China—a poor country—was *financing the U.S. government's large annual budget deficits* caused by its tax cuts and military spending. In addition, by supplying the United States with large amounts of loaned funds, China was helping to *keep American interest rates low*. The interest rate is the "price" paid for borrowing money, and by making loanable funds more plentiful in the United States, China kept interest rates low. For another way of looking at how China's pegging of the yuan affected American interest rates, see the *You Decide* box.

So China's pegging of the yuan supported a huge surge in consumer spending in the United States, in three ways: it kept interest rates for consumers low, it financed tax cuts by the U.S. federal government, and it made a vast amount of cheap imported goods available to American consumers.

But China's "cheap yuan" policy was strongly criticized in the United States (and other countries) because it contributed to a large increase in Chinese exports that was seen as a threat to jobs in those countries. China was accused of unfair trading practices, and there were threats of retaliatory trade barriers against Chinese goods. As time passed, the pressure on China to revalue the yuan intensified.

Finally, in July 2005, the Bank of China announced that the yuan would no longer be pegged to the U.S. dollar, but rather that it would be "managed" against a weighted average of a basket of currencies. This began the gradual upward movement of the exchange rate of the yuan, which can be seen after mid-2005 in Figure 11-3. By mid-2008, the international price of the yuan had increased by 21 percent against the U.S. dollar. When the U.S. recession of 2008–09 threatened Chinese exports to the USA, China again pegged the yuan until 2010, as Figure 11-3 also shows; after mid-2010, China allowed the yuan to rise against the U.S. dollar. By mid-2011, the yuan was 28 percent higher against the U.S. dollar than it had been six years earlier.

However, even after the exchange rate of the yuan was increasing, critics in the United States and other countries argued that the yuan was still being manipulated (that is, held down) by the Chinese government in order to gain a competitive advantage for its exports.

The International Macroeconomic Effects of China

As noted earlier, China's emergence had a big impact of the global economy not only because of its huge, cheap workforce, but also because China is unusually open to trade. By adding to the global economy a low-cost competitor, a large source of sup-

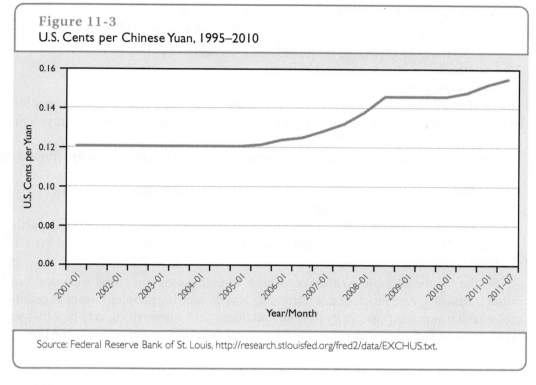

Figure 11-3
U.S. Cents per Chinese Yuan, 1995–2010

Source: Federal Reserve Bank of St. Louis, http://research.stlouisfed.org/fred2/data/EXCHUS.txt.

ply of low-cost goods, and a large source of capital, China had important and diverse effects on a broad macroeconomic global scale, including

1. *lower inflation rates*, due to China's exports of low-priced goods into other countries;
2. *lower interest rates*, due to China's large-scale purchases of U.S. government bonds and due to low inflation rates;
3. *encouragement of consumer spending*, by providing cheap goods and by keeping interest rates low, especially in the United States;
4. *slower employment growth* in other countries, due to China's cheap imports that compete with their industries;
5. *slower growth of wages* in other countries, due to cheap Chinese imports that compete with their industries; and
6. *changes in relative prices*—falling prices for the manufactured goods that China exports, and rising prices for goods that it imports, especially oil and raw materials.

So for a typical American, the entry of China into the global economy meant that your pay increases were slow, but so was inflation, and you could buy inexpensive imported consumer goods on easily available credit at low interest rates. Gasoline prices increased more rapidly, but so did the value of your home—and it was easy to borrow money at low interest rates, using your home as security for the loans. And both you and your country's government were going deeper into debt with each passing year.

The United States

The position of the United States in the world economy for the first few years after 2001 was also unusual, but in very different ways from China's position. The main aspects of the United States' situation were

1. *a strong economic boom*, with very high consumption spending, very heavy borrowing, and very low saving by Americans,
2. *large federal government budget deficits*, financed largely by borrowing from foreign lenders, especially China,

3. *very large trade deficits* (excesses of imports over exports), and
4. a surprisingly high, but declining, international value of the U.S. dollar.

Each of these will be explained in the following sections.

1. The economic boom of 2004–07

The 2004-07 period saw a strong economic boom in the United States, which was led by very rapid increases in consumer spending. But this boom was unusual in several ways that were influenced by China:

- The rate of inflation remained low, largely due to massive imports of low-priced goods from China.
- Workers' incomes did not rise much, partly due to the depressing effect of Chinese (and Indian) competition on wages worldwide.
- Interest rates remained low, partly because inflation rates were low, and partly because of the vast supply of funds flowing into the American financial system from China.

So the source of rapidly-rising consumer spending was not rising incomes, but rather borrowing. And much of this borrowing was done using people's homes as collateral, which was made possible by the fact that home prices were rising very rapidly—so rapidly that in fact a housing price "bubble" was developing, as described in the box.

YOU DECIDE

The Housing Price Bubble and Subprime Mortgages

For several years after 2001, interest rates were exceptionally low in the United States. Such low interest rates, combined with a U.S. tax system that allowed deduction of mortgage interest from taxable income and exempted up to $500 000 of capital gains on sale of a house from taxation, generated very high demand for housing and rapidly-rising house prices.

Home buying requires borrowing, so there was an explosion of mortgage lending. Many mortgage loans were made to "subprime" borrowers; that is, people whose employment record, low incomes, and lack of assets (or even a down payment) made them bad credit risks. Home buying by such borrowers added greatly to the demand for housing, generating sharp increases in home prices, which led to a "bubble" in the housing market.

A "bubble" in the price of an asset occurs when many people buy that asset *because they believe that its price will rise*, so that they can sell it for a profit. If this belief is strong, the rising prices of such assets *will create even higher demand for them*. People will pay very high prices for such assets, and borrow heavily to buy them. It was estimated that over 20 percent of home purchases in the United States were by people who had no intention of living in the house—they were only buying it as an asset, in order to resell it. This speculative buying added to demand, driving housing prices to extremely high levels—a classic "bubble".

A similar bubble developed in the stock market. During the boom, very high profits led to sharp increases the prices of corporate shares. Often taking advantage of plentiful credit at low interest rates, speculators added greatly to the demand for shares, generating a bubble in stock prices similar to that in the housing market. ■

QUESTIONS

1. Suppose that the bubble were to end, and the prices of housing and stocks were to fall sharply.
   (a) Why might this happen?
   (b) How would this affect consumers and the American economy?

The rapidly rising price of their homes encouraged many American families to stop saving out of their current income, because the rising prices of their homes seemed to be accumulating assets for their future, including their retirement. It also encouraged them to finance increases in their consumption spending by borrowing against their homes. In the words of some observers, Americans were using their homes as ATMs, or as piggy banks. Such borrowing was encouraged and assisted by America's very highly-developed and aggressive financial sector, which extended credit even to people with low incomes who were poor credit risks. As a result, the average personal saving rate of Americans decreased to nearly zero, and was even negative at times. (Of course, some Americans were saving, but their saving was outweighed by the heavy borrowing of others.) So consumption spending soared to a record-high 71 percent of U.S. GDP, and the personal debt of American households increased rapidly, to very high levels.

There are over 1.3 billion credit cards in the U.S., more than 11 per household.

2. Large federal government budget deficits, financed by foreign borrowing

After 2001, the U.S. federal government decided upon an historically unique combination of large increases in military spending and large tax cuts. The result was very large budget deficits, meaning that the U.S. government was engaging in "negative saving"—it needed to borrow, and borrow heavily.

With American households not saving money for it to borrow, where was the U.S. government getting the funds to finance its large budget deficits? The funds were coming from foreign lenders, mostly China, which was buying large amounts of U.S. government bonds. This served the purposes of both countries—Chinese lending financed the budget deficits of the American government, and by selling its currency to buy U.S. dollar bonds, China kept the international price of the yuan from rising, which sustained its exports to the vast U.S. market, which brings us to the next point.

3. Very large U.S. trade deficits

Not surprisingly, the huge volume of imports into the United States generated very large deficits (well over $2000 per year for every American citizen) in the U.S.A.'s trade in goods and services with other countries, as shown in Figure 11-4.

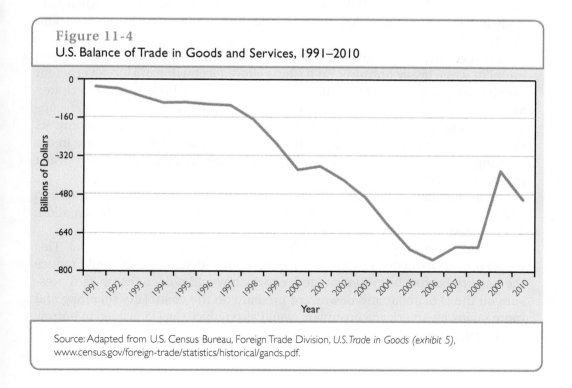

Figure 11-4
U.S. Balance of Trade in Goods and Services, 1991–2010

Source: Adapted from U.S. Census Bureau, Foreign Trade Division, *U.S. Trade in Goods* (exhibit 5), www.census.gov/foreign-trade/statistics/historical/gands.pdf.

Figure 11-4 also shows how the U.S. balance of trade deficits grew dramatically after 2001, when China joined the World Trade Organization. This period saw a rapid increase in imports to the United States, partly due to the surge in spending by American consumers, and partly due to the low international price of the Chinese yuan and the high international value of the U.S. dollar. The trade deficits shrank considerably in 2009 when the recession cut into purchases of imports by American consumers, but began to grow again as early as 2010.

Imbalances in the Global Economy

In summary, by 2005-08, there were unusually large imbalances in the global economy. On the supply side, the world's production capacity had been increased considerably by the entry of China into the world economy. On the demand side, global demand for goods and services was being sustained largely by American consumers, who were financing their spending by borrowing against their homes, and were in deep and rising debt. Many had mortgages with "teaser" interest rates that were low for a year or two, then would increase, making payments on their homes unaffordable.

The United States had very low saving and very high borrowing needs, while Asia (especially China) had surpluses of capital. Large amounts of capital were being loaned by China, a poor country, to the United States, a rich country. Those flows of capital from China to the United States were keeping the exchange rate of the U.S. dollar high, and the exchange rate of the Chinese yuan low. And this exchange rate imbalance, together with America's high spending and low saving, were generating very large trade American trade deficits.

The U.S. government owes China over a trillion dollars, which amounts to over $3000 for every U.S. citizen.

What Could Be Done?

Most international economic authorities believed that various changes would be needed in order to restore balance to the global economy, including the following.

1. *An increase in the international value of the Chinese yuan/ reduction in the exchange rate of the U.S. dollar* was considered a key element in remedying the trade imbalances in the global economy—both the Chinese trade surpluses and the American trade deficits.

   However, there were dangers in a too-rapid increase in the yuan. The U.S. government was a heavy borrower, so if China slowed its buying of U.S. government bonds too rapidly, interest rates in the United States could rise, *unless* the United States increased its saving at the same time. And higher interest rates could jeopardize economic growth in the United States and in the global economy, as explained in the *You Decide* box. Therefore, the much-anticipated increase in the exchange rate of the yuan was considered likely to happen slowly, probably over a period of at least 10 years.

   So an increase in the yuan would be neither a quick nor simple solution. In addition, it would require changes in the economic fundamentals of the situation, as explained in the next two sections.

2. *An increase in saving in the United States* was considered to be essential. This would require reductions in the U.S. federal budget deficit, which would reduce the need to borrow from foreign lenders, which would reduce the upward pressure on the U.S. dollar and downward pressure on the yuan. Less spending and more saving by American consumers would also reduce the USA's need to borrow from foreign lenders.

YOU DECIDE

Beware of Simple Solutions

Many people in America and Europe believed that the problem with China was simple—that the low-priced yuan made China an unfair competitor. For them, the solution to this problem was equally simple: a large and rapid increase in the exchange rate of the yuan.

But *would* a rapid and large increase in the international price of the yuan really benefit Americans economically, by protecting their jobs against Chinese imports?

Suppose a United States government bond that pays interest of $60 per year is presently selling for $1000, so it is paying an annual interest rate of 6 percent. Now suppose that China decides to allow the exchange rate of the yuan to increase. So the Bank of China reduces its purchases of U.S. government bonds considerably, which causes the price of those bonds to fall to $930. ∎

QUESTIONS

1. How would such a reduction in Chinese purchases of U.S. government bonds affect interest rates?
2. How would a considerably higher exchange rate of the yuan affect American consumers?
3. Why might this change in interest rates have potentially negative effects on many American consumers and on the world economy?

Such increases in saving in the U.S. economy were considered important because this would reduce the dependence of the United States on borrowing from foreign lenders such as China.

3. *An increase in consumer spending in the Chinese economy* was also considered to be a key part of the solution, because this would make China less dependent on exports, which in turn would make a higher exchange rate for the yuan less of a problem for China.

For several years, large-scale capital investment projects had been the driving force behind the rapid growth of the Chinese economy. But there were growing signs of overinvestment, making it likely that the pace of investment would be slowed. In that event, the Chinese economy would need additional demand, most of which could come from Chinese consumers.

Consumption spending was estimated to amount to only about 35 percent of the output of the Chinese economy, leaving plenty of room for it to increase. The Chinese government could take various steps to encourage higher spending by Chinese consumers. Such measures could include easier access to consumer credit, and a stronger social "safety net" such as better health care and pension coverage that would reduce the need for people to save, enabling them to spend more.

4. *Energy conservation measures* in the United States, particularly for motor vehicles, would also be helpful. A major source of America's high balance of trade deficits has been its very high consumption of fuel, much of which has to be imported.

The 2008–09 Global Recession

Some of the adjustments described in the previous section did begin to happen. By 2009, the exchange rate of the yuan was about 20 percent higher than in 2005, when it was unpegged from the U.S. dollar (see Figure 11-3). And the U.S. balance of trade deficit stopped growing in 2007, and even decreased somewhat, as Figure 11-4 shows.

But before the necessary changes in the international economy could take effect, events took a serious turn for the worse, starting in the United States.

First, the housing bubble burst. Price bubbles inflate because buyers believe that prices will rise and rise, but after a certain point, people begin to believe that prices will stop rising or even fall. At that point, more and more people will be anxious to sell, but there will be *no one who wants to buy.* So the U.S. housing bubble burst, and prices fell sharply, starting in 2006-07. This left many U.S. families with mortgage debts that were greater than the value of their homes. The downturn in the U.S. housing market was made worse by defaults on subprime mortgages—after one year, 20 percent of subprime borrowers were unable to make the payments on their mortgages, after two years, 50 percent had defaulted, and after three years, 80 percent had lost their homes. Their houses were seized by lenders and put up for sale, which put additional downward pressure on prices. To make matters worse, as the economic outlook deteriorated, the stock market plunged as nervous investors sold their shares.

These developments took American consumers by surprise, and left them shell-shocked. Consumer confidence plunged, taking consumption spending with it. American consumers suddenly lacked both the confidence and the collateral (that is, the value of their homes) to continue borrowing, and the economy slipped into recession.

Then the financial crisis struck. Those large numbers of "subprime" mortgage loans (on which 80 percent of borrowers would be defaulting in three years) had been packaged together into securities with names like "collaterized debt obligations" and "structured investment vehicles", and large amounts of these securities had been bought by banks, insurance companies, mutual funds, pension funds, and so on. In short, the financial system of the United States and many other nations had become "infected" with assets of uncertain (or little) value. Major financial institutions went bankrupt, others had little idea of their real financial condition, and for a while, lenders became afraid to make new loans and investments. So the financial system was faltering at its primary economic task, which is to provide the credit (loans) that make the economic system work on a day to day basis—not just mortgage loans, but also all sorts of consumer loans (including car loans and credit card loans), loans to businesses to finance their operations (including meeting their payrolls), loans to students, and so on.

At this point, the financial crisis spilled over to the real economy, making the recession worse by restricting credit and dragging aggregate demand further downwards. But the recession was also making the financial crisis worse, by forcing some borrowers to default on past loans and by making lenders more reluctant to make new loans, due to the increased risk. So there was a recession ***plus*** a financial crisis, with each making the other worse, in a sort of downward spiral.

These problems were not restricted to the United States—similar problems occurred in many countries in which financial institutions had used similar lending practices to those in the USA and/or invested in securities that largely consisted of American subprime mortgage-backed "assets". The Canadian banking system was not badly affected by the subprime mortgage crisis, partly because of stronger government regulation in Canada of the assets in which banks can invest, and partly because of the more cautious lending and investing practices of Canadian banks.

But this did not mean that Canada was unaffected—like many countries, Canada "imported" the U.S. recession in the form of falling exports to the United States. And so the U.S. recession and financial crisis spread, and grew into a global recession. And because so many consumers in so many nations were so seriously in debt relative to the newly-depreciated value of their assets, there was concern that there could be a quite long period of economic stagnation, as consumers held down their consumption spending in order to pay down their debts and rebuild their assets.

The Government Response

The extraordinary problem of a major recession combined with a once-in-a-lifetime financial crisis caused the governments of almost all major nations to respond with unusual haste and force. In almost every case, this consisted of three major components:

- massive financial support for banks and other financial institutions,
- dramatic reductions in interest rates, and
- large-scale anti-recession policies (assistance to the unemployed, infrastructure spending, tax reductions, etc.).

The first of these measures was considered essential to restoring the ability of the banking and financial system to make the loans to consumers and businesses that are essential for the economy's operations on a day-to-day basis, and the second was undertaken in an attempt to minimize the damage caused by the recession, and hopefully to shorten the duration of the recession. But this was a serious "balance sheet recession", and the very high levels of consumer debt associated with it (especially in the United States, but also in much of Europe) meant that the recovery would be slow due to weak consumer spending, and could take several years.

The Post-Recession Global Economy: More Imbalances

Until 2008, spending by American consumers had dominated the demand side of the world economy. However, following the 2008–09 recession, both the United States and Europe were facing a long and slow recovery, with ongoing high unemployment likely as their governments' policy stance reversed, from policies of recession-fighting budget deficits to cutbacks in government spending intended to reduce deficits.

In sharp contrast, the economies of emerging nations, led by the BRIC group (Brazil, Russia, India and China) were growing considerably faster than the USA and Europe. And there was growing agreement that this was not just due to the recession, but rather that it represented a long-term shift in global economic growth and power toward emerging nations[1].

It was believed that economic recovery and growth in the USA and Europe was being made more difficult by China's policy of holding the exchange rate of the yuan artificially low in order to secure a competitive advantage in international trade. China was doing this through purchases of U.S. dollars (mostly U.S. government bonds) and by restrictions on inflows of foreign capital, to prevent these from pushing the exchange rate of the yuan upwards.

With U.S. interest rates already very low and fiscal policy planned to switch after 2011 from recession-fighting to deficit-fighting, the U.S. Federal Reserve turned in 2010–11 to a last-resort policy described as "quantitative easing", through which the Federal Reserve purchased U.S. government bonds—a policy more commonly known as "printing money".

---

[1]For an excellent account of these long-term economic trends, read *The Post-American World* by Fareed Zakaria.

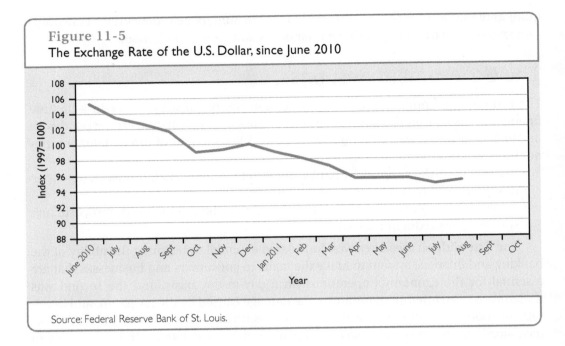

Figure 11-5
The Exchange Rate of the U.S. Dollar, since June 2010

Source: Federal Reserve Bank of St. Louis.

With U.S. monetary policy so loose and investors concerned about government debt defaults in Europe (see the box "The EU and the Euro—More Problems"), there was an outflow of capital from America and Europe into the economies of the more rapidly growing emerging nations, where it could earn higher returns.

But such inflows of funds into the emerging nations would increase their exchange rates, and quite possibly generate inflation in their economies, both of which would hurt their exports. This was an unwelcome development for the governments of these emerging economies. In their view, having failed to stimulate its ailing economy with monetary and fiscal policies, the United States was deliberately manipulating the exchange rate of the U.S. dollar downwards in an attempt to boost its economy by increasing exports and decreasing imports. Figure 11-5 shows the exchange rate of the U.S. dollar against a "basket" of currencies of major U.S. trading partners, which fell by 10 percent from mid-2010 to mid-2011.

The governments of some emerging nations (including Japan, South Korea, Taiwan, Thailand, Indonesia, Malaysia, Brazil, Colombia, and Israel) responded with Chinese-style policies, including the buying of foreign currencies and restrictions and taxes on inflows of foreign capital, particularly short-term capital, or the "hot money" that we saw in Chapter 10.

So while China and other emerging market governments were alleging that the United States' policy of "quantitative easing" was really intended to reduce the exchange rate of the U.S. dollar at the expense of their exports, there were accusations from the United States that the real problem was that China was manipulating its currency so as to maintain an unfair competitive advantage and threats to retaliate by imposing tariffs on Chinese exports to the USA.

This raised concerns that economic conflict between America and China and emerging nations could escalate into "currency wars" and trade wars. According to the Managing Director of the International Monetary Fund in late 2010, "There is clearly the idea beginning to circulate that currencies can be used as policy weapons". But one way to retaliate against a nation that manipulates its currency downward is to impose tariffs on its exports—for instance in 2010, the U.S. House of Representatives passed legislation that would allow the imposition of import tariffs to retaliate for exchange rates deemed to be artificially low. And this raised the possibility of retaliatory tariffs, which could escalate into a trade war, which generated concerns that the world might be heading toward a 1930s-style international economic conflict as described on the first page of this chapter.

Finally, if an international currency conflict were to develop, the International Monetary Fund could do little to prevent it. The IMF has traditionally been able to influence nations' economic policies because those nations were in serious economic trouble and needed to borrow from the IMF. However, most of the countries that would be involved in a currency conflict after 2011 would have ample foreign exchange reserves and no need to borrow.

YOU DECIDE

The EU and the Euro—More Problems

A fundamental structural weakness of the European Union is that it is a free trade area of very diverse countries in terms of their economic development, 16 of which are committed to using a single currency—the euro. Another problem is that the EU has no central government and quite ineffective rules governing the extent to which the governments of member countries can borrow and accumulate debt.

As a result, the governments of less-advanced members, such as Greece and Portugal that lagged in their ability to compete with other nations, borrowed heavily in order to subsidize their producers and consumers, and wound up with very large government budget deficits and rising government debt, most of which was owed to foreign lenders. Before the euro, such nations could let the exchange rate of their currencies fall, which would improve their ability to compete with other nations, and so improve employment and incomes in their countries and the budget situations of their governments. (The trade-off, of course, would be higher import prices and a lower standard of living.)

However, because they were part of the EU and committed to using the euro, they could not let their exchange rates fall; the main way to become more competitive would be through reductions in business costs, through lower wages and salaries. But this was politically impossible, so their government budget deficits and debt grew, to the point where, in the case of Greece, it seemed possible that the government might default on its debts. But a default would have serious repercussions across the EU, because many of the Greek bonds were held by European banks and investment funds whose financial condition was already weakened due to the 2008–09 financial crisis and recession. This generated pressure on other EU countries to provide financial assistance in order to "bail out" Greece as a debtor (and many European banks, as holders of Greek bonds) so as to avoid another financial crisis.

However, in other EU nations there was strong opposition to using public funds to bail out Greece (which was regarded as having borrowed excessively in order to provide its people with benefits that they had not earned) and to bail out banks (which were regarded as having made unwise loans to the governments of Greece and other nations). This political opposition was heightened by suspicions that both Greece and the banks that had loaned to it might have been counting on EU governments to bail them out when things reached the crisis point.

As of late 2011, it was unclear how this situation would be resolved, if at all. In the meantime, concerns over possible government financial crises, not only in Greece but also in Portugal, Ireland, Italy, and Spain, were generating considerable economic uncertainty in Europe and around the world.

QUESTION

1. What further developments have occurred regarding the government financial problems within the EU? Try Google searches using keywords such as *European Union, Europe + sovereign debt,* and *euro.*

Developments through 2011

As of late 2011, progress on the American and Chinese aspects of the major global economic imbalances described earlier was occurring, but slowly.

Regarding the exchange rate of the yuan, China was allowing the exchange rate of the yuan to rise, but gradually. From 2005 to 2011, the yuan had risen by 28 percent against the U.S. dollar, but a 2010 International Monetary Fund report said that the yuan was still "substantially undervalued". So criticisms continued from the USA that China was manipulating its currency, together with threats of tariffs on Chinese imports.

Regarding the problem of U.S. government budget deficits so as to reduce its dependence on borrowing from foreign lenders (particularly China), progress was also slow. One political party would not agree to any deficit-reducing policy that included cuts to social welfare programs and insisted on some tax increases, and the other party refused to accept any policy that included increases in taxes and insisted on spending cuts to social programs; the result was a stalemate in the short run and much uncertainty about the outcome in the longer run.

The situation was complicated by the slowness of the recovery from the recession, which was making China cautious about allowing its yuan to become more costly to foreign buyers of its exports, and the United States more cautious about deficit-reducing policies that would slow the recovery and possibly cause another recession.

Updates on Website

Updates to the recent events in Chapter 11 are available on the http://www.pearson custom.com/can/micro_macro_econ website.

Chapter Summary

1. The Great Depression of the 1930s showed the dangers of government policies that try to protect their domestic industries by increasing tariffs and manipulating their exchange rates. (L.O. 1)

2. The General Agreement on Tariffs and Trade (GATT, renamed the World Trade Organization (WTO) in 1995) made substantial progress in reducing tariffs and promoting international trade through multilateral negotiations. (L.O. 2)

3. In 2001, the Doha Round of WTO trade negotiations was launched, with the main objective of helping developing countries by opening up the markets of rich

countries to their products, especially agricultural ones. Progress was slow, and as of 2009 the outcome of the negotiations was uncertain. (L.O. 3)

4. Trading blocs are trade agreements between groups of nations outside of the WTO agreement. Some observers believe that the world might evolve into three major regional trade and currency blocs: Europe, the Americas, and Asia. (L.O. 4)

5. In 1945, the major nations of the world established a system of pegged exchange rates under the supervision of the International Monetary Fund (IMF). However, it proved impossible to freeze exchange rates, and the pegged system was abandoned in 1973. In place of the pegged system, nations adopted various exchange rate systems, the most common of which was the *dirty float*. (L.O. 5)

6. In the 2001–08 period, the Chinese economy was characterized by very high investments in heavy industry, a very high saving rate, and large volumes of exports to the United States. (L.O. 6)

7. Large-scale purchases of U.S. government bonds (U.S. dollars) by China helped to hold down the exchange rate of the Chinese yuan, which contributed to the growth of Chinese exports to the U.S. market. (L.O. 6)

8. In the 2001–08 period, the U.S. economy was characterized by a strong consumer-led boom, with very low saving rates and heavy borrowing by American consumers against the rising value of their homes. (L.O. 6)

9. The U.S. economy was also characterized by large trade deficits and large government budget deficits that were largely financed by borrowing from China. (L.O. 6)

10. By 2005–08, there were large imbalances in the world economy. The U.S. economy had very high consumption, very low saving, and a large trade deficit. China had large savings that were being loaned to the United States, which kept the exchange rate of the Chinese yuan down and the U.S. trade deficit high. (L.O. 7)

11. Most observers believed that the adjustments to these imbalances would involve increased saving in the U.S., increased consumption in China, a decrease in the exchange rate of the U.S. dollar, and an increase in the exchange rate of the yuan. (L.O. 7)

Questions

1. On the supply side of the global economy, the most important development since 2000 has been
   (a) the growth of Japan's manufacturing sector.
   (b) the rapid growth of the European Union's industrial capacity.
   (c) the emergence of China as a very large source of low-wage labour and low-cost goods.
   (d) a slowdown in U.S. capital investment due to high interest rates caused by rapid inflation.
   (e) the development of mass-production manufacturing industries in India.

2. On the demand side of the global economy, the main source of demand until the 2008-09 recession was
   (a) rapidly rising consumption spending by Chinese households.
   (b) heavy capital investment spending by U.S. corporations.
   (c) high and rising aggregate demand in the Japanese economy.
   (d) high consumption spending by U.S. households.
   (e) high and rising aggregate demand in the European Union.

3. Two of the more remarkable aspects of the world economic scene as of 2005–07 were that U.S. households were saving almost nothing while Chinese households were saving roughly 25 percent of their disposable income, and that China was lending the United States large amounts of money. What explains these apparent anomalies?

4. By 2004–07, the United States was importing about six times as much from China as it was exporting to China. Many Americans believed that the solution to this imbalance was to force China to revalue its currency (the yuan) upward by perhaps 25 percent.
   (a) Why would they believe that this change would be a solution to the China–U.S. trade imbalance?
   (b) What danger did this proposed course of action overlook?

5. "If it were not for China's lending of vast amounts of money to the U.S. government, the United States would probably have had a serious recession by 2005, triggered by rapidly rising interest rates." Explain the reasoning behind this statement. Why would interest rates probably have risen rapidly, and what impact would this probably have had on the U.S. economy?

6. "The higher the Japanese yen went in the 1980s, the more likely it was to stop rising." Explain the reasoning behind this statement. What were the consequences for Japan of the rapid increase in the exchange rate of the yen?

7. Has the international value of the U.S. dollar decreased since 2011? The U.S. exchange rate against a basket of other currencies can be found at **http://research .stlouisfed.org/fred2/series/TWEXBMTH/105/10yrs**.
   (b) Has the international price of the Canadian dollar in terms of the U.S. dollar increased or decreased since August 2011, when it was about $1.00 Canadian = $1.01 US.? Visit www.statcan.gc.ca, and under "Find statistics", click on "Summary tables" and search for "Exchange rates", then click on "Exchange rates, interest rates, money supply and stock prices".

8. In 2005, the international price of the Chinese yuan was 12.1 cents U.S., a rate at which the yuan had been pegged for several years by the Chinese government. By mid-2011, the yuan had increased in price by 28 percent to 15.5 cents U.S. Has the international price of the Chinese yuan continued to increase against the U.S. dollar? Recent statistics can be found at **http://research.stlouisfed.org/fred2/data/ EXCHUS.txt**.

Study Guide

Review Questions (Answers to these Review Questions appear in Appendix B.)

1. During the Great Depression of the 1930s, governments practised two types of economic policies that made the depression even more severe. Identify from the following list those *two* policies.
   (a) They manipulated the international values of their currencies downward in attempts to make their products more competitive internationally.
   (b) They introduced government budget deficits and borrowed heavily in attempts to stimulate aggregate demand.

(c) They reduced interest rates too far in attempts to increase their money supplies rapidly, causing severe inflation.

(d) They increased tariffs on imports in attempts to protect domestic jobs against import competition.

(e) Government took over ownership of most large corporations and required them to hire many workers in attempts to increase employment.

2. Which *two* organizations were established after the end of the Second World War in 1945 in order to avoid a return to the problems described in the previous question?
   (a) the International Monetary Fund and the General Agreement on Tariffs and Trade
   (b) the International Monetary Fund and the World Bank
   (c) the World Bank and the General Agreement on Tariffs and Trade
   (d) the United Nations and the International Monetary Fund
   (e) the United Nations and the General Agreement on Tariffs and Trade

3. Under the rules of the World Trade Organization (WTO),
   (a) governments must not subsidize their producers.
   (b) "dumping" of products into other nations' markets is not allowed.
   (c) nations may impose tariffs on imports from low-wage nations.
   (d) nations with high unemployment rates may impose tariffs on imports.
   (e) Answers (a) and (b).

4. Under WTO rules, final decisions concerning trade disputes between nations are to be made
   (a) by a meeting of the governments of the nations involved.
   (b) by the president of the WTO.
   (c) by a panel of neutral experts in trade and trade law.
   (d) by the World Court.
   (e) None of the above.

5. As of mid-2011, the Doha Round of WTO trade negotiations was
   (a) proceeding on schedule toward a groundbreaking agreement.
   (b) close to an agreement in which the developed countries would sharply reduce their farm subsidies that were making it impossible for farmers in poor nations to compete.
   (c) terminated without an agreement.
   (d) regarded as unlikely to succeed, in part over the issue of whether the developed nations would reduce their farm subsidies.
   (e) None of the above.

6. State whether each of the following accurately describes the economic situation in China as of 2005–11.
   (a) _____ There were large-scale investments in basic industry by government enterprises.
   (b) _____ Foreign corporations were investing heavily in industrial plant and equipment in China.
   (c) _____ The personal saving rate of Chinese households was very low.
   (d) _____ The economy was in a boom due to high consumption spending by Chinese households.
   (e) _____ High exports were a key to the growth of the Chinese economy.
   (f) _____ China was lending large amounts to the United States.

7. Which of the following describes the situation concerning the international price of China's currency (the yuan) over the 2001–11 period?
    (a) The yuan was under upward pressure due to inflows of investment capital from foreign businesses.
    (b) The yuan was under upward pressure due to China's large volume of exports.
    (c) The yuan was under upward pressure due to inflows of funds from speculators who anticipated an increase in its value.
    (d) Large-scale purchases of U.S. government bonds by the Chinese government were holding the exchange rate of the yuan down, and keeping Chinese exports high.
    (e) All of the above.

8. Which of the following describes the effects of China on the global economy?
    (a) Inflation rates were kept lower by the large supply of low-cost goods exported from China.
    (b) Interest rates were increased by China's large demand for capital.
    (c) Wage rates and employment in manufacturing industries were held down by competition from China.
    (d) The prices of crude oil and gasoline were increased by rapidly-growing Chinese demand.
    (e) a, c, and d.

9. The U.S. economic boom of 2004–07 was unusual in that
    (a) unemployment remained high through the boom.
    (b) the rate of inflation remained low through the boom.
    (c) interest rates remained low through the boom.
    (d) b and c.
    (e) None of the above.

10. The U.S. economic boom of 2004-07 was unusual in that
    (a) the average income of Americans did not increase by much.
    (b) the rapid growth of consumer spending was largely financed by people's borrowing, using their homes as collateral for the loans.
    (c) a and b.
    (d) interest rates increased earlier and faster than in most booms.
    (e) the government raised income taxes early in the boom.

11. Another unusual aspect of the U.S. economic boom of 2004-07 was that
    (a) consumer confidence began to decrease quite early in the boom.
    (b) consumption of imported of goods grew less rapidly than consumption of U.S.-made goods.
    (c) the U.S. federal government had large budget deficits during the boom.
    (d) there were many mortgage loans made to high-risk borrowers with low incomes and few assets.
    (e) c and d.

12. The U.S. government financed its large budget deficits largely by
    (a) borrowing from the World Bank.
    (b) selling large amounts of government bonds to China.
    (c) selling large amounts of government bonds to Americans.
    (d) increasing taxes on Americans.
    (e) None of the above.

13. Because the U.S. government financed its budget deficits in the way described in the previous question,
    (a) consumer spending by U.S. households fell as consumer confidence weakened.

(b) the international value of the U.S. dollar was supported at a higher level than otherwise would have prevailed.

(c) the international price of the Chinese yuan was held down, which kept Chinese exports of goods to the big U.S. market high.

(d) interest rates in the U.S. economy were kept low, which kept consumption spending high.

(e) Answers (b), (c), and (d).

14. The imbalances that existed in the world economy by 2005–11 included
    (a) very high saving in China.
    (b) large budget deficits of the U.S. federal government.
    (c) very low saving by American consumers.
    (d) rapid increases in the international value of the yuan.
    (e) a, b, and c.

15. Which of the flowing would <u>not</u> help to correct the imbalances that existed in the world economy by 2005–11?
    (a) an increase in the international value of the yuan.
    (b) lower income taxes in the United States.
    (c) a decrease in the international value of the U.S. dollar.
    (d) an increase in saving by American consumers.
    (e) increased consumption spending in China.

Critical Thinking Questions

(Asterisked questions 1 to 4 are answered in Appendix B; the answers to questions 6 to 10 are in the Instructor's Manual that accompanies this text.)

*1. Figure 11-5 shows a falling international value of the U.S. dollar that many people expected to continue. If the exchange rate of the U.S. dollar continued to decrease, what would be the effect on:
    (a) Canadian consumers?
    (b) employment and unemployment in Canada?

*2. "As the value of the yen rose in the 1980s, the probability that Toyota and Honda would build automobile manufacturing plants in North America rose with it." Explain the reasoning behind this statement.

*3. Explain the following summary of the economic effects of China on the global economy. "You can buy cheaper clothes, electronic equipment, and manufactured goods, and you will pay a lower interest rate on your mortgage and the price of your home will rise faster. On the other hand, it may be harder to find a job, your pay raises will probably be smaller, and you will have to pay more for gasoline."

*4. "The multilateral approach of the WTO is no longer able to make progress toward free trade. The future of free trade does not lie with the WTO, but rather with trading blocs and bilateral agreements." Explain why the speaker would believe this. Do you agree?

5. Explain to someone who has never taken an economics course why in a rich country like the United States the personal saving rate is nearly zero, while in a poor country like China households save about 25 percent of their disposable income.

6. The Chinese government owns a vast amount of U.S. government bonds.
    (a) If China were to sell large amounts of those bonds on the open market, what would probably happen to the international value of the U.S. dollar, U.S. interest rates, U.S. consumers, and the U.S. economy?
    (b) Why is it extremely unlikely that China would sell its U.S. government bonds in this way?

7. Oil-producing nations also owned large amounts of U.S. government bonds, which they had purchased with their high revenues (petrodollars) due to high oil prices. But, unlike in China, these funds were not part of countries' official foreign exchange reserves—they were owned by oil stabilization funds, whose aim was not to stabilize countries' currencies, but rather to earn the maximum possible return.

    (a) Why would these funds pose a much greater threat to the stability of the U.S. dollar than China's vast holdings of U.S. bonds?

    (b) What danger would exist in this situation if the exchange rate of the U.S. dollar started to decrease again?

8. By 2005, the United States was importing six times as much from China as it was exporting to China. Some U.S. politicians were demanding that the U.S. government threaten to impose restrictions on Chinese exports to the U.S. unless China agreed to a sharp increase in the exchange rate of the yuan—as much as perhaps 25 percent. But economists cautioned that by forcing a rapid appreciation of the yuan, the United States would risk creating a recession in its own economy. How could a rapid increase in the international value of the yuan possibly cause a recession in the United States?

9. Some observers expected that a united Europe would overtake the United States in terms of global economic power. But there is an interesting difference between Europe and the United States in the area of demographics. Europe's fertility rates fell sharply after the 1950s, so its population is growing slowly and will be aging. In contrast, the U.S. fertility rate reversed its decline in the 1980s, so the United States has a population that is growing faster than was expected and will stay much younger than Europe's. What impact will these demographic differences have on the future prospects for these two economies?

Use the Web   (Hints for these Use the Web exercises appear in Appendix B.)

1. Visit the WTO website at **www.wto.org**, search for *Leading exporters and importers in world merchandise trade*.

    (a) Since 2009, which of the world's largest exporters have seen the most rapid increases in their exports?

    (b) What changes have occurred in the World Trade Organization's ranking of the world's largest exporters?

2. Do a Google search for "Doha." How successful has the Doha Round of World Trade Organization negotiations been? What accounts for the success (or lack thereof) of the negotiations?

3. As the recession deepened in 2009, there were concerns that in attempts to protect jobs within their borders, countries would enact *protectionist* measures that restricted imports, and that retaliation by other nations could lead to a "trade war" of the sort that made the Great Depression much worse during the 1930s.

Did protectionism in fact become the problem that some feared? Google "protectionism", and see what recent developments you can find concerning this matter.

12

Canada in the Global Economy

LEARNING OBJECTIVES

After studying this chapter, you should be able to

1. State the purpose and the main features of Canada's National Policy of 1879, and explain its various effects upon the Canadian economy.

2. Explain why the productivity of Canada's manufacturing sector tended to be low, and why it fell farther behind other nations' productivity in the 1980s.

3. State four factors that pressed Canada in the 1980s to change its traditional trade policy of protecting its manufacturing sector.

4. Describe the major terms of the Canada–U.S. Free Trade Agreement of 1989 regarding tariffs and settlement of trade disputes.

5. Describe the strategic significance of the North American Free Trade Agreement (NAFTA) for the U.S., and the expected economic effect of NAFTA on Canada.

6. Explain three business strategies that can help Canadian producers compete internationally.

7. Explain why the exchange rate of the Canadian dollar decreased in the 1990s, and the positive and negative economic effects of this trend on Canadians.

8. Explain why the exchange rate of the Canadian dollar increased sharply after 2002, and why this trend caused concern in Canada.

9. Explain why it was expected that in the future, Canada's trade and exports would become more diversified among nations other than the United States.

10. Apply the facts and concept of this chapter to various situations.

Economically, Canada is a small country in a big world, with one-half of one percent of the world's population and a GDP that is less than 3 percent of total world output. Canada's market of 34 million people is smaller than the state of California, and not large enough to support the economies of scale achievable in large markets such as the United States and Europe.

Canadians are made to feel even smaller by the fact that their nearest neighbour, the United States, has the largest and richest economy in the world. On the other hand, Canadians enjoy a high standard of living, which has been made higher by Canada's very active economic relationships with other countries, especially the United States. This relationship includes very high levels of both exports and imports, and large amounts of investment flowing in both directions.

Being situated next to the United States has always presented Canada with something of a dilemma. To Canada, the U.S. has always seemed to represent *both*

- an economic *opportunity*, in the form of the vast market that the United States presents to Canadian firms, and
- an economic *threat*, in the form of competition from the U.S.'s large and highly efficient producers.

For Canadian governments, the threat of U.S. competition has presented an argument for *trade restrictions*, to protect Canadian producers from American imports. On the other hand, the proximity of the large U.S. market has made a policy of *freer trade* more enticing for many Canadian firms wanting access to that market. Efficient Canadian exporters have urged the government to adopt free trade, while industries threatened by imports have argued that protectionism is in Canada's interests. Obviously, this has placed Canadian policy-makers in a contradictory position between protectionism and free trade, and for many years Canada's trade policy consisted of a search for a balance between these two positions. As we will see, for many years the nation's trade policy emphasized protection of Canadian industries; however, it shifted gradually toward freer trade over time, and has moved much more rapidly in that direction since the mid-1980s.

Part A: Trade and Trade Policy

A Brief Historical Background

In 1854, the British colonies that were to become Canada were given access to the U.S. market through a trade treaty with the States. However, the Americans cancelled that treaty in 1866, leaving these colonies in a difficult position economically. In 1879, the government of the new nation of Canada introduced a nation-building program known as the **National Policy**, the key economic component of which was a system of protective tariffs.

National Policy

A set of nation-building policies introduced in Canada in 1879, the key economic aspect of which was protective tariffs to foster the development of Canadian industry.

The tariffs of the National Policy were of the *infant industry* type described in Chapter 9—they were meant to protect Canada's manufacturing industries, which were just starting to develop at this time. By placing a tariff barrier along the Canada–U.S. border, the National Policy intended not only to develop a Canadian manufacturing sector but also to shape trade links along east–west lines rather than the north–south links with the United States that would otherwise have prevailed. The tariffs also provided the government with tax revenue that was used to finance the building of the railroad that was crucial to the forging of east–west links. For over a century, Canadian manufacturers would enjoy considerable tariff protection against competition from imports, trade would be pushed into an east–west direction, and the railroad would be a symbol of Canada's nationhood.

Effects of Tariff Protection

The tariff protection initiated under the National Policy would shape the Canadian economy for over a century. Unquestionably, the tariffs fostered the development of a *larger manufacturing sector* than would otherwise have existed in many industries, from breakfast foods to footwear to automobiles. And this manufacturing sector grew into a major employer, especially in Ontario and Quebec. In this sense, the tariff policy achieved its basic objective.

On the other hand, the tariff protection meant *higher prices* for Canadian consumers. The tariffs not only added to the prices of imported products, but also allowed Canadian firms to charge higher prices for their products. In effect, the protected manufacturers were being subsidized by consumers. This situation was intended to be temporary—as the infant industries matured and became more efficient, it was expected that less tariff protection would be needed.

In addition, Canada's tariff policy led many foreign manufacturers, especially American firms, to establish **branch plants** in Canada in order to avoid paying the Canadian tariffs. As a result, *foreign ownership* of Canadian industry became very high. These various effects of Canada's tariff policy are summarized in Figure 12-1.

branch plants
Manufacturing plants established in a nation by a foreign-owned firm in order to avoid tariffs on imports by producing their products inside that nation.

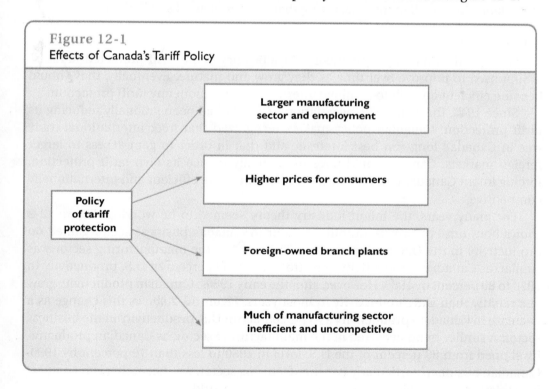

Figure 12-1
Effects of Canada's Tariff Policy

- Policy of tariff protection
  - Larger manufacturing sector and employment
  - Higher prices for consumers
  - Foreign-owned branch plants
  - Much of manufacturing sector inefficient and uncompetitive

The Manufacturing Productivity Problem

Figure 12-1 refers to another problem that would become more serious with the passage of time—much of the manufacturing sector that developed under tariff protection was relatively inefficient and not competitive internationally. Two factors were limiting the productivity of Canadian manufacturers—Canada's own policy of tariff protection and the small size of the Canadian market.

For many years, tariffs protected much of Canada's manufacturing sector from foreign competition and from pressures to become more efficient. And due to

Canada's tariffs and its lack of a free trade agreement with other nations (until 1989), many Canadian manufacturers and foreign-owned branch plants were producing mostly for the Canadian market, which is very small by international standards. By the mid-1980s, with international trade and competition increasing rapidly, Canada was the only high-income country in the northern hemisphere that did not have something approximating secure tariff-free access to markets of 100 million people or more, either domestically or through trade.

The small market available to many Canadian manufacturers restricted their use of modern mass-production technology. Since the average Canadian manufacturing plant was significantly smaller than its counterparts in the United States, Europe, and Japan, it was less able to develop the productive efficiency associated with large-scale operations (economies of scale). While this was not a problem in all industries, it was a disadvantage in many.

But the problems of Canadian manufacturing went beyond small plant size. Whereas a plant producing for the vast U.S. market could specialize in mass-producing a single product very efficiently, plants (often branch plants) producing only for the small Canadian market had to produce an entire range of products, each on a small scale. This required that the Canadian plants switch from producing one product to another several times in a year, a costly process that reduced efficiency. Studies indicated that this problem of *short production runs* was often a greater source of inefficiency in Canadian manufacturing than the problem of small plant size.

The Problem of Lagging Productivity

According to the infant industry theory, the efficiency of the tariff-protected "infants" is supposed to improve over time as they grow and mature. Eventually, they should become efficient enough to compete internationally without any tariff protection.

Since 1947, through GATT negotiations, Canada had been gradually reducing its tariff protection. Canadian policy-makers recognized that freer international trade was in Canada's long-run best interests, and that in order to gain access to larger foreign markets, Canada would have to gradually reduce its own tariff protection, forcing infant Canadian manufacturers to become more efficient and internationally competitive.

For many years, the infant industry theory seemed to be working. Figure 12-2 shows how, until the 1980s, output per hour in Canada's business sector gained on productivity in the U.S. business sector. The trend in the manufacturing sector was similar, as Canadian productivity grew from about 60 percent of U.S. productivity in 1950 to 80 percent by 1980. However, after the early 1980s, Canadian productivity grew less rapidly than U.S. productivity in most years. Figure 12-2 shows this change as a decrease in Canadian productivity as a percentage of U.S. productivity in the business sector. A similar trend occurred in the manufacturing sector, as Canadian productivity slipped from 80 percent of the U.S. level in 1980 to less than 70 percent by 1990. Canadian business, particularly its manufacturing sector, was becoming less competitive relative to the United States and the rest of the world.

The most basic reason for this problem is believed to lie in the phenomenon of *globalization* described at the end of Chapter 9. In the 1980s, globalization led to a combination of increased competition and larger markets that increased the productivity of producers in many nations. However, many Canadian manufacturers were still operating on a small scale in the tariff-protected Canadian market, and so failed to keep up with productivity advances in other nations. This weak productivity performance and declining international competitiveness of Canadian manufactur-

www.csls.ca

Figure 12-2
Output per Hour in the Canadian Business Sector as a Percentage of the U.S. Level, 1961–2003

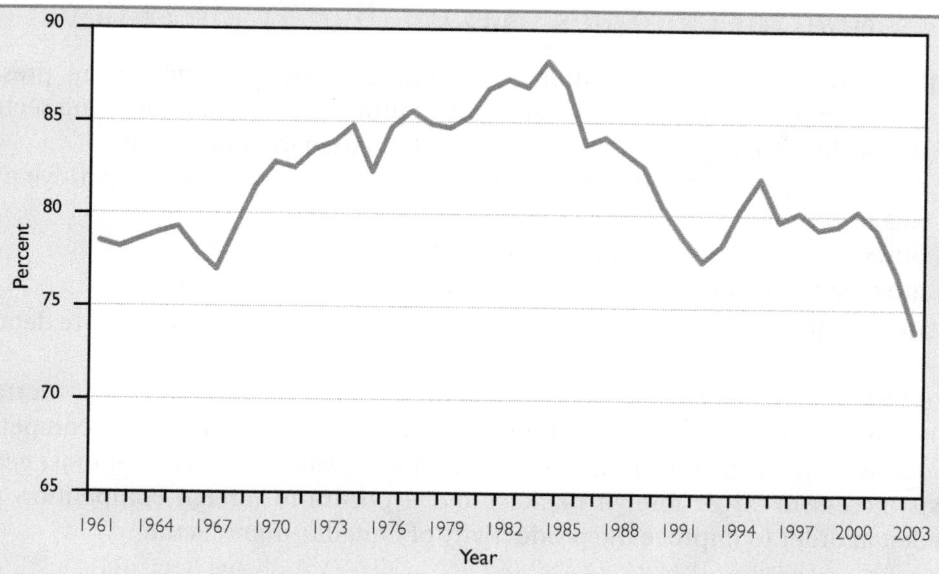

Source: Andrew Sharpe, Centre for the Study of Living Standards, *International Productivity Monitor*, Number 8, Spring 2004: "Recent Productivity Developments in Canada and the United States: Productivity Growth Deceleration versus Acceleration."

ers became an increasing concern of Canadian government policy-makers during the 1980s (see Chapter 3 for additional details).

The Automobile Industry—A Noteworthy Exception

The automobile industry was an interesting exception to the tendency of Canadian manufacturers to be inefficient. After 1965, the auto industry operated under a sort of "free trade" agreement between Canada and the United States, known as the **Auto Pact**. Under the Auto Pact, the Canadian and U.S. governments encouraged and supported continent-wide specialization of auto plants, to increase efficiency, and the Canadian auto industry was transformed from a relatively inefficient branch-plant industry to a world-class industry—in fact, one of the showpieces of the Canadian economy. Canadian auto plants now specialize in the production of a few cars, most of which are exported to the United States. On the other hand, many cars bought in Canada are imported from similarly specialized plants in the United States. The Auto Pact showed that Canadian industry could succeed in international competition, and it provided a model that other industries would follow in future years.

Auto Pact
The 1965 agreement between Canada and the United States that provided for free trade in automotive vehicles, products, and parts.

Consequences of Uncompetitiveness

As the 1980s progressed, the costs of Canada's weakness in productivity and competitive performance became apparent. Canada's share of world trade was declining, and economic studies indicated that this was almost entirely because of a deterioration in Canada's ability to compete. The studies indicated that Canada enjoyed the opportunity for export success by being so close to the vast U.S. market and producing an appropriate range of manufactured goods, but had not taken advantage of that opportunity.

Pressures for Changes to Canadian Trade Policy

In this new, globalized international environment, several factors were pressing Canada to change from its traditional policy of protecting its manufacturing sector:
- the declining competitiveness of much of Canadian manufacturing,
- the growing costs to consumers and exporters of protecting uncompetitive manufacturers,
- outflows of Canadian business investment capital, and
- growing protectionism in the United States.

In the following sections, each of these four factors is examined in more detail.

The Declining Competitiveness of Much of Canadian Manufacturing

As outlined above, much of the Canadian manufacturing sector lost competitive ground relative to the rest of the world during the 1980s. In the view of most economists, access to larger foreign markets and exposure to foreign competition were needed in order to improve the productivity of Canada's manufacturers.

The Growing Costs of Protecting Uncompetitive Manufacturers

As productivity fell further behind that of other nations, the costs to Canadians of protecting Canada's manufacturing sector increased. These costs took two forms—the costs to consumers of having to pay high tariff-supported prices for goods, and the costs to Canadian exporters of retaliatory measures by other nations.

Costs to consumers consisted of higher prices due to tariffs. By the mid-1980s, these costs were estimated to be as high as $200 000 for each job saved by tariffs. Such figures raised the question of whether continued protection of some Canadian industries was economically justifiable, particularly when those industries were losing ground to foreign competition even with such costly protection.

Costs to exporters were more difficult to estimate, but were considered to be important. Canada's more efficient and successful industries needed more access to larger foreign markets in order to grow and realize their potential. However, it was difficult to gain this access as long as Canada maintained its protection of many of its own industries, often through questionable trade restrictions. For instance, GATT found Canada's protection of its wine, beer, and some food-processing industries to be in violation of international trade agreements, exposing Canada to retaliatory action by other nations and making it more difficult for Canada to negotiate reductions in other countries' tariffs.

Outflows of Business Investment Capital

Partly because they could not gain secure access to larger foreign markets, a growing number of Canadian firms turned to establishing branch operations in foreign countries. Historically, Canada had experienced a *net inflow* of business investment capital; however, after the mid-1970s this turned into a net outflow, mainly due to increased investment abroad by Canadian firms. And with the outflow of investment capital along went the associated jobs.

Growing Protectionism in the United States

In the mid-1980s the United States, the market for roughly three-quarters of Canada's exports, was becoming more *protectionist*. Faced with stronger foreign competition from various quarters, U.S. authorities moved toward restrictions on imports—including imports from Canada—as a means of protecting American industries and jobs.

Under U.S. law, American industries could obtain government protection from foreign competition by filing complaints with U.S. authorities. Several American industries used this law to obtain government action against Canadian imports, using questionable statistics and economic arguments in the process. Canada could only appeal such actions through U.S. courts, with very little chance of success.

These practices affected only a small proportion of Canada's exports, but they were threatening, and created uncertainty for Canadian firms. Also, fear of U.S. import restrictions was leading a growing number of Canadian firms to build branch operations in the United States, rather than in Canada. This outflow of Canadian business capital—and jobs—was a growing concern in Canada.

Figure 12-3 summarizes these pressures for change to Canadian trade policy. As a result of these factors, Canada in 1985 announced its interest in negotiating a free trade agreement with the United States, and in 1989, the Canada–U.S. Free Trade Agreement (FTA) came into effect.

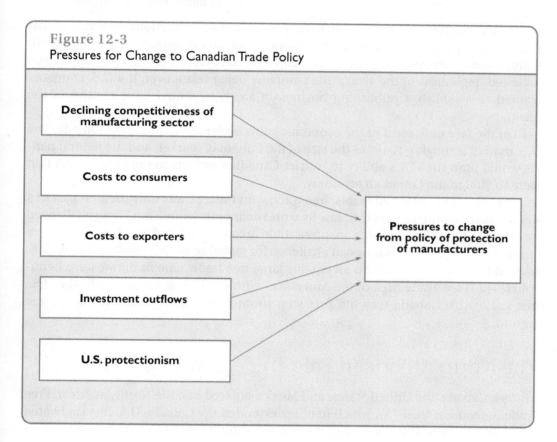

Figure 12-3
Pressures for Change to Canadian Trade Policy

- Declining competitiveness of manufacturing sector
- Costs to consumers
- Costs to exporters
- Investment outflows
- U.S. protectionism

Pressures to change from policy of protection of manufacturers

The 1989 Canada–U.S. Free Trade Agreement (FTA)

Contrary to common belief, the FTA did not represent a sudden breakthrough to free trade between the two nations. Tariffs between Canada and the U.S. had been gradually coming down for decades, and at the time the FTA came into effect, three-quarters of Canada–U.S. trade was already tariff-free and the average tariff was only 12 percent.

From the Canadian perspective, the main features of the agreement were as follows:

- Tariffs between the two countries were to be eliminated—about 15 percent of them immediately and the rest over the next 5 to10 years. The highest tariffs, which applied mainly to the more heavily protected consumer goods, were to be phased out over 10 years in 10 equal stages.

- Canada obtained more secure access to the U.S. market, mainly through better protection against the sorts of arbitrary restrictions on Canadian exports described earlier. Under the FTA, such actions by the U.S. could be appealed by Canada to a neutral board (or panel) consisting of five members drawn from a roster of international trade experts. These neutral experts can review and over-turn decisions by the U.S. (or Canadian) government if American (or Canadian) law has been applied incorrectly or unfairly. Because of the increasing use of such measures by the United States, many observers considered this appeal mechanism to be the key feature of the FTA from Canada's viewpoint.

- Canada relaxed its restrictions on foreign investment, and provided assurances that in the event of energy shortages, Canada would not discriminate against American users of Canadian energy with respect to either price or supply.

Both countries would continue to maintain existing restrictions on foreign own-ership in the communications sector (broadcasting) and transportation. In Canadian cultural industries, such as publishing, proposed takeovers by foreign firms had to be reviewed, regardless of the size of the company being taken over. If a U.S. company wanted to establish a publishing business, Canadians would have control of the business.

On the face of it, most of the economic gains under the FTA went to Canada. The U.S. market is roughly 10 times the size of the Canadian market, and the neutral pan-els would limit the U.S.'s ability to restrict Canadian exports to the U.S. market that were so vital to the Canadian economy.

However, to the United States, free trade with Canada was only the first part of a much broader strategy. The U.S. saw its world economic leadership being challenged by Europe's plan to establish a vast free trade area by 1992 and to adopt a common currency. To counter the European challenge for global economic leadership, the U.S. wanted to eventually establish an equally large free trade zone in the western hemi-sphere—a "Free Trade Area of the Americas," with the U.S. at its centre. To the U.S., free trade with Canada was the first step toward this goal; Mexico would be the second.

The North American Free Trade Agreement (NAFTA)

In 1994, Canada, the United States, and Mexico entered into the North American Free Trade Agreement (NAFTA), which in effect extended the Canada–U.S. free trade area to include Mexico. This agreement created the world's largest free trade zone, with a market of about 360 million people.

Background on Mexico

Compared to Canada, Mexico has a much larger population (about 114 million to Canada's 34 million), but this country is only about one-quarter as economically wealthy as Canada, as measured by GDP per person. Unlike Canada, however, Mexico had been until quite recently relatively isolated from the broader international economy.

Like Canada, Mexico had traditionally used high tariffs to protect its infant industries from foreign competition, especially the United States. Unlike Canada, however, Mexico did this in the context of a socialist state, with what is regarded as the world's first socialist constitution (1917).

The result was an economic system that was not only highly protected from foreign competition but also highly regulated by its government. Much of Mexican industry was either government-owned or heavily regulated; in many cases, government regulations prevented competition, leaving many key industries under the control of monopolies. With so little competition and so much regulation, productivity and living standards in the Mexican economy were very low.

Not having joined the General Agreement on Tariffs and Trade (GATT), Mexico remained quite isolated from the globalization trend of the 1980s. It staked most of its hopes for economic prosperity on oil exports, and reaped considerable benefits when oil prices were very high from 1979 to 1985. But the collapse of world oil prices in 1986 sharply reduced Mexico's oil-export revenues and left it near bankruptcy from its huge foreign debt, mostly loans made by international banks that had counted on high prices for Mexico's oil.

At this point, Mexico's government decided upon a basic change in strategic economic direction, from an inward-looking, protected, and regulated economy to one that was market-oriented and an active participant in the world economy. The Mexican government privatized and deregulated many of the nation's industries in order to improve their efficiency. In 1987, Mexico signalled its intention of participating in the world economy by taking the very large step of joining the GATT.

From 1987 to 1993, Mexico's average tariff on imports dropped from 45 percent to 9 percent, and Mexico's international trade grew rapidly, especially with the United States. Mexico signed an agreement with five Central American nations to form a regional free trade zone, and in 1991 sought a free trade agreement with Canada and the United States—the North American Free Trade Agreement (NAFTA).

Key Terms of NAFTA

Under NAFTA, tariffs were to be eliminated over periods of up to 15 years; however, virtually all of the tariffs between Canada and Mexico were to be phased out over a maximum of 10 years. On some products, tariffs were to be eliminated immediately, while tariffs on sectors that were more vulnerable to import competition (such as Canada's apparel, footwear, toys, and miscellaneous manufactured articles) would be phased out over 10 years. Both Canada and Mexico would have the right to take safeguard measures that allowed them to re-impose tariffs to protect producers from surges of imports, should these occur.

Most restrictions on investment were also to be phased out over a period of time, although Canada would retain the right to review foreign takeovers of larger Canadian companies, as it previously had the right to do so under the FTA. Canada would retain its exemption for its cultural industries under the FTA and its social and health services would be protected, also as it had the right to do under the FTA.

Finally, the mechanism for resolving trade disputes would be essentially the same as under the FTA. Disputes could be referred to a panel of neutral trade experts that would have the power to overturn a country's decisions that were contrary to its trade laws and NAFTA. As the "In the News" box shows, there is reason to believe that these panels have often worked to the advantage of Canada.

IN THE NEWS

NAFTA Has Helped Curb U.S. Protectionism

The United States can be quite aggressive in protecting its industries against foreign competition, and Canadians are sometimes pessimistic about their chances of prevailing in any trade dispute with their giant neighbour.

But in about two-thirds of cases that it has appealed under NAFTA rules, Canada has won either a rollback or elimination of U.S. duties or tariffs. According to Patrick Macrory, a trade lawyer and lecturer based in Washington, "It [NAFTA] has been quite effective in curbing what Canadians believe to be the overzealous enforcement of anti-dumping and countervailing duty laws by U.S. authorities."

So, Canada actually has been quite successful in appealing U.S. protectionist actions to NAFTA's panels of neutral experts. Finally, trade disputes such as these should be kept in perspective—they affect only a very small proportion of Canada–U.S. trade. ■

QUESTIONS
1. Why do you think Canada's appeals to NAFTA panels have so often been successful?
2. In some of the decisions by NAFTA panels, Americans sitting on the panels have voted in favour of Canada. What might explain this?

The Economic Impact of NAFTA on Canada

Canada's two-way trade with Mexico is very small—only about 2 percent of its trade with the United States. For this reason, it was expected that the effect of NAFTA on Canada would not be large, at least in the short-to-medium term.

According to the International Trade Commission, Mexico would gain the most from NAFTA, Canada would gain slightly, and the United States would gain the least. Canada's gains would be small for a variety of reasons, the most important of which was that Canada already had a free trade agreement involving the large U.S. market, while its trade with Mexico was much smaller.

In addition, roughly 85 percent of Canada's imports from Mexico were already tariff-free, and the tariffs on the remaining 15 percent were on average not very high. And Mexico's low wages did not give it a general competitive advantage, since productivity in Mexico was only about one-sixth of Canadian productivity.

NAFTA would increase export opportunities for a number of Canadian industries, mostly those that could provide goods and services related to the modernization of Mexico, such as telecommunications, engineering consulting and construction, transportation, and financial institutions. In addition, under NAFTA Mexico would open up the growing Mexican market to imports of Canadian- and U.S.-built cars. On the other side of the picture, Canada could expect increased competition from Mexico in labour-intensive industries such as apparel, auto parts, textiles, and various manufactured goods, and Mexico could provide Canada with competition for U.S. and foreign business investment.

While the prospective economic gains for Canada under NAFTA were not large, it was considered strategically important for Canada to be part of the deal. If the United States had *separate* free trade agreements with Canada and Mexico, only companies located in the United States would have had free access to the markets of *all three* countries, giving the United States a significant advantage in attracting business investment capital. So while being in NAFTA would not bring large economic gains for Canada, *not* being in it could have resulted in significant losses in terms of investment and jobs. According to the C.D. Howe Institute, "the overall macro-economic impact of NAFTA is not going to be big for Canada, but we would have lost a lot if we were not in it."

The Chile Free Trade Pact

In 1996, Canada and Chile concluded a trade agreement that provided for the elimination of tariffs on 80 percent of Canadian exports to Chile. Remaining tariffs were phased out over the 1997–2002 period. Chile is a small country of 16 million, and Canada trades more with the United States in a single day than it does with Chile annually. However, Canadian mining companies see opportunities in Chile, and Canada is one of the largest foreign investors in Chile.

On a strategic level, signing a trade agreement with Chile was seen as one more step in extending NAFTA throughout the western hemisphere. However, the United States was not part of this agreement, as political opposition there had stalled that nation's progress toward its long-term goal of a broader free trade area of the Americas.

Canada Enters the Global Economy: Adjusting to Change

The 1990s saw great changes in Canada's trade policy from its traditional stance of protectionism. The most dramatic change was the Canada–U.S. Free Trade Agreement, which was followed by NAFTA in 1994 and the agreement with Chile in 1996. In the meantime, the GATT/WTO Uruguay Round agreement came into effect in 1995.

The more rapid movement toward free trade would have significant economic effects on Canadians. There would be an *acceleration of change* in the Canadian economy, as some industries expanded and others contracted more rapidly than they otherwise would have. As an illustration of the extent of this change, in real terms (measured in 2002 dollars), from 1989 to 2008

- Canada's GDP grew by 61 percent,
- Canada's exports grew by 131 percent, and
- Canada's imports grew by 155 percent.

From 1989 to 2005, exports increased from 25 percent of GDP to 35 percent, and imports from nearly 26 percent of GDP to 33 percent. As these changes happened, some industries had to cope with unprecedented foreign competition, while others enjoyed unprecedented export success.

Such changes involved a substantial adjustment process for both workers and industries, as product lines, production methods, and skill requirements were affected. Some export industries would thrive and grow, while other industries affected by imports would rationalize, downsize, or disappear. Production technologies would change, and workers would have to move to new industries, jobs, or locations.

The most basic adjustment provision in the trade agreements was the fact that tariffs were to be eliminated gradually, generally over a period of 5 to 15 years. This was intended to give companies and workers adequate time to adapt to free trade, which presented dangers for some and opportunities for others. In addition, various retraining programs were available in Canada, and a retraining element was added to the employment insurance program.

Strategies for Success I—World Product Mandating

One of the concerns about free trade was the fate of Canada's foreign-owned branch plants. As we have seen, the small size of the Canadian market meant that these branch plants were often much less efficient than the plants of their parent in the United States. The original reason for U.S. parent firms establishing and operating branch plants in Canada was to avoid paying Canadian tariffs. This fact raised concerns that free trade would mean the closing of many Canadian branch plants and the shifting of production back to the United States. These dire consequences would have been much less likely if the Canadian plants were *specialized* in the production of one or a few products so that they could be fully efficient; however, the small size of the Canadian market had precluded that for most companies.

world product mandating
An arrangement whereby a branch plant acquires a mandate from its foreign parent company to manufacture and market a particular product or products for the world market.

An interesting approach to making branch plants more specialized and efficient is **world product mandating**. Under such an arrangement, a Canadian branch plant acquires a mandate to manufacture and market a particular product for the world market on behalf of the parent company. That is, branch plants would no longer produce, on an inefficiently small scale, the full range of their parents' product lines. Instead, they would concentrate on one or a few selected products for a wider market. With greater specialization and longer production runs, Canadian manufacturers could become more efficient and internationally competitive.

The automobile industry provides the best example of a successful world product mandating strategy, as described earlier in this chapter. But world product mandating has also been successful for a number of companies that have utilized it, including Westinghouse Canada, DuPont, Kodak, Procter & Gamble, Garrett Manufacturing, Litton Systems Canada, Gandalf Technologies, GTE Sylvania, Heron Cable, Hughes Aircraft, Polymer International, and others.

World product mandating provides a way to channel the economic resources of foreign multinational corporations into the development of a more specialized manufacturing sector that is better able to compete in both Canadian and export markets.

Strategies for Success II—Niche Marketing

niche marketing
Marketing to small segments of a market.

Another concern regarding free trade was that smaller Canadian manufacturers could not succeed in head-to-head competition with large U.S. mass-production manufacturers. Under a strategy of **niche marketing**, Canadian firms avoid competing directly with big U.S. companies for the mass market. Instead, they target smaller volumes of production into relatively small segments, or niches, of the market. The market for many consumer products is not really a single market, but rather consists of several segments, with a large segment for medium-quality mass-produced products at the centre of the market, and various relatively small segments (niches), such as high-end products targeted at specific buyer groups. In a small market such as Canada's, such niches are often very small indeed, but in a vast one such as the United States, they can be large enough to offer significant opportunities to niche producers. In addition, the above-average prices in such niche markets can offset the higher production costs of Canadian producers.

Because the U.S. market is approximately 10 times the size of Canada's, a 1-percent share of the American market involves as many sales as a 10-percent share of the Canadian market. For example, in the apparel industry, Canadian firms have done very well by producing high-quality men's suits and high-fashion women's wear for the U.S. market, where those firms enjoy healthy demand and high prices.

Strategies for Success III—Partnering

Another strategy for Canadian firms is to *partner* with larger foreign firms in ways that benefit both of them. For example, Stroh Brewing of the United States wanted a premium product for the high end of the U.S. market, and Sleeman Brewing of Guelph, Ontario, produced just such a beer. After signing an agreement under which Stroh would distribute Sleeman's beer in Michigan, John Sleeman was quoted as saying, "All we have to do is get 1 percent of the Michigan market and we've got to build a couple more breweries."

Canada's Trade Since the Agreements

Canada's export performance following the trade agreements was more impressive than many had expected. In particular, exports to the United States grew strongly, as reflected in Figure 12-4. Figure 12-4 shows the *balance* of exports and imports, so the positive numbers for Canada's trade with the USA indicate that Canada's exports to the USA were larger than imports. Conversely, the negative numbers for Canada's trade with the rest of the world show that for countries other than the United States, Canada was importing more than it was exporting.

Certainly, Canada's economy became more closely *tied to the United States'*, as two-way trade between the nations reached $1.8 billion per day in merchandise alone (excluding services). An interesting measure of the links between the two economies is that estimates suggest that well over half of the trade between them consists of transactions between parent companies and their subsidiaries.

While Canada's exports to the United States grew strongly, it should be noted that most of Canada's exports came from a relatively small number of companies. The export success of these few large companies illustrates the importance of *economies of scale* as discussed earlier in this chapter; "the rest of the story" is that there are large numbers of medium- and small-size Canadian firms that are not yet enjoying export success.

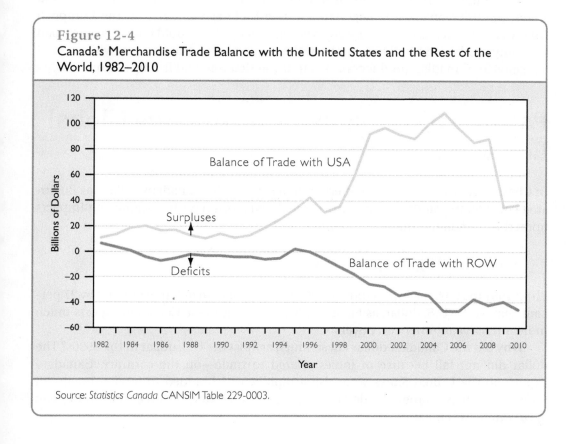

Figure 12-4

Canada's Merchandise Trade Balance with the United States and the Rest of the World, 1982–2010

Source: *Statistics Canada* CANSIM Table 229-0003.

However, Figure 12-4 also shows that Canada's trade situation was changing. Exports to the United States had been boosted by the low cost of the Canadian dollar in the 1990s, and then by the booming U.S. economy in the 2003–07 period. However, the exchange rate of the Canadian dollar increased considerably after 2002, and when the American economic boom turned into a serious recession, Canada's exports to the USA plunged by 20 percent.

More Diversified Trade in the Future?

Canada has benefited greatly from its exports to the vast U.S. market, which were a key factor in Canada's economic booms of the 1990s and the 2003–07 period, when the United States was the market for more than 80 percent of Canada's exports.

More recently, however, a smaller proportion of Canada's exports has been going to the USA, and many observers are expecting that Canada's trade, and especially its exports, will become more diversified among various other trading partners. In part, this is due to the fact that the Canadian dollar has become considerably more costly for American buyers, and in part it is due to the expectation that U.S. economic growth will be slower than in the past.

A more fundamental factor, though, is the shift in world economic growth discussed in Chapter 11, as the most rapid growth rates are being achieved by emerging nations that have not in the past been major players in international trade. The most prominent of these are known as the "BRIC" countries—Brazil, Russia, India, and China, and it expected that Canada's trade with these nations will grow more rapidly than its trade with the United States in the future. And as these countries' economies grow, they will become more important participants in world trade, and quite possibly more important markets for Canadian exporters.

In another effort to strengthen trade ties with countries other than the United States, in 2011 Canada was negotiating a free trade agreement with the European Union. A combined Canada-EU study said that such a deal would boost the Canadian economy by about $12 billion, or about three-quarters of one percent, with most of the gains for Canadian producers going to the agriculture and fishing sectors.

> "... with the globalization of financial markets, which have exploded in the last 10 to 15 years, it's financial flows which drive the currency."
>
> — JAMES FRANK, CHIEF ECONO-MIST, THE CONFERENCE BOARD OF CANADA

Part B: The Canadian Dollar in the Global Economy

In Chapter 10, we saw how the international price of the Canadian dollar has fluctuated considerably in the recent past. These fluctuations have had significant impacts upon the Canadian economy since the early 1990s.

The Diving Dollar in the 1990s

From 1991 to 2002, the international value of the Canadian dollar decreased by 27 percent against the U.S. dollar, as Figure 12-5 shows. This made Canadian exports much more attractive to American buyers.

Why did the Canadian dollar fall so much against the U.S. dollar in the 1990s? The dollar did not fall because of forces related to trade—on the contrary, Canadian exports to the United States were rising rapidly, which added to foreign buying of Canadian dollars. Rather, the dollar was pushed downward by forces related to *flows of capital* between nations.

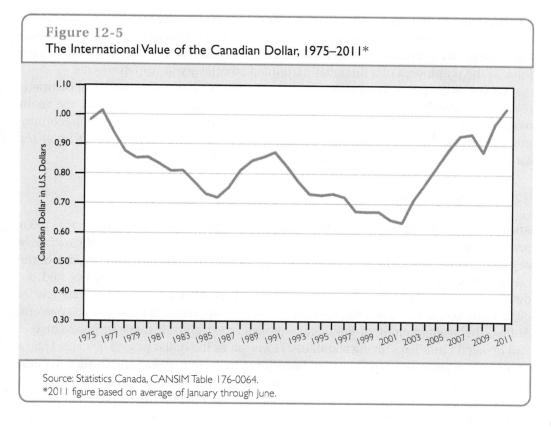

Figure 12-5

The International Value of the Canadian Dollar, 1975–2011*

Source: Statistics Canada, CANSIM Table 176-0064.
*2011 figure based on average of January through June.

One of these forces was *interest payments on Canada's large debt to foreign lenders,* which was discussed in Chapter 8. The payment of the interest on this foreign debt generated sales of about 30 billion Canadian dollars in many years of the 1990s. In the second half of the 1990s, *outflows of investment funds* added to the downward pressure on the Canadian dollar. We saw in Chapter 11 how the U.S. dollar was pushed to high levels by heavy inflows of foreign capital into the U.S. stock market in the second half of the 1990s. Over this period, Canadians bought large volumes of shares on U.S. stock markets—almost $95 billion from 1998 to 2000 alone. This large outflow of capital from Canada put downward pressure on the Canadian dollar while adding to the upward pressure on the U.S. currency. So, the decrease in the value of the Canadian dollar against the U.S. dollar after the mid-1990s was in large part due to the remarkable surge in the value of the U.S. dollar that was described in Chapter 11.

So, from 1991 to 2002, the international value of the Canadian dollar decreased by 27 percent against the U.S. dollar. What did this mean for Canadians?

Effects of the Low Dollar on Canadians

The low international value of their dollar had two major consequences for Canadians. The bad news was that it depressed Canadians' living standards, by increasing the cost of imports. The good news was that with the Canadian dollar so cheap to foreigners, Canadian exports increased sharply.

From 1990 to 2002, exports grew by 111 percent in real terms, more than three times the 34-percent growth for the economy as a whole (GDP). Over the same period, exports increased from 27 percent of GDP to 43 percent. In addition, as we have seen, a growing proportion of Canada's exports consisted of manufactured goods.

So, it was exports that led Canada out of the recession of the early 1990s and into a long economic boom. During this boom, the unemployment rate reached its lowest point in 26 years—6.4 percent in 2000.

However, there was a trade-off for these gains in jobs—the lower Canadian dollar meant higher prices for imports, which depressed the standard of living of Canadian consumers.[1] In a sense, it was as if Canadians had taken a "pay cut" in order to save jobs, as the employees of a financially troubled company will sometimes do.

With exports performing strongly, concerns over Canada's international competitiveness diminished. But beneath the surface, there were concerns that the main reason for Canada's export success was not that Canadian industry was becoming more productive and competitive, but rather that *the low international price of the Canadian dollar* was making its products attractive to foreign buyers.

The Rising Dollar, 2002–08

After 2002, the forces that had pushed the Canadian dollar downward in the 1990s reversed themselves. As we saw in Chapter 11, there was a sharp decrease in the exchange rate of the U.S. dollar, which led to a very large increase in the international price of the Canadian dollar. In addition, strong exports of resources at high prices boosted the demand for the Canadian dollar. In the two years after reaching a record low of 62.02 cents U.S. in January 2002, the Canadian dollar appreciated by roughly 30 percent. At first, this strengthening of the dollar was welcomed, since it made imports cheaper and boosted Canadians' living standards. However, as the dollar passed 80 cents U.S., a new concern arose—would Canadian firms (both those that export and those that compete with imports) be able to compete internationally with such a high dollar?

While free trade with the United States and Mexico had reduced the tariff protection of Canadian manufacturers, the falling Canadian dollar of the 1990s had provided a different form of protection for them. Figure 12-6 shows that after decreasing from 2001–2003 under the pressure of a slowing U.S. economy and the high Canadian dollar, exports grew again in 2004–05. However, much of the strength in Canada's exports in this period was in resource and energy products, for which the world market was strong. In the more competitive area of manufactured goods, Canada's exports were lagging, and there was continuing uncertainty over the ability of many Canadian manufacturers to compete internationally with the Canadian dollar well above 80 cents U.S. Figure 12-6 also shows how the high Canadian dollar eroded the balance of trade surplus of exports over imports after 2003.

The Canadian Dollar as a Source of Uncertainty

After mid-2008, the exchange rate of the Canadian dollar again fell below 80 cents U.S. as the global recession cut deeply into both the prices and volumes of Canada's resource exports. As explained in Chapter 10, such a retreat of the Canadian dollar during a recession was welcome as a cushion, or "shock absorber" for the Canadian economy.

However, there was considerable uncertainty and concern over whether the Canadian dollar might return in the future to the high levels that caused problems in 2006-08. One concern was that if global economic conditions improved again, high and rising demand for Canadian resource exports would drive the dollar considerably higher. Another concern was that if the 2008-09 problems with the United States' financial system and economy were to continue, foreign investors might move funds out of U.S. dollars, pushing the U.S. dollar lower—and a lower U.S. dollar would mean

---

[1] The burden did not just fall on consumers. For Canadian businesses that imported capital equipment, the falling dollar meant higher costs.

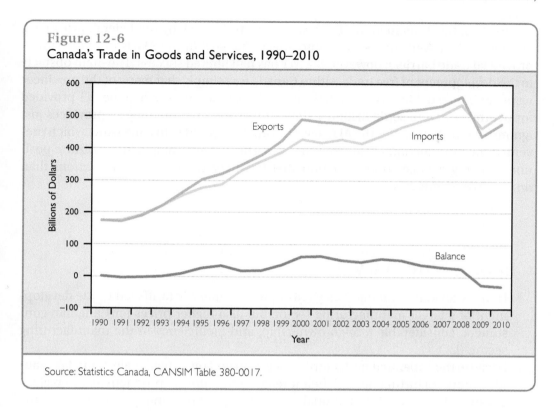

Figure 12-6
Canada's Trade in Goods and Services, 1990–2010

Source: Statistics Canada, CANSIM Table 380-0017.

a higher Canadian dollar, to the discomfort of Canadians in industries that export or compete with imports.

In summary, the extreme ups and downs of the Canadian dollar over the past two decades, including the setting of all-time records for *both* the lowest level (in 2002) and the highest level (in 2007) were bringing home to Canadians both the importance of the exchange rate of their currency, and the extent to which that exchange rate was beyond Canada's control, for better or for worse.

A Final Trade Question: Will We Ever Have Free Trade *Within* Canada?

As the world moved toward globalization, Canada was still far from having free trade among its own provinces. The movement of goods, workers, and investment capital between provinces was restricted by a complex web of hundreds of provincial government regulations designed to protect each province's producers and workers against out-of-province competition. The most common such restrictions required governments and their agencies to buy only from suppliers located in that province, often at higher costs to the taxpayer. Other examples of restrictions are Quebec's refusal to allow the sale of butter-coloured margarine and Prince Edward Island's prevention of the sale of milk from Nova Scotia. Other restrictions included standards and rules that excluded out-of-province products or workers.

In 2005, an interprovincial panel ruled that Quebec must open its borders to butter-coloured margarine, ending a Quebec ban on this product enacted in 1987.

According to various studies, these restrictions cost Canadians as much as $6.5 billion annually. A more subtle cost of these restrictions has been that they subdivided the already small Canadian market into even smaller regional segments, making Canadian producers even more inefficient and less competitive internationally. In the words of a GATT report in 1994, "Inter-provincial trade barriers have become a major problem for Canada, hampering economic growth and job creation, as well as reducing competitiveness of Canadian-based firms."

In 1995, the Agreement on Internal Trade (AIT) struck by the federal, provincial, and territorial governments came into effect. The goal of the AIT is to reduce inter-provincial trade barriers; however, the AIT has had limited success. The main obstacle to the development of free trade within Canada was simply that many of the provinces were not interested in giving up their protectionist measures. While the AIT provided for neutral panels to settle disputes, their rulings were not binding, so provinces just ignored them. Also, under the AIT, just one province could veto a measure, which prevented the introduction of valuable changes. This has left Canada in the bizarre position of being a major trading nation that has freer trade *with other nations* than *among its own provinces*.

Chapter Summary

1. Under Canada's National Policy (1879), infant industry tariffs led to the development of a larger manufacturing sector, but also higher prices for Canadian consumers, considerable foreign ownership, and inefficiency in the manufacturing sector. (L.O. 1)
2. Because they operated under tariff protection and on a small scale, Canada's manufacturers fell further behind their foreign competitors in productivity when globalization increased international trade, competition, and productivity in the 1980s. (L.O. 2)
3. Pressures for change in Canadian trade policy arose from the decreasing international competitiveness of much of Canadian manufacturing, the growing costs to Canadian consumers and exporters of protecting uncompetitive manufacturing, outflows of business investment capital, and rising protectionism in the United States. (L.O. 3)
4. In 1989, the Canada–U.S. Free Trade Agreement eliminated tariffs between Canada and the United States over a period of time and established a dispute-settlement process that would provide Canada with more secure access to the U.S. market. (L.O. 4)
5. In 1994, the North American Free Trade Agreement (NAFTA) extended the Canada–U.S. free trade area to Mexico. This was strategically important to the U.S.'s plan for a much wider free trade area to counter the European Union; however, its short-run economic effect on Canada was expected to be quite small. (L.O. 5)
6. Business strategies for succeeding in highly competitive international markets include world product mandating, niche marketing, and partnering with foreign firms. (L.O. 6)
7. The value of the Canadian dollar decreased considerably during the 1990s, largely due to outflows of funds to pay interest to foreign lenders and to invest in U.S. stocks. The lower dollar depressed Canadians' living standards, but helped exports to grow and unemployment to decrease. (L.O. 7)
8. From 2002 to 2008, the exchange rate of the Canadian dollar increased very sharply. The higher dollar made imports less costly, but also caused concerns over the ability of Canadian producers to compete internationally. (L.O. 8)
9. In the future, it expected that a growing proportion of Canada's exports will go to nations such as the BRIC group, which are less wealthy but are growing rapidly economically. (L.O. 9)

Questions

1. For most of the twentieth century, Canada's trade/tariff policy (which originated with the National Policy of 1879)
   (a) was intended to foster the development of the manufacturing sector of the Canadian economy.
   (b) was a policy of quite high tariff protection of the Canadian manufacturing sector.
   (c) was intended to keep the prices that consumers paid as low as possible.
   (d) was basically a policy of free trade.
   (e) Both (a) and (b).

2. By the mid-1980s, there was considerable concern that productivity in Canada's manufacturing sector was low and that many manufacturers were internationally uncompetitive. Which of the following factors contributed to these problems?
   (a) the relatively small Canadian market
   (b) short production runs
   (c) tariffs that protected manufacturers from import competition
   (d) relatively small plants
   (e) All of the above.

3. Which of the following factors led Canada to seek a free trade agreement with the United States?
   (a) Canadian manufacturers would have secure access to larger markets that would allow them to achieve lower production costs through economies of scale.
   (b) Most Canadian manufacturers were more efficient than their U.S. competitors, and so would benefit immediately from free trade.
   (c) Exposure to competition from imports would force Canadian manufacturers to become more efficient.
   (d) The cost to Canadian consumers of tariff protection for inefficient Canadian manufacturers was growing.
   (e) Answers (a), (c), and (d).

4. The decrease in the international value of the Canadian dollar during the 1990s led to proposals that the Bank of Canada fix or *peg* the value of the Canadian dollar relative to the U.S. dollar. Suppose that the Bank of Canada had been committed to keeping the Canadian dollar at 75 cents U.S. after 1993.
   (a) How could the Bank of Canada have fixed the Canadian exchange rate in this way?
   (b) What would have been the effects of such a policy upon Canadians and the Canadian economy?

5. In 2004–05, unemployment in the Canadian economy was low, and the international price of the Canadian dollar was increasing. As the Canadian dollar rose toward 85 cents U.S., there were demands that the Bank of Canada hold the exchange rate *down*.
   (a) Why would these proposals to hold down the international price of the dollar be made?
   (b) How could the Bank of Canada have held the Canadian exchange rate down?
   (c) Why do you think the Bank of Canada did *not* take action to hold down the exchange rate of the Canadian dollar at that time?

6. If Canada's productivity were to fall further behind the productivity of its major trading partners in the future, what would be the likely effect upon
   (a) the international value of the Canadian dollar?
   (b) the standard of living of Canadians?

7. Over the past few years, what have been the trends regarding
    (a) Canada's merchandise exports to/imports from the United States?
    (b) Canada's merchandise exports to/imports from the rest of the world?

    What seem to be the reasons for these trends?

    Statistics on Canada's merchandise trade with the U.S. and the rest of the world can be found on Statistics Canada's website at **www.statcan.gc.ca**. Search for "Imports, exports and trade balance of goods and services on a balance-of-payments basis, by country or country grouping".

8. Visit the website for the Centre for the Study of Living Standards, (**www.csls.ca**) and find the most recent studies that compare Canada's productivity performance to other nations. What have been the most recent trends, and what are the reasons for them?

Study Guide

Review Questions (Answers to these Review Questions appear in Appendix B.)

1. The presence of the large U.S. economy immediately to the south has always represented
    (a) an opportunity to all Canadian producers.
    (b) a threat to less competitive Canadian producers.
    (c) an opportunity for efficient Canadian producers.
    (d) an opportunity for Canadian consumers.
    (e) Answers (b), (c), and (d).

2. As a result of the economic realities in the previous question,
    (a) the vast majority of Canadians have favoured a policy of free trade with the United States.
    (b) some Canadians have favoured a policy of free trade with the United States, while others wanted a policy of tariff protection.
    (c) Canada's trade policy with the United States has always been controversial politically.
    (d) Answers (b) and (c).
    (e) None of the above.

3. State whether each of the following statements concerning the trade/tariff policy that Canada followed for most of the twentieth century (originating with the National Policy of 1879) is *true* or *false*.
    (a) It was successful in generating growth of the manufacturing sector of the Canadian economy. _____
    (b) It caused foreign companies to establish branch manufacturing plants in Canada. _____
    (c) It caused prices to consumers across Canada to be higher than they otherwise would have been. _____
    (d) It protected many inefficient and internationally uncompetitive Canadian manufacturers from foreign competition. _____
    (e) It reduced foreign ownership of Canadian industry. _____
    (f) It increased competition in the Canadian economy. _____

4. By the mid-1980s, it had become apparent that the productivity and international competitiveness of Canada's manufacturing sector was
   (a) below that of Canada's trading partners, and falling further behind them.
   (b) higher than that of Canada's trading partners.
   (c) lower than that of Canada's trading partners, but improving more rapidly and gaining on them.
   (d) about the same as most of Canada's major trading partners.
   (e) None of the above.

5. By the mid-1980s, there was widespread agreement that the solution to the most basic economic problems faced by Canada's manufacturing sector was to
   (a) buy back control of foreign-owned firms.
   (b) increase the productive efficiency of the manufacturing sector.
   (c) break up the large manufacturing firms known to be monopolizing some industries.
   (d) slow down the pace of technological change in manufacturing so as to protect the jobs of workers.
   (e) raise tariffs on foreign goods.

6. Which of the following was regarded as a major step toward the solution referred to in the previous question?
   (a) buying back control of Canada's manufacturing sector from foreign owners
   (b) a policy of freer trade that would expose Canadian manufacturers to more foreign competition
   (c) a policy of freer trade that would give Canadian producers more access to larger markets
   (d) Both (b) and (c).
   (e) increased tariff protection for Canadian manufacturers facing strong foreign competition

7. A consideration that spurred Canada on to negotiate the Free Trade Agreement of 1989 with the United States was that
   (a) under such an agreement, the U.S. would no longer be able to place any restrictions on Canadian exports to the U.S. market.
   (b) it was generally agreed among economists that a market of at least 100 million people is needed in order to be able to realize the full benefits of efficient production.
   (c) the U.S. was becoming increasingly restrictive (or protectionist) with respect to imports, including those from Canada.
   (d) the Canadian public was overwhelmingly in favour of free trade with the U.S.
   (e) Answers (b) and (c).

8. State whether each of the following was a provision of the Canada–U.S. Free Trade Agreement. Answer *true* or *false*.
   (a) Canada was to gain more secure access to the U.S. market through protection against unfair U.S. trade restrictions. _____
   (b) Both countries agreed not to impose any restrictions whatsoever on imports from each other. _____
   (c) There was to be some relaxation of Canadian restrictions on U.S. investment in Canada. _____
   (d) Trade disputes between Canada and the United States were to be resolved by the decision of a panel of neutral trade experts. _____
   (e) Most tariffs between the two countries were to be phased out over a 10-year period. _____

9. *World product mandating* can strengthen Canada's manufacturing sector by
    (a) specializing the Canadian branch plants of foreign companies in the production of particular products, most of which would be exported into larger foreign markets.
    (b) government restrictions on the importation of certain types of products, thereby giving Canadian producers a mandate to serve that part of the Canadian market.
    (c) providing government subsidies to Canadian companies seeking to export into world markets.
    (d) negotiating tariff reductions on Canadian manufactured products around the world in exchange for increased access by foreign nations to exports of vital Canadian natural resources.
    (e) Both (b) and (c).

10. *Niche marketing* can be an effective strategy for Canadian producers in international markets because
    (a) by selling their products at premium prices, Canadian producers of such products can recover their higher production costs per unit.
    (b) a niche market in the United States can generate many more sales than a niche market in Canada.
    (c) Answers (a) and (b).
    (d) they can use mass-production technology and achieve very low production costs per unit due to economies of scale.
    (e) None of the above.

11. The Tilley Company of Canada produces specialized and unique clothing products that are marketed at high prices to consumers across North America. This strategy for success is an example of
    (a) economies of scale.
    (b) niche marketing.
    (c) world product mandating.
    (d) direct marketing.
    (e) None of the above.

12. An automobile company decides to use one of its plants in Ontario to produce its Trailer Blazer truck for sale across North America. This strategy for success is known as
    (a) niche marketing.
    (b) economies of scale.
    (c) world product mandating.
    (d) direct marketing.
    (e) None of the above.

13. According to the International Trade Commission (ITC), the likely economic effect of the North American Free Trade Agreement (NAFTA) on Canada would be
    (a) small and positive.
    (b) small and negative.
    (c) large and positive.
    (d) large and negative.
    (e) None of the above.

14. From 1991 to 2002, the international value of the Canadian dollar
    (a) increased considerably.
    (b) increased slightly.
    (c) remained almost stable.

(d) decreased slightly.

(e) decreased considerably.

15. How did the change in the international value of the Canadian dollar from 1991 to 2002 affect

(a) Canadian exporters?

(b) Canadian consumers?

16. The increase in the exchange rate of the Canadian dollar from 2005 to 2008 represented a threat to

(a) Canadian consumers.

(b) Canadian retirees who spend their winters in Florida.

(c) National Hockey League teams in Canadian cities.

(d) Canadian manufacturers.

(e) None of the above.

Critical Thinking Questions

(Asterisked questions 1 to 4 are answered in Appendix B; the answers to questions 5 to 8 are in the Instructor's Manual that accompanies this text.)

*1. Suppose that, due to concerns about inflation in its own economy, the U.S. government increased American interest rates.

(a) How would this probably affect the international value of the Canadian dollar?

(b) What two options would the Bank of Canada have in these circumstances?

(c) What would be the consequences for the Canadian economy of each of these options?

(d) What would probably decide which option the Bank of Canada would select?

*2. If Canada's manufacturing productivity were to increase rapidly over the next few years, what would be the likely effect upon

(a) the international value of the Canadian dollar?

(b) the standard of living of Canadians?

*3. Much attention has been paid to how a higher international price of the Canadian dollar works to the disadvantage of Canadian manufacturers in competing with foreign producers. How could the rapid increase in the international value of the Canadian dollar provide an *opportunity* for Canadian businesses that are seeking to improve their efficiency?

*4. Many observers believe that by signing the Canada–U.S. Free Trade Agreement in 1989, the federal government was giving Canadian manufacturing industries a wake-up call that globalization was on the way. Explain why such a wake-up call was considered necessary, and *two* ways in which the Canada–U.S. Free Trade Agreement of 1989 could be expected to increase the productive efficiency of Canada's manufacturing industries.

5. "One reason why the productivity of many Canadian manufacturers has lagged behind their foreign counterparts is that they haven't been *forced* to become more efficient. Until 1989, they had tariff protection, then for more than a decade after 1991, the exchange rate of the Canadian dollar gave them protection."

(a) Explain the reasoning behind this statement.

(b) If the speaker is correct, what should happen to Canadian manufacturing productivity with the value of the Canadian dollar above $1.00 U.S., as it was in 2011?

6. "Free trade with the United States has proven to be a great error on the part of Canada and a major source of Canada's loss of manufacturing jobs and high unemployment since the early 1990s."
   (a) What factors should be considered in assessing the accuracy of this statement?
   (b) Having considered those factors, do you agree with the statement? Why?

7. Suppose that Canada and the United States were considering adopting a common currency, as was done in the European Union.
   (a) What advantages might a common currency provide for Canada?
   (b) What would be some of the key questions that would have to be worked out, and what obstacles would there be to such a measure?

8. Suppose a Canadian family spends $4000 per month, 20 percent of which is spent on imports. Suppose also that the Canadian dollar were to fall over a period of time from 80 cents U.S. to 72 cents U.S., and by a similar amount against other currencies.
   (a) Estimate the cost of this decrease in the exchange rate of the Canadian dollar to this family, both in dollars per month and as a percentage of its total consumption.
   (b) What economic benefits for Canada could be claimed as an offset to this reduction in living standards?
   (c) What could this family do to reduce the effect of the lower Canadian dollar on its standard of living?

Use the Web (Hints for these Use the Web exercises appear in Appendix B.)

1. Visit Statistics Canada's website at **www.statcan.gc.ca** and search for "Canada's balance of international payments", then click on "Canada's balance of international payments", and check the current account.
   (a) Over the past few years, what have been the trends regarding Canada's total exports and imports of goods and services, and balance of trade (the difference between exports and imports)?
   (b) What seem to be the reasons for these trends?

2. Following are the flows of direct business investment into and out of Canada from 2004 to 2010, in billions of dollars.

Year	Canadian Direct Investment Abroad	Foreign Direct Investment into Canada	Net Flow of Direct Investment
2004	− 56.4	− 0.6	− 57.0
2005	− 35.9	+ 32.7	− 3.2
2006	− 52.4	+ 68.4	+ 16.0
2007	− 62.0	+ 123.1	+ 61.1
2008	− 85.1	+ 61.0	− 24.1
2009	− 47.6	+ 24.4	− 23.2
2010	− 39.7	+ 24.1	− 15.6

"+" indicates flows of funds into Canada
"−" indicates flows of funds out of Canada

Update these statistics using data from Statistics Canada's website **www.statcan.gc.ca**. Search for "Canada's balance of international payments", then click on "Canada's balance of international payments", and check the capital and financial account. Do the statistics show any trends in the flows of direct investment into and out of Canada? If so, what might explain these trends?

Into the Future

After studying this chapter, you should be able to

1. Define the term *resource wealth mentality* and explain how this mentality could apply to Canadian attitudes and government policies in the past.

2. Explain why the globalization of the world economy occurred, and how it presented Canada with both opportunities and challenges.

3. State four characteristics that help to make a nation's economy attractive to investment in high-technology industries in the globalized world economy.

4. Explain three ways in which Canada was not well prepared for the globalization trend of the 1980s.

5. Describe four basic changes in Canadian government economic policy since the late 1980s, and explain the purpose of each of these changes.

6. Explain four ways in which the 1990s were a period of difficult transition for Canadians.

7. Explain four ways in which Canada emerged from the 1990s in a stronger economic condition.

8. Explain four major challenges facing Canada's economy in the future.

9. Apply the facts and concepts of this chapter to various situations.

It could be said that the 1990s were the decade between Canada's past and its future—the period during which Canada came to grips with the phenomenon of globalization that was sweeping across much of the world.

Accordingly, the 1990s saw many fundamental economic changes: free trade agreements that opened up foreign markets to Canadian exporters and exposed Canadian producers to import competition, the Bank of Canada's anti-inflation policies that forced the economy into a "downshift" from an environment of high inflation rates to one of low inflation rates, and the federal government's anti-deficit policies that brought an end to a 20-year period of government spending programs financed by borrowing and escalating government debt. As we will see, these changes did not occur independently of each other; they were all related to Canada's adjustment to the new, globalized world economy. And perhaps reflecting the extent of change in the 1990s, the decade began with high inflation, high interest rates, a recession, high unemployment, and massive government budget deficits, and it ended with low inflation, low interest rates, a boom, low unemployment, and budget surpluses.

However, the transition during the 1990s from the past to these new conditions was a difficult one. To understand why this transition was so challenging, we need to review the nature of the Canadian economy and government policy orientation that existed prior to these changes.

Canada Before the 1990s

Traditionally, Canadians have lived in a relatively insulated environment brought about by paternalistic government policies, a history of market protection, and the accumulated attitudes and experiences of both individuals and businesses.

This old economic order, as we call it, was a system where many prospered. However, because the old order generally provided insulation from external pressures and fostered limited internal pressures, many of the critical requirements for upgrading to more sophisticated and sustainable competitive advantages in Canadian industry have been missing or are only weakly present.[1]

Michael Porter describes a Canada that had traditionally relied upon exports of natural resources and resource products as its basic source of economic prosperity. These exports, together with substantial inflows of foreign (mainly U.S.) business capital investment, provided Canadians with the foreign currency with which they purchased the imported goods and services that supported their high living standards. By making Canadians among the most prosperous people in the world, these advantages also made it possible for them to support a relatively inefficient tariff-protected manufacturing sector, by paying high prices for its products.

With economic wealth so readily provided by resource exports and foreign investment, government policy tended to be relatively unconcerned with *creating wealth*. Rather, government policies focused on promoting a *fair distribution of wealth* by providing assistance to individuals, businesses, and regions that needed it. Over the years, governments established a wide variety of social welfare programs for individuals and families (from education and health care to income support systems such as unemployment insurance, welfare, and pensions), an extensive support system for weaker and

---

[1] Professor Michael E. Porter, *Canada at the Crossroads: The Reality of a New Competitive Environment* (October 1991; a study prepared for the Business Council on National Issues and the Government of Canada).

less efficient producers (including tariff protection for manufacturers, subsidies for farmers, and assistance of various sorts to corporations in difficulty), and various forms of assistance to economically weaker regions (including equalization payments, regional development grants, and subsidies to people and businesses in those regions).

According to some critical observers, Canada had developed a **resource wealth mentality**—the view that economic wealth is not something that you *create* so much as something that *happens to you*, through possessing and selling resources. With wealth seemingly so easily available that it could be taken for granted, the main role of government became to ensure that the nation's wealth was distributed fairly among its entire people. As a result, government policy became more concerned with the *distribution* of economic welfare than with incentives for the efficiency that *creates* wealth. So while Canadians were generally quite *prosperous* economically, they were not (with the exception of their natural resource sector and certain other industries) particularly *efficient* or *competitive internationally*.

resource wealth mentality
The view that society's economic wealth is derived mainly from the sale of natural resources, rather than from efficiency in the production of goods and services.

Pressures for Change: Globalization and Competition

During the 1980s, a variety of factors combined to generate such a major increase in international trade, competition, and investment that this phenomenon came to be known as the *globalization* of markets. Some of the factors that contributed to this change were lower tariff barriers and improved computer, communications, and transportation technology that facilitated trade and investment on a global scale. Also, there were increasing numbers of "players" in the marketplace as less developed countries entered into world markets. With globalization came increased international competition, which increased productivity and pushed costs and prices downward.

These changes were especially significant to Canada, which relies heavily upon trade and exports for its economic prosperity. To some Canadian industries, the opening of world markets meant opportunities to export, while to others, it meant foreign competition that presented serious threats.

Canada was slow to respond to the situation as globalization spread during the 1980s. As we saw in Chapter 12, after decades of operating in the small Canadian market behind tariff protection, much of Canada's manufacturing sector was not very efficient and was ill-prepared for stronger international competition. And, despite the importance of trade to its economy, Canada was slow to adapt to this new, more competitive international environment. Rather than look outward to the opportunities presented by the global economy, Canada sought to maintain the "old economic order" described by Michael Porter, by continuing to protect its less efficient producers against competition with tariffs and government subsidies. So, during the 1980s, the efficiency of Canadian industry failed to keep pace with improvements in other nations, and Canada became less internationally competitive, especially in manufacturing.

And as the 1980s unfolded, the costs of Canada's policy of protecting its producers against foreign competition became higher and higher. These included costs to consumers (in the form of higher prices), costs to Canadian exporters (as foreign nations retaliated against Canadian protectionism with barriers against Canadian exports), and lost business investment (as a growing number of successful Canadian businesses expanded into other countries in order to gain access to larger markets). In short, Canada was slow to adapt to the new realities of globalization by becoming more efficient and competitive, and the costs of this failure were mounting as the decade wore on.

The Challenge of Globalization

"We are using Russian engineers living in Israel to design (computer micro) chips that are made in America and then assembled in Asia."

— PETER J. SPRAGUE, CHAIR, NATIONAL SEMICONDUCTOR CORPORATION.

In this new, globalized world economy, multinational corporations search the world for the most economical locations for their investment capital and operations. If a country can attract business investment and the jobs and production that it brings, that country will prosper economically. If it fails to attract investment, it will lag behind economically.

What makes a country an attractive location for business investment? Many people think that the answer is "cheap labour," but the matter is not nearly as simple as that. Cheap labour is only important for labour-intensive manufacturing industries such as clothing and footwear; however, in most industries, such low-wage, semi-skilled labour has been replaced to a great extent by technology. To modern, high-technology industries, the key attraction is not *cheap* labour, but rather *skilled people* with *specialized knowledge*. In addition, a nation needs to have excellent *transportation and communication links* to the rest of the world in order to function effectively as part of the new world economy. According to this view, a nation's key strategic assets economically are now its *education and training systems* and its *transportation and communications infrastructure*—the knowledge and skills of its people and the support systems for bringing the productive use of those skills into play in the global economy.

If a country has a skilled labour force and a sound infrastructure, it will tend to gain business investment and prosper economically. Its skilled workforce will earn high incomes, and its economy will provide its government with a strong tax base, which can be used to invest further in better schools, research, and transportation and communications systems. These features will attract more investment, and the cycle of prosperity can be continued.

In addition, it is advantageous for a country to provide a *stable macroeconomic environment* of solid government finances, low inflation, and low interest rates. Such an environment is more likely to develop a strong saving–investment process and the business confidence (of both domestic and foreign investors) that will generate investment, rising productivity, competitiveness, and prosperity. By contrast, economies with problems of large government deficits and debt, high inflation, and high interest rates are not as attractive a location for business investment, and tend to fall behind in both productivity and competitiveness. So the globalization of the world economy also puts pressure upon governments to pursue moderate and stable macroeconomic policies.

Canada in the 1980s

"The outstanding question at the beginning of 1985 is whether Canada will ride the wave of change or be swamped by it."

— EDWARD CARMICHAEL, C.D. HOWE INSTITUTE

During the 1980s, Canada's economic environment and policies were not well suited to the challenges of globalization. Canadian manufacturers were still protected against import competition by relatively high tariffs, and were falling further behind their foreign counterparts. Canada's rate of inflation was higher than most of its trading partners', and by the late 1980s it was increasing again. And Canada's federal and provincial governments had very large budget deficits and high and rising debt. These problems made Canada less likely as a base for successful businesses in the globalized world economy, and a less attractive destination for investment by multinational corporations.

The Shift in Policy

By the late 1980s, the changing international economic situation was forcing Canada to make some fundamental changes to its economic policies. The first—and most symbolic—such change involved Canada's *trade policy*, with the conclusion in 1989 of the *Canada–U.S. Free Trade Agreement*. This change was a landmark in that it signalled Canada's intention to participate more fully in the increasingly globalized markets of the world. As such, it also signalled a basic shift in Canadian policy toward an emphasis on productivity, competitiveness, and an outward-looking internationalism, rather than on the more inward-looking nationalistic policies that had for many years sheltered Canadian industries and workers from international competition. The Free Trade Agreement was regarded as just the first step in Canada becoming more productive and competitive on a global scale. The expansion of the agreement to include Mexico in the North American Free Trade Agreement in 1994 continued this process, as did the 1995 World Trade Organization agreement. In all of these agreements, Canada gained wider and more secure access to large foreign markets, but had to reduce its own tariffs that had been protecting Canadian producers. This increased exposure to international competition made it particularly important that Canada establish a macroeconomic environment that would help Canadian producers to compete internationally.

To improve Canada's international competitiveness and to make Canada more attractive to investors, much more emphasis was placed on *keeping inflation in check* than had been the case in the past. During the late 1980s and early 1990s, the Bank of Canada determinedly pursued an anti-inflation policy of high interest rates, the effects of which can be seen in the decrease in the rate of inflation in Figure 13-1.

And after the Bank of Canada had pushed the rate of inflation down to about 2 percent, the federal government and the Bank of Canada announced in 1993 their

"For the first 100 years after Confederation, Canada lived off its resources. For the past 16 years, we have lived off our credit. Now we must live off our skills, our wits, our energy and our initiative."
— MICHAEL WILSON, MINISTER OF FINANCE, 1984

"What we've learned is that you have to keep your inflation rate low. That's the only way you're going to keep your interest rates low."
— GORDON THIESSEN, GOVERNOR OF THE BANK OF CANADA, NOVEMBER 1996

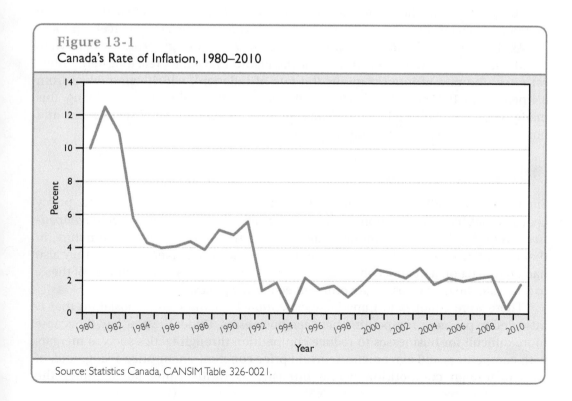

Figure 13-1
Canada's Rate of Inflation, 1980–2010

Source: Statistics Canada, CANSIM Table 326-0021.

"Maintaining these (inflation) targets will allow
markets and investors to
plan with confidence,
knowing that Canada will
remain a low-inflation environment."

— PAUL MARTIN, MINISTER OF
FINANCE, MAY 2001

"For years, governments
have been promising more
than they can deliver, and
delivering more than they
can afford. That has to end.
We are ending it."

— PAUL MARTIN, MINISTER OF
FINANCE, 1994

intention to *keep* the rate of inflation below 3 percent per year. This was a signal that Canada was committed to maintaining a low-inflation environment, in which more stability and *lower interest rates* could be expected in the future. Such an environment would be more favourable to business investment and productivity growth, which would improve Canada's international competitiveness and attractiveness to investors.

The third basic change in economic policy was the federal government's plan to *eliminate its budget deficits*. Setting out its plans in a similar manner as it had done concerning inflation, the government stated its targets for deficit reduction over several years, so as to build confidence that Canada would indeed provide a more stable financial environment than it had in the past.

By the early 1990s, the situation concerning government finances had become critical. The combined budget deficits of all levels of government in Canada amounted to over $50 billion per year. Canada's foreign debt, about half of which was owed by Canadian governments, was by far the largest in the world and rising rapidly. Foreign lenders were beginning to demand higher interest rates because of the risks associated with the financial condition of Canadian governments.

The federal government's budget of 1995 announced large reductions in federal spending over a period of several years. Most of the cuts were to *federal transfer payments to the provinces* for health care, post-secondary education, and welfare. This reduction in provincial revenues led to a series of major spending cuts by the provincial governments on their own programs. Hospital services were reduced, grants to colleges and universities were cut, and welfare benefits were reduced.

At the same time as federal spending was being cut, faster economic growth generated strong increases in federal tax revenues. The result of this combination of spending cuts and rising tax revenues was a sharp reduction in federal budget deficits.

The federal deficit was eliminated in fiscal year 1997–98. In the years that followed, there were budget surpluses, which were partly used to reduce government debt. The federal government's net debt peaked at $609 billion in 1997, and had decreased to $516 billion by 2008. When viewed as a percentage of GDP, the reduction in debt is more dramatic, as Figure 13-2 shows—from 72 percent of GDP in 1996 to 32 percent in 2008.

As the rate of inflation came down and concerns about government debt were eased, interest rates were able to come down. Figure 13-3 shows real long-term interest rates (the rate of interest minus the rate of inflation), which came down from 8.4 percent in 1994 to below 3 percent. By reducing the real cost of borrowing, this made long-term financial undertakings such as business capital investment and home-buying considerably more attractive.

Other Policy Changes

Since the mid-1980s, governments had been introducing various economic policy changes that had the common objective of *increasing the productivity and competitiveness* of the Canadian economy. Many of these were microeconomic in nature, in that they affected specific sectors of the economy; however, taken together, they also had an impact on a macroeconomic scale. The following are some examples of these, to illustrate the new thrust of government economic policy.

There were changes to Canada's *competition legislation*—the legislation that is intended to promote competition between businesses. Under the new law, it became more difficult for businesses to reduce competition through tactics such as mergers with competitors and agreements to avoid price competition, or price-fixing. And, of course, foreign competition would intensify as tariffs came down under the Canada–U.S. Free Trade Agreement, NAFTA, and the 1995 WTO agreement.

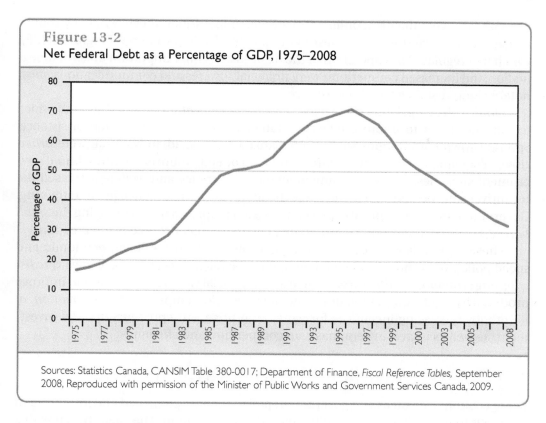

Figure 13-2
Net Federal Debt as a Percentage of GDP, 1975–2008

Sources: Statistics Canada, CANSIM Table 380-0017; Department of Finance, *Fiscal Reference Tables,* September 2008, Reproduced with permission of the Minister of Public Works and Government Services Canada, 2009.

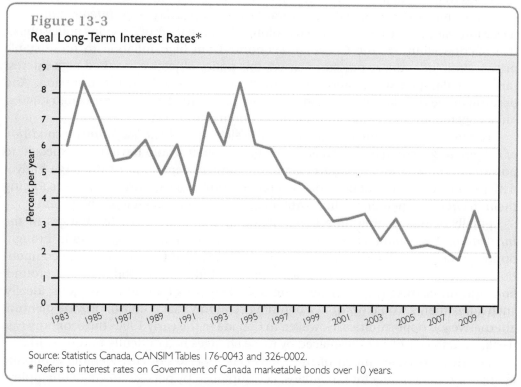

Figure 13-3
Real Long-Term Interest Rates*

Source: Statistics Canada, CANSIM Tables 176-0043 and 326-0002.
* Refers to interest rates on Government of Canada marketable bonds over 10 years.

There was also the **deregulation** of some industries. Over the years, Canada had accumulated a large body of government regulations on business, many of which controlled prices and production and restricted the entry of new competitors into some industries. Many of these regulations had the unintended effect of reducing competition and efficiency in the regulated industries. To improve productivity performance, the government *deregulated* some industries. The most notable examples of such

deregulation
Policies to reduce the extent of regulation of business by government, with the intention of promoting efficiency through increased competition.

deregulation were the dismantling of the Foreign Investment Review Agency (FIRA), which had restricted foreign investment, and the National Energy Program (NEP), which had regulated the operation of the oil industry. Other important areas of deregulation and increased competition were financial services and communications, most notably long-distance telephone service.

www.aircanada.ca

Along with deregulation came *reductions in government subsidies* to business, which forced businesses to improve efficiency rather than rely on government assistance. Several Crown corporations such as Air Canada and Canadian National were *privatized*, or sold to private interests, forcing them to operate more efficiently without government subsidies. Changes to unemployment insurance and welfare increased the incentives for people receiving these benefits to work or engage in retraining. Government policy-makers also placed increased emphasis on encouraging the *small business sector* of the economy, which had become a major source of job creation.

These new policies represented a significant shift in Canadian economic and social policy. Government policies had in the past been directed largely toward *redistributing economic wealth*, through an extensive social welfare system. But to improve productivity and competitiveness, the new policies emphasized the *creation of wealth*, by increasing incentives for work, enterprise, entrepreneurship, and investment, as well as increasing emphasis on competition and efficiency.

The 1990s—A Difficult Period of Transition

These economic changes and government policy changes coincided and interacted in the 1990s to make that decade a difficult period of transition. The 1990s began with a recession that was prolonged by several factors, especially *high interest rates*. The recession was partly caused, and also prolonged, by the Bank of Canada's policy objective of "downshifting" the Canadian economy from high inflation to more stable prices. Until inflationary pressures eased, this policy objective required high interest rates that dampened demand and slowed the recovery from the recession. And because of the time lags involved in monetary policy, the effects of these high interest rates lingered for some time, slowing the economy's recovery.

The recovery from the recession was also slowed by the *weak financial condition of Canadian governments*. Ordinarily, the government would have been expected to boost the recovery with budget deficits to stimulate demand. But the large budget deficits and rising debt of both the federal and provincial governments were forcing them to *cut* their spending, which prolonged the period of high unemployment.

Finally, it was at this time that Canada also had to adjust to changes in the *international economic environment*. While globalization and freer trade brought opportunities for Canadian producers, they also brought increased foreign competition. Many efficient firms enjoyed faster growth, but weaker producers lost ground. For some firms, this meant restructuring and downsizing that eliminated jobs. Ideally, such adjustments would occur in a booming economy that is able to provide plentiful alternative job opportunities. However, in Canada in the early 1990s the economy was weak, so many employees displaced by these changes had difficulty finding work.

For these reasons, much of the 1990s was a period of considerable economic change and uncertainty for Canadians, accompanied by persistently high unemployment rates until quite late in the decade.

As an indication of the extent of change that was taking place over this period, from 1988 (the year before the Canada-U.S. Free Trade Agreement) to 2000, Canada's:

• GDP grew by 76 percent,
• imports grew by 173 percent,

• total exports grew by 199 percent, and
• exports to the United States grew by 241 percent.

This is a picture of an economy undergoing a great deal of change in a quite brief period, at a pace to which Canadians were unaccustomed. Exports were growing very rapidly and imports were penetrating the Canadian market at a greatly increased pace, while at the same time the protections provided by tariffs and government income support programs were being reduced.

Through the Transition

By the late 1990s, economic conditions in Canada had improved considerably. Led by rapidly rising exports to the booming U.S. economy, the Canadian economy had recovered strongly by the late 1990s. In this more stable and positive economic environment, consumer and business confidence improved and aggregate demand gained momentum, pushing the unemployment rate to its lowest level in more than 25 years.

These improvements led the International Productivity Monitor to say, "Canada has performed remarkably well within its peer group of OECD (Organisation for Economic Co-operation and Development) countries since the mid-90s, finally reversing the country's 15-year economic swoon that began at the end of the 1970s."

> Canada's recent macroeconomic performance has been enviable, and has reflected the benefits of sound institutions and a strong policy framework.
> — INTERNATIONAL MONETARY FUND, 2004

Challenges for the Future

By the early 2000s, Canadians could look back with satisfaction from having successfully tackled three major economic challenges in less than a decade: bringing the rate of inflation down after a long period of high inflation rates, ending a 25-year period of government budget deficits and escalating debt, and adjusting from a regime of tariff protection to one of freer trade.

In addition, Canada had the top-rated banking system in the world, relatively sound government finances, and a good labour force.

Looking ahead, it was generally agreed that Canada faced various economic challenges, including

• how to sustain high levels of exports in the face of a higher exchange rate of the Canadian dollar,
• how to diversify its exports among more international markets,
• how to maintain prosperity as growing numbers of baby boomers reached retirement age, and
• how to improve productivity in the Canadian economy.

1. The Higher Exchange Rate of the Canadian Dollar

The low international price of the Canadian dollar during the 1990s that can be seen in Figure 13-4 was a major factor in the strong growth of Canada's exports during that period.

However, as Figure 13-4 also shows, the international price of the Canadian dollar rose after 2002, eventually passing $1.00 U.S. in 2011. This created a much more challenging situation for many Canadian exporters, especially manufacturers.

> An increase in the Canadian dollar from $0.90 US to $1.00 US means that foreign buyers must pay 11 percent more for Canadian dollars.

2. Diversifying Canadian Exports

The combination of the 1989 Canada-U.S. Free Trade Agreement and low exchange rate of the Canadian dollar in the 1990s generated very strong increases in Canada's

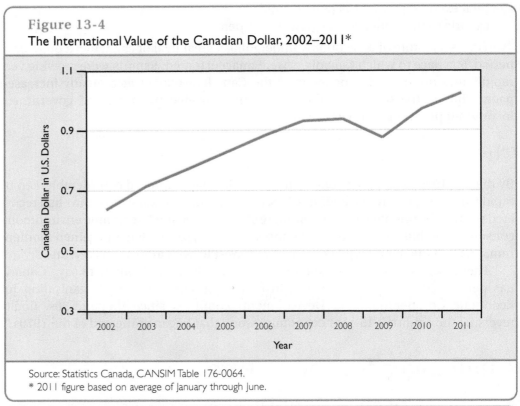

Figure 13-4
The International Value of the Canadian Dollar, 2002–2011*

Source: Statistics Canada, CANSIM Table 176-0064.
* 2011 figure based on average of January through June.

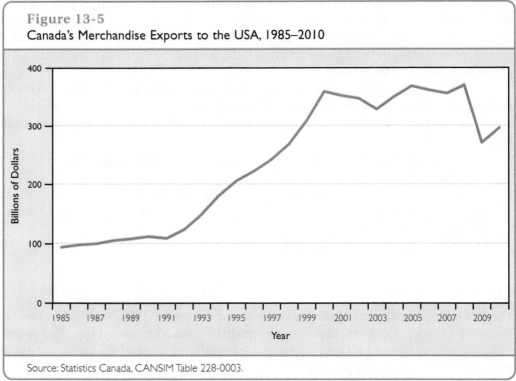

Figure 13-5
Canada's Merchandise Exports to the USA, 1985–2010

Source: Statistics Canada, CANSIM Table 228-0003.

exports to the United States, as can be seen in Figure 13-5. Canada's economic ties to the USA grew to the point that, from 1999 to 2002, nearly 84 percent of all of Canada's exports went to the USA.

However, Figure 13-5 also shows that Canada's exports to the United States stopped increasing after 2000, largely due to the high cost of the Canadian dollar to

Americans, then decreased sharply in 2009–10, due to the severe U.S. recession. With the Canadian dollar expected to remain high against the U.S. dollar (partly because the U.S. dollar was widely expected to weaken due to the USA's economic problems), and with the American recovery from the 2008–09 recession expected to be long and slow, many strategists recommended that Canada seek to diversify its exports to other markets. Recently, the most rapid growth rates have been achieved by emerging nations such as the "BRIC" countries—Brazil, Russia, India, and China, and it expected that Canada's trade with these nations will grow more rapidly than its trade with the United States.

3. The Retirement of the Baby Boomers

The oldest baby boomer reached age 65 in 2011, and many baby boomers will retire before then. For about 20 years, there will be an unusually large number of retirements from Canada's labour force. This will have two effects that will put downward pressure on Canadians' living standards:

- slower growth of the labour force, which would limit the economy's output; and
- a higher proportion of retired people for the working population to support.

4. The Importance of Productivity Improvements

Various steps could be taken that would help to deal with both the productivity and competitiveness of Canadian industry and the retirement of the baby boomers. However, one basic change that would help to address *both* of these challenges would be more rapid productivity growth in Canada.

Higher productivity would hold down the labour costs per unit of Canadian producers, and so help them to compete both in export markets and with imported products. Higher output per worker would certainly help to keep output growing despite slower growth of the labour force as the baby boomers retire. And more output per working Canadian could only help with the country's challenge of supporting a growing number of retired people.

While faster productivity growth would be an excellent solution to various challenges that Canada faces, achieving this goal may not be an easy task. In the words of Peter J. Nicholson, ". . . weak productivity growth, both absolutely and relative to the United States, has been the Achilles' heel of the Canadian economy for the past 25 years."[2]

So productivity growth, which was discussed back in Chapter 3 as a key requirement for economic prosperity, will be a key to Canada's economic future.

Chapter Summary

1. Traditionally, Canada relied on natural resource exports for economic wealth, while government policies were more concerned with redistributing income and providing social welfare programs than with promoting productivity and competitiveness. (L.O. 1)

---

[2] *The Growth Story: Canada's Long-Run Economic Performance and Prospects*, International Productivity Monitor, Fall 2003.

2. The globalization of the world economy presented Canada with great opportunities in the form of larger markets, and great challenges in the form of foreign competition. (L.O. 2)

3. In the globalized world economy, business investment tends to be attracted by a high-quality labour force, strong communication and transportation links to the rest of the world, and a stable economic environment in terms of low inflation rates, low interest rates, and sound government finances. (L.O. 3)

4. Canada was not well prepared for globalization in the 1980s because its industries were protected by tariffs, and it had a high inflation rate and a problem of large government budget deficits and debt. (L.O. 4)

5. In response to globalization, Canada made the following basic changes to its economic policies:

   (a) a commitment to freer trade,
   (b) a commitment to lower inflation,
   (c) a commitment to end federal budget deficits, and
   (d) a variety of other changes intended to strengthen incentives, competition, and productivity. (L.O. 5)

6. The 1990s were a difficult period of transition during which the following developments interacted: a recession, the adjustment to freer trade, the Bank of Canada's anti-inflation policies, and the federal government's spending cuts to end its budget deficits. (L.O. 6)

7. Canada emerged from this transition with a low rate of inflation, sound federal government finances, much lower interest rates, and stronger consumer and business confidence. (L.O. 7)

8. On the negative side, there were continuing concerns about how Canada's weak productivity performance and a higher value of the Canadian dollar would affect Canada's international competitiveness in the future. (L.O. 8)

Questions

1. Briefly describe Canada prior to the 1990s in terms of
   (a) the basic source of its economic wealth, and
   (b) the general thrust of its government economic policies.

2. Globalization presented Canada with both
   (a) opportunities, in the form of _____, and
   (b) threats, in the form of _____.

3. State whether each of the following statements concerning the globalization of the world economy is *true* or *false*.
   (a) _____ Canada responded quickly to globalization pressures in the 1980s.
   (b) _____ Canada's manufacturing sector was generally well-prepared to take advantage of the opportunities presented by globalization in the 1980s.
   (c) _____ In today's world economy, education and training systems are key strategic assets for countries.
   (d) _____ The key attraction for business investment in high-technology industries in the globalized world economy is cheap labour.
   (e) _____ It is important that countries provide a stable macroeconomic environment in terms of low inflation rates and sound government finances.

(f) _____ Canada could not ignore globalization, because Canada relies heavily on exports for its economic prosperity.

(g) _____ In order to adjust to globalization, Canada had to make several basic changes to its economic policies.

4. How did the 1989 Canada–U.S. Free Trade Agreement symbolize a fundamental shift in the direction and goals of Canadian economic policy, and how did the new policy objectives differ from those of the past?

5. In the view of economists, the game (industry) of professional hockey provides a good example of how globalization, or the internationalization of markets, presents Canadians with both challenges and opportunities. Explain why this is the case, taking into account the perspectives of both players and teams.

Study Guide

Review Questions (Answers to these Review Questions appear in Appendix B.)

1. Prior to the 1980s, Canada's traditional source of economic prosperity was in the
   (a) export of manufactured goods.
   (b) export of natural resources.
   (c) inflow of foreign business investment.
   (d) establishment of social welfare programs.
   (e) Answers (a) and (c).

2. A *resource wealth mentality*
   (a) refers to the view that in order to prosper economically, a society must use *all* of its economic resources (labour, capital, and land) efficiently and effectively.
   (b) refers to the view that economic prosperity comes mainly from processing and selling natural resources, rather than efficient and effective production of goods and services.
   (c) can lead to the belief that the government's role is to ensure that the country's economic wealth is distributed fairly among its citizens.
   (d) Answers (b) and (c).
   (e) None of the above.

3. Which of the following factors contributed to *globalization*?
   (a) lower tariffs
   (b) improved communications technology
   (c) lower transportation costs
   (d) more countries entering the global market
   (e) All of the above.

4. When globalization was spreading in the 1980s, much of Canada's manufacturing sector was
   (a) world leaders in technological development and efficiency.
   (b) small scale.
   (c) protected by tariffs against foreign competition.
   (d) inefficient by world standards.
   (e) Answers (b), (c), and (d).

5. State whether each of the following statements is *true* or *false*. Globalization pushed Canadian governments more toward the goal of
   (a) keeping the rate of inflation low. _____
   (b) providing more generous social welfare benefits for those who were adversely affected by globalization. _____
   (c) eliminating government budget deficits. _____
   (d) increasing the efficiency of Canadian producers. _____
   (e) maintaining low interest rates. _____

6. Which of the following factors is usually most important to multinational high-technology corporations in deciding in which countries to locate their production facilities?
   (a) sources of cheap raw materials.
   (b) low wage rates
   (c) a highly educated and skilled workforce.
   (d) Answers (a) and (b).
   (e) None of the above.

7. To improve Canada's ability to compete in the globalized world economy, it was necessary for governments to place more emphasis on policies that would
   (a) improve the productivity of Canadian industry.
   (b) control the growth and market power of large corporations.
   (c) redistribute income from the rich to the poor.
   (d) provide more protection for Canadian jobs against foreign competition.
   (e) None of the above.

8. Which of the following measures were used by Canadian governments to achieve the goal of increased productivity?
   (a) deregulation and competition legislation.
   (b) privatization of government enterprises.
   (c) increased competition from imports.
   (d) reduction of subsidies to businesses.
   (e) All of the above.

9. For Canada, the 1990s could be described as a period of
   (a) steadily rising unemployment.
   (b) large adjustments to changes in the international economic environment.
   (c) increasingly severe inflation.
   (d) increasing protectionism against competition from imports.
   (e) avoiding change.

10. Which of the following statements are *true* and which are *false*? By 2004–08,
   (a) _____ Canada's rate of inflation was remaining low, and within the target range established by the Bank of Canada and the federal government.
   (b) _____ Canada's unemployment rate was still high (nearly 10 percent).
   (c) _____ The federal government continued to have large budget deficits.
   (d) _____ Productivity growth was slow.
   (e) _____ Federal government debt had been reduced from about 70 percent of GDP to less than 35 percent of GDP.

Critical Thinking Questions

(Asterisked questions 1 to 3 are answered in Appendix B; the answers to questions 4 to 7 are in the Instructor's Manual that accompanies this text.)

*1. Some economists argue that a higher international value of the Canadian dollar should be expected to actually *improve* the productivity performance of Canadian industry. Can you think of two logical reasons for believing this?

*2. Over the 2000–2005 period, the federal government introduced a series of cuts to personal and corporate income that by 2004–05 were to reduce personal income taxes by $22.3 billion and corporate income taxes by $4.4 billion. Explain how these tax cuts could be viewed as part of a strategy for improving the performance of the Canadian economy.

*3. Chapter 13 refers to how the federal government used its budget surpluses to pay down the government's debt.

   (a) What are the two other basic types of uses for the government's surpluses?
   (b) How could the government's surpluses be used to promote faster growth of productivity in Canada?

4. What changes to Canada's educational system would you suggest in order to help Canada to meet its economic challenges and achieve its potential?

5. If the federal government began to have large budget deficits again, how would you expect this to affect interest rates in Canada? Why?

6. Because productivity in Canada has been growing more slowly than in the United States, the Conference Board of Canada foresees Canada as being "a comfortable place to live, but in gentle decline relative to the United States." Is it your impression that this is the case, or do you feel that Canada is doing better than that? Why?

7. Canada's economy will face an unusual supply-side challenge when the baby boomers retire. In 2001, 13 percent of Canada's population was over 65 years of age. It was forecast that by 2030, the over-65 group would be 22 percent of the population, and by 2050, 42 percent.

   (a) What are the implications of these forecasts for the living standards of Canadians? (*Hint: think in terms of output* per Canadian *rather than* per worker.)
   (b) What changes could Canada make that would help to avoid the problems in part (a)?

Use the Web   (Hints for these Use the Web exercises appear in Appendix B.)

1. Visit the Industry Canada website at **www.ic.gc.ca**. What services and programs do you see that are intended to help Canadian industry to be more efficient and competitive? Explain how each service or program could help Canada to meet the challenges of being competitive in the globalized world economy.

2. How has productivity growth in Canada's manufacturing sector compared to its U.S. counterpart in recent years? Statistics are available on the website for the U.S. Bureau of Labor Statistics at **www.bls.gov**; click on *Productivity*, then *International Comparisons*.

Answers to Boxed Questions

Chapter 1: What Is Economics?

YOU DECIDE: **Opportunity Cost**

1. Four kilograms of fruit per day. To produce three more kilograms per day of fish would require the transfer of one person from fruit production, where average output per worker was 4 kg per day.
   (a) Your car will not be fixed.
   (b) Your mother will be *very* disappointed—which may or may not involve more severe consequences for you than a broken-down car.

Chapter 2: Introduction to Macroeconomics

IN THE NEWS: **Recent Price Increases**

1. The price of cigarettes increased rapidly due to tax increases that were part of the government's anti-smoking campaign. The most basic factor in tuition fee increases was decreasing government financial support for colleges and universities, which forced them to increase their fees. Rising gasoline prices would explain the increase in transportation costs.
2. A likely explanation of the price decreases is increases in imports of low-cost appliances, clothing and computers. In the case of computers, a special factor was in play—increases in quality, which are recorded by Statistics Canada as if they were price decreases. So if the laptop you buy is the same price but 30 percent more powerful than the 'same' laptop a year ago, this is interpreted as a 30 percent decrease its price.
3. Two factors that tend to push down on the prices of goods more than on the prices of services are increases in the efficiency of producing them (usually due to technology) and imports of lower-cost goods. Services are more difficult to 'automate', and are not traded internationally as much as goods are.

Chapter 3: Sources of Economic Prosperity: The Supply Side

YOU DECIDE: **Sally's Taxes**

1. Sally's marginal rate is 40 percent—the percentage of her extra income (form her second job) that goes to taxes.
2. The marginal tax rate of 40 percent is the key to her incentive to do *additional work*, because this tax rate determines how much of the income from that extra work she will take home (60 percent of it). Sally needs the income from her regular job, so she would not decide to quit that job because the taxes on the income from it were too high. But if her marginal tax rate were too high, she might decide not to work at the second job, because the after-tax income wasn't high enough to make it worth working at a second job.

Chapter 4: Sources of Economic Prosperity: The Demand Side

IN THE NEWS: **Trends in Saving**

1. *Decreasing interest rates* were a key factor underlying the falling saving rate. From 1991 to 2004, the interest rate on a one-year mortgage fell from 10.2 percent to 4.6 percent, and the rate on consumer loans fell from 13.8 percent to 9.2 percent. As lower interest rates encouraged consumer borrowing and spending, less was saved (remember, saving is what's left out of disposable income after spending on consumption). Another factor was the *rising value of households' assets*—corporate

stocks in the late 1990s and early 2000s, and their homes in 2003–05. If the value of their assets is rising, people tend to feel less of a need to save out of their current year's income in order to build assets. A third reason for saving less of their disposable income was the *slow growth of real disposable income* of many families, which meant that to increase their consumption as desired, they had to save less.

2. A negative personal saving rate means that households *as a group* are spending more than their disposable income. This does not mean that *all* households are doing this; indeed, many are saving. But if low interest rates and high consumer confidence lead enough households to borrow and spend, the saving rate for households as a group can be negative.

3. The recession of 2008–09 increased the saving rate, as declining consumer confidence meant that many people would be spending less in general, and cutting back on borrowing to buy "big-ticket" items in particular.

IN THE NEWS: Demand in the Recession
1. Exports decreased the most sharply, because of the severe recession in the United States.

2. Investment spending by business decreased sharply in 2009, while consumption spending continued to grow, although much more slowly. Consumers have to spend most of their income on necessities, whereas businesses do not need to spend on capital investment—they will only do so when they expect that such investments will be profitable, which is not the case during a recession.

3. Government spending was the least affected by the recession, largely because most government spending is on basic public services such as health care and education, the need for which is not reduced by a recession. Also, government spending on programs such as employment insurance and welfare will actually increase during a recession (more on this in Chapter 7).

Chapter 5: Money and the Economic System

YOU DECIDE: Electronic Cash?
1. Consider your own spending patterns and estimate the advantages and disadvantages *for you* of using a cash card. The cost (service charge)

was estimated to be around $3 per month.

2. It has been reported that the cash cards were not as widely used as had been hoped by the banks. One possible reason is that people still found cash more convenient for the large number of small purchases they make in a day. Another is that for larger purchases, they simply used their debit cards, which most people already had.

3. Those who view the "cashless society" as inevitable see it as the final step in the long evolution of money as described in this chapter. Some who see it as impossible stress the *technical difficulties*—would every bubblegum machine, pay toilet, and babysitter in the country have a computer terminal? Others who see it as impossible focus on *psychological obstacles*—many people like the feel of "hard money" in their pockets, and quite a few others might not be keen on having every transaction they ever made recorded on a computer somewhere. Cash is a conveniently private form of payment for various transactions that are frowned upon by the law (and others).

Chapter 6: Booms, Recessions, and Inflation

YOU DECIDE: Where Are We Now?
1. The Output Gap graph will show two important things: first, the *level* of actual GDP relative to capacity output (whether actual GDP is above or below capacity, and by how much), and second, the *trend* of actual GDP relative to capacity output (whether actual GDP is rising or falling relative to capacity output). The actual GDP figures in the output gap graph are for grand total GDP only—they do not break GDP down into its component parts.

2. Statistics Canada's GDP by expenditure figures do break the trends in output and demand down into their component parts, which helps us to understand why the trends shown in the Output Gap are happening.

For example, in the fourth quarter of 2008, the Output Gap showed actual total output falling relative to capacity output, as the recession set in. And Statistics Canada's GDP by expenditure figures showed that this downturn was being caused mainly by decreases in exports, and also by decreases in business investment spending (and spending on new housing, if the figures were examined in more detail).

Chapter 7: Stabilizing the Economy: Government Monetary and Fiscal Policies

IN THE NEWS: Fiscal Policy and the Recession of 2008–09

1. From the quite large size of the projected budget deficits in 2011–12 and 2012–13, it does not appear that the government was expecting the recovery from the recession to be quick.

Chapter 8: Perspectives on Macroeconomic Policy

YOU DECIDE: The 2008–09 Recession and Jobs

1. The recession had the most negative effects upon males and young people, with young males the most severely affected. Males were most affected because the industries that were hit the hardest by falling exports to the USA were the manufacturing industries that employ many males, with automobile manufacturing providing the best example. Construction, which also employs mainly males, also suffered a serious decline. Employment of young people in general is more affected by recessions, because under seniority rules, junior employees are the first to be laid off, and many employers generally discontinue hiring of new entrants to the work force during recessions; in manufacturing during the 2008-09 recession, this was generally the case.

Females were less affected mainly because most women work in service industries, which are usually less affected by recessions and most of which did not rely on exports to the USA.

Chapter 10: The Canadian Dollar in Foreign Exchange Markets

IN THE NEWS: Exchange Rate Changes and Competitive Balance

1. Not forever—sooner or later, the high demand for China's currency from buyers of its exports would drive the price of the currency up, making its exports less attractive. *However*, this may take quite a long time—for reasons that are covered in Chapter 11, it may take 20 years or more for China's yuan to increase to a longer-term equilibrium level. From 2001 to mid-2011, the yuan rose by 28 percent against the U.S. dollar.

IN THE NEWS: The Floating Canadian Dollar as a "Shock Absorber"

1. Many Canadian tourist operators near the U.S. border rely heavily on business from American vacationers. The operators would be delighted (or, at least relieved) by the fact that visits to their facilities would cost Americans about 20 percent less than last year.

2. For Canadian consumers, the situation would be the opposite—they would pay more for goods imported from the United States, and for visits to the USA. For Canadians who spent a lot of time and money in the USA (such as "snowbirds"), the extra cost could be significant.

3. If the Canadian dollar had stayed around $1.00 U.S., the pain of the recession would have been concentrated more on Canadian businesses that sell to Americans, and on the employees of those businesses. Their sales would have been lower, and they would have had to lay off more employees. On the other hand, Canadian consumers would not have had to pay higher prices for U.S. goods and services.

The decline of the Canadian dollar by about 20 percent against the U.S. dollar would mean that the pain of the recession would be spread more widely among Canadians—those businesses and their employees would suffer less, while Canadian consumers would suffer more.

IN THE NEWS: Tar Sands Oil and the Canadian Dollar as a "Petro-Currency"

1. Additional development of the oil sands would increase the international value of the Canadian dollar, for two reasons. First, if foreign capital were used for investment in oil sands projects, the inflow of foreign funds would push the Canadian dollar upwards. And second, the exporting of much of the oil would put additional upward pressure on the Canadian dollar.

2. All Canadians would benefit economically from the higher international value of their currency, which would make imports less costly.

3. If the oil sands developments were on a large enough scale to push the Canadian dollar upwards to a significant extent, the higher dollar could make it more difficult for Canadian manufacturers (most of which are located in central Canada) to export, because foreign buyers would have to pay more for Canadian dol-

lars. A higher Canadian dollar would also make it harder for Canadian manufacturers to compete with imports, which would be made cheaper for Canadians by the higher dollar.

Chapter 11: The Global Economy

YOU DECIDE: **The Bond Price–Interest Rate Connection**

1. The bonds pay interest of $60 per year. So as the price of the bonds goes up, the interest rate that the bonds paid decreases. As the question notes, someone who bought one of these bonds for $1000 would earn an interest rate of 6 percent ($60 ÷ $1000 × 100). But someone who paid $1070 for that bond would only be earning 5.6 percent ($60 ÷ $1070 × 100). Large purchases of U.S. government bonds by China would push the price of those bonds higher, which would make interest rates lower.

2. Bond prices and interest rates move in opposite directions. Higher bond prices mean lower interest rates, and vice-versa. Viewed from the other direction, the higher interest rates go, the lower bond prices go, and vice-versa.

YOU DECIDE: **The Housing Price Bubble and Subprime Mortgages**

1. (a) The housing bubble was likely to burst, and it did. Price bubbles inflate because buyers believe that prices will rise and rise, but after a certain point, people begin to believe that prices will stop rising or even fall. At that point, more and more people will be anxious to sell, but there will be *no one who wants to buy*. So the U.S. housing bubble would burst, and prices would fall sharply. This started in 2006-07.

(b) Many Americans found that the value of their assets (mainly homes) had fallen, but their debts were still there, as large as ever. They no longer had the collateral (equity in their homes) to support further borrowing, and some even found that the mortgage debt on their homes was greater than the market value of the homes. American consumer confidence plunged dramatically, and consumer spending fell as many people switched suddenly from borrowing and spending to saving and paying down debt, which led the U.S. economy into a recession.

YOU DECIDE: **Beware of Simple Solutions**

1. If China reduced its purchases of U.S. government bonds, the prices of those bonds would fall due to lower demand for them. And as the price of U.S. government bonds fell, the interest rate on them would rise. This is the exact opposite of the situation in the previous box on the bond price–interest rate connection—if China is less willing to supply loanable funds to the U.S., the price of borrowing (the interest rate) will be higher. In this example, the interest rate would increase to 6.5%, calculated as $60 ÷ $930 × 100.

2. A higher value of the yuan would mean that U.S. consumers would have to pay higher prices for the quite large amounts of Chinese consumer goods that they were buying. This would reduce their standard of living.

But there would be a second effect, which is less well understood but potentially more serious—the increase in interest rates that would probably accompany the upward movement of the yuan.

3. U.S. consumers were very heavily in debt by late 2005. Much of this debt was short-term in nature (credit cards and short-term mortgage loans), which would mean that an increase in interest rates would hit these households with higher interest costs very quickly.

If interest rates went up by a significant amount, the effects on many U.S. households could be serious. At the very least, they would have to cut back on their consumption of goods and services in order to make higher monthly interest payments; more likely, they would also focus on paying down debt rather than borrow more to finance consumption spending. In short, spending by American consumers would decrease.

And since U.S. consumers were the main source of demand for goods and services in the world economy, aggregate demand could be depressed not only in the U.S., but around the world.

Chapter 12: Canada in the Global Economy

IN THE NEWS: **NAFTA Has Helped Curb U.S. Protectionism**

1. The short answer is that in the case of most Canadian appeals, the U.S. has been in the

wrong, but the real question is *why* this has so often been the case. A key reason is that U.S. law almost encourages American industries to file complaints of unfair import competition, as a tactic to harass successful foreign competitors. And once such a complaint has been filed, U.S. authorities have tended to pursue it without much critical examination. Even if the complaint is thrown out when appealed to a neutral panel, this process can take a long time, during which obstacles are put in the way of the imports. Canada (and other nations) has protested this as a "hit and run" harassment tactic, and neutral panels have often agreed with them.

2. The neutral parties who sit on the panels that hear these appeals are members of a small professional community of highly respected experts in their field. They are aware of the sort of problems described in the answer to the previous question, and would not want to tarnish their respective reputations for objective neutrality by taking the side of their own country when that country is clearly in the wrong.

Answers to Study Guide Questions

Chapter 1

REVIEW QUESTIONS

1. c
2. e
3. a
4. a
5. d
6. b
7. c
8. b
9. d
10. e
11. c
12. e
13. (a) True
    (b) True
    (c) False
    (d) True
    (e) False
14. (a) False
    (b) True
    (c) True
    (d) False
    (e) True
15. c

CRITICAL THINKING QUESTIONS

1. Not at all—Rupinder has many more dollars, but still has only has a limited number of dollars. Every dollar that Rupinder spends on one thing means that there is one less dollar available to spend on other things.

2. The opportunity cost consists of the other things that you could have had if you had not devoted your resources to attending school. The obvious opportunity costs involve the *money* spent on school (tuition, books, and so on); however, you must also include the opportunity cost of the *time* devoted to school. For instance, if you could have worked and earned $25 000 instead of attending school, that should be considered an opportunity cost.

3.
(a) Improve *both* efficiency and effectiveness, by giving employees a financial incentive to perform better in *all* ways.

(b) Improve *both* efficiency and effectiveness, by reducing labour costs (efficiency) and eliminating imprecision in the production process (effectiveness).

(c) Improve efficiency by increasing the productivity of servers, as measured by the number of tables served per server. Another way of measuring the increase in efficiency would be the decrease in labour cost per table (or per meal) served.

4. Competition among producers pushes producers to use resources effectively and efficiently but also forces them to *keep prices down*. If there were no competition (that is, a monopoly), the producer could charge much higher prices. The same idea applies to producers getting together and agreeing on their price, which is illegal in Canada. Probably the most attractive aspect of the market system is that it does a good job of benefiting consumers, who are portrayed as "kings of the marketplace." However, if there were no competition, producers, not consumers, would be the dominant force in markets.

5.
(a) Market element: Consumers are directing the use of economic resources by buying more goat meat, which will cause its price to increase, which will encourage more production of goat meat. No government action is involved.

(b) Command element: Governments are directing the use of economic resources toward education by using tax funds to finance education at no cost to users.

(c) Market element: The oversupply will drive prices down, which will encourage buyers to buy more computers, and producers to adjust their production. No government action is involved.

(d) Command element: Due to concerns that the merger of two such large firms would create monopoly-like power in the marketplace, the government is directing that the merger not take place.

(e) Command element: The government is directing that the market's distribution of income ("division of the economic pie") be altered so that lower-income citizens receive a larger share.

(f) Market element: This situation was essentially the negotiation of a price (the compensation of players) by private buyers (the hockey clubs) and private sellers (the players). The decision was made by these parties, not the government.

USE THE WEB

1. A search for *productivity* is likely to turn up some good information. On the other hand, a search the words *effectiveness* and *efficiency* is less likely to be productive, since articles are unlikely to use these exact terms. Instead, look at an item and ask yourself whether you can apply the concepts of effectiveness and efficiency to it.

Chapter 2

REVIEW QUESTIONS

1. the market value of the total annual output of final goods and services produced
2. c
3. d
4. a
5. b
6. d
7. The general level of prices has increased.
8. b (money GDP increased by 3 percent, but prices increased by 4 percent, so real GDP decreased by 1 percent)
9. b
10. 130.0 (125.0 × 1.04)
11. how fast prices are *rising* (in percentage terms)

12.
(a) 50
(b) 10 (500 000 unemployed out of a labour force of 5 000 000)

13.
(a) structural
(b) frictional
(c) cyclical
(d) seasonal
(e) structural

14. a

15. c

CRITICAL THINKING QUESTIONS

1. The economy is in a boom, the most basic cause of which would be high and rising aggregate demand.

2. The economy is in a recession, the most basic cause of which would be low and falling aggregate demand.

3.
(a) 2000: 2.7 percent, 2001: 2.6 percent, 2002: 2.2 percent
(b) the CPI went *up*, but the rate of inflation went *down*
(c) In each of 2001 and 2002, the CPI *went up*, but it went up *more slowly* than the previous year. In other words, the CPI itself went up, but its rate of increase (the rate of inflation) *decreased*.

4. (a)

Year	Labour Force (000)	Employed (000)	Unemployed (000)	Unemployment Rate
2002	16 580	15 308	1 272	7.7%
2003	16 954	15 665	1 289	7.6%

(b) In 2003, the number of unemployed people increased, while the unemployment rate decreased.

(c) The size of the labour force increased, so that even though more people were unemployed, they represented a small percentage of the (larger) labour force.

5.
(a) The participation rate probably decreased because as unemployment increased some people gave up looking for work because they did not expect to find any.

(b) The 1993 unemployment rate would have been 13.7 percent rather than the 11.4 percent that was actually recorded. If the participation rate had been at the 1989 level of 67.2 percent, the labour force would have been 14 904 758 and unemployment would have been 2 047 758. The calculations follow:

	1993 (actual)	1993 with 1989 participation rate
Population 15 years and over	22 179 700	22 179 700
Participation Rate	65.4%	67.2% (same as in 1989)
Labour Force	14 504 500	14 904 758
Employment	12 857 000	12 857 000
Unemployment	1 647 500	2 047 758
Unemployment Rate	11.4%	13.7%

USE THE WEB

1. To assess trends, look at the *percentage increases* in the GDP and in the various components of the GDP. Using percentages allows you to compare changes in numbers of very different sizes. The releases from Statistics Canada usually provide explanations of why the various components of GDP changed as they did.

2. The releases from Statistics Canada normally state whether inflation is speeding up or slowing down, and identify which components of the CPI are causing any trend.

Chapter 3

REVIEW QUESTIONS

1. c
2. a
3. b
4. b
5. a
6. c
7. d
8. d
9.
(a) the profit motive
(b) competition
10.
(a) 95 percent—the taxman took 19/20ths of their additional income.
(b) No, this tax rate did not apply to *all* of their income—only the highest "slice" of their income was taxed at that rate (the income *above* the level at which the 95 percent marginal tax rate started to be applied).
(c) Excessively high tax rates can be self-defeating, in the sense that the government's tax revenues can actually be *reduced* by them, as people find

ways to avoid paying such high taxes. In the extreme, people may leave the high-tax jurisdiction, as the Rolling Stones did. Or people may evade the taxes, by not declaring income or by engaging in black market activity.

11.
(a) 22.0 percent
(b) 33.3 percent
12. 40 percent ($8000 of additional tax on $20 000 of additional income)
13.
(a) 100 (10 workers each producing 10 units per day)
(b) increase the number of people working (if all 15 people of working age each produced 10 units per day, real GDP would be 150 units per day)
(c) increase output per worker (if the current 10 workers each produced 15 units per day, real GDP would be 150 units per day)
14.
(a) 1.6
(b) 1.4
(c) 3.0
15. e

CRITICAL THINKING QUESTIONS

1.
(a) Economic resources could be used to produce consumer goods or capital goods. Consumer goods provide benefits to people *in the present*, while capital goods provide benefits *in the future*, by increasing productivity. By doing without some consumer goods now ("saving"), people can make resources available for the production of capital goods that will increase their standard of living in the future.
(b) There are two aspects to this process—saving and investment. Governments can encourage people to save with tax incentives such as registered retirement saving plans, and lower taxes on profits would leave businesses with more "business savings." Tax incentives could also be used to encourage businesses to invest in capital equipment. And since new productive technologies often spring from research, government tax incentives for research and development spending by businesses and government support for basic research can also promote investment.
2.
(a) Most people focus on how such investments benefit the businesses (lower costs, increased production capacity, and so on). However, if

Canadian businesses are more efficient and more effective, Canadians in general will benefit as consumers, due to lower prices, better service, and so on.

(b) The opportunity cost of this investment is the other things that could have been produced instead—perhaps the resources devoted to the corporate computers could have been used to produce more of the companies' consumer goods.

3.

(a) What they mean is that for every five hours of overtime that they work, the income from two of those hours is taken by taxes, so they get to keep the income from three of those hours.

(b) 40 percent (two hours out of every five goes to taxes)

4.

(a) 80 000 units of output per year (200 workers × 400 units each)

(b) 83 232 units of output per year (204 workers × 408 units each)

(c) 4.0 percent (the increase is 3232 units, which is 3232/80 000 = 4.0 percent)

(d) 82 416 units of output per year (204 workers × 404 units each)

5. Canada's productivity performance has been lagging behind that of its major trading partners, which increases the risk that Canadian producers may have difficulty competing with their foreign counterparts who are growing more efficient more rapidly. Also, if Canada's productivity growth continues to lag behind that of other nations, the standard of living of Canadians will fall further behind those nations. There is also the risk that a nation with low productivity might be a less attractive destination for job-creating investment by multinational business firms.

USE THE WEB

1. This source will provide productivity statistics for Canada's business sector for each quarter (a quarter is a three-month period), and usually compares recent Canadian productivity growth with past growth rates and with productivity growth in the United States.

Chapter 4

REVIEW QUESTIONS

1. d

2. total spending in the economy on goods and services

3.

(a) 60

(b) disposable income

(c) consumer confidence and interest rates

4. saving is $20 billion; 4 percent

5.

(a) lower personal saving rate, because lower interest rates encourage more borrowing and consumer spending, which means less saving

(b) higher personal saving rate, because lower consumer confidence means less borrowing and consumer spending, which means more saving

6. b

7. d

8.

(a) spending by business on capital goods

(b) 10–12 percent

9. b

10.

(a) decrease (This will make it more costly for business to borrow.)

(b) increase (This will increase business confidence.)

(c) decrease (This will make investment projects less profitable after taxes, and will reduce the after-tax profits available for investment.)

11. Investment increases productivity, which increases the standard of living.

12.

(a) consumption

(b) saving (income not spent on consumption)

(c) consumption

(d) investment

(e) consumption

(f) saving (income not spent on consumption)

(g) consumption (purchase of the service of the stockbroker)

13.

(a) 21 percent

(b) public services (health care, education, security, etc.)

14. b

15. e

CRITICAL THINKING QUESTIONS

1.

(a) increases aggregate demand, because consumer spending will increase.

(b) increases aggregate demand, because investment spending will increase.

(c) decreases aggregate demand, because consumer spending will decrease.

(d) decreases aggregate demand, because of less spending on Canadian-made goods.

(e) decreases aggregate demand, because borrowing and spending by consumers and businesses will be decreased.

(f) decreases aggregate demand, because consumer and business confidence and spending will be decreased.

(g) increases aggregate demand, because consumer spending will increase.

(h) increases aggregate demand, because exports to the United States will increase.

2.

(a) Aggregate demand would increase even further, and get even closer to the economy's capacity output.

(b) (i) Real GDP would rise rapidly until it reached capacity. After aggregate demand had reached capacity, the rate of growth of real GDP would be limited to roughly 3 percent per year (the rate at which capacity output can increase).

(ii) Employment would increase until the economy reached capacity and full employment was reached. After that, employment could only increase at about the same pace as the economy could grow, as explained in (i).

(iii) The rate of inflation would increase (i.e., prices would rise faster) as aggregate demand approached the economy's capacity output. If aggregate demand exceeded the economy's capacity output, prices would increase very rapidly.

3.

(a) Aggregate demand would decrease further, and fall farther below the economy's capacity output.

(b) (i) Real GDP would decrease due to falling demand.

(ii) Employment would decrease due to falling demand, and unemployment would increase.

(iii) The rate of inflation would fall (i.e., prices would increase less rapidly), due to the lack of demand in the economy.

4. New automobiles are costly, so purchases of them are often financed by borrowing money. Consumers are more willing to borrow when economic conditions are good and their confidence is high. During recessions, many consumers are less willing to take on debt. Also, for many people, the purchase of a new car can be postponed—if they are uncertain about borrowing, they can "make do" with their current car until economic conditions improve.

5. This is because output is rising *in response to an increase in demand*. If output were to rise spontaneously, *without* an increase in demand, there would indeed be downward pressure on prices. This happens in markets for individual products, such as when there is a large harvest of corn. However, on a macroeconomic scale, increases in the total output of the economy are typically caused by higher aggregate demand, often accompanied by greater inflationary pressures.

USE THE WEB

1. Look for two aspects of recent consumer spending trends—*what* are the trends, and *why* are these trends happening?

2. Compare the trends in consumer confidence and business confidence—are they moving in the same direction, and why?

Chapter 5

REVIEW QUESTIONS

1. b

2. d

3.

(a) medium of exchange (used for making purchases)

(b) standard of value (for comparing the values and costs of items)

(c) store of value (a way of saving purchasing power)

4.

(a) store of value

(b) medium of exchange

(c) standard of value

(d) store of value

5. e

6. bank deposits

7. c

8. d

9. 5 percent ($25/$500)

10. $200 ($12 billion/.06)

11.

(a) True

(b) False

(c) False

(d) False

(e) True

(f) False

12.

(a) False

(b) True

(c) True

(d) False (books entries can be money, if people agree to use them as money)

(e) False (they are by far the largest single form of money)

13. e

14. e

15.

(a) M1 = $480 billion

(b) M2 = $1000 billion

CRITICAL THINKING QUESTIONS

1. Like other businesses, banks earn profits on the services that they provide. On their loans, their profit comes from the difference ("spread") between the interest rate that they pay on deposits and the interest rate that they charge on their loans. However, what is *very different* about banks is that when they make loans, the amount of money in circulation (in the form of book-entry money in the accounts of people and businesses) increases, which means that the money supply of the country increases. Because of this, banking, unlike other businesses, has far-reaching effects on the economy.

2.

(a) The person who paid with cash is the only one who actually paid with money that could be spent immediately. A cheque is not money; it is an instruction to a bank to pay money that is in the dress buyer's bank account to the store. The bank credit card is not money; it just sets in motion a process in which the bank will pay the merchant and in effect lend the purchase price to the buyer of the dress, who will repay the bank at a later date.

(b) In the case of the cheque, the store receives a written instruction to the dress buyer's bank to pay the store the amount of the purchase. In the case of the bank credit card, the store receives assurance that the bank will pay the store for the amount of the purchase.

3.

(a) The declaration of the government that, "This note is legal tender" certainly helps to make the $20 bank note acceptable. However, the real key

to the acceptability of the bank note is the confidence that other people will accept it as payment for $20 worth of goods and services. And underlying this confidence is faith in the monetary authorities of Canada (the Bank of Canada)—confidence that they are issuing "good" money that will hold its value.

(b) The actual value of a $20 bill is what it will buy, or its *purchasing power*. The purchasing power of the $20 bill would increase if the general level of prices fell, and it would decrease if (more probably) the general level of prices increased.

4. Many merchants feel that if a customer says he or she (really) has funds in a bank account and is prepared to write a cheque on it, why shouldn't the customer be prepared to just have the funds electronically withdrawn on the spot using a debit card?

5. If a recession were expected, banks would become more concerned about the risk that borrowers might be unable to repay loans. People who had borrowed might be laid off, and businesses might suffer financial difficulties that prevented them from repaying loans. These concerns might cause banks to be more cautious, and reluctant to make loans, which would further depress aggregate demand and the money supply, which would increase the risk that the recession would become more severe.

USE THE WEB

1. This is a research question.

Chapter 6

REVIEW QUESTIONS

1. fluctuations in aggregate demand—during recessions, aggregate demand falls below the capacity output of the economy, while at other times aggregate demand rises past the capacity output of the economy, and causes inflation.

2. b

3. e

4. a

5. d

6. a

7. b

8. c

9. d

10. c

11. b

12. c

13. a
14. d
15. c

CRITICAL THINKING QUESTIONS

1. Building materials manufacturers, because they produce capital goods. Business spending on capital goods generally decreases considerably during recessions.

2. Automobile manufacturing, because during recessions, people tend to cut back on purchases of such big-ticket items, the purchasing of which usually requires borrowing.

3.

(a) Assembly line workers in auto manufacturing plants would probably suffer high unemployment. During a recession, low consumer confidence causes the demand for "big-ticket" items such as cars to fall, as people are more reluctant to borrow.

(b) Servers in exclusive restaurants would probably not be affected that much. Most of the people who eat at such restaurants (professionals, executives, etc.) would not be seriously affected by a recession.

(c) Workers 25 years of age and older would be less affected than younger workers. In a recession, many employers lay off younger workers first, either because of union agreements or a desire to retain experienced workers.

(d) Young people (age 15–24) would suffer higher unemployment in a recession, for the reasons in part (c). Also, during a recession the fact that many employers are not hiring new employees hits younger workers just entering the labour force especially hard.

(e) Female workers (in general) do not suffer as large an increase in unemployment as male workers. The industries that are hardest hit by a recession (construction, steel, automobile manufacturing, etc.) are major employers of males, while most females work in office and service industries, which suffer less severe employment downturns in recessions.

(f) Young male workers are particularly severely affected by recessions, for the reasons in parts (d) and (e)—many young males work in industries that are more severely affected by recessions, and their youth makes them more vulnerable to layoffs and to the fact that employers are not hiring.

4.

(a) It would be logical to expect that the unemployment rate would increase. The leading indicator provides an "advance indication" of the direction of aggregate demand, so decreases in it would make a downturn of demand likely in the near future.

(b) It would be logical to expect that the rate of inflation would decrease, because a downturn of demand seems likely.

(c) It would be logical to expect that interest rates would decrease. When the economy slows down, interest rates tend to decrease—lenders become less concerned about inflation, and they need to reduce interest rates to induce people to borrow money when confidence is reduced by concerns about recession.

5. Inflation could grow more severe because of various factors. The respending effect of the multiplier would be adding to already-high levels of demand, pushing aggregate demand higher. The accelerator effect could kick in as rising consumer spending generates investment, adding to aggregate demand. High levels of consumer and business confidence would probably generate considerable borrowing, which would boost the money supply and add to aggregate demand. And if the rate of inflation increased to the point that people became concerned about inflation, *inflation psychology* could become a problem—if people tried to protect themselves against inflation by getting large pay increases and by buying now before prices rose, they would add to inflationary pressures.

USE THE WEB

1. This is a research question, the answers to which will vary depending on when the research is done.

2. This site will show only the graph of the statistics, so you will need to interpret the graph. The horizontal line labelled *0* represents capacity output, and the other line represents the level of aggregate demand. Is the level of demand below or above capacity output, and is it rising or falling?

3. This is a research question, the answers to which will vary depending on when the research is done.

Chapter 7

REVIEW QUESTIONS

1. stabilize the economy (smooth out fluctuations in aggregate demand; reduce the severity of the business cycle)

   Monetary policy uses changes in interest rates and the money supply to influence the level of aggregate demand; fiscal policy uses changes to the government's budget.

2. e
3. d
4. a
5. e
6. d
7. c
8. d
9. a
10. b
11. c
12. d
13.
   (a) deficit
   (b) increase
   (c) recession (high unemployment)
14. b
15.
   (a) surplus
   (b) decrease
   (c) inflation
16. e
17. a
18. c

CRITICAL THINKING QUESTIONS

1.
(a) The Bank of Canada wants to slow down inflation (reduce the rate of inflation).
(b) Any industry or occupation that would be particularly affected by higher interest rates—for example, housing construction and construction workers, capital goods and workers in such industries, real estate, steel, and so on.
(c) It would probably have a negative effect on stock prices, by creating expectations of an economic slowdown due to higher interest rates.
(d) The effect may be through interest rates on student loans or credit card balances, or through the effect of higher interest rates on the availability of part-time work for students or the effect on family finances.

2. About $10 billion, calculated as follows: with aggregate demand at $800 billion, a 2-percent decline would mean a loss of about $16 billion in demand (2 percent of $800 billion). If the government injected $10 billion of additional spending into the economy, a multiplier of 1.6 would magnify its effect to $16 billion in about one year, filling the shortfall in demand. The amount of spending needed would be calculated as follows:

   Increase in spending $\times$ 1.6 = 16 billion
   Increase in spending = $16 billion/1.6
   = $10 billion

3. The Bank of Canada could reduce interest rates. Lower interest rates would boost aggregate demand in the Canadian economy generally, and would contribute to a lower international price of the Canadian dollar, which would make Canadian exports less costly to foreign buyers. It would also make imports more costly to Canadian buyers, increasing the probability that they would buy Canadian-made goods.

4. It would make it more likely that the Bank of Canada would reduce interest rates. The decrease in the U.S. leading indicator makes an economic downturn in the United States more likely, and since much of Canada's output is exported to the United States, this could depress aggregate demand in the Canadian economy. To offset such a reduction in demand, the Bank of Canada could reduce interest rates in Canada.

5.

   The key to this phenomenon is that when making their decisions, investors do not look *at the present*, but rather *at the future*. Seeing the boom grow even stronger can lead them to expect *more inflation and higher interest rates* in the near future.

   Higher interest rates would drive stock prices lower, for two reasons. First, higher interest rates increase the probability of an economic slowdown, in which business profits would fall. Second, people's savings can be invested in two basic ways: in shares of companies or in interest-earning investments such as bonds. Higher interest rates make bonds relatively more attractive as an investment. This pulls more savings toward bonds as an investment, leaving less for the buying of stocks, which in turn depresses the demand for stocks, causing their prices to fall.

Knowing this, many investors will seek to sell their shares *before* stock prices fall. As a result, the stock market often falls *before* a boom turns into a slowdown or a recession, making stock prices one of the "leading indicators" described in Chapter 6. The opposite tends to happen during a recession, as lower interest rates lead to higher stock prices *before* the economy has really recovered.

USE THE WEB

1. In looking for relationships between variables (statistics) over a period of time, it can be useful to draw a simple graph of the statistics over a period of a few years. To make the statistics comparable from year to year, be sure to use the *unemployment rate* (the *percentage* of the labour force unemployed) and the *rate of inflation* (the *percentage increase* in the consumer price index from year to year).

Chapter 8

REVIEW QUESTIONS

1. b
2. a
3. d
4. b
5. c
6. a
7. e
8. d
9. a
10. (a) True
(b) True
(c) False
(d) True
(e) True
11. increase, because these policies work by depressing aggregate demand.
12.

Year	Government Spending	Tax Revenues	Budget Deficit (–) or Surplus (+)	National Debt
1	$20	$20	$0	$100
2	24	21	−3	103
3	29	24	−5	108
4	27	28	+1	107

13.
(a) Yes
(b) No
(c) Yes
(d) No
(e) Yes

14. b
15. e

CRITICAL THINKING QUESTIONS

1. Frictional unemployment should increase during a boom, because with employment high and rising, there are more job openings into which people can move.

2.
(a) The main economic problem is a high and rising rate of inflation—the rate of inflation is nearly 4 percent per year (above the Bank of Canada's 3-percent ceiling) and is still rising. Don't be misled by the fact that the unemployment rate of 7 percent is higher than the inflation rate—7 percent is considered to be "full employment," and the unemployment rate is still falling.
(b) Aggregate demand is very high, and seems to have reached the capacity output of the economy.
(c) A tight money policy of higher interest rates would slow down borrowing and spending, which would hold down the rate of inflation by depressing aggregate demand in the economy.
(d) A budget surplus (government tax revenues in excess of government spending) would help to hold down the rate of inflation, by depressing aggregate demand in the economy.
(e) These policies would probably cause higher unemployment, because they depress the level of aggregate demand in the economy.

3.
(a) The government could pay down its debt, increase spending on government programs, or reduce taxes.
(b)
(i) $291 per Canadian for the year ($9 600 000 000/33 000 000)
(ii) 80 cents per Canadian per day ($291/365)

4. One reason for this expectation was that if the rate of inflation were lower and more stable, lenders would be willing to accept lower interest rates because they would be less concerned about the effect of inflation on the purchasing power of their capital. Another reason for expecting lower interest rates was that if the federal government's finances were visibly under better control, lenders would regard Canadian government debt as less risky and would be willing to accept lower interest rates on it.

5. Suppose the government had a balanced budget when a decrease in aggregate demand caused

unemployment to increase. This would have an automatic negative effect on the government's budget in two ways: it would increase government spending on employment insurance, and it would reduce government tax revenues because unemployed people pay less income tax because their incomes are lower. The result would be that the government would now have a budget deficit.

If the government were required by law to balance its budget, it would now be forced to reduce government spending and/or increase taxes in order to prevent a budget deficit from happening. However, a reduction in government spending or a tax increase would push aggregate demand lower, making the recession more severe. And as more jobs were lost, the government would have to cut its spending and/or increase taxes further, creating a downward spiral of falling demand, employment, and incomes.

USE THE WEB

1.
(a) Check the statistics for the most recent five years, and look for trends.
(b) Economic conditions (such as a boom or recession) can affect the employment rate, the unemployment rate, and the participation rate.

Chapter 9

REVIEW QUESTIONS
1. b
2. c
3. a
4. d
5. b
6. d
7. b
8. e
9. c
10. c
11. d
12. b
13. b
14.
(a) lowering of trade barriers (freer trade)
(b) improvements in communications technology

(c) reductions in transportation costs
(d) entry of members of the former Soviet bloc into the world economy
15. d

CRITICAL THINKING QUESTIONS
1. This question involves a recap of many of the key points in this chapter, such as the following:
   - Such action would be a violation of trade agreements and would probably be appealed by our trading partners and overturned by a neutral panel of experts.
   - It would expose Canada to retaliation that would hurt our export industries and jobs in those industries.
   - As a nation that is highly dependent upon exports, it is not in Canada's interest to get into trade disputes, much less start them.
   - The industry has been sheltered by tariffs for many years and should have become more competitive by now.
   - Some foreign competition will force it to become more efficient and competitive.
   - Tariffs would mean that consumers would have to pay higher prices.
2. The problem with this proposal is that Canada's trading partners could (and would) retaliate by imposing tariffs on Canadian exports to their countries, which would increase unemployment in Canada's export industries (as well as cause higher prices in Canada). Such action by Canada would be a violation of trade agreements, under which Canada's trading partners would be legally allowed to retaliate with tariffs of their own.
3. Because free trade increases productivity and reduces production costs, trade makes it possible for all involved to enjoy a higher standard of living. A trade war (which might be more accurately called a tariff war) has the opposite effect—in all countries participating in the trade war, tariffs reduce competition and increase prices. Furthermore, the economies of scale made possible by larger export markets are lost, pushing production costs and prices higher. The overall effect is that the standard of living in all nations that are party to a trade war will be reduced. The loss of jobs associated with reductions in exports would also be costly and disruptive.

4. The simplest explanation is merely national-ism, which generates an us-versus-them view of international matters. A more sophisticated explanation would be based on concerns that, due to differences regarding various factors such as wages, labour standards, environmen-tal laws, and so on, there may not be a level playing field between producers in different countries. That said, economic nationalists always seem to manage to identify factors that *reduce* the competitiveness of their country's producers, while overlooking their nation's advantages and ignoring statistics that refute their arguments, which takes the discussion back to the emotional us-versus-them basis.

5. This statement is supported by the available statistical evidence. After years of freer trade and technological change, the unemployment rate in Canada was lower after 2000 than in pre-vious years, and reached a 32-year low in 2006. But the new jobs that were being created were different from the jobs of the past—the vast majority were in service industries rather than goods-producing industries, and most of the new jobs involved higher skills than in the past.

These changes on the demand side of the job market led to shortages of many types of skilled workers that caused their incomes to increase faster. But due to technology and freer trade, the number of jobs for less-skilled work-ers grew slowly or even decreased in some cases, so their incomes grew slowly (or even fell, when adjusted for inflation). The result has been a gradual widening of the pay gap between skilled and less-skilled workers.

USE THE WEB

1. In looking for explanations any trends in exports or imports, consider broad economic forces such as booms or recessions. For instance, it was expected that in 2009, the recession would depress not only exports, but also imports. Also, remember that the export and import statistics are in dollars, so they are affected not only by changes in the *amount* of exports or imports, but also by changes in their *prices*. Price changes can be important with respect to Canada's exports of natural resources such as crude oil, the price of which soared dur-ing the economic boom of 2007, then collapsed in the second half of 2008.

Chapter 10

REVIEW QUESTIONS

1. The international price of the Canadian dollar would
   (a) fall, due to increased selling of Canadian dollars.
   (b) rise, due to increased buying of Canadian dollars.
   (c) fall, due to increased selling of Canadian dollars.
   (d) rise, due to increased buying of Canadian dollars.
2. d
3. a
4. c
5. *rise*, which would cause payments to *increase* and receipts to *decrease*.
6. c
7.
(a)
   (i)   False
   (ii) True
   (iii) False
   (iv) False
(b) deficit
(c) fall
(d) exporters—paying less for Canadian dollars would make Canadian exports more attractive to foreign buyers.
(e) consumers (or importers)—the prices of imports would increase.
(f) The lower Canadian dollar would cause receipts (e.g., from exports) to increase and payments (e.g., from imports) to decrease; eventually, the receipts and payments would be in equilibrium, and the dollar would stabilize at a new, lower level.
(g) Import prices might rise rapidly, which would reduce the standard of living of Canadians and might cause inflation to accelerate.
(h)
   (i) buy Canadian dollars
   (ii) increase interest rates
8.
(a)
   (i)   True
   (ii) False
   (iii) False
   (iv) False

(b) surplus

(c) rise

(d) consumers (or importers)—the prices of imports would decrease.

(e) exporters—paying more for Canadian dollars would make Canadian exports less attractive to foreign buyers.

(f) The higher Canadian dollar would cause receipts (e.g., from exports) to decrease and payments (e.g., from imports) to increase; eventually, the receipts and payments would be in equilibrium, and the dollar would stabilize at a new, higher level.

(g) Exports might fall, causing unemployment to increase.

(h) (i) sell Canadian dollars

 (ii) decrease interest rates

9. c

10. b

11. e

12. e

13. c

14. a

15. b

CRITICAL THINKING QUESTIONS

1.

(a) It would be more likely that the international value of the Canadian dollar would decrease, because a global recession would depress Canadian exports in general and the prices of resource exports in particular. This would depress the demand for Canadian dollars, and the international price (value) of the Canadian dollar.

(b) The lower exchange rate of the Canadian dollar would help to "cushion" the Canadian economy against the impact of lower foreign demand for Canadian exports, by making those exports less costly to foreign buyers. On the other hand, it would also mean that Canadian buyers of foreign imports would pay more for those.

2.

(a) Foreign exchange speculators would be more likely to buy Canadian dollars, in the expectation that the exchange rate of the Canadian dollar would increase soon.

(b) If speculative buying of the Canadian dollar drove its international price too high, Canadian producers could find it more difficult to compete in international markets, which could cause an increase in unemployment in Canada.

(c) The Bank of Canada could sell Canadian dollars on foreign exchange markets, in an attempt to depress its value. This might discourage the speculators, if they believed that the Bank of Canada would not allow the exchange rate of the dollar to increase further. The Bank of Canada could also reduce interest rates; however, this would increase aggregate demand in the Canadian economy, which the Bank of Canada may not want to do if demand were already high.

3. On balance, there was a substantial net outflow of investment income from Canada of $16 billion. This outflow (payment) would generate selling of Canadian dollars, which would push the international value of the Canadian dollar downwards.

4.

(a) The international price of the yuan would have increased, due to heavy buying of the yuan by foreigners who were buying large amounts of Chinese exports.

(b) China was rapidly developing its industry, and needed to export large amounts of goods to the vast U.S. market. By keeping the price of the yuan low relative to the U.S. dollar, China could keep its products cheap for U.S. buyers.

(c) China sold large volumes of its own currency, and bought U.S. dollars (actually, China bought large amounts of U.S. government bonds). China also kept its interest rates low enough relative to U.S. interest rates to keep the yuan at a low level relative to the U.S. dollar.

5. if the exchange rate of the Canadian dollar were to rise rapidly, it would become less likely that the Bank of Canada would increase interest rates soon. The main reason is that a rapidly-rising dollar could threaten Canada's exports and the jobs associated with them. Increasing Canadian interest rates would cause the dollar to rise faster, posing an even greater threat to exports. And even if the Bank of Canada were concerned about inflation, a rising Canadian dollar would make it less urgent that the Bank of Canada raise interest rates, because the higher dollar would itself be slowing down aggregate demand in the economy by depressing exports.

USE THE WEB

1. Answers will vary depending on economic conditions at the time.

Chapter 11

REVIEW QUESTIONS

1. a and d
2. a
3. e
4. c
5. d
6.
(a) True
(b) True
(c) False—the personal saving rate was about 25 percent.
(d) False—the economy was booming due to high investment spending.
(e) True
(f) True
7. e
8. e
9. d
10. c
11. e
12. b
13. e
14. e
15. b

CRITICAL THINKING QUESTIONS

1. A falling international value of the U.S. dollar would mean a rising value of the Canadian dollar against the U.S. dollar.
(a) This would make American goods and services (such as trips to the USA) less costly for Canadian consumers.
(b) However, it would make it more difficult for many Canadian producers (especially manufacturers) to compete in the U.S. market, and by making imports less costly, it would make import competition more severe for Canadian firms. Both of these effects would increase unemployment in Canada.

2. The high and rising international price of the yen made it increasingly difficult for Japanese auto makers to manufacture cars in Japan and export them. Eventually, it became economically necessary for them to build automobile manufacturing plants outside of Japan.

3. These descriptions of the diverse effects of China on the global economy are all accurate. China exports low-priced clothes, electronic equipment, and manufactured goods. By lending vast amounts of money to the United States, China helps to keep interest rates low in the United States and other countries. Since low interest rates boost the demand for houses, China also contributed to the boom in housing prices in many countries. However, the inflow of Chinese imports reduced employment in various North American manufacturing industries, which made it harder for workers to find a job, and competition from China held down prices and wages in some North American industries. Finally, China's rapid economic development generated a rising demand for energy, which helped to push the prices of crude oil and gasoline to high levels.

4. Pessimists concerning the WTO's future progress toward free trade point to various obstacles, the most basic one of which may be the fact as of the start of 2006, the WTO included 149 nations, *all* of which must agree if an agreement is to be reached. To this obstacle is added the problem that WTO negotiations no longer focus on relatively simple matters such as tariffs on manufactured goods, but rather on more complex matters such as non-tariff barriers and trade in services. Finally, there was the growing problem of the insistence of developing nations that developed nations reduce their agricultural subsidies that made it impossible for developing nations to export their agricultural products, and the refusal of some developed nations to do so.

USE THE WEB

1. It is easier to see trends and compare nations if you use the percentage increases in exports. Check how the percentage increase in Canada's exports compares to the average percentage increase for the top ten exporters.

2. As of mid-2011, hope for a successful conclusion to the Doha Round was fading. Negotiations were at an impasse, and while another meeting was scheduled for December 2011, it was not expected to result in any progress, so the question would be whether the delegates would decide to try again in 2012 or terminate the negotiations.

3. As of 2011, the outlook regarding protectionism was unclear. Most national governments were reaffirming their heartfelt commitment to free trade; however, some were nonetheless

instituting protectionist measures such as subsidies for troubled producers and "buy at home" rules for government agencies.

Chapter 12

REVIEW QUESTIONS

1. e
2. d
3.
(a) True
(b) True
(c) True
(d) True
(e) False
(f) False
4. a
5. b
6. d
7. e
8.
(a) Yes
(b) No
(c) Yes
(d) Yes
(e) Yes
9. a
10. c
11. b
12. c
13. a
14. e
15.
(a) Exporters benefited because the decrease in the international price of the Canadian dollar made their products more attractive to foreign buyers.
(b) Consumers had to pay higher prices for imported goods and services.
16. d

CRITICAL THINKING QUESTIONS

1.
(a) The international value of the Canadian dollar would be depressed, as higher U.S. interest rates made the U.S. dollar a more attractive currency in which to place short-term funds.
(b) The Bank of Canada's choices would be to follow the U.S. lead and increase Canadian interest rates, or not to do so.

(c) If the Bank of Canada did not increase Canadian interest rates, the Canadian dollar would fall against the U.S. dollar. This would boost Canadian exports, but it would also depress Canadians' living standards, through higher prices of imports.

If the Bank of Canada did increase Canadian interest rates, the Canadian dollar would not fall against the U.S. dollar and import prices would not increase. On the other hand, higher interest rates would slow down the Canadian economy, generating higher unemployment than would otherwise have existed.

(d) The general condition of the Canadian economy would very likely be the deciding factor. If unemployment were high, the Bank of Canada would probably not follow the U.S. lead on interest rates, and would let the Canadian dollar fall in order to boost exports and employment. On the other hand, if inflation were a concern, the Bank of Canada would probably increase Canadian interest rates.

2.
(a) An increase in Canada's manufacturing productivity (output per worker per hour) would mean lower production costs per unit, which would enhance the ability of Canadian industry to compete internationally. Exports would increase, which would increase the demand for the Canadian dollar, and imports would decrease, which would reduce the supply (selling) of Canadian dollars. Together, these changes would tend to increase the international value of the Canadian dollar.

(b) The standard of living of Canadians would be increased. Canadian consumers would benefit from a higher exchange rate of the dollar, because the prices of imports would be lower. Also, Canadians in general would benefit from higher productivity, which would reduce production costs and prices.

3. Many of the capital goods used by Canadian industry to improve efficiency are imported, and a higher exchange rate of the Canadian dollar makes it less costly for Canadian firms to import them. By late 2005, a Canadian dollar that bought 40 percent more U.S. dollars than it did in early 2002 was encouraging a consider-

able increase in capital investment by Canadian firms on imported machinery and equipment.

4. By the 1980s, it was apparent that the productivity and international competitiveness of Canadian manufacturing industries was lagging behind Canada's trading partners and competitors. It was believed that the Canada–U.S. Free Trade Agreement would increase the productive efficiency of Canadian manufacturers in two ways. First, with secure access to the big U.S. market, Canadian firms could achieve economies of scale by increasing investment in capital equipment and increasing production. And second, being exposed to competition from American producers in both the U.S. and Canadian markets would force Canadian manufacturers to become more efficient.

USE THE WEB

1. (a) To get a clearer picture of recent trends, draw graphs of exports and imports of both goods and services, and calculate the percentage change in exports and imports in recent years.

(b) The two most likely reasons for changes in these trends are changes in the international value of the Canadian dollar and changes in economic conditions in the United States.

2. As the table in the question shows, flows of direct investment both into and out of Canada fluctuate widely from year to year. For an indication of the reasons for such fluctuations, visit **www.statcan.ca** and search *The Daily* for "direct investment."

Chapter 13

REVIEW QUESTIONS

1. b
2. d
3. e
4. e
5.
(a) True
(b) False
(c) True
(d) True
(e) True

6. c
7. a
8. e
9. b
10.
(a) True
(b) False
(c) False
(d) True
(e) True

CRITICAL THINKING QUESTIONS

1. First, a higher international value of the Canadian dollar would make it more difficult for Canadian producers to compete with foreign firms, both in export markets (because foreign buyers would have to pay more for Canadian dollars) and in the Canadian market (because a higher Canadian dollar means lower-priced imports). This increased competitive pressure should be expected to push Canadian producers to become more efficient.

   Second, a higher international value of the Canadian dollar would provide Canadian producers with an opportunity to purchase productivity-improving capital equipment from foreign suppliers at a lower cost.

2. Most people would probably think of the tax cuts in terms of their effect on spending and aggregate demand in the economy. However, the tax cuts could also strengthen the supply side of the economy—Canada's high taxes had for some time been regarded as a drag on economic activity in Canada in general, and on business investment and productivity in particular. This was more of a concern because Canada's taxes were higher than taxes in the United States, where productivity was rising more rapidly than in Canada.

3.
(a) The surpluses could also be used for increased spending on government programs, or for tax reductions.

(b) Productivity growth could be enhanced both by spending and by tax reductions. For example, spending on education, on training and skills development, and on research and development could boost productivity growth. Tax reductions on business profits or cuts to capital taxes could encourage business investment, and reductions in personal income taxes might provide incentives for work and for saving and investment.

USE THE WEB

1. Answers will depend on the government policies that are implemented.
2. Answers will vary depending on productivity trends in Canada and the United States.

Glossary

accelerator effect The effect whereby rising consumption spending causes rapid increases in induced investment, and a slowing down or levelling off of consumption spending causes sharp declines in induced investment.

aggregate demand Total spending on goods and services by all buyers of the economy's output.

aggregate demand Total spending on goods and services, consisting of consumption spending, investment spending, government spending, and net exports $(C + I + G + X - M)$.

aggregate supply curve A graphical representation of the supply side of the economy showing how the production cost per unit changes as the level of output is increased toward its potential.

appreciation of a currency Increases in the international value of a currency.

Asia–Pacific Economic Co-operation (APEC) A group of 21 nations that border the Pacific Ocean and intend to form a free trade area by 2010.

Auto Pact The 1965 agreement between Canada and the United States that provided for free trade in automotive vehicles, products, and parts.

automatic stabilizers Government spending and taxation programs that have the effect of automatically supporting aggregate demand during recessions and depressing aggregate demand during periods of boom/inflation.

balance of payments deficit A situation in which a nation's payments exceed its receipts.

balance of payments equilibrium A situation in which a nation's receipts and payments are equal to each other.

balance of payments surplus A situation in which a nation's receipts exceed its payments.

balance of payments A summary of all of a nation's receipts and payments for a given year.

balanced budget A government budget in which tax revenues and expenditures are equal.

bank Rate The rate of interest charged by the Bank of Canada on loans (advances) it makes to banks and other financial institutions.

bankers' deposit rate The rate of interest paid by the Bank of Canada on the chartered banks' deposits at the Bank of Canada.

boom psychology People's expectation of a future boom that makes them more willing to borrow to buy big-ticket items and capital goods.

branch plants Manufacturing plants established in a nation by a foreign-owned firm in order to avoid tariffs on imports by producing their products inside that nation.

budget deficit A government budget in which expenditures exceed tax revenues.

budget surplus A government budget in which tax revenues exceed expenditures.

business cycle The fluctuation of the economy between booms and recessions.

business savings Profits retained in a business after taxes have been paid and dividends have been paid to shareholders. (Also known as **retained earnings**.)

capacity output The maximum amount of output the economy can produce without generating excessively rapid increases in production costs and prices.

capital account Balance of payments items involving flows of investment funds (capital) between countries.

capital equipment The tools, equipment, machinery, and factories used to increase production per worker, and thus improve living standards.

capital taxes Taxes levied on the amount of a corporation's assets, or its capital.

cash reserve ratio The percentage of total deposits that a bank keeps as cash reserves.

cash reserves That amount of cash kept on hand by a bank to cover day-to-day withdrawals of cash.

central bank A government agency with responsibility for monetary policy, as well as other financial functions, on behalf of the government.

consumer confidence The degree to which consumers feel optimistic (or pessimistic) about their future economic prospects.

consumer indebtedness Consumer debt as a percentage of disposable income.

consumer price index (CPI) A weighted average of the prices of a "basket" of goods and services purchased by a typical urban family.

consumption spending Spending by households on consumer goods and services.

consumption Consumer goods and services that are used up by consumers for present enjoyment.

countercyclical fiscal policy A policy of using fiscal policy (budget deficits during recessions and surpluses during periods of inflation) to smooth out the economic fluctuations associated with the business cycle.

currency war The deliberate manipulation of the exchange rates of currencies downwards, in order to gain a competitive advantage in trade.

current account Balance of payments items relating to day-to-day transactions in goods and services.

cyclical unemployment Unemployment that is caused by periodic cyclical weaknesses in aggregate demand associated with recessions.

cyclical unemployment Unemployment that is caused by periodic cyclical weaknesses in aggregate demand associated with recessions.

deflation A decrease in the general level of the prices of goods and services.

demand side The purchasers of society's output of goods and services.

depreciation of a currency Decreases in the international value of a currency.

deregulation Policies to reduce the extent of regulation of business by government, with the intention of promoting efficiency through increased competition.

devaluation A reduction in the level of a pegged exchange rate.

direct investment Investments in business enterprises which are sufficiently concentrated to constitute control of the concern.

dirty float A situation in which a government influences the exchange rate.

dumping The practice of exporting a product at a price below the cost of producing it, or below the price charged in the country in which it is produced.

easy money policy Monetary policy directed toward making interest rates lower in order to stimulate aggregate demand.

economic boom High levels of output and employment in the economy as a whole.

economic resources Labour, capital equipment, and natural resources that are used to produce goods and services.

economies of scale The achievement of increased efficiency as a result of larger-scale productive operations and reductions in production costs per unit made possible by large-scale production and mass-production technology.

effectiveness A measure of how well an economy performs in terms of producing goods and services that meet the needs and wants of people.

efficiency A measure of how well an economy performs in terms of producing high volumes of goods and services at a low cost per item.

employment rate The percentage of the working-age population that is employed.

euro A common currency adopted by 12 of the 15 countries of the European Union.

European Union (EU) A very large trading bloc consisting of 27 European countries.

exchange rate management Government policies to moderate fluctuations in exchange rates. See **dirty float.**

exchange rate The international price, or value, of a currency in foreign exchange markets.

fiat money Money that a government has declared to be legal tender.

fiscal policy The use of government spending and taxes (the government's budget) to influence the level of aggregate demand and thus the performance of the economy. Also known as *budget policy.*

floating exchange rate A situation in which the international value of a currency is allowed to fluctuate freely with the supply of and demand for it.

foreign exchange markets Markets, conducted through banks, in which currencies of different nations are bought and sold (exchanged for each other).

foreign exchange reserves Holdings of foreign currencies and gold maintained by governments for the purpose of stabilizing their exchange rates through purchases and sales of their currencies.

frictional unemployment Unemployment arising from people being temporarily out of work because they are in the process of changing jobs.

frictional unemployment Unemployment arising from people being temporarily out of work because they are in the process of changing jobs.

full employment The lowest rate of unemployment that can be achieved without generating unacceptable inflation in the economy.

General Agreement on Tariffs and Trade (GATT) An international agreement under which many nations, following 1947, negotiated reductions in tariffs in order to promote freer trade.

globalization The trend toward more international trade and investment that has characterized the world economy since the early 1980s.

gross domestic product (GDP) Total value of goods and services produced (and incomes earned) in a country in one year.

gross domestic product (GDP) The total value of goods and services produced and incomes earned in a country in one year.

hidden unemployment People who are unemployed but are not counted in the unemployment statistics because they have given up looking for work.

hot money Short-term funds that can be moved readily from one currency to another.

import quotas Legal limits on the volume of particular goods that may be imported into a nation.

induced investment Capital investment spending undertaken by business in response to increases in sales that have brought production to near-capacity levels and that are expected to continue.

infant industries Industries protected by government from foreign competition until they have matured to the point of becoming internationally competitive without protection.

inflation psychology People's expectation of future inflation that leads them to seek larger wage increases and to make purchases of some big-ticket items quickly, before prices rise further.

inflation An increase in the general level of the prices of goods and services.

inputs The same as economic resources.

interest rate Percentage of borrowed money paid by a borrower (and received by a lender) annually.

International Monetary Fund (IMF) An international agency established to oversee and maintain the system of pegged exchange rates set up in 1945.

investment The production of capital goods that make possible increased production in the future.

labour force Those Canadians of working age who are either employed or are unemployed and both available for work and seeking work.

labour The largest single productive input available to any economy, labour includes all of the productive talents of the people of a society, mental as well as physical.

land Short form for all the natural resources available to a society's economy as economic inputs.

leading economic indicators Economic statistics that tend to increase or decrease in advance of increases or decreases in the pace of economic activity, thus giving advance notice of changes in economic trends.

M1 The narrowest definition of the money supply, including only currency (bank notes and coins) outside the banks plus demand deposits (current chequing account deposits).

M2 A wider definition of the money supply, including M1 plus personal savings deposits plus non-personal notice deposits.

M2+ A wider definition of the money supply, including M2 plus deposits at trust and mortgage loan companies, credit unions, and caisses populaires.

marginal tax rate The percentage of any *additional* income received that goes to taxes.

market power The ability to raise one's price; usually associated with a dominant or monopolistic position in a market.

market system An economic system in which economic decisions are made in a decentralized manner mainly by consumers and privately owned producers.

monetary policy The Bank of Canada's use of interest rates and the money supply to influence the level of aggregate demand in the economy.

money GDP GDP in current dollar terms; that is, including any price increases due to inflation.

money supply The total volume of money in circulation.

multiplier effect The effect whereby fluctuations in spending (for instance, investment spending) spread by means of the respending effect through the economy, with the total impact on GDP and incomes being considerably larger than the initial fluctuations in spending.

national debt A measure of the indebtedness of the federal government; specifically, the difference between the government's liabilities (mostly outstanding bonds) and its net recorded assets.

National Policy A set of nation-building policies introduced in Canada in 1879, the key economic aspect of which was protective tariffs to foster the development of Canadian industry.

niche marketing Marketing to small segments of a market.

nontariff barriers Other methods (besides tariffs) of restricting imports, including quotas and licences for imports, preferential purchasing policies, and subsidies for domestic producers.

North American Free Trade Agreement (NAFTA) Free trade agreement involving Canada, the United States, and Mexico.

oligopoly An industry that is dominated by a few firms.

operating band The one-half percentage point range established by the Bank of Canada for the overnight rate; the top of the range is the bank rate and the bottom of the range is the bankers' deposit rate.

opportunity cost The concept that the real economic cost of producing something is the forgone opportunity to produce something else that could have been produced with the same inputs.

output The goods and services produced by a society using its productive inputs.

overnight loans Very short-term loans between financial institutions to cover temporary shortfalls in areas such as settlement balances.

overnight rate The rate of interest on one-day loans made by banks, investment dealers, and other financial institutions to each other.

participation rate The percentage of the population of working age that is working or seeking work.

payments International transactions in which a nation pays funds to other countries.

pegged exchange rates Exchange rates that are prevented by their respective governments from moving from their fixed levels in relation to others.

personal disposable income Personal income less personal taxes, or after-tax personal income; may be spent or saved.

personal saving rate The percentage of personal disposable income that is saved.

personal saving Personal disposable income not spent on consumption.

productivity Output per worker per hour; one measure of efficiency.

profits Those funds left from a business's sales revenues after all expenses have been paid; such funds are therefore available (after taxes have been paid) for dividends to shareholders and reinvestment in the business.

real GDP GDP statistics that have been adjusted to eliminate the effects of price increases, the result being a statistic that measures only changes in real output. Also called *GDP in constant dollars* or *GDP at 1997 prices.*

real income The purchasing power of income (as distinct from its dollar value).

real interest rate The rate of return earned by a lender after inflation is taken into account.

receipts International transactions in which a nation receives funds from other countries.

recession psychology People's concerns regarding recession and unemployment that lead them to curtail their spending, especially on big-ticket items that require borrowing.

recession A period when the economy is producing considerably less than its potential output, and unemployment is high. Formally defined as two consecutive quarters (a quarter being three months) of declining output.

resource wealth mentality The view that society's economic wealth is derived mainly from the sale of natural resources, rather than from efficiency in the production of goods and services.

saving Doing without (forgoing) consumer goods; disposable income not spent on consumption.

scarcity The problem that, while economic inputs (and thus potential output) are limited in availability, people's wants and needs are apparently unlimited.

seasonal unemployment Unemployment arising from seasonal downturns in employment in some industries.

settlement balances Deposits (at the Bank of Canada) of the commercial banks and other financial institutions that are used to settle debts and transactions between them.

speculation The buying of an asset (here, a currency) with the objective of reselling it for a higher price in the future.

standard of living A measure of the economic prosperity of the people of a society, usually expressed in terms of the volume of goods and services consumed per person per year.

structural budget deficits Deficits arising from a built-in imbalance between government expenditures and revenues that results in deficits even when the economy is in a period of boom.

structural unemployment Unemployment arising from a mismatch between the skills required by employers and those of unemployed people.

subsidies Government financial assistance to a firm or industry, through grants, loans, or reduced taxes.

supply side The producers of a nation's output of goods and services.

tariffs Taxes, or import duties, levied by a nation on products imported from foreign countries.

theory of comparative advantage The theory that even if one nation is more efficient in the production of all items than another nation, it can still be to the economic advantage of both nations to specialize in what they produce most efficiently (items in which each has a "comparative advantage"), and trade with each other.

tight money policy Monetary policy directed toward making interest rates higher in order to slow the growth of aggregate demand.

trade war Retaliatory escalation of trade barriers by nations against each other's exports.

trading blocs Groups of nations that have a trade agreement among themselves outside of the WTO agreement.

unemployment rate The percentage of the labour force that is unemployed.

world product mandating An arrangement whereby a branch plant acquires a mandate from its foreign parent company to manufacture and market a particular product or products for the world market.

World Trade Organization (WTO) Successor to the GATT as of 1995.

Index

MACROECONOMICS SCOREBOARD

CANADA'S TOP MERCHANDISE EXPORT MARKETS, 2010

SOURCE: INDUSTRY CANADA, TRADE DATA ONLINE

	BILLIONS OF $
United States	$299.1
United Kingdom	16.4
China	13.2
Japan	9.2
Mexico	5.0
Germany	3.9
South Korea	3.7
Netherlands	3.3
Brazil	2.6
Norway	2.5

LARGEST MERCHANDISE IMPORTERS INTO CANADA, 2010

SOURCE: INDUSTRY CANADA, TRADE DATA ONLINE

	BILLIONS OF $
United States	$203.4
China	44.5
Mexico	22.1
Japan	13.5
Germany	11.3
United Kingdom	10.7
South Korea	6.1
France	5.4
Italy	4.7
Taiwan	3.0

CANADA'S UNEMPLOYMENT RATE, 2000–2010

2000	6.8
2001	7.2
2002	7.7
2003	7.6
2004	7.2
2005	6.8
2006	6.3
2007	6.0
2008	6.1
2009	8.3
2010	8.0